Interpersonal Processes

SAGE ANNUAL REVIEWS OF COMMUNICATION RESEARCH

SERIES EDITORS

Robert P. Hawkins, *University of Wisconsin—Madison*
John M. Wiemann, *University of California, Santa Barbara*
Suzanne Pingree, *University of Wisconsin—Madison*

EDITORIAL ADVISORY BOARD

Books in This Edited Series:

Volume 14

SAGE ANNUAL REVIEWS OF COMMUNICATION RESEARCH

Interpersonal Processes:
New Directions in Communication Research

MICHAEL E. ROLOFF

and

GERALD R. MILLER

Editors

SAGE PUBLICATIONS
The International Professional Publishers
Newbury Park   London   New Delhi

For information address:

SAGE Publications, Inc.
2455 Teller Road
Newbury Park, California 91320

SAGE Publications Ltd.
6 Bonhill Street
London EC2A 4PU
United Kingdom

SAGE Publications India Pvt. Ltd.
M-32 Market
Greater Kailash I
New Delhi 110 048 India

Printed in the United States of America

Library of Congress Cataloging-in-Publication Data

Main entry under title:

Interpersonal processes.

(Sage annual reviews of communication research; v. 14)
1. Interpersonal communication.   I. Roloff, Michael E.
II.   Miller, Gerald R.   III. Series.
BF637.C45I65   1987   153.6   87-9639
ISBN 0-8039-2654-5
ISBN 0-8039-2655-3 (pbk.)

92   93   94   10   9   8   7   6   5   4

CONTENTS

EDITORS' INTRODUCTION

Michael E. Roloff and Gerald R. Miller

IN 1976, THE FIFTH Sage Annual Review of Communication Research, *Explorations in Interpersonal Communication,* appeared. It was a project in which we both participated (Gerry as editor and contributor and Mike as contributor) and about which we feel great pride. At that time, the quantitative study of interpersonal communication was beginning to flourish but lacked a sense of definition. Few attempts had been made to identify the range of phenomena studied under the rubric of interpersonal communication. Consequently, research within a given domain continued with only limited awareness of what was going on in other areas. If nothing else, *Explorations* showcased a variety of research areas and, through example, provided a picture of the larger enterprise.

Ten years later, scholarship in interpersonal communication has grown in both breadth and depth. We believe that beyond mere definition, *Explorations* contributed to this development. Some of the chapters grew into entire volumes (e.g., Berger & Bradac, 1982; Cushman & Cahn, 1985; Pearce & Cronen, 1980) and many continue to be cited a decade later. While we believe the chapters hold up rather well, the rapid escalation in the volume of research and theory (due in part to their own influence) has inevitably limited their usefulness.

Consequently, we proposed an edited volume that might extend beyond the first. In doing so, we asked some of the original contributors to update their earlier chapters with the intent of identifying new insights and, where necessary, making revisions in their original thinking. Other scholars were asked to contribute manuscripts focused on topics not included in the original volume. Our goal was to establish a mixture of chapters that would be linked to the content of *Explorations* and recognize the emergence of new research areas.

The chapters of this volume can be clustered into three groups. The first four chapters focus on the functions of interpersonal communication. Roloff examines interpersonal communication from a social exchange perspective. Within that framework, interpersonal communication is a means by which individuals control their environment by obtaining resources through direct exchanges within interactions or by negotiating future exchanges. These processes are thought to vary with the intimacy level of a relationship.

Berger updates a chapter in *Explorations*. His uncertainty reduction theory is predicated on the notion that communication helps individuals understand

and predict each other's behavior. Uncertainty reduction theory has stimulated a great deal of research, and Berger reviews that research with an eye toward its implications for his original perspective and directions for the future.

Symbolic interactionism, with its focus on the self-concept, is a perspective with much appeal for communication scholars. Using his role-identity model as a base, McCall examines the reciprocal nature of interpersonal communication and self-related processes. He notes that interpersonal communication is a means by which the self-concept is formed and that such self-related processes guide interpersonal communication. Furthermore, the self-concept may itself be a communication process.

Berscheid focuses upon interpersonal communication and emotion. This topic is important for understanding interpersonal communication but there has been little research on it. Berscheid argues that interpersonal communication and emotion are in an interdependent relationship. Consequently, individuals experiencing emotion may seek others with whom to communicate but during the interaction find themselves experiencing other and perhaps unanticipated emotions.

The next six chapters represent a cluster focused upon interaction phenomena. Each describes a perspective related to a specific set of behaviors that might be observed within conversations. Miller, Boster, Roloff, and Seibold examine issues related to compliance-gaining interactions. In 1976, these authors wrote an article that played a part in the burgeoning volume of literature focused on the selection and generation of compliance-gaining strategies. This chapter critiques subsequent research and points to its theoretical limitations and potentially low generalizability to interactions. Based upon the critique, new directions are suggested.

Millar and Rogers offer an update of their chapter in *Explorations*. They summarize their thinking about dimensions of interpersonal relationships and about research focused upon the establishment of relational control within conversations.

Sillars and Weisberg raise several issues related to the skills approach to conflict interactions. Specifically, they question the assumption that openness is always beneficial within conflicts. Instead, they cite studies indicating that some measure of conflict avoidance occurs even among satisfied relational partners. Furthermore, open confrontation is not evaluated similarly by all societal subgroups.

Derlega, Winstead, Wong, and Greenspan focus on one of the more studied aspects of interpersonal communication: self-disclosure. Their chapter examines the types of attributions associated with self-disclosive statements and the influence of those attributions on subsequent self-disclosures. The results of two original studies are presented.

While self-disclosed information is an important part of interactions, personal data are not the only type of information exchanged in conversations. Kellermann posits a model of information exchange that relies in part upon the conversational and relational history of interactants to predict behavior. Although cognitive processes are at the heart of the model, it also incorporates affect as a major determinant and consequence of information exchange.

Poole, Folger, and Hewes contribute a chapter about a topic not included in *Explorations:* methodology. As the number of content areas studied has proliferated, so too has the number of methods. These authors offer a review of quantitative and qualitative approaches to studying interaction, including an assessment of the strengths and weaknesses of each.

The final two chapters examine relational issues and interpersonal communication. Taylor and Altman review research related to their social penetration theory. This theory is frequently used to predict developmental processes in relational formation. Although the theory is over a decade old and has been quite influential, the authors note that not all parts of the theory have been tested and few studies have employed longitudinal methods.

Duck explores the dynamics of relational disengagement. He suggests that interpersonal communication influences and is influenced by relational disengagement. He urges researchers to move beyond demographic analyses of relational breakups and study communication patterns, styles, contexts, and orderings that might be related to disengagement.

Although, the chapters present a wide array of topics, certain content themes tie them together. First, most of the chapters recognize interdependency between communication and other relational processes. Intimacy, uncertainty, the self-concept, emotion, and relational definition are among the concepts that both influence and are affected by interpersonal communication processes such as compliance gaining, self-disclosure, and information exchange. This approach recognizes the causal ambiguity inherent in much of our research and will hopefully force more refined explanations of interpersonal phenomena.

Second, the authors by and large share an interest in interaction. It is the interface between two individuals that is the defining characteristic of interpersonal communication and is therefore the focus of interpersonal communication research. However, this focus is a broad one. Research in this domain may include microanalyses of coded interaction behaviors, self-reports of interaction tendencies, or anticipation of interaction phenomena. Thus the content focus allows for a variety of methodologies.

Finally, while interpersonal communication occupies a central role in the communication discipline, it is by no means of limited interest to individuals not residing in communication departments. Our different academic backgrounds make interdisciplinary research exciting. We believe this excitement is evidenced by this volume.

As we noted earlier, *Explorations* remains an important volume. We believe this one will have a similar impact.

REFERENCES

Berger, C.R., & Bradac, J.J. (1982). *Language and social knowledge: Uncertainty in interpersonal relations.* London: E.E. Arnold

Cushman, D.P., & Cahn, D.D., Jr. (1985). *Communication in interpersonal relationships.* Albany: State University of New York Press.

Pearce, W. B., & Cronen, V. (1980). *Communication, action, and meaning.* New York: Praeger.

Chapter 1

COMMUNICATION AND RECIPROCITY WITHIN INTIMATE RELATIONSHIPS

Michael E. Roloff

In the intercourse of social life, it is by little acts of watchful kindness recurring daily and hourly, by words, tones, gestures, looks, that affection is won and preserved.

—George Augustus Sala (1828-1895)

Life is made up, not of great sacrifices or duties, but of little things, in which smiles and kindnesses, and small obligations, given habitually, are what win and preserve the heart and secure comfort.

—Sir Humphrey Davy (1778-1829)

ALTHOUGH OF RELATIVELY ancient vintage, the above quotations provide important insights into contemporary human relationships. An important part of interpersonal relations is the exchange of benefits. As implied by the quotations, acts interpreted as kind or rewarding prompt reactions that are affectionate or have survival value for the giver. In essence, rewards beget rewards. If rewarding behavior is absent, the relationship is placed in jeopardy. Indeed, research reveals that the perceived quality of resources (e.g., information) received from relational partners accounts for approximately 35% of the variance in relational satisfaction among couples engaged in casual or intimate dating (Lloyd, Cate, & Henton, 1982) and 75% of wives' and 57% of husbands' marital satisfaction scores (Rettig & Bubolz, 1983).

The quotations also imply that the rather ordinary rewards one receives daily are critical for maintaining relationships. Indeed, two studies in which married couples kept daily records of their spouse's relational behavior found that individuals in distressed marriages perceived that their spouses engaged in more behavior that had a negative impact on the respondents and less behavior associated with positive outcomes (Birchler, Weiss, & Vincent, 1975; Jacobson, Follette, & McDonald, 1982). In addition, Jacobson et al. (1982) reported that a spouse's marital satisfaction score on a *particular day* was correlated with the perceived frequency of positive and negative behaviors enacted by the partner on the *same day*. Specifically, individuals were happiest with their relationship on days when they perceived their spouse performed positive behaviors for them and avoided negative ones. This reactivity to recent actions was especially strong among couples who were generally distressed with their marriages.

Finally, the quotations imply that interpersonal communication can be an important source of rewards for relational partners. Consistent with this position, Lloyd et al. (1982) found that the perceived quality of information communicated by one's intimate dating partner was the best predictor among relational resources of satisfaction with the dating relationship, and Rettig and Bubolz (1983) reported that the perceived quality of spousal communication was significantly correlated with both husbands' and wives' marital satisfaction. Similarly, Jacobson, Waldron, and Moore (1980) discovered that in nondistressed marriages, the best predictor ($r = .56$) of a wife's daily marital satisfaction was how frequently she perceived her husband engaged in positive interactions with her; and among distressed husbands and wives, the best predictor was how frequently they engaged each other in negative interactions ($r = -.40, -.39$, respectively).

Given these results, it is not surprising that social exchange theories have been seized on by scholars seeking to predict and explain relational phenomena. These theories primarily focus on the exchange of resources between individuals. Despite their seeming popularity, their implications for interpersonal communication have been limited to a few phenomena such as self-disclosure. This chapter is the third installment of a series of papers aimed at exploring more fully the relationship between social exchange and interpersonal communication. Earlier publications focused on the assumptions of basic social exchange approaches (Roloff, 1981) and the importance of reciprocity within interactions (Roloff & Campion, 1985). Here, I will posit a more specific approach to the norm of reciprocity and draw links between reciprocity and the functions of interpersonal communication.

NORM OF RECIPROCITY

Observers of the human condition have long noted the existence of a culturally based dictum that the receiver of a benefit is morally obligated to return a benefit in kind. As Aristotle (1943) observed in the *Nicomachean Ethics*,

> People seek to return either evil for evil or good for good. It seems like slavery to them not to return an evil; and if they do not return a good, there is no interchange of services; and it is this interchange that holds society together. Therefore men build a temple of the Graces in their streets to encourage reciprocity of ser-

vice, for that is characteristic of grace, to return the services of one who has been gracious to others. (pp. 161-162)

Twentieth-century scholars have also underscored the existence of such an exchange standard. In his analysis of gift giving in primitive cultures, Mauss (1954, p. 1) concluded that "in theory such gifts are voluntary but in fact they are given and repaid under obligation." In addition, Simmel (1950, p. 387) observed that "all contacts among men rest on the schema of giving and returning equivalence."

Despite its ancient vintage, the norm of reciprocity remained a vaguely defined concept until 1960, when Alvin Gouldner made his classic attempt at formally defining it. According to Gouldner (1960, p. 170), the norm of reciprocity makes two minimal demands: "(1) People should help those who have helped them, and (2) people should not injure those who have helped them." In essence, the norm of reciprocity states that the receiver of a benefit is obligated to provide benefits to the giver.

In one sense, this obligation only requires the recipient to be grateful to the giver until the repayment is made. However, being indebted may not always be desirable. A debtor may feel that the right to freely criticize or evaluate the creditor is severely constrained, for to express disapproval or lack of support might imply ingratitude for the services rendered. In addition, the creditor might believe that those to whom the debt is owed have a legitimate right to exercise control over, or at least monitor, the debtor's resource expenditure until the debt is retired. The debtor may fear that expenditures will be viewed as frivolous given outstanding debts. In short, the debtor may feel that the obligation is a threat to independence and to freedom of choice. Consequently, Greenberg (1980) has argued that indebtedness often stimulates increased discomfort, which in turn makes the individual sensitive to ways of reducing the obligation.

An often overlooked but critical aspect of Gouldner's analysis is that the norm of reciprocity does not precisely specify the resources to be exchanged in particular situations; instead, it is simply a moral code suggesting that, in general, people should return benefits. Gouldner (1960, p. 175) notes,

> Unlike specific status duties and like other general norms, this norm [of reciprocity] does not require highly specific and uniform performances from people whose behavior it regulates. Instead, the concrete demands it makes change substantially from situation to situation and vary with the benefits which one party receives from another.

In other words, behaviors consistent with the norm of reciprocity may vary widely across situations. Thus the norm of reciprocity is cast at such a high level of abstraction that it does not predict precise behaviors.

Befu (1980) has made a similar argument in which he suggests the existence of exchange rules specifying a range of acceptable kinds and quantities of resources to be exchanged. Befu notes,

> Rules of exchange as defined here differ from the norm of reciprocity in that the latter refers to a generalized expectation to reciprocate, irrespective of what is being given or returned, whereas rules of exchange vary precisely on the basis of the nature of what is to be exchanged. (p. 203)

Rules of exchange represent acceptable methods of operationalizing the norm of reciprocity. They are more precise than the norm of reciprocity but provide flexibility by noting *ranges* of acceptable exchange behavior rather than a single option: The recipient of a benefit feels some obligation because of the norm of reciprocity and from a set of actions specified by exchange rules devises a strategy for repaying the debt.

Unfortunately, Befu provides no examples of exhange rules, and Gouldner does not precisely indicate how patterns of behavior consistent with the norm of reciprocity may vary across situations. Thus we are left with a framework but no specific content. Without such content, the utility of the framework is restricted since no testable hypothesis can be derived from it. The rest of this section will attempt to specify the components of exchange rules and to indicate how these components vary across relationships.

COMPONENTS OF EXCHANGE

Befu (1980, p. 203) noted that the range of acceptable behaviors specified in exchange rules "varies from one circumstance to another." Given this situation, it seems reasonable to begin by specifying what components of an exchange might vary across situations. A social exchange is defined as the voluntary transfer or sharing of resources between relational partners. Based upon the writings of social exchange theorists, one can identify eight components of an exchange.

First, it is possible to focus on the degree to which the resources involved in an exchange are *homeomorphic*. Gouldner (1960) noted that reciprocity takes one of two forms: homeomorphic or heteromorphic. Homeomorphic reciprocity requires that the recipient of a benefit should return a resource of the same form. The "dyadic effect" observed in self-disclosure research (e.g., Jourard, 1971) is similar to this concept; that is, when one is self-disclosed to, there is a tendency to self-disclose back. Heteromorphic reciprocity permits the exchange of resources of different form as long as they are of similar value. Consequently, the receiver of self-disclosure might choose not to self-disclose in return, but instead, express sympathy for the communicator, and this exchange would be acceptable as long as the two behaviors are perceived to be of similar value (Berg & Archer, 1980). Exchange rules specifying homeomorphic reciprocity are more restrictive than those allowing for heteromorphic exchanges. In both cases, the individual must return something of similar value, but in the former case, the return must reside in the same resource domain.

Second, exchange rules may vary in the amount of time the receiver of a benefit is allowed to repay a debt. Blau (1964) noted that individuals offering a social reward to another rarely specify an expected repayment time in advance. This lack of an explicit time frame does not mean that the giver and receiver have none in mind; it simply means they may be reluctant or feel no particular need to express it. This lack of specification stems partially from exchange rules that suggest time limits for repayment. While exchange rules might not specify the exact moment when the return must be made, they may specify a general time frame when repayment is required. Furthermore, it is hypothesized that this general time frame will vary across situations.

Third, exchange rules may vary in the degree to which they require return of a resource of equivalent value. Gouldner (1960) noted that there may be specific standards of reciprocity requiring that a resource of the exact value be returned, whereas others may allow for "rough equivalence" wherein a resource slightly more or less valuable than the initial one is repaid. He suggests that "exact equivalence" is a more restrictive requirement and may make reciprocation difficult.

Fourth, exchange rules may differ in the extent to which they require a contingent relationship between the resource given and the resource returned. By "contingent" is meant a clear link between the two resources. Phenomenologically, that link may be evidenced in a perception on the part of the giver or receiver that a returned resource is intended to serve as repayment for a particular debt (e.g., Roloff & Campion, 1985). Therefore, unless a partner perceives such a link, feelings of indebtedness may remain despite the provision of a resource. Noncontingent exchange focuses on the overall frequency with which resources are provided, regardless of the particular link between any two of them. This form of exchange mandates that the overall frequency of resources provided one another be highly correlated even though the specific pattern of returns is random. For example, two individuals who occupy interdependent roles may enact a variety of helpful behaviors toward one another—for example, one spouse may be responsible for cooking, cleaning, and shopping while the other takes care of repairs, bill-paying, and security. While the completion of any given role duty does not obligate the other to perform a specific duty (e.g., fixing lunch is not linked specifically to fixing a faucet, paying a bill, or checking for a prowler), the overall performance of the role obligates the other to perform successfully his or her duties. Thus neither a phenomenological nor a statistical link may exist between any two specific behaviors but the overall frequency of such behaviors is correlated. The noncontingent approach is less restrictive since it does not require parties to specifically "keep count" of each obligation.

Fifth, some exchange rules may limit the types of resources that may be used in an exchange. This component is different than the first one discussed since it suggests that certain resources may not be appropriate either as gifts *or* returns within some contexts. For example, the relationship between a student and a professor sanctions certain types of exchanges while prohibiting others. When students pay tuition for a specific class, they obligate the professor to provide information related to the class topic. Students who demonstrate competency over a given information domain obligate the professor to award a grade indicative of their mastery of that material. Some graduate students may be awarded graduate assistantships that obligate them to perform certain research or teaching services in return for monetary compensation. However, an offer or return of intimate sexual behavior constitutes a counternormative exchange and is viewed as undesirable (Forgas & Dobosz, 1980). This does not mean that such actions never occur but instead suggests that those engaged in such behavior may take preventive action to avoid formal or informal reprimands. For example, even a voluntary romantic relationship between a professor and student may be kept secret, or at least not advertised, until the role relationship changes. Or, the two may avoid situations where the professor evaluates the student for fear that an exchange of love for status or money might be inferred. These measures may be employed even if the student and professor are married to one another. It should be noted that within the same academic context, it is not inappropriate for two students to become involved in a romantic relationship (Forgas & Dobosz, 1980).

Sixth, exchange rules may focus on the degree to which an obligation is transferable from one person to another. An obligation may be extended in two ways. One involves a situation where the benefit provided to an individual not only obligates the receiver to the particular giver but to those who are closely connected to the giver. For example, if one receives a favor from another, one may feel some obligation to help the spouse or children of the giver. In such cases, one repays the debt by benefiting those closely connected to the giver. A second transference of obligation occurs when those connected to a receiver of a benefit also feel obligated toward the giver. A spouse may be indirectly obligated when a good turn is done for the partner. Or a spouse directly rewarded by another may feel that the marital partner should feel some degree of obligation toward the giver.

Seventh, exchange rules may differ in the degree to which individuals feel obligated to initiate exchanges. Thus far, attention has been focused on the responsibility to return a received benefit. Exchange rules may also focus on responsibility to start an exchange. That obligation may take the form of offering assistance to a needy person without that person having to ask or granting a request for a resource from another. On the other hand, a person needing a resource may feel obligated to initiate exchanges with particular others. Significant others may feel affronted if an individual does not come to them for assistance in time of need. Furthermore, a needy individual may feel obligated to accept an offer of assistance from another even though that offer implies a debt. To refuse a gift may imply a negative evaluation of the giver. Consequently, social mechanisms may trigger exchanges. Indeed, Mauss (1954, p. 10) observes that the concept of exchange "not only carries with it the obligation to repay gifts received, but it implies two other equally important: the obligation to give presents and the obligation to receive them." Although Mauss's assertion implies that such obligations are universal, the degree of obligation may vary across exchange rules.

The eighth component focuses upon the degree of unilateral indebtedness that is permissible before sanctions are employed. Since the norm of reciprocity is a moral standard, violations may prompt the use of sanctions. If a person does not repay obligations, a giver may refuse to grant further favors until previous debts are retired, or may demand strict repayment of all future debts (i.e., refuse credit). Individuals may find that they are permitted to "run up a larger tab" in some relationships than in others.

Having identified several components of an exchange that may vary across exchange rules, the obvious next step is to seek insight into factors that cause such variation. While exchange rules may by influenced by a number of factors, I will focus primarily upon their variance across types of relationships.

RELATIONAL DETERMINATION OF EXCHANGE RULES

Just as scholars have noted that the exchange of benefits is critically important for relationships, they have also observed that relationships tend to differ in the underlying basis for the exchange. For example, Aristotle noted in the *Nicomachean Ethics* that some relationships are based on the utility or pleasure derived from that which relational partners provide, and involve little affection or concern between partners.

> People then who love for utility's sake are moved to affection by what is good for themselves, and people who love for pleasure, by what is pleasant to themselves. They love a person for not what he is in himself, but only for being useful or pleasant to them. Such friendships then are friendships incidentally only; for the person loved is not loved for being what he is, but merely for being a source of some good or pleasure. (1943, p. 197)

Other relationships involve concern between relational partners. Aristotle noted that "those who wish the good of their friends for their friend's sake are in the truest sense friends, since their friendship is the consequence of their own character, and not an accident" (1943, p. 198). In essence, the exchange of benefits within a true friendship stems from mutual concern for each other's welfare rather than accumulation of individual profits. While true friendship appears to be a very desirable relationship, Aristotle noted that such relationships are effortful, and therefore rare. They are reserved for those with whom we have much contact and intimate knowledge.

Margaret Clark and Judson Mills employ similar logic when they describe differences between *exchange* and *communal* relationships (Clark & Mills, 1979; Mills & Clark, 1982). Exchange relationships are based primarily on utility or pleasantness. Exchange partners provide resources with an expectation that the recipient will feel obligated to return a resource of comparable form or value. Such relationships are driven by the desire to attain resources and to reduce personal indebtedness. Communal relations are based upon a mutual concern for each other's welfare. While both exchange and communal partners provide one another benefits, those in communal relationships do so because of the obligation implied by their concern for each other rather than debts incurred from receiving previous benefits.

Clark and Mills provide a useful beginning point for identifying exchange rules. They argue that the rules for giving and receiving benefits are different in exchange and communal relationships and identify some of these differences. The approach taken here is congruent with theirs but different in that it posits the degree of intimacy associated with a relationship as a primary predictor of exchange rules, rather than whether a relationship is communal or exchange-oriented. Based on ordinary usage of the term "intimacy," Chelune, Robison, and Kommor (1984, p. 14) describe an intimate relationship as "a relational process in which we come to know the innermost, subjective aspects of another, and are known in a like manner." In essence, intimacy implies mutual sharing of personal information. Chelune et al. also hypothesize that intimate relationships embody the qualities of trust, commitment, and caring. Intimates believe that the other can be trusted to act nonexploitatively and that each will try to meet the other's needs.

Obviously, relatively intimate relationships share characteristics with communal relations, and less intimate relationships are similar to exchange-oriented relations. Indeed, Clark (1983a, 1983b) noted that communal relations are those people usually identify as close—namely, friends, family, and romantic partners—while exchange relationships are more distant—such as clients, or acquaintances. Despite the similarities, use of the term "intimacy" provides important advantages. First, "intimacy" has a relatively standardized meaning among ordinary people, and hence may provide greater insight into how they see exchange rules differing across relationships *they* define as different. Research indicates that intimacy is a dimension used by people to discriminate among types of interpersonal relationships (e.g., Marwell & Hage, 1970; Wish, Deutsch, & Kaplan, 1976) and that intimacy has shared meaning for people in the general population (Waring, Tillman, Frelick, Russell, & Weisz, 1980). It is not known, however, whether the terms "communal" and "exchange" have meaning beyond the academic community and, more important, whether they are used in a fashion similar to that of Clark and Mills. Indeed, ordinary people may associate communal relations with an alternative lifestyle rather than a particular type of relationship. If researchers are interested in studying how people make sense of their everyday relationships, or, in essence, describing their implicit theories of social relationships (Wegner & Vallacher, 1977), a term with some meaning among the general population is most useful.

Second, focusing on the degree of intimacy associated with a relationship makes it possible to move beyond prototypical categories to more continuous variables. While communal and exchange relations are useful heuristic devices, they imply that people divide their relationships into two discrete categories; actually, people appear to order relationships on relatively continuous dimensions (Wish et al., 1976). Also, exchange rules probably differ in emphasis across relational dimensions. Rather than relational partners being concerned with *either* receiving repayment for a specific benefit *or* meeting the needs of their partner, they may differ in the emphasis placed on both. For example, while Clark (1983b) notes that close relationships tend to be communal, "most people tend to have very weak communal relations with everyone and are willing to provide low-cost help without expecting anything in return" (p. 211). On the other hand, parties to close relationships may also expect repayment for specific actions. Greenberg, Bar-Tal, Mowrey, and Steinberg (cited in Greenberg & Westcott, 1983) found that when asked to describe an incident where they felt indebted to someone, 75% of the respondents described an obligation to a relative or close friend who provided financial help or a service. Furthermore, Argyle and Henderson (1984, p. 218) discovered that among rules identified by people as being important for friendship were the necessity to "repay debts, favours or compliments no matter how small" and to "volunteer help in time of need." Interestingly, the latter rule was judged more important than the former. Thus in less intimate relations partners are less concerned with meeting each other's needs and place more emphasis on repayment of specific debts; in more intimate relationships, the opposite is true.

Hence there apparently exists a general expectation that persons in more intimate relationships should have higher levels of mutual knowledge and should feel greater levels of mutual trust, caring, and commitment than those in less intimate relationships.[1] This expectation may result from socializing children to discriminate among people with whom they have contact, and it is likely tested through experiences with actual relationships.

Implied in this expectation are two exchange obligations. First, people in intimate relationships are more obligated to provide one another needed resources than are people in casual acquaintanceships. The increased knowledge and caring associated with intimacy suggests that intimates should be better able to help their partners and to provide assistance without external inducements—such as pleas or prior or anticipated benefits. Second, people involved in intimate relationships are more obligated to provide resources under a "good faith" principle than are nonintimates. By "good faith" is meant that intimates are more obligated to accept benefits that are less valuable than those given, keep less accurate counts of whether anything has been returned, and forgive instances where their partners obviously failed to help or repay debts. These two obligations should have an impact on the appropriateness of the behaviors associated with each of the exchange components identified earlier. Eight hypotheses will be advanced to specify these impacts.

First, as the degree of intimacy associated with a relationship increases, the appropriateness of heteromorphic exchange increases. Because intimates are more concerned with meeting each other's needs than repaying specific debts, they should be willing to return needed resources regardless of whether the benefit is identical to the one initially received. Often, the intimate who provided a benefit does not need or want an identical benefit in return; for example, though a friend who owns a snowblower may offer snow removal to a friend who does not, it is unlikely that the former would want, need, or expect to receive snow removal in return. In fact, such an offer might be viewed as odd and undesirable. Clark (1981) discovered that the return of identical resources is perceived as repayment of debts and implies less of a friendship. Indeed, Clark (1984a) has hypothesized that the exchange of identical resources may threaten the communal basis of a relationship.

In less intimate relationships, need is less important than reducing indebtedness. Given lower trust, partners may strive to return something similar because it appears to be of equal value. Indeed, Pruitt (1981) contends that individuals are often reluctant to accept dissimilar resources as repayment and may even demand greater quantities because of the difficulty of determining their relative worth. Consistent with this view, Beach and Carter (1976) discovered that returns of resources that are in the same domain (e.g., services) come closer to being of equivalent value than dissimilar resources.

To clarify, I am not arguing that homeomorphic exchanges necessarily will be viewed more skeptically as intimacy increases, or, that in more intimate relationships, homeomorphic exchange will be less appropriate than heteromorphic. In some cases, a needed resource may be identical to the one given. If the friend's snowblower breaks, he or she may want the debtor to help with snow. Indeed, Clark (1984a) has suggested that the return of comparable benefits will not threaten a communal relationship if the same resource is urgently needed. In addition, there is evidence that people prefer to receive resources perceived to be in the same or similar resource domain as that which was given regardless of whether they define themselves as strangers, acquaintances, or friends (Brinberg & Castell, 1982; Foa & Foa, 1974, pp. 182-183). I am only suggesting, then, that the exchange of different resources will be more tolerated across degrees of intimacy and that as intimacy increases, exchanges of dissimilar behaviors within the same resource category will be viewed as more appropriate (e.g., snowblowing for grass cutting).

Second, as the degree of intimacy associated with a relationship increases, the amount of time to return a benefit becomes more variable. In intimate relationships, the appropriateness of a return is based more upon the relational partner's need than the time elapsed since the earlier benefit was given. This implies that intimates may wait to return a benefit until they perceive it is needed. Since needs may emerge at any time, intimates may be required to provide benefits soon after receiving one or much later. To some extent, they are "on call."

In less intimate relationships, partners may feel compelled to "pay as they go." Since the degree of trust is relatively low, nonintimates may feel they should return benefits sooner rather than later to document their reliability. This seems particularly true if a nonintimate wishes to build a trusting relationship. From the opposite perspective, nonintimates may wish to repay debts sooner if they have some animosity toward the other, since they feel they should avoid being perceived as ungrateful or critical until the debt is retired. In such cases, a person may return a resource so as to end any future basis for interaction.

Third, as the degree of intimacy associated with a relationship increases, the appropriateness of exchanging roughly equivalent resources increases. As noted earlier, to be obligated to return a resource of exact equivalence can make reciprocation difficult. In cases where one has received a very valuable benefit, it may be harmful to reciprocate unless one has an adequate supply of valuable resources to return. Consequently, intimates may be especially tolerant of returns that are less valuable if their partners can ill-afford to return something of exactly equal value. In such cases, the positive intent behind a return of assistance may compensate for the fact it was unneeded or of lower quality. Regardless of the reason, there is evidence that intimates are willing to tolerate some discrepancy in the worth of what is given and received. Beach and Carter (1976) found that friends did not expect to repay or to be repaid with a resource of exactly equal value.

In less intimate relationships, individuals have less knowledge of one another; consequently, they cannot be certain that a return of less value is the result of inability to pay or is even accompanied with goodwill. They may be more inclined to view such repayments as inadequate and may even view them as attempts at exploitation.

As with the first hypothesis, a disclaimer is necessary. I am not arguing that in intimate relationships, returns of exact equivalence will be judged less appropriate than those of rough equivalence, or, that as intimacy increases, the appropriateness of returns of exact equivalence decreases. Intimates may appropriately return resources of exact equivalence when the giver and recipient both have similar needs and the recipient can afford to make a return of equivalent value. For example, two friends may decide to alternate driving their children to school. Assuming that they both have cars and are available at the appropriate times, such an exchange would appear both exactly equivalent and acceptable.

Fourth, as the degree of intimacy associated with a relationship increases, the appropriateness of noncontingent exchanges increases. This hypothesis implies that in intimate relationships, the explicit link between pairs of resources is less important than the perceived correlation between the total amounts of resources provided by each partner. Intimates may not expect that each service they provide will be specifically linked to a returned service, but they do expect that if they generally meet their partner's needs, the partner will reciprocate. Thus, partners do not have to keep exact counts of what was given and what, if anything, was returned. Indeed, Clark (1984b) found that individuals working on a joint task were less likely to keep records of exact contributions if they were working with someone with whom they desired to form a communal rather than an exchange relationship. The trust associated with intimate relationships obviates the need for explicit linkages.

This does not mean, however, that contingent exchanges are less appropriate in more intimate relationships. In some cases, intimates may reach an agreement to trade services and the link between their actions is made explicit. For example, a mother and father may agree to alternate baby-sitting so that each will have some time to pursue individual interests. Such an agreement indicates specific responsibilities, the repeated violation of which could cause conflict. While this exchange is contingent, it has a coordination advantage in that each knows what he or she is obligated to do and when. However, not all intimate exchanges require such an explicit link.

In less intimate relationships, trust is lower and partners may try to keep tabs on their exchanges. Explicit linkages between gifts and returns become important for demonstrating that a debt has been retired. Greenberg, Mowrey, Steinberg, and Bar-Tal (cited in Greenberg, 1980) found that 53% of the respondents felt they would remain at least somewhat indebted if they provided assistance to a benefactor and if the benefactor was unaware that they had been the source of the assistance. Consequently, noncontingent exchange may leave too much ambiguity as to the degree to which indebtedness has been reduced.

Fifth, as the degree of intimacy associated with a relationship increases, the range of acceptable resources to be exchanged increases. Given the range of needs experienced by a person, it should not be surprising that intimates assist each other in numerous areas. In addition, the trust and affection accompanying intimacy may allow an individual to risk exchanging resources of a private or personal nature. Consistent with this hypothesis, intimates do share a wider variety of resources than nonintimates. Teichman (cited in Foa & Foa, 1974, pp. 159-160) found that when compared to work or client relationships, parent-child relationships were expected to be higher in exchange of love, status, information, goods, and services. Only money was used less in exchange. In addition, Argyle and Furnham (1983) discovered that people reported a higher degree of satisfaction with the instrumental rewards (e.g., financial, support, goods/property), emotional support (e.g., discussion of personal problems), and shared interests (e.g., doing things together) received from their more intimate partners (e.g., spouse, parents, same- and opposite-sex friends) than from nonintimates (e.g., work superiors or colleagues, neighbors).

Sixth, as the degree of intimacy associated with a relationship increases, the transferability of obligation increases. In more intimate relationships, partners come to view themselves and are often viewed by others as a unit rather than two distinct individuals. Consequently, when one partner engages in an exchange external to the relationship, it may have consequences for the other. Since the partners are interdependent, someone who promotes the well-being of one may possibly also benefit the other, and the benefited other should therefore feel some gratitude toward the partner's benefactor. In addition, intimate partners may feel obliged to their partner's surrogate for returns, since a benefit received by one indirectly benefits the other. Indeed, a refusal to help an intimate partner's significant other may result in serious conflict, for it may be perceived as a rejection of the partner.

In less intimate relations, the unit relationship is weaker. One's debts should be less transferable, and one may not acquire the debts of others or feel as obligated toward the nonintimate's significant others. An important exception should be noted. If nonintimates cannot return assistance to the person who helped them, they may substitute a similar other as a target of repayment. Greenberg et al. (cited in Greenberg, 1980, p. 19) discovered that in such cases, the significant other of a nonintimate is a better surrogate than a mere acquaintance, but research indicates that substitutions for nonintimates result in lower quality assistance than would be given directly to the person who initiated the exchange (Shumaker & Jackson, 1979).

Seventh, as the degree of intimacy associated with a relationship increases, partners become more obligated to initiate exchanges with each other. Because intimates care about one another, they should feel a strong urge to come to each other's aid. This implies they will monitor each other's needs and will offer assistance without their partners requesting it. For example, Argyle and Henderson (1984) found a strong rule of friendship, which mandated that a friend should *volunteer* help in time of need. Violation of this rule was serious enough to destroy the friendship. In addition, intimates may feel affronted if they are available to help and their partners seek assistance from a less intimate partner, or if their offer to help is rejected. Such actions may imply their partner does not view the relationship as an intimate one.

In less intimate relationships, there is less presumption of obligation. Consequently, a potential donor may need to see some future benefit arising from his or her actions before supplying assistance. At least two studies have found that resources are more likely to be given to unacquainted others if they have the potential to give a resource back (Enzle & Lowe, 1976; Pruitt, 1968). Furthermore, nonintimates may be reluctant to seek or accept help unless they can reciprocate. Greenberg and Shapiro (1971) found that college students were less likely to request or accept offers of assistance when reciprocation, and hence reduced indebtedness, was impossible.

Eighth, as the degree of intimacy associated with a relationship increases, the more obligated are the partners to be tolerant of asymmetric distributions of resources. This hypothesis implies that intimates should be less disturbed and less likely to employ sanctions if one partner has been the recipient of a disproportionate share of benefits. In some cases, one party's needs are greater than the other's and as a result, the needier partner receives larger amounts of resources. For example, an unemployed or ill intimate may be cared for by a partner despite an inability to reciprocate. In such instances, the needier partner may express gratitude toward the benefactor; and, after the crisis subsides, will return to former levels of contribution. In addition, the needier partner may feel an obligation to provide future unilateral assistance if a crisis should befall the partner.

Even when asymmetry is due to thoughtlessness, some degree may be forgiven. As noted earlier, intimates are more concerned their partners be there when needed than with having each benefit returned. As long as an intimate partner meets the other's needs, occasional slights may be overlooked. For example, Clark and Waddell (1985) found that failure to repay a debt produced negligible feelings of exploitation among communal partners while failure to respond to a partner's needs increased such feelings considerably. Furthermore, Argyle and Henderson (1984) found that 26% of their respondents felt that failure to repay debts and favors was at least moderately important in causing a friendship to collapse, while 44% attributed strong importance to failure to volunteer help in a time of need.

Of course, in intimate relationships, tolerance for asymmetry is not limitless. Repeated failure to show gratitude or at least acknowledge receipt of a benefit may result in feelings of exploitation. Even if gratitude is expressed or different needs exist, asymmetry may harm the relationship. Asymmetry implies that one partner is sacrificing resources and perhaps need fulfillment for the other. If extended for long periods of time, even gratitude may not be enough compensation for real losses of resources.

In less intimate relationships, asymmetry is not likely to be as tolerable. Need is less important than repayment of debts. While nonintimates may feel some sympathy for needy others and may even feel obligated to provide a modest degree of unilateral assistance, if returns are not forthcoming feelings of exploitation may increase and further benefits will not be provided. For example, Clark and Waddell (1985) reported that failure to repay a debt resulted in greater feelings of exploitation in exchange relationships than in communal ones.

Thus behaviors perceived to be consistent with the norm of reciprocity are hypothesized to vary with the relationship's intimacy. In some ways, it is easier to conform to the norm in more intimate relationships. Returns need not be explicitly linked to gifts and may be of different forms or values. In addition, repayment time is more variable and partners are more understanding of occasional failure to repay or meet needs. On the other hand, increased intimacy entails greater obligation. Intimates are expected to initiate exchanges whenever their partners are in need and may be required to provide very valuable and personal resources. Furthermore, intimates may incur the debts of their partners. Consequently, increased intimacy implies a mixture of leniency in combination with high expectations.

At this point, I have dealt only with the obligation to perform certain exchange behaviors. In the next section, I will examine communication patterns implied by these obligations.

FUNCTIONS OF INTERPERSONAL COMMUNICATION

All humans face the challenge of survival. To tackle this challenge alone compounds the problem significantly. At its extreme, self-sufficiency implies an individual can survive without the assistance of others. In such cases, exchange is unnecessary since the individual can create all needed resources. While such a notion appeals to some romantics, reality dictates that individuals rely upon others for resources. Consequently, systems have emerged to link potential resource persons. One such system is communication. In general, the function of communication is to facilitate the acquisition of resources needed to control one's environment. Specifically, communication serves as a means by which resources are offered, transferred, or shared between individuals, and it is also an instrument for negotiating the exchange of resources.

Scholars have noted that the concepts "communication" and "relationship" are interrelated (e.g., Hinde, 1979). Communication helps define the nature of a relationship, and relational characteristics influence the nature of interactions. This section focuses on how the degree of intimacy associated with a relationship influences both exchanges within an interaction and interpersonal negotiation processes.

INTERACTION AS AN EXCHANGE PROCESS

Interaction is partially composed of a series of offered resources *or* offers of resources. By "offered resource" is meant that an interactant may directly provide another with some symbolic resource during a conversation. Scholars have noted that such symbolic resources as love, status, and information are often exchanged during an interaction (Foa & Foa, 1974; Longabaugh, 1963). "Offers of resources" suggests that individuals may offer to provide resources at some *future time* without explicit prior request. These offers may involve symbolic resources or more tangible items—such as money, goods, or services. Thus an interaction is a mechanism for conveying or offering resources.

Given the reciprocal nature of relationships and interactions, it is hypothesized that the exchanges contained within an interaction will vary with the intimacy associated with the larger relationship. Based upon the previous section, several specific hypotheses are advanced that relate intimacy to conversational exchange.[2]

The first hypothesis focuses on the probability that an interaction will be initiated. Specifically, *when an individual discovers or anticipates that a person is in need, the more intimate the relationship, the greater the probability that interaction will be initiated.* The hypothesis rests on the notion that intimates are more obligated than nonintimates to volunteer help *spontaneously* in time of need. Consequently, intimates may periodically "check in" with each another to insure all is well, and such behavior is more likely when there are indications a need may exist.

Nonintimates have less obligation to volunteer resources or anticipate when needs exist. Indeed, nonintimates may fear such initiations will be perceived as "prying." This does not mean that nonintimates never initiate interaction when perceiving a need of another. It is hypothesized that individuals in nonintimate relationships are more likely to initiate interaction with a needy other when (a) they have an outstanding obligation to the other; (b) they have had successful exchanges with the other; (c) the other is perceived as willing and able to return a resource of comparable value; (d) the needed resource is not too costly; (e) the needy individual has no available partner of greater or equal intimacy; and/or (f) they desire to form a more intimate relationship with the needy other. Parts a through d suggest that nonintimates will initiate interactions when they perceive the act can reduce their indebtedness, result in attainment of resources, or at least is not too costly. Part e implies nonintimates may respond if they perceive that no one of greater obligation (i.e., intimacy) is present to help. Consequently, a stranger may try to comfort a crying child if the child appears to be lost but may not intercede if a parent is present. Part f notes that nonintimates may initiate interaction as a means of escalating the relational intimacy. Such behavior may express a willingness to provide assistance to another even though the costs are high and there is no obligation to do so.

After an interaction begins, the intimacy of a relationship will also guide the process. Specifically, *as the degree of intimacy associated with a relationship increases, the degree of need assessment interaction behavior increases.* Though most conversations start with questions such as "How is it going?"

or "How are things today?" such questions are more thoroughly pursued in intimate relationships. Individuals in intimate relationships are more likely to assess perceived needs directly via questions and to follow up such inquiries with probes seeking more explicit answers. In essence, intimates seek greater informational depth. In addition, intimate need assessment may involve greater topic breadth. Intimates may be freer to inquire about private problems or needs. Such inquiries among nonintimates may be taboo and may result in rejections (e.g., "None of your business!"). Baxter and Wilmot (1985) have noted that certain topics may be "off limits" even in highly intimate relationships. In such cases, less obtrusive measures may be employed to acquire the information.

Intimates are also obligated to disclose their needs to a greater extent than nonintimates. It is hypothesized that *as the degree of intimacy associated with a relationship increases, the extent to which individuals disclose their needs in response to their partner's need assessment behavior increases.* Intimate partners are obligated to help one another, and such help is difficult if no information about needs is disclosed. However, in some cases even intimates may be reluctant to describe their needs. Specifically, *needy* intimate partners are less likely to disclose needs if they (a) anticipate that their need fulfillment may deplete their partner's supply of resources; (b) perceive that their needs may damage their relationship with the partner; and/or (c) believe that their partners should have known their needs without being told.

This qualifying hypothesis first suggests that needy intimates may conceal their needs from the partner because they believe the partner cannot afford to sacrifice the needed resources. Consequently, withholding of need-based information may stem from a desire to avoid increasing the needs of an intimate partner who seeks to give assistance. In addition, intimates may fear that voicing needs reflects badly upon them and subsequently threatens the relationship. To admit need may imply inability or at least failure to perform expected relational duties and may also prompt rejection by the partner. Finally, intimates may feel their partners should be sufficiently sensitive so that open admission of needs is unnecessary. In essence, an intimate might feel that if a partner were meeting relational obligations, no open admission would be necessary and resource deficiencies might not even have occurred.

Nonintimates are under less obligation to disclose their needs and may feel such behavior is undesirable unless certain conditions exist. It is predicted that individuals in nonintimate relationships are more likely to disclose needs to another if (a) the other has an outstanding obligation to them; (b) they perceive they can repay the other's help; (c) the cost of the needed resource is low; (d) they have no available partners of greater intimacy; and/or (e) they do not fear exploitation by the other. Parts a through c assume that nonintimates will express their needs if they know another owes them some obligation, a new obligation can be readily met, and the obligation is not likely to be large.

Part d simply notes that disclosure may occur when one has few alternative partners who are more obligated, and part e recognizes that nonintimates may fear that disclosure of needs will make them vulnerable to exploitation.

Not only might intimates seek and provide information about needs but they are also obligated to offer resources aimed at reducing expressed or perceived needs. Therefore, it is predicted that *as the degree of intimacy associated with a relationship increases, the likelihood of offering a resource to a needy partner increases.* To ascertain a need but to do nothing about it is likely to be viewed as negatively as not perceiving the need at all. Consequently, an intimate is obligated to go beyond processing information about the partner's needs and to provide some resource either during the conversation or afterward. When one intimate wants to aid the other in need satisfaction but they disagree as to the best resource for meeting the need, conflict often ensues. In such cases, the resource that is offered may be unsatisfactory to the needy individual.

This hypothesis also assumes that if no current needs exist, conversational resources may be provided that will prove interesting or useful in the future. In such cases, interaction serves as a means of preventing resource deficits.

Again, there are several conditions under which nonintimates may offer resources. It is hypothesized that individuals in nonintimate relationships are more likely to offer resources to a needy other when (a) they have an outstanding debt to the other; (b) they have had successful exchanges with the other; (c) the other is perceived as willing and able to return a resource of comparable value; (d) the needed resource is not too costly; (e) the needy individual has no available partner of greater or equal intimacy; and/or (f) they desire a more intimate relationship with the other. Parts a through c propose that nonintimates will sometimes alleviate each other's needs when they believe that they owe such assistance and when they believe a resource will be returned. Part d proposes that low-cost resources may be forthcoming in nonintimate interactions, that nonintimates may share advice and low levels of social support and affection while conserving more valuable or personal resources. Part e suggests that resources will be provided if the other has no one else available, and part f suggests that such resources may be used as bait for relational escalation.

Intimates are also obligated to *accept offered resources. Specifically, as the degree of intimacy associated with a relationship increases, the greater the likelihood that an individual will accept an offered resource.* By "acceptance" is meant that an individual will acknowledge receipt of a resource and indicate a willingness to accept or act upon it. As noted earlier, intimates are expected to accept offers of assistance from their partners, for refusal may be viewed as rejection of the relationship or a lack of trust, either of which may result in conflict.

This does not mean that nonintimates will always reject offers of resources. If certain conditions are met, the probability of acceptance increases. Specifically, individuals in nonintimate relationships are more likely to accept offers of resources if (a) their partners are indebted to them; (b) they perceive they could repay the resource; (c) the resource is not too costly; (d) they do not fear exploitation; and/or (e) they have no available partner of greater intimacy. Thus if nonintimates can avoid becoming grossly in debt or have no alternative intimate partners, resources will be acknowledged and accepted.

After resources have been accepted, partners sometimes express gratitude. Polite "thank yous," open acknowledgments of gratitude, and even expressions of indebtedness may be tendered the benefactors. Such gratitude is more likely to occur when intimacy levels are low. Specifically, *as the degree of intimacy associated with a relationship increases, the degree of expressed gratitude for receipt of a resource decreases.* Since there is greater obligation to provide needed resources as intimacy increases, offers of resources within intimate relationships are expected. Given low levels of intimacy, such offers are not obligatory, particularly if given without prior inducements. Even though nonintimate givers may anticipate something in return, they do have to respond to the needs. Consistent with this reasoning, Bar-Tal, Bar-Zohar, Greenberg, and Hermon (1977) reported that individuals felt nonintimates were less obligated to provide assistance than were intimates and were more grateful for help from nonintimates than intimates.

Expressed gratitude may occur under some conditions within highly intimate relationships. Individuals in intimate relationships are more likely to express gratitude if (a) their partners provide an unusually valuable resource; and/or (b) they have recently been the recipient of a high degree of asymmetry of resource distribution. Intimates may need to express gratitude when their partners have expended an abnormal amount of effort and time to provide a resource. This implies that the resources received on a typical basis may not be overtly acknowledged. In addition, if the recent flow of resources has been decidedly one-sided, intimate partners may strongly need to acknowledge verbally their gratitude and indebtedness; indeed, the benefactor may demand it. Parents may at least require verbal "thanks" from children for the many resources they are given.

Finally, the conversations of intimates are more likely to be characterized by an asymmetrical flow of resources. *In the case of unilateral needs, as the degree of intimacy associated with a relationship increases, the greater the asymmetry of the flow of resources.* This hypothesis posits that when one of the intimates has greater needs, more offers will be directed toward the needy individual. This is consistent with the notion that one major obligation of relational intimacy is to provide needed resources without concern for immediate return. When needs are mutual, however, the intimate interaction usually manifests a greater bidirectional flow.

Since nonintimates are less obligated to provide resources, even in cases of unilateral needs, the needy individual will seek to reciprocate within the interaction. As noted in the previous hypothesis, a reciprocation may only consist of expressed gratitude or open acknowledgment of one's indebtedness, or it may involve an offer of some type of compensation.

Thus, some conversations are focused on need fulfillment or need prevention. In more intimate relationships, individuals will generally work harder to ascertain, disclose, and meet each other's needs. If needs are asymmetrical, then intimates will act to alleviate them even if nothing can be returned. When needs are equal, both parties will strive to reduce the other's needs, and, if no immediate needs are observed, conversational resources thought to be useful in the future are provided. Nonintimates, who are less obligated to act on the other's needs, will generally do so only when external inducement is provided, costs of resources are low, or no alternative partners of greater or equal intimacy are available.

INTERPERSONAL NEGOTIATION

Even one's most intimate partner cannot always ascertain or volunteer needed resources. Some needs cannot be identified unless they are specifically expressed. Since some needs consume costly resources, a relational partner may demand justification before providing such resources. Consequently, individuals may have to educate partners and convince them to provide resources. Such is the stuff of *interpersonal negotiation: a process* wherein needy individuals try to conclude exchange agreements with relational partners.

It seems reasonable that needy individuals will seek resources from those who both possess the needed resources *and* are likely to grant the request. Such persons are likely to be intimate partners. Specifically, it is hypothesized that *as the degree of intimacy associated with a relationship increases, the greater the likelihood that persons will seek needed resources from their relational partner.* The obligations inherent in intimate relationships make such partners reasonable targets. Even if intimates lack sufficient skills to provide a service, they are obligated to try to help and at a lower cost than nonintimates. Indeed, research indicates that people are more likely to seek needed resources from intimates than from nonintimates (e.g., Griffin, 1985; Shapiro, 1980).

Nevertheless, intimate partners may, in certain situations, be reluctant to seek resources from their partners. Individuals in intimate relationships will avoid seeking resources if (a) they fear it will endanger the relationship; (b) they have been the recent recipient of asymmetrical flows of resources; (c) their partners cannot afford to provide such resources; and/or (d) the particular resource should be given spontaneously. Parts a,b, and c flow from similar logic presented in prior sections. Intimates do not want to harm their relationship or create needs for their partners. Part d rests on different reasoning. Blau (1964) has argued that resources such as social approval, interpersonal attraction, and respect cannot be bargained for without reducing their value. Such resources must be given spontaneously lest they appear to be contrived and insincere. These are important resources in intimate relationships, and partners may feel that they should be given freely without explicit requests.

In addition, nonintimates may become persuasive targets under certain circumstances. Individuals in nonintimate relationships are more likely to seek needed resources from each other when (a) the other has an outstanding obligation to the requester; (b) they have had successful exchanges with one another; (c) they are able to repay the resource if it is provided; (d) the resource is of low value; (e) they have no available partners of greater or equal intimacy who can provide the resources; and/or (f) they do not fear exploitation. Parts a through d imply that the debt incurred by seeking a resource from a nonintimate may be less if the other owes the requester, a history of successful exchanges exist if the resource is of low value, and the requester feels able to provide a resource in return. These conditions are especially important, for research indicates a greater feeling of indebtedness occurs when a resource is requested than when it is offered freely (Greenberg & Saxe, 1975). Consequently, anything that increases trust or lowers the debt should reduce reticence about making the request. Parts e and f suggest that if one has no choice of sources or does not fear excessive demands, then resources will be sought from a nonintimate.

It is expected that individuals will structure their requests differently across relationships of varying degrees of intimacy. Specifically, *as the degree of intimacy associated with a relationship increases, the fewer the number of (a) explanations for the requests, (b) apologies, and/or (c) external inducements that will be included with the request.* Explanatory statements provide reasons for requesting the resources, and may include the extent of need, causes of the need, and how the specific resource will alleviate the need. Apologies express regret for making the request, and external inducements offer resources in exchange. External inducements include promises of specific resources at a later time, or resources offered in the conversation itself, such as compliments. Explanatory statements and external inducements are persuasive devices for convincing the individual to provide the resources. In intimate relationships, such devices are less important since the target is usually obligated in advance of the request to honor it. Apologies prevent the needy individual from appearing presumptuous. Since no prior obligation exists in nonintimate relationships, individuals may fear they appear to be imposing upon the other, which alone would warrant rejection.

Nevertheless, intimates may utter such statements when they fear rejection. Individuals in intimate relationships will provide greater numbers of explanatory statements, apologies, and/or external inducements when (a) the resource is of unusually great value and/or (b) the requester has recently been the recipient of asymmetrical flows of resources. This hypothesis assumes that even the obligations of intimates have limits. If atypical time and energy are involved or the requester has been receiving much while returning little, the requester may feel compelled to offer justification in excess of the obligation inherent in the relationship.

This analysis also predicts that compliance gaining attempts will be differentially effective across relationships of varying intimacy. *As the degree of intimacy associated with a relationship increases, the probability of granting a request increases.* Simply put, the prior obligation of intimacy increases compliance with requests. Still, intimates may choose to not comply in certain situations. Individuals in intimate relationships will not comply with a request if (a) the need does not appear to be legitimate; (b) the resource will not meet the need; (c) the requester has recently been the recipient of an asymmetrical flow of resources; and (d) the needed resource is quite costly. Intimates can reject requests that are excessive—that is, when the need is exaggerated, the resource will not meet the need, or the demand requires too much of the target—or if the partner has apparently taken advantage of the relationship by not making returns.

Individuals in nonintimate relationships will grant requests to the extent that they (a) have an outstanding obligation to the requester; (b) have had successful exchanges with the requester; (c) perceive the requester is willing and able to return a resource of comparable value; (d) perceive the resource to be of low cost; (e) perceive that the requester has no alternative suppliers of greater or equal intimacy; and/or (f) desire to increase the degree of intimacy associated with the relationship. This hypothesis is similar to earlier ones about how nonintimates decide to help others when they perceive a need. In essence, nonintimates need external inducement and perceptions that only they can help.

As noted earlier, compliance will not always be forthcoming. When rejection of a request occurs, the structure of the rejection will vary with intimacy. *As the degree of intimacy associated with a relationship increases, the greater the likelihood that a rejection will be accompanied by* (a) *apologies,* (b) *refutations,* (c) *excuses, and/or* (d) *counteroffers.* The obligation to provide resources decreases the likelihood that an intimate will simply refuse. Since they have violated a relational expectation, intimates must offer some response that minimizes damage to the relationship. These responses include apologies, such as expressions of regret or sorrow; refutational statements, which attack the legitimacy of the need or the ability of the resource to meet the need; excuses, which cite external reasons why the target is willing but unable to provide the resource; and counteroffers, which suggest alternative resources or alternative suppliers of resources.

Nonintimates may also choose to amplify upon their rejections in certain circumstances. Individuals in nonintimate relationships will include apologies, refutations, excuses, and/or counteroffers when (a) they have outstanding obligations to the requester; (b) they have had successful exchanges with the requester; (c) the need is legitimate; and/or (d) they want to maintain an exchange relationship with the requester. Parts a and b assume that if a nonintimate has received a nonreciprocated resource or has a history of successful exchanges, then an obligation to honor a request exists. Thus refusal mandates an attempt to reduce the perception that one does not honor one's obligations. Part c assumes that nonintimates may feel a request is a legitimate reflection of the need and therefore demands a detailed response, and part d assumes that a flat rejection may reduce the likelihood that even an exchange relationship will be continued.

Since intimate partners are expected to comply, a rejection is likely to upset the requester. Indeed, research indicates that individuals are more upset when a request is turned down by family and friends than by strangers and acquaintances (Bar-Tal et al., 1977). This negative affect is likely to be reflected in the communication behavior of the requester. *As the degree of intimacy associated with a relationship increases, there is an increase in the likelihood that rejection will be responded to with* (a) *information seeking;* (b) *counterpressure;* (c) *external inducements; and/or* (d) *coercive statements.*

Information seeking implies that intimates will try to determine the grounds for rejection. Since it has already been predicted that the target will provide some justification for the rejection, this hypothesis assumes probing of stated and unstated reasons. Counterpressure implies persistence. Intimates may simply repeat their need for the resource, amplify upon the extent of need, or refute the stated reasons, excuses, or counteroffers offered by the target. External inducements suggest that intimates may add promises or compliments to the request to motivate compliance. Coercive statements include threats, insults, or invoking prior debts owed by the target. These are attempts to *force* compliance and may not occur until information seeking, counterpressure, and external inducements have failed. All of the above communicative tactics are reactions to unexpected rejection and reflect attempts to overcome resistance.

While research indicates that intimates are more negative in their mutual influence attempts (Fitzpatrick & Winke, 1979), boundary conditions reduce this action. Individuals in intimate relationships are less likely to follow rejection with information seeking, counterpressure, external inducements, or coercive statements if (a) their partner's refutations, excuses, or counteroffers are perceived to be legitimate; (b) other intimate sources of benefits are available and willing to help; (c) further argument may endanger the relationship; and/or (d) the requester has been the recent recipient of an asymmetric distribution of resources. Part a implies that a negative overt reaction may be averted if the rejection is adequately explained. Recall that it was argued that intimates are obligated to overlook occasional unresponsiveness. If that transgression can be smoothed over, no further argument is likely to occur. Parts b and c suggest that less pressure will occur if alternative sources are readily available and further argument could damage the entire relationship. Finally, part d implies that requesters will not pursue additional resources aggressively when they know they have already received disproportionate resources.

Since nonintimates are under little prior obligation to provide assistance, rejection is less likely to be questioned. On some occasions, however, nonintimates may also choose to pursue rejections. Individuals in nonintimate relationships may follow rejection with information seeking, counterpressure, external inducements, and/or coercive statements if (a) the target has an outstanding obligation to the requester; (b) the target and requester have completed exchanges; (c) the request was role-based; and/or (d) few alternative sources are available. Parts a and b assume that pressure results when the target owes the requester a favor and the rejection is thus a refusal to reciprocate, or when prior successful exchanges imply a willingness to engage in future exchanges. Part c recognizes that some roles such as salesperson or solicitor require nonintimates to pursue rejections so that the sale or donation may be consummated. Part d implies that if nonintimates have no other alternatives, they will strive to overcome resistance. In any case, persistence still is likely to be irritating to the nonintimate target.

Thus interpersonal negotiation in intimate relationships starts with a needy person seeking resources from an obligated partner. Consequently, unless resistance is anticipated, the request is typically unadorned with communicative blandishment. In most cases, intimate partners will grant requests; and when they refuse, they will try to communicate in ways that minimize relational damage. Intimates will respond negatively to rejection unless they are convinced by the target's reasons for the rejection or they fear that argument will harm the relationship.

Nonintimates work harder for their resources. They usually provide more information about the need and request, and offer inducements to comply. This is necessary because the partner is less obligated to comply. If the target is indebted to the nonintimate requester, the solicitation may be granted. If a nonintimate target refuses a request, conflict will occur if the target refuses to honor a previous obligation or seeks to terminate exchanges. However, such conflict is less likely in nonintimate relationships and partners are more likely to turn to alternative sources.

SUMMING UP

As noted throughout this chapter, approaches that view human affairs from an exchange perspective are of ancient vintage. Exchange will doubtless continue to be used as an explanation for human behavior, including behavior occurring in interpersonal relationships. Despite some appeal, these approaches have had limited utility for communication researchers, both because of imprecision in operationalizing the norm of reciprocity across situations and because of limited and often tangential application to communication variables. This chapter seeks to rectify both deficiencies.

Gouldner's explication of a general moral principle that requires individuals to repay favors and to be supportive of benefactors until repayment is achieved was adopted as a starting point. While this principle is applicable across situations, it is implemented through exchange rules that vary with the situation. As the degree of intimacy associated with a relationship increases, partners become more obligated to meet each other's needs and to provide such resources under a "good faith" principle. These two obligations were hypothesized to influence eight components of an exchange such that individuals in more intimate relationships are required to *volunteer* needed resources, even of a highly personal nature. Moreover, such obligations are transferable to the partner's significant others. Intimates do have some flexibility in meeting other's needs; returned resources may be of different form, of only roughly equivalent value, and not specifically linked to any prior act.

In less intimate relationships, there is less obligation to provide needed resources. Consequently, benefits are provided when they reduce the giver's prior debts to the recipient or when they increase the indebtedness of the receiver to the giver. Since there is less trust inherent in the relationship, exchanges tend toward a *quid pro quo*. Thus, the same exchange behavior may be viewed as less acceptable if it occurs in a nonintimate rather than an intimate relationship.

In terms of communication, the degree of intimacy associated with a relationship affects exchanges occurring in an interaction and influences how future exchanges will be negotiated. In general, intimates are more obligated to be sensitive to their partner's needs before and during interaction and to offer needed resources freely. In addition, intimates are more likely to disclose their needs to one another and to accept offered resources, but they are less likely to express gratitude for resources. When negotiating exchange agreements, intimates are less likely to offer verbal support for their requests and are more likely to follow repeated refusals with pressure. All of these hypothesized exchange behaviors include qualifications under which the obligations in the relationship might be legitimately violated.

NOTES

1. This discussion assumes that intimacy is a trait individuals attribute to relationships. Clearly, some relationships imply greater intimacy than others. For example, the terms "stranger," "acquaintance," "friend," and "spouse" imply increasing but not necessarily equal increments of intimacy. *Within each type* of relationship, intimacy

varies. For example, Fitzpatrick's (1977) research documents the commonsense notion that all marriages are not equally intimate. Indeed, some marriages may be equally or less intimate than friendships. For purposes of this discussion, however, examples implying that family and friendship are more intimate than stranger and acquaintance relationships will be used.

2. Two things should be noted about subsequent hypotheses. First, each hypothesis assumes that individuals in intimate relationships are motivated to keep their relationships at current levels of intimacy. If an individual is not, the likelihood of need-related behavior may be reduced to levels of nonintimate relationships or, perhaps, may be contrary to need-fulfillment. For example, individuals desiring to disengage from their relationships are less likely to self-disclose about various topics including needs (Baxter, 1979), and less adjusted marrieds are less sympathetic to each other's external problems (Cousins & Vincent, 1983). Second, each hypothesis assumes that individuals in intimate relationships are subject to transferability of obligation such that they incur the debts of their partners and feel an obligation to help needy significant others of their intimate partners. For clarity of statement, these phrases were deleted from the wording.

REFERENCES

Argyle, M., & Furnham, A. (1983). Sources of satisfaction and conflict in long-term relationships. *Journal of Marriage and the Family, 45* 481-493.

Argyle, M., & Henderson, M. (1984). The rules of friendship. *Journal of Social and Personal Relationships, 1,* 211-237.

Aristotle. (1943). *On man in the universe.* Roslyn, NY: Walter J. Black, Inc.

Bar-Tal, D., Bar-Zohar, Y., Greenberg, M. S., & Hermon, M. (1977). Reciprocity behavior in the relationship between donor and recipient and between harm-doer and victim. *Sociometry, 40,* 293-298.

Baxter, L. A. (1979). Self-disclosure as a relationship disengagement strategy: An exploratory investigation. *Human Communication Research, 5,* 215-221.

Baxter, L. A., & Wilmot, W. W. (1985). Taboo topics in close relationships. *Journal of Social and Personal Relationships, 2,* 253-269.

Beach, L. R., & Carter, W. B. (1976). Appropriate and equitable repayment of social debts. *Organizational Behavior and Human Performance, 16,* 280-293.

Befu, H. (1980). Structural and motivational approaches to social exchange. In K. Gergen, M. Greenberg, & R. Willis (Eds.), *Social exchange: Advances in theory and research* (pp. 197-214). New York: Plenum.

Berg, J.H., & Archer, R.L. (1980). Disclosure or concern: A second look at liking for the norm breaker. *Journal of Personality, 48,* 245-257.

Birchler, G. R., Weiss, R. L., & Vincent, J. P. (1975). Multimethod analysis of social reinforcement exchange between maritally distressed and nondistressed spouse and stranger dyads. *Journal of Personality and Social Psychology, 31,* 349-360.

Blau, P. (1964). *Exchange and power in everyday life.* New York: John Wiley.

Brinberg, D., & Castell, P. (1982). A resource exchange theory approach to interpersonal interactions: A test of Foa's theory. *Journal of Personality and Social Psychology, 43,* 260-269.

Chelune, G. J., Robison, J. T., & Kommor, M. J. (1984). A cognitive interactional model of intimate relationships. In V.J. Derlega (Ed.), *Communication, intimacy, and close relationships* (pp. 11-40). New York: Academic Press.

Clark, M. S. (1981). Noncomparability of benefits given and received: A cue to the existence of friendship. *Social Psychology Quarterly, 44,* 375-381.

Clark, M. S. (1983a). Reactions to aid in communal and exchange relationships. In J. D. Fisher, A. Nadler, & B. M. DePaulo (Eds.), *New directions in helping* (Vol. 1, pp. 281-303). New York: Academic Press.

Clark, M. S. (1983b). Some implications of close social bonds for help-seeking. In B. M. DePaulo, A. Nadler, & J. D. Fisher (Eds.), *New directions in helping* (Vol. 2, pp. 205-229). New York: Academic Press.

Clark, M. S. (1984a). Implications of relationship type for understanding compatibility. In W. Ickes (Ed.), *Compatible and incompatible relationships* (pp. 119-140). New York: Springer-Verlag.

Clark, M. S. (1984b). Record keeping in two types of relationships. *Journal of Personality and Social Psychology, 47,* 549-557.

Clark, M. S., & Mills, J. (1979). Interpersonal attraction in exchange and communal relationships. *Journal of Personality and Social Psychology, 37,* 12-24.

Clark, M. S., & Waddell, B. (1985). Perceptions of exploitation in communal and exchange relationships. *Journal of Social and Personal Relationships, 2,* 403-418.

Cousins, P. C., & Vincent, J. P. (1983). Supportive and aversive behavior following spousal complaints. *Journal of Marriage and the Family, 45,* 679-682.

Enzle, M. E., & Lowe, C. A. (1976). Helping and social exchange. *Social Behavior and Personality, 4,* 261-266.

Fitzpatrick, M. A. (1977). A typological approach to communication in relationships. In B. Ruben (Ed.), *Communication yearbook 1* (pp. 263-275). New Brunswick, NJ: Transaction Books.

Fitzpatrick, M. A., & Winke, J. (1979). You always hurt the one you love: Strategies and tactics in interpersonal conflict. *Communication Quarterly, 27,* 3-11.

Foa, U. G., & Foa, E. B. (1974). *Societal structures of the mind.* Springfield, IL: Charles C Thomas.

Forgas, J. P., & Dobosz, B. (1980). Dimensions of romantic involvement: Towards a taxonomy of heterosexual relationships. *Social Psychology Quarterly, 43,* 290-300.

Gouldner, A. W. (1960). The norm of reciprocity: A preliminary statement. *American Sociological Review, 25,* 161-178.

Greenberg, M. S. (1980). A theory of indebtedness. In K. Gergen, M. Greenberg, & R. Willis (Eds.), *Social exchange: Advances in theory and research* (pp. 3-26). New York: Plenum.

Greenberg, M. S., & Shapiro, S. P. (1971). Indebtedness: An adverse aspect of asking for and receiving help. *Sociometry, 34,* 290-301.

Greenberg, M. S., & Saxe, L. (1975). Importance of locus of help initiation and type of outcome as determinants of reactions to another's help attempt. *Social Behavior and Personality, 3,* 101-110.

Greenberg, M. S., & Wescott, D. R. (1983). Indebtedness as a mediator of reactions to aid. In J. D. Fisher, A. Nadler, & B. M. DePaulo (Eds.), *New directions in helping* (Vol. 1, pp. 85-112). New York: Academic Press.

Griffith, J. (1985). Social support providers: Who are they? Where are they met? And the relationship of network characteristics to psychological distress. *Basic and Applied Social Psychology, 6,* 41-60.

Hinde, R. A. (1979). *Towards understanding relationships.* New York: Academic Press.

Jacobson, N. S., Follette, W. C., & McDonald, D. W., (1982). Reactivity to positive and negative behavior in distressed and nondistressed married couples. *Journal of Consulting and Clinical Psychology, 50,* 706-714.

Jacobson, N. S., Waldron, H., & Moore, D. (1980). Toward a behavioral profile of marital distress. *Journal of Consulting and Clinical Psychology, 48,* 696-703.

Jourard, S. M. (1971). *Self-disclosure: An experimental analysis of the transparent self.* New York: John Wiley.

Lloyd, S., Cate, R., & Henton, J. (1982). Equity and rewards as predictors of satisfaction in casual and intimate relationships. *Journal of Psychology, 110,* 43-48.

Longabaugh, R. (1963). A category system for coding interpersonal behaviour as social exchange. *Sociometry, 26,* 319-344.

Marwell, G., & Hage, J. (1970). The organization of role relationships: A systematic description. *American Sociological Review, 35,* 884-900.

Mauss, M. (1954). *The gift.* New York: Free Press.

Mills, J., & Clark, M. S. (1982). Exchange and communal relationships. In L. Wheeler (Ed.), *Review of personality and social psychology* (Vol. 3, pp. 121-144). Newbury Park, CA: Sage.

Pruitt, D. G. (1968). Reciprocity and credit building in a laboratory dyad. *Journal of Personality and Social Psychology, 8,* 143-147.

Pruitt, D. G. (1981). *Negotiation behavior.* New York: Academic Press.

Rettig, K. D., & Bubolz, M. M. (1983). Interpersonal resource exchanges as indicators of quality of marriage. *Journal of Marriage and the Family, 45,* 497-509.

Roloff, M. E. (1981). *Interpersonal communication: The social exchange approach.* Newbury Park, CA: Sage.

Roloff, M. E., & Campion, D. E. (1985). Conversational profit seeking: Interaction as social exchange. In R. L. Street, Jr. & J. N. Cappella (Eds.), *Sequence and pattern in communicative behaviour* (pp. 161-189). London: Edward Arnold.

Shapiro, E. G. (1980). Is seeking help from a friend like seeking help from a stranger? *Social Psychology Quarterly, 43,* 259-263.

Shumaker, S. A., & Jackson, J. S. (1979). The aversive effects of nonreciprocated benefits. *Sociometry, 42,* 148-158.

Simmel, G. (1950). *The sociology of Georg Simmel* (K. H. Wolff, Ed.). New York: Free Press.

Waring, E. M., Tillman, M. P., Frelick, L., Russell, L., & Weisz, G. (1980). Concepts of intimacy in the general population. *Journal of Nervous and Mental Disease, 168,* 471-474.

Wegner, D., & Vallacher, R. (1977). *Implicit psychology: An introduction to social cognition.* New York: Oxford University Press.

Wish, M., Deutsch, M., & Kaplan, S. J. (1976). Perceived dimensions of interpersonal relations. *Journal of Personality and Social Psychology, 33,* 409-420.

Chapter 2

COMMUNICATING UNDER UNCERTAINTY

Charles R. Berger

UNCERTAINTY PLAYS AN enormously important role in many spheres of social life. Galbraith (1977) has argued we live in an "age of uncertainty" that is unlike previous historical epochs. Past political and economic life, according to Galbraith, was considerably more predictable than it is today. In addition, the advent of the nuclear age has raised current international stakes to such a degree that governments spend huge sums each year to uncover the future actions of both friends and foes. Consider the following statistics. During fiscal 1985, it is estimated that the Central Intelligence Agency will spend $99,300,000 on its operations, while the National Security Council will spend $4,605,000. In addition, the National Security Agency, with its classified budget, will spend millions more dollars on intelligence-gathering efforts. Most likely, the U.S.S.R. spends approximately equal numbers of rubles to support its intelligence community.

Not only does the U.S. government spend large amounts of tax money to try to reduce its international uncertainties, individual citizens are willing to pay dearly to reduce their uncertainties about the future course of stocks and other investment vehicles. It is estimated that Americans spend some $100,000,000 a year to obtain investment information (*Wall Street Week,* 1985). In addition, consider the substantial sums paid by businesses to economic forecasters and it becomes apparent that uncertainty reduction itself is a major business.

When individuals and corporations cannot reduce business and personal uncertainties, they spend large amounts of money to hedge against negative outcomes that may loom over the horizon. In 1983, $109 billion in net property and casualty insurance premiums were paid by individuals and corporations (A. M. Best, 1984a). During the same period, $119 billion in net premiums were paid for life and health insurance policies, excluding premiums paid to

AUTHOR'S NOTE: The author would like to thank Robert A. Bell, Kathy Kellermann, Gerry Miller, and Michael Roloff for their comments on an earlier version of this chapter.

Blue Cross-Blue Shield (A. M. Best, 1984b). These figures demonstrate that as the importance of the outcomes increases in a situation, persons and institutions are willing to invest considerable resources to try to predict and hedge against future events that may affect their outcomes. So pervasive are these uncertainty-reduction activities that decision making under uncertainty is a growing area of research in such academic disciplines as business (Hogarth, 1980) and cognitive psychology (Kahneman, Slovic, & Tversky, 1982). These investigators, as well as others, have sought to understand the strategies individuals employ to make judgments and decisions when complete information is unavailable to them.

Although economists, political scientists, sociologists, and psychologists have recognized the centrality of uncertainty in human affairs, communication researchers in general and interpersonal communication researchers in particular have only recently begun to acknowledge the importance of uncertainty in human communication. Early communication researchers (e.g., Berlo, 1960) did discuss Shannon and Weaver's (1949) mathematical theory of information, which deals with uncertainty in communication systems, however, such discussions did little to motivate either theory building or empirical research aimed at exploring the role played by uncertainty in human communication. Several psychologists (Heider, 1958; Kelly, 1955; Thibaut & Kelley, 1959) discussed the role played by uncertainty in interpersonal relationships, but these discussions had little impact upon communication researchers interested in the study of interpersonal processes. Thus, the main impact of Thibaut and Kelley's (1959) analysis of interpersonal relationships was their explication of the roles played by exchanges of rewards and costs in relationship development (e.g., Roloff, 1981). Their discussion of uncertainty was virtually ignored by communication researchers.

This state of affairs changed in 1975 when Calabrese and I (Berger & Calabrese, 1975) advanced an axiomatic theory designed to explain certain communication phenomena that we observed during initial interactions. We felt then, as we feel today, that a number of events occurring in such initial encounters can be explained in terms of uncertainty and uncertainty reduction. Although the theory was originally developed to explain certain initial interaction phenomena, it has recently been expanded to explain aspects of established romantic relationships (Parks & Adelman, 1983) and intercultural encounters (Gudykunst, Yang, & Nishida, 1985). These studies, as well as several others, have demonstrated three important points: First, uncertainty levels are important in relationships beyond the initial stages of their formation. Second, uncertainty is also important in communication contexts other than interpersonal ones. Third, and not surprisingly, the theory, as proposed by Berger and Calabrese (1975), contains some propositions of dubious validity.

A decade has elapsed since publication of the original theory, and it seems appropriate to see what directions it has taken and to sketch how it might be developed in the future. Thus the two primary goals of the present chapter are to assess the evolution of the theory since its inception and to plot some potential courses of future development. When the theory was first discussed (Berger & Calabrese, 1975), there was no official name given to it. Some dubbed it "initial interaction theory" while others called it "uncertainty theory." More recent discussions have used the term "uncertainty reduction theory" (URT). This more inclusive label seems to capture best the evolutionary direction of the theory.

THEORETICAL EVOLUTION

THE NATURE OF UNCERTAINTY

Just as it is the bane of political and economic decision-makers, uncertainty is also a potential hobgoblin of interpersonal relationships. The task of interacting with a stranger, who in theory can behave and believe in a very large number of alternative ways and whose actions and beliefs remain to be explained, presents interactants with complex predictive and explanatory problems. These problems pertain both to understanding the other person in an interaction and understanding oneself. To interact in a relatively smooth, coordinated, and understandable manner, one must be able both to predict how one's interaction partner is likely to behave, and, based on these predictions, to select from one's own repertoire those responses that will optimize outcomes in the encounter. Uncertainty is not reduced for its own sake. Political and economic planners as well as communicators seek to reduce their uncertainties about their environments so that they can respond to these environments in ways that will assure goal achievement (e.g., Miller & Steinberg, 1975).

The idea that uncertainty is a function of the number of alternatives present in a situation and their relative likelihood of occurrence is, of course, taken directly from information theory (Shannon & Weaver, 1949). However, Berger and Calabrese (1975) extended this notion of uncertainty to include explanation. Thus uncertainty is a function of both the ability to predict and the ability to explan actions of other *and* of self. This explanatory component was added because of the importance accorded causal explanation by various attribution theorists (Heider, 1958; Jones & Davis, 1965; Kelley, 1967, 1971). This broader conceptualization of uncertainty holds that persons obtain information that allows them to increase their predictive certainty before they become concerned with the problem of why certain behaviors have or have not occurred. Berger, Gardner, Parks, Schulman, and Miller (1976) pointed out that obtaining the knowledge necessary for reducing explanatory uncertainty might be both more difficult and time consuming than acquiring information necessary for the reduction of predictive uncertainty. A similar discussion of levels of knowing was presented by Miller and Steinberg (1975) at about the same time.

This basic conceptualization of the uncertainty construct remains intact. Furthermore, Berger (1975) was able to demonstrate how information exchanged early in interactions can foster predictions about unknown attributes of the other (*proactive attributions*) and explanations of subsequent conduct during ongoing interactions (*retroactive attributions*). This distinction between proactive and retroactive attributional activity was incorporated into Clatterbuck's (1979) CLUES scale, which has been employed in a number of studies examining the relationships between uncertainty and other variables. Recently, Gudykunst and Nishida (1986) have modified the CLUES scale to increase its cross-cultural generalizability. Both the original and modified versions of the scale are displayed in the Appendix.

COMMUNICATION AND UNCERTAINTY

Given the many combinations of verbal and nonverbal behaviors and the ranges of subtle modulations of these behaviors available to most normal interactants, it is amazing persons are able to carry out as many meaningful interactions with others as they apparently do. Of course, psychotherapists, organizational and media consultants, and others whose job it is to improve communication skills are quick to point out that persons playing a variety of roles fail to discharge their duties as they should because of "communication breakdowns" or "failures to communicate." Though such breakdowns and failures are certainly real and should be expected given the complex nature of communicative transactions, more often than not persons are able to achieve their interaction goals successfully. If the reader doubts the veracity of this assertion, consider all of the mundane interactions that most of us have during the course of an average day. Encounters with shopkeepers, ticket agents, waiters, coworkers, and a host of others usually go off without a hitch.

Communication and uncertainty are inextricably intertwined. Communicative actions are those things interactants frequently wish to predict and less frequently seek to explain, and it is through observations of communicative conduct that predictions and explanations are derived. This reciprocal relationship is central to URT. Axioms of the original theory posited reciprocal causal relationships between amount of communication and uncertainty and between nonverbal affiliative expressiveness and uncertainty; specifically, uncertainty is reduced as these variables increase, and decreases in uncertainty are responsible for increases in both verbal and nonverbal communication.

Although these relationships still seem somewhat plausible, Berger and Bradac (1982) recognized that there are circumstances under which communicative action might actually increase uncertainty. Persons are perfectly capable of acting in ways calculated to cloud their intentions in the eyes of others. Goffman (1969) presents an insightful analysis of how persons employ *covering moves* to mask their true intent and how observers employ *uncovering moves* to ascertain actual intentions. However, persons can deploy *counter-uncovering moves* to foil the uncovering moves made by observers. This process of increasing uncertainty through communicative action may not be intentional. Given certain combinations of alternative choices and specific contexts, some communicative choices might actually increase uncertainty because of the number of alternative interpretations available to observers. As Jones and Davis (1965) have argued, since positive actions can be motivated by either sincere or ulterior motives, they are not as reliable for making inferences about underlying dispositions as are negative behaviors that we assume are not motivated by ulterior motives.

In addition to the above possibilities, Planalp and Honeycutt (1985) have studied events that increase uncertainty in ongoing relationships. In their survey, respondents had little difficulty thinking of events that increased their uncertainty about persons whom they thought they knew well. These events—namely, competing relationships, unexplained loss of close contact, sexual behavior, deception, change in personality and values, and betraying confidence—exerted strong impacts upon cognitive, affective, and communication variables. In addition, a majority of the relationships studied became more distant or were terminated as a result of the events. Unfortunately, the way in which participants were asked to report on uncertainty-increasing events in their relationships may have biased them toward thinking about negative rather than positive events, although a few respondents did report positive events. This is an improtant point since persons can be pleasantly surprised by certain events in such relationships. Nevertheless, this study is significant because it supports the notion that communication does not always act to reduce uncertainty in relationships.

It is probably safe to assume that reduced communication between persons can impair their ability to predict and explain each other well. This prediction challenges the well-known aphorism, absence makes the heart grow fonder. Under the present view, absence and reduced interaction between persons are likely to lead to increased relational difficulties, especially when the individuals involved in the relationship are experiencing considerable change in their individual lives. There is some evidence to support this line of reasoning. Ayres (1979) found that both stranger and friend dyads asked each other about an equal number of questions during the initial few minutes of their interactions; however, friends asked significantly more evaluative questions of each other when compared with strangers. Thus sheer volume of information seeking in the two types of dyads was the same, but the kinds of information sought differed. Ayers's findings suggest that even friends may have reduced their uncertainties about each other each time they interact. Unfortunately, Ayres

(1979) did not measure the length of time since the last interaction between the friends he studied. Had he done so, we would have expected question frequency to increase with time elapsed since the last interaction.

The relationship between uncertainty and communication is not simple. Lack of opportunity to communicate most certainly has the effect of raising uncertainty levels; however, the opportunity to interact may or may not produce reductions in uncertainty. Although it is safe to assume that communication is necessary for the reduction of uncertainty—unless, of course, one believes uncertainty can be reduced through ESP—the relationships between uncertainty and communication posited here differ from those advanced by Berger and Calabrese (1975). Moreover, the present discussion suggests that sheer volume of communication is probably not a good predictor of uncertainty reduction. Indeed, the quality rather than the quantity of information exchanged between interactants should have a greater impact upon the reduction of mutual uncertainties.

SOCIAL CONTEXT AND UNCERTAINTY REDUCTION

Berger and Calabrese (1975) suggested that the social context of interactions might provide uncertainty-reducing information. For example, persons first meeting at a political rally might begin their conversation by talking about the candidate rather than exchanging the usual biographic and demographic information; however, exchanges of such information might occur later in the same interaction. In this situation uncertainty is reduced by both parties making inferences about the reasons for the other's presence at the rally. Most likely, persons would assume that others present at such a rally support the candidate, thus making the candidate a safe topic for a conversational opening.

Rubin (1977) varied the interaction context to see how it would affect the number and types of questions asked by interactants. In the ambiguous condition, persons were asked to form a general impression of others by asking them questions. In the specific condition, persons were asked to form impressions of their partners in terms of how they thought the partners would perform on a library job. Persons in the latter condition also were told to form their impressions by asking questions. This study revealed two findings relevant to the present issue: First, more questions were asked in the ambiguous context; second, more demographic questions were asked in the ambiguous context. In addition to these findings, Rubin (1979) reported that interactions in the ambiguous context lasted significantly longer than those in the specific context, and postinteraction ratings revealed that persons in the ambiguous context felt they had greater insight into their partners' personalities.

These findings support the notion that uncertainty can be reduced by the context of the interaction. Interactants in the ambiguous context faced the problem of reducing their uncertainties about their partners along many more dimensions than those in the specific context. To accomplish this task, they had to spend more time interacting with their partners and they had to ask them more questions. In addition, the questions they asked were primarily biographic and demographic. Answers to these broad background questions can be used to make inferences about attitudes and opinions not yet revealed in the conversation (Berger, 1975). Interestingly, the increased interaction time in the ambiguous context led interactants to feel they had a better grasp of their partners' personalities than did interactants in the specific context. This finding is not too surprising given the conversational task in the specific condition—that is, to form an impression of a person as a potential library assistant.

Although Rubin's findings clearly show the uncertainty-reducing properties of interaction contexts, the social context may increase interactants' uncertainty levels under certain conditions. One can imagine circumstances in which persons might structure interaction situations to maximize the uncertainty levels of the persons involved. Individuals may be intentionally misled so they do not discover a hidden agenda, or so many potential agendas are rendered possible that persons have a difficult time understanding exactly which one is operating at a given time. Thus the social context, like communicative action, can sometimes be used to raise uncertainty levels.

UNCERTAINTY REDUCTION STRATEGIES

Thus far we have examined the roles played by both communication and the interaction context in the uncertainty reduction process. There are, however, additional routes to uncertainty reduction. First, persons bring considerable knowledge with them to any interaction situation: information about persons in the form of person prototypes (Cantor & Mischel, 1977), role schemas, and typical event sequences or scripts (Abelson, 1981; Schank & Abelson, 1977). This knowledge enables the individuals to begin to understand others involved in the social situation and provides the procedural knowledge necessary to conduct the interaction. Such knowledge is vital for the conduct of most interactions (Abelson, 1981; Schank, 1982; Schank & Abelson, 1977; Winograd, 1980). Also in this long-term memory are schemas for the acquisition of new knowledge (i.e., procedural routines for acquiring new information). Obviously, such new information *must* be acquired if a relationship is to develop. This kind of procedural knowledge is extremely powerful because it enables us to acquire new knowledge. It is to these knowledge acquisition routines that I now turn.

In the original version of URT, Berger and Calabrese (1975) were not concerned with strategies for reducing uncertainty. Subsequently, attention was directed toward these knowledge acquisition strategies (Berger, 1979; Berger & Bradac, 1982; Berger et al., 1976). These presentations advanced a typology of information-gaining strategies consisting of three broad strategy classes: passive, active, and interactive. *Passive* strategies are those in which the uncertainty reducer gathers information about a target through unobtrusive observation. *Active* strategies involve the observation of targets' responses to manipulations of the interaction environment but no direct interaction between observers and targets. Also included in this category is the acquisition of information about a target from third-party sources. Finally, *interactive* strategies involve direct, face-to-face contact between the information seeker and the target.

It is tempting to speculate which of these three classes of strategies is most effective in acquiring information. One might argue, for example, that interactive strategies are superior because the uncertainty reducer can control the target and can ask probing questions. However, it could also be argued that passive approaches are more effective because the observer can attend more closely to the target. In the passive mode, observers do not have to be concerned about their conduct during the interaction. No research energy has been expended on this issue, but it is an important one to study from both theoretical and methodological points of view. Since researchers frequently make judgments of research participants after observing their interactions on videotape (passive mode), we might ask: Would these judgments correspond to those that would have been made had the observer actually interacted with the person (interactive mode)? My suspicion is that there would be significant changes in judgments as a function of shifts in observational context.

Research conducted to investigate knowledge acquisition strategies has revealed several important findings. Studies aimed at illuminating the passive strategies (Berger & Douglas, 1981; Berger & Perkins, 1978, 1979) suggest that when persons wish to acquire information about a target person using unobtrusive observation, they prefer to observe the target in social rather than solitary situations. In addition, social situations in which the target is highly involved in interaction with others are judged to be more informationally rich than social situations in which the target is relatively uninvolved with the others present. Finally, persons anticipating interaction with the target person consider informal social contexts to be potentially more informative than formal contexts. These findings suggest that informal, active social contexts are perceived to place fewer situational constraints on target persons and thus to be more informative about the target persons; in short, one can find out more about individuals conversing with others at a party than by observing them at a funeral or sitting in a room alone.

To date, little work has been done on active strategies of information acquisition. Obviously, this paradigm of information acquisition is widely employed in behavioral science research (i.e., the investigator manipulates a set of conditions and then observes participant responses to these manipulations). Whether persons perform such "experiments" in their everyday lives is an issue worthy of research. While little research has been done in the area of "naive social experimentation," some work has been reported that is germane to the question of how persons evaluate information about target persons that they receive from third parties. Hewes, Graham, Doelger, and Pavitt (1985) found that both college students and non-college students obtain about 65% of their information about others in their social networks from direct contact, with about 30% of their information being obtained from third-party sources. Though directly acquired information was rated significantly more useful than indirectly obtained information, the latter was judged to be "somewhat useful." This study also revealed that persons are quite aware of the possibility that information obtained from third-party sources is biased, and about 71% of the respondents claimed they were able to take these biases into account in interpreting these messages. Thus naive social actors and actresses may be somewhat more sophisticated at debiasing information they receive than the work of some psychologists suggests (Kahneman et al., 1982; Nisbett & Ross, 1980).

The Hewes et al. (1985) study represents an important step in the investigation of active strategies of information acquisition. Persons who study interpersonal communication tend to focus on exchanges occurring within dyads or groups that they observe. Obviously, face-to-face encounters are ideal for studying many communication phenomena. Nevertheless, it is naive to assume that persons gather all their information about each other in such contexts. In the early stages of dating relationships, for example, indirect modes of information acquisition may be more prevalent than direct ones and more significant types of information may be exchanged through indirect channels (e.g., "Do you think she *really* likes me?" or "Could you find out from him whether he really enjoyed our date last weekend?"). Certainly, when there is considerable self-presentational activity in a relationship, more accurate information may be available through third-party channels. Thus in organizational settings, a boss may give an unrealistically positive evaluation to a subordinate, but disclose his or her true evaluation of the subordinate to a confidant. The confidant, in turn, may disclose the boss's true evaluation to the subordinate. Such "informational triangles" are probably quite common in both formal organizations and relatively informal social networks. Obviously, these triangles are critical for uncertainty reduction and the evaluation of social information.

Interactive strategies for knowledge acquisition have received the bulk of our recent research attention. In a series of studies (Berger & Kellermann, 1983, 1985; Kellermann & Berger, 1984) we have sought to discover the information-seeking devices used during face-to-face interactions. Berger and Kellermann (1983) found three principal strategies: question asking, disclosure, and relaxation of the target. Interestingly, persons attempting to acquire large amounts of information do not necessarily ask any more questions than persons seeking to have a "normal conversation." Instead, persons in the high information-seeking mode ask their targets more questions concerned with explanations for their behavior and their future goals and plans. Moreover, persons interested in knowledge acquisition take advantage of floor possession to ask questions of their targets.

Kellermann and Berger (1984) found that persons seeking information tended to employ more positive nonverbal behaviors during their interactions than did persons unconcerned with information acquisition. These findings led to the hypothesis that strategy selection is governed by two main considerations: the efficiency of the strategy and its social appropriateness. Question asking, disclosure, and relaxing the target are ordered with respect to both dimensions; question asking is most efficient but potentially most intrusive, and relaxing the target least efficient but also least threatening. This line of reasoning suggests that there may be a tradeoff between these two dimensions when selecting information-gaining strategies. Furthermore, the significance of these dimensions extends beyond the selection of information-gaining strategies. For example, Rosenfeld (1966) and Mehrabian and Williams (1969) found that approval-seekers and persons attempting social influence displayed more positive nonverbal behaviors than persons not attempting to achieve these social goals. Their findings are quite similar to those obtained for our high information seekers (Kellermann & Berger, 1984). In general, these studies suggest that when persons attempt to achieve social goals, people try to induce their targets to like them in order to facilitate goal achievement.

Berger and Kellermann (1985) have discovered a series of *offensive* and *defensive* tactics that persons use to foil information-seeking attempts of others during the parry and thrust of conversations. Offensive tactics include focusing the conversation on the information seeker and asking the information seeker as many questions as possible. Such tactics prevent the seeker from querying the target. Defensive tactics include giving minimal and ambiguous responses to questions and giving off unaffiliative nonverbal behaviors. We are currently in the process of examining how information seekers respond to the communicative parries employed by their conversational partners. We suspect that patterns of strategy and countermeasure deployment emerge over time. One critical focus of this research is upon the *iterative mechanisms* underlying these exchanges through time.

For persons to conduct relatively coordinated interactions with others, they need person, role, and procedural knowledge. If the relationship is to progress beyond an initial interaction, interactants must acquire more specific information about each others' personalities, attitudes and preferences, and values. Persons can employ perceptual, cognitive, and communicative routines to acquire the needed information for understanding both their relational partners and themselves. Since the acquisition of such information is vital for continuance of the relationship, researchers need to gain an understanding of the strategies persons use to acquire it. Studies of these strategies will both add to our fund of knowledge about uncertainty reduction and enable us to aid those who have difficulty gaining understanding of others and themselves.

UNCERTAINTY AND RELATIONSHIP DEVELOPMENT

Our discussion of uncertainty reduction strategies quite naturally leads to consideration of the role uncertainty plays in the development, maintenance, and dissolution of personal relationships. In the original statement of URT, Berger and Calabrese (1975) argued that uncertainty reduction leads to increases in attractiveness and that continued high levels of uncertainty in a relationship should produce lowered levels of attraction. Clatterbuck (1979) reported the findings of numerous investigations examining the relationship between uncertainty as measured by his CLUES scale and attraction. He found consistent correlations between CLUES and various attraction measures; in general, persons who felt they knew more about their relational partners were more attracted to them. The correlations across these studies were in the .20 to .35 range. Gudykunst et al. (1985) found consistent positive relationships between the CLUES attributional confidence measure and interpersonal attraction across acquaintance, friend, and dating relationships in a multicultural study involving persons from Japan, Korea, and the United States. Clatterbuck (1979) also reported consistently positive correlations between CLUES and the length of time persons had known each other. Similarly, using the Gudykunst et al. (1985) data, I found that across all three cultures levels of uncertainty were twice as high in acquaintance as in friend relationships.

The data collected by Clatterbuck (1979) as well as by Gudykunst et al. (1985) involved the use of self-report questionnaires. Laboratory investigations have revealed that uncertainty as manifested in speech behavior declines as interactions progress. For example, Lalljee and Cook (1973) reported that filled pause rate decreased and speech rate increased as interactions between strangers progressed. Sherblom and Van Rheenen (1984) found that mean word length, type-token ratio, and linguistic diversity all increased as interviews between strangers progressed. Conversely, several indices of immediacy (Mehrabian & Wiener, 1966) did not show expected changes. These findings, coupled with those cited above, provide some support for the notion that as relationships progress, uncertainty tends to be reduced; however, in light of the earlier discussion concerning the relationships between communication and uncertainty, it is possible that uncertainty levels can escalate at later stages of relationships (Planalp & Honeycutt, 1985).

While the notion that uncertainty is reduced over time seems reasonable, as long as persons involved in the relationships remain in contact with each other, the claim that the reduction of uncertainty leads to increased attraction is considerably more controversial. Scheidel (1977) has pointed out that persons can come to know things about others that trigger dislike. Furthermore, the uncertainty involved in romantic relationships might actually be a source of excitement and attraction (Livingston, 1980). Once it is reduced, the relationship might move to a less exciting, mundane level. These arguments cast doubt on one proposition advanced in the original version of URT. Thus some alternative possibilities will be considered here. In discussing them, it should be remembered that in its original form, URT was solely concerned with explaining events occurring during initial interactions. However, since some researchers have found that uncertainty plays an important role in more developed relationships (Gudykunst et al., 1985; Parks & Adelman, 1983; Parks, Stan, & Eggert, 1983; Sunnafrank, 1986), it seems worthwhile to extend URT in this direction.

Persistently high uncertainty levels should put considerable strain on relationships. Under conditions of high uncertainty, interaction is effortful and difficult; thus over a protracted time period, persons should develop negative affect toward the relationship. Even so, uncertainty with respect to various actions and beliefs may not always have a profound negative impact upon relationships; indeed, uncertainty in areas of peripheral concern enhance novelty and may actually be experienced as pleasant (Berlyne, 1960). Thus if a relational partner dresses unpredictably, and manner of dress is not important in the relationship, uncertainty in this domain should have little impact upon relational outcomes. If, however, a relational partner is subject to unpredictable mood changes, uncertainty in this domain might eventually undermine the relationship.

Uncertainty about another can also be reduced in such a way as to become certain that the other possesses numerous unattractive attributes. Obviously, such knowledge strains the relationship and increases pressures for its dissolution. Furthermore, uncertainty can be reduced in such a way that positive outcomes are predicted, thus fueling relational growth. Once these affective responses are formed, they will influence further efforts to reduce uncertainty. Persons will continue to reduce uncertainty about liked others and cease to reduce uncertainty about disliked others. This reasoning suggests a reciprocal relationship between uncertainty and attraction, with continued uncertainty reduction a function of the valence of affect toward one's partner.

Though correlational data (Clatterbuck, 1979; Gudykunst et al., 1985) support such a relationship between uncertainty and attraction, they cannot address the issue of the *sequence* of events involved in the relationship—that is, which of the two variables starts the process. On the one hand, initial affective responses to another that are related to judgments of physical attractiveness or other "surface features" may be responsible for driving the desire to reduce or not to reduce uncertainty. Zajonc (1980) opts for the primacy of affect over cognition in many judgment and decision-making situations. By contrast, it is possible that one must find out what another believes and how another behaves over time before affective judgments can be made. Most likely, initial global affective responses based upon readily observable attributes of the other are responsible for the presence or absence of initial uncertainty reduction attempts; however, if the interaction progresses beyond beginning stages, knowledge acquired through uncertainty reduction will very likely alter these initial global affective responses.

In support of the above reasoning, Parks and Adelman (1983) found that persons in romantic relationships who communicated more frequently with and received more support from members of their romantic partners' social networks demonstrated lower levels of uncertainty about their partners and were less likely to experience breakups of their relationships. It is important to reemphasize that in long-term relationships lack of interaction will probably have deleterious effects on the relationship because of rising uncertainty levels, but heightened levels of communication may or may not have positive effects on relational outcomes depending upon the nature of such interactions. Communication may act to reduce or increase uncertainty, as we noted earlier, and even when communication reduces uncertainty the nature of the interaction will determine affective outcomes.

Baxter and Wilmot (1984) investigated the strategies persons use to find out how their relational partners view the relationship. These "secret tests" are uncertainty reduction strategies designed to reveal how committed one's relational partner is to the relationship. Baxter and Wilmot (1984) focused upon opposite-sex relationships, although such "tests" are also used in same-sex relationships. For opposite-sex relationships, Baxter and Wilmot (1984) identified seven distinct types of strategies: asking third parties, triangles, directness tests (asking direct questions), separation tests (not interacting), endurance tests (testing limits, self-putdown), public presentation (presenting partner to others), and indirect suggestion (joking, hinting). These seven strategies can be classified in terms of the passive, active, and interactive strategy types of information acquisition strategies discussed earlier. Baxter and Wilmot (1984) also reported that use of the seven "secret tests" varied in platonic, potentially romantic, and romantic relationships. Furthermore, females report using more "secret test" strategies than did males.

Although Baxter and Wilmot (1984) dealt with relationships in their relatively early stages, persons in established relationships are also likely to use some of these strategies to reduce uncertainties about their relational partners. The concept "established relationship" is something of a misnomer, since *any relationship*, no matter how long-lived or stable, is subject to the vagaries of uncertainty-producing events. When uncertainties surface in long-term relationships, such strategies as triangles, directness tests, and indirect suggestion might be used to reduce them, although some of the other strategies discussed above might not see extensive use in long-term relationships. The important point to recognize is that even long-term relationships are subject to potential undermining by uncertainty, and when uncertainty levels rise, persons in these relationships will generally take steps to reduce uncertainties about their relational partners.

UNCERTAINTY IN INTERCULTURAL ENCOUNTERS

Some intercultural communication researchers have found uncertainty to be a fruitful starting point for their research. Gudykunst and Kim (1984) note the likelihood of elevated uncertainty when persons interact interculturally. This fact has been frequently invoked to explain the dismal history of U.S.-U.S.S.R. relations since World War II. This line of reasoning implies that relationships between the two superpowers would be considerably more amiable if persons on both sides gained greater understanding of the history and culture of the other nation. Such an understanding would presumably facilitate communication between the two nations and lower the probability of aggression.

Intuition suggests that uncertainty should be more pervasive in intercultural interactions; however, uncertainty and the strategies for its reduction probably vary across cultures. Some research has addressed this particular issue. Gudykunst (1983) employed Hall's (1976) notions of high- and low-context communications to examine cultural differences in the way uncertainty is handled in relationships. In distinguishing between high- and low-context communications, Hall (1976) asserts,

> A high-context (HC) communication or message is one in which most of the information is either in the physical context or internalized in the person, while very little is in the coded, explicit part of the message. A low-context (LC) communication is just the opposite, i.e., the mass of information is vested in the explicit code. (p. 79)

In Hall's system, such Asian cultures as those of China, Korea, and Japan are high-context cultures while those of the United States, Germany, Switzerland, and Scandinavia tend to be low context.

Gudykunst (1983) compared the responses of members of HC and LC cultures to a hypothetical situation which asked them to indicate what they would do upon meeting a stranger from their own culture at a party. Results revealed that members of HC cultures (1) are more cautious in initial interactions with strangers, (2) make more assumptions about strangers, and (3) ask more questions of strangers than do their LC culture counterparts. These findings led Gudykunst (1983) to conclude that while there are differences in uncertainty reduction strategies between HC and LC cultures, members of both types of cultures reduce their uncertainties by seeking background information from their interactive partners.

Gudykunst and Nishida (1984) reported that Japanese and American students asked to imagine themselves interacting with a stranger from a different culture indicated they would be more likely to ask questions of their partner and disclose more information about themselves than did persons asked to imagine themselves interacting with a stranger from their own culture. These findings support the idea that intercultural interactions are more uncertainty prone than intracultural interactions. Gudykunst and Nishida (1984) found no support for the proposition that cultural similarity by itself is related to interpersonal attraction. Instead, they found that the combination of cultural and attitudinal dissimilarity tends to lower estimates of interpersonal attraction, suggesting that in the intercultural context, similarities and attraction are not related in simple ways.

In a study already cited, Gudykunst et al. (1985) found consistent relationships between uncertainty and attraction across three kinds of relationships within three cultures. Attraction was positively associated with reduced uncertainty. We have noted, however, that under some conditions, reduced uncertainty might not lead to increased attraction; in fact, Gudykunst et al.'s (1985) version of URT suggests that attraction determines uncertainty reduction (i.e., we find out more about persons whom we like and less about persons whom we dislike). While this relationship is quite plausible, there is most likely some kind of complex, reciprocal relationship between these two variables. Nevertheless, the evidence adduced in this study, as well as that reported by Clatterbuck (1979), is impressive in its consistency across relationship types and cultures.

In addition to the relationship between uncertainty and attraction, Gudykunst et al. (1985) found no support for the propositions that (1) amount of communication reduces uncertainty, and (2) perceived similarities between persons reduce uncertainty. We have already considered why amount of communication may not be a good predictor of uncertainty reduction. Why perceived similarity fails to predict uncertainty reduction is not clear, although Clatterbuck (1979) noted that the similarity variable did not perform well as a predictor of CLUES scores. Perhaps similarity has a direct impact upon attraction which, in turn, affects uncertainty reduction with similarity exerting no direct effect on uncertainty. Further research is needed to resolve this particular problem. Finally, Gudykunst et al. (1985) report that the use of interactive strategies of uncertainty reduction is associated with increased attributional confidence. This finding coincides with Gudykunst and Nishida's (1984) finding that persons experiencing uncertainty in a culturally dissimilar interaction employ interactive strategies to a greater extent than do persons interacting with others from similar cultures.

Anyone who has traveled in another culture knows the havoc that uncertainty creates in daily living. Action sequences that are routine in one's own culture become obsolete. Driving, riding buses, making telephone calls, and ordering food may require learning new routines. Such learning requires considerable energy; thus, the fatigue that frequently plagues foreign travelers, usually attributed to "jet lag," may also result from the increased cognitive effort required to cope with new uncertainties. Moreover, even interethnic interactions within one's own country may be rendered effortful by uncertainty. As Simard (1981) pointed out in her study of Canadian Francophones and Anglophones, both groups "perceive it as more difficult to know how to initiate a conversation, to know what to talk about during the interaction, to be interested in the other person, and to guess in which language they should talk" (p. 179) when they interact with each other. The potential stress engendered by uncertainty in such encounters is worthy of research attention in its own right.

UNCERTAINTY AND SOCIAL SUPPORT

As just suggested, uncertainty can breed both stress and anxiety. It is also the case that uncertainty reduction can alleviate these aversive states. When persons are unsure of what is likely to occur, they are unable to respond adaptively so as to control their outcomes in the situation. Consider the individual who has been biopsied for a suspicious lump. The critical question is whether the growth is malignant; however, given no knowledge of the biopsy results, the individual can do little but worry about them. Once the individual knows the test findings, he or she can take action. Obviously, if the lump is benign, no action is necessary; however, even if it is malignant the individual can act to deal with the situation. Persons apparently find waiting for such results *more* stress provoking than receiving bad news. URT would predict that knowing is preferable to not knowing since persons can try to control outcomes when they are certain of their options. It is also obvious, however, that in the biopsy example, learning that one has cancer would probably increase stress and anxiety. What is being argued here, however, is that stress and anxiety will be greater when the results are unknown because of inability to respond adaptively to the situation.

Albrecht and Adelman (1984) have suggested that the positive role played by social networks in reducing stress and anxiety can be explained by uncertainty reduction. They propose that when persons communicate with others who share their plight, stress is alleviated because uncertainty is reduced by such interactions. Support networks provide the distressed individual with information that makes the environment more stable and predictable. When persons share their problems, they can assist each other in developing cognitive and action strategies; for example, persons may literally *learn* how to be parents of terminally ill children or how to deal with a terminal illness of their own. The acquisition and internalization of such information enable persons to respond to their environments more adaptively, and hence to gain more control over their outcomes.

THE UNCERTAINTY HEURISTIC

It seems appropriate to conclude this tenth anniversary presentation of URT by discussing some directions the approach might take researchers in the future. A number of potentially fruitful areas of inquiry are suggested by URT. Several of these have already been reviewed in this chapter; however, some additional areas of study are yet to be explored.

RELATIONAL INSURANCE

At the outset of this chapter, I pointed out that governments, businesses, and individuals are not only willing to spend large sums of money to try to reduce their uncertainties, but also to hedge against potential negative outcomes. The insurance industry rests on the notion that one should be willing to spend money to avoid financial jeopardy when disasters occur. It is interesting to consider whether persons employ similar hedges in their personal relationships. After all, one can never be absolutely sure that one's current relational partner will forever remain true, whether that partner be a friend or a lover.

Thibaut and Kelley (1959) invoked the concept of comparison level for alternatives (or CL_{alt}) as one hedge against potentially negative relational outcomes. Persons with numerous attractive alternative relationships are less likely to be dependent upon any particular relationship than are persons who have few available alternative relationships. Another hedge closely related to CL_{alt} is one's level of involvement in the relationship. Persons who are highly involved in a relationship are more vulnerable to the negative consequences of its demise than are less involved persons. This notion has been labeled by Waller and Hill (1951) as the "principle of least interest."

There appear to be other ways beside CL_{alt} and the principle of least interest for persons to insure themselves against the negative consequences of relational demises. For example, married persons with sufficient incomes to sustain themselves have a form of relational insurance. Other resources such as status and education also serve as forms of social insurance. Persons may employ still other means to minimize the likelihood of relational termination. For example, people sometimes require long periods of acquaintanceship before they are willing to commit themselves to a friendship. In the domain of romantic relationships, it is possible to opt for a long courtship before making a marriage commitment. Such strategies aim at reducing uncertainty about one's relational partner as much as possible before making serious commitments. This strategy appears effective in view of the apparently robust inverse relationship between amount of time known and uncertainty mentioned earlier in this chapter (Clatterbuck, 1979; Gudykunst et al., 1985). Finally, in recent years, some married couples have explicitly faced the possibility of divorce at the time of their marriage by entering into contracts that if violated become grounds for divorce. Moreover, these contracts may specify how property is to be divided between the ex-spouses in case of divorce. While this approach to marital relationships may strike some romantics as overly pessimistic and mechanical, the relatively high divorce rate suggests its potential adaptiveness.

UNCERTAINTY AND RELATIONAL TRAJECTORIES

Earlier it was pointed out that most communication researchers studying relationship development have employed some variant of social exchange theory (see Roloff, 1981) to explain why relationships develop and decline over time. In general, these theories explain relational growth by arguing that when rewards exceed costs for relational partners, relationships tend to escalate. Conversely, relational deescalation results from unfavorable reward/cost ratios. These explanations are both parsimonious and intuitively appealing; moreover, they can be facilely invoked post hoc to explain why particular relationships have grown or declined.

From the perspective of the communication researcher, one difficulty with such explanations is that they bypass the communication process and focus attention on outcomes; in other words, interest is directed not at communicative conduct per se but rather at the net result of interactions. Communication as a process is *assumed* to be influential but is not studied. This chapter has stressed the importance of considering the interactions between cognitive activity and affect to understand relational growth and decline. Exclusive concern with affect or rewards and costs tells us little about how persons in relationships think about these exchanges or how they actually communicate about them to each other.

The position taken here is that URT is a more useful approach to the study of personal relationships for communication researchers than are the social exchange approaches. The URT perspective on personal relationships fosters questions about relationship development that center more directly on communicative action than do the research questions suggested by exchange theories. To determine what one's relational partner finds rewarding or costly, it is necessary to gather information using passive, active, or interactive strategies. Since any stimulus can constitute a reward or a cost depending upon individual interpretation, it is necessary to determine a person's meaning for a stimulus. For example, while most people find verbal praise rewarding, some low self-esteem individuals may interpret such praise as punishing or costly; they may interpret compliments directed at them as aversive. Only through uncertainty reduction can interactants determine which stimuli are rewarding and which are costly to their partners. When persons make such statements as "I like X" or "I dislike Y," they are indicating what is potentially rewarding or costly to them. Hence, uncertainty reduction is a necessary condition for the definition of the currency of social exchange, and it is through communicative activity that uncertainty is reduced.

The above argument does not imply that communication researchers should avoid studying interaction outcomes and focus their research efforts solely on communication process. What it does suggest, however, is that URT is more likely to encourage the study of communicative processes that produce outcomes, rather than simply explaining outcomes by recourse to reward/cost ratios without investigating communication. Moreover, URT recognizes the futility of studying reward and costs defined in some "objective," outside-observer sense. It is implausible to assume that persons have highly uniform definitions of the behaviors that are rewarding and costly in relationships: One person's meat may indeed be another person's poison. Thus subjective definitions of rewards and costs are essential to the workings of social exchange machinery. Subjective definitions become known through uncertainty reduction processes. What gives individuals the ability to exert control in relationships is the *knowledge* of what is rewarding and costly to their interaction partners and to themselves.

Finally, we pointed out earlier that uncertainty can be both a symptom and a cause of relationship decline. Communicative awkwardness may be symptomatic of underlying relational difficulties, and people involved in awkward relationships may find their partners increasingly unattractive precisely because it is so difficult to interact with them. Uncertainty increases communicative work to the point that persons retire from the relationship, either temporarily or permanently. Of course, after relationships have terminated, persons may expend considerable effort trying to reduce their uncertainty about the causes of the relationship demise. Considerable evidence indicates that persons engage in these uncertainty reduction activities after divorces and other relational endings (Harvey, Wells, & Alvarez, 1978; Orvis, Kelley, & Butler, 1976). Interestingly, though social exchange theories may have something to say about why relationships terminate, they appear to have little to say about post-termination behaviors.

UNCERTAINTY BEYOND INTERPERSONAL RELATIONSHIPS

Even though discussions of URT have generally focused on interpersonal and intercultural communication, URT is also relevant to such areas as organizational and mass communication. New employees face prediction and explanation problems similar to those faced by strangers in informal relationships, and the stakes may be considerably higher in the organizational context. As a result, new employees might be expected to take out larger relational insurance policies than strangers meeting in a more informal context. New employees should be particularly careful in revealing information about themselves when compared to strangers at a party. Moreover, new employees may be more reticent to befriend fellow employees for fear of affiliating with the "wrong" persons. As pointed out earlier, when the stakes are high persons will spend resources to hedge against negative outcomes. Jablin and Krone (in press) have presented a very lucid account of the processes by which new employees reduce their uncertainties in organizational contexts. Lester (1987) has developed an axiomatic theory designed to explain how new employees reduce their uncertainties in organizational cultures. This model serves to organize findings in the organizational socialization area in a systematic and coherent manner. It also offers a number of hypotheses concerning the role that uncertainty plays in this process.

In the domain of mass communication, several functional approaches, as well as the uses and gratifications approach, assert that one important function of media is to provide information that enables people to orient themselves in an uncertain world (Blumler & Katz, 1974). Most of these approaches also recognize, however, that the media serve a number of additional functions such as passing time, entertainment, escape, and companionship (Greenberg, 1974). From the perspective of URT, it is important to note that interacting with mass media can both reduce uncertainties and raise them. Furthermore, research needs to be directed toward the strategies that media consumers employ to gain information from the media. Can persons "de-bias" media information along the lines suggested by Hewes et al. (1985)? A number of research questions concerning media are suggested by URT.

Hewes and Planalp (1982) have asserted that while notions such as uncertainty are useful in communication inquiry, it is important to understand more specific mechanisms available to persons for information processing. I agree strongly with their view. Although the present chapter has not delved into these specifics, I think it has demonstrated the general potential of such an approach for the study of human communication. What could be more basic to the study of communication than the propositions that (1) adaptation is essential for survival (2) adaptation is only possible through the reduction of uncertainty, and (3) uncertainty can be both reduced and produced by communicative activities?

APPENDIX

CL7 Attributional Confidence Scale (Clatterbuck, 1979)
    (1) How confident are you of your general ability to predict how he/she will behave?
    (2) How certain are you that he/she likes you?
    (3) How accurate are you at predicting the values he/she holds?
    (4) How accurate are you at predicting his/her attitudes?
    (5) How well can you predict his/her feelings and emotions?

(6) How much can you empathize with (share) the way he/she feels about himself/herself?

(7) How well do you know him/her?

Revised Version of the Attributional Confidence Scale (Gudykunst & Nishida, 1986)

People vary in the degree to which they can predict how other people behave and think. Please answer each of the following questions with respect to your ability to predict selected aspects of the behavior of the person you answered the previous question about. Answer each question using a scale from zero (0) to one hundred (100). If you would have to make a total guess about the person's behavior or feelings you should answer "0"; if you have total certainty about the other person's behavior you should answer "100." Feel free to use any number between 0 and 100.

(1) How confident are you in your general ability to predict how he/she will behave?

(2) How confident are you that he/she likes you?

(3) How accurate are you at predicting his/her attitudes?

(4) How accurate are you at predicting the values he/she holds?

(5) How well can you predict his/her feelings?

(6) How much can you empathize with (share) the way he/she feels about him/herself?

(7) How well do you know him/her?

(8) How certain are you of his/her background?

(9) How certain are you that he/she will behave in a socially appropriate way when this is important?

(10) How certain are you that he/she can understand your feelings when you do not verbally express them?

(11) How certain are you that you understand what this person means when you communicate?

(12) How confident are you that this person will make allowances for you when you communicate?

REFERENCES

Abelson, R. (1981). Psychological status of the script concept. *American Psychologist, 36,* 715-729.

Albrecht, T. L., & Adelman, M. B. (1984). Social support and life stress: New directions for communication research. *Human Communication Research, 11,* 3-32.

A. M. Best Inc. (1984a). *Best aggregates and averages: Property and casuality.* New York: Author.

A. M. Best Inc. (1984b). *Best industry composite of life and health companies.* New York: Author.

Ayres, J. (1979). Uncertainty and social penetration theory expectations about relationship communication: A comparative test. *Western Journal of Speech Communication, 43,* 192-200.

Baxter, L. A., & Wilmot, W. W. (1984). "Secret tests": Social strategies for acquiring information about the state of the relationship. *Human Communication Research, 11,* 171-201.

Berger, C. R. (1975). Proactive and retroactive attribution processes in interpersonal communication. *Human Communication Research, 2,* 33-50.

Berger, C. R. (1979). Beyond initial interaction: Uncertainty, understanding, and the development of interpersonal relationships. In H. Giles & R. St. Clair (Eds.), *Language and social psychology* (pp. 122-144). Oxford: Blackwell.

Berger, C. R., & Bradac, J. J. (1982). *Language and social knowledge: Uncertainty in interpersonal relations.* London: E. E. Arnold.

Berger, C. R., & Calabrese, R. J. (1975). Some explorations in initial interaction and beyond: Toward a developmental theory of interpersonal communication. *Human Communication Research, 1,* 99-112.

Berger, C. R., & Douglas, W. (1981). Studies in interpersonal epistemology III: Anticipated interaction, self-monitoring and observational context selection. *Communication Monographs, 48,* 183-196.

Berger, C. R., & Kellermann, K. A. (1983). To ask or not to ask: Is that a question? In R. N. Bostrom (Ed.), *Communication yearbook 7* (pp. 342-368). Newbury Park, CA: Sage.

Berger, C. R., & Kellermann, K. A. (1985). *Personal opacity and social information gathering: Seek, but ye may not find.* Paper presented at the annual convention of the International Communication Association, Honolulu, HI.

Berger, C. R., & Perkins, J. (1978). Studies in interpersonal epistemology I: Situational attributes in observational context selection. In B. Ruben (Ed.), *Communication yearbook 2* (pp. 171-184). New Brunswick, NJ: Transaction Books.

Berger, C. R., & Perkins, J. (1979). *Studies in interpersonal epistemology II: Self-monitoring, involvement, facial affect, similarity and observational context selection.* Paper presented at the annual convention of the Speech Communication Association, San Antonio, TX.

Berger, C. R., Gardner, R. R., Parks, M. L., Schulman, L. W., & Miller, G. R. (1976). Interpersonal epistemology and interpersonal communication. In G. R. Miller (Ed.), *Explorations in interpersonal communication* (pp. 149-171). Newbury Park, CA: Sage.

Berlo, D. K. (1960). *The process of communication.* New York: Holt, Rinehart & Winston.

Berlyne, D. (1960). *Conflict, arousal, and curiosity.* New York: McGraw-Hill.

Blumler, J. G., & Katz, E. (Eds.). (1974). *The uses of mass communication: Current perspectives on gratifications research.* Newbury Park, CA: Sage.

Cantor, N., & Mischel, W. (1977). Traits as prototypes: Effects on recognition memory. *Journal of Personality and Social Psychology, 35,* 38-48.

Clatterbuck, G. W. (1979). Attributional confidence and uncertainty in initial interaction. *Human Communication Research, 5,* 147-157.

Galbraith, J. K. (1977). *The age of uncertainty.* Boston: Houghton-Mifflin.

Goffman, E. (1969). *Strategic interaction.* Philadelphia: University of Pennsylvania Press.

Greenberg, B. S. (1974). Gratifications of television viewing and their correlates for British children. In E. Katz & J. Blumler (Eds.), *The uses of mass communications.* Newbury Park, CA: Sage.

Gudykunst, W. B. (1983). Uncertainty reduction and predictability of behavior in low- and high-context cultures: An exploratory study. *Communication Quarterly, 31,* 49-65.

Gudykunst, W. B., & Kim, Y. Y. (1984). *Communicating with strangers.* Reading, MA: Addison-Wesley.

Gudykunst, W. B., & Nishida, T. (1984). Individual and cultural influences on uncertainty reduction. *Communication Monographs, 51,* 23-36.

Gudykunst, W. B., & Nishida, T. (1986) Attributional confidence in low- and high-context cultures. *Human Communication Research, 12,* 525-549.

Gudykunst, W. B., Yang, S. M., & Nishida, T. (1985). A cross-cultural test of uncertainty reduction theory: Comparisons of acquaintances, friends, and dating relationships in Japan, Korea, and the United States. *Human Communication Research, 11,* 407-455.

Hall, E. T. (1976). *Beyond culture.* Garden City, NY: Doubleday.

Harvey, J. H., Wells, G. L., & Alvarez, M. D. (1978). Attribution in the context of conflict and separation in close relationships. In J. H. Harvey, W. J. Ickes, & R. F. Kidd (Eds.), *New directions in attributional research* (Vol. 2, pp. 235-260). Hillsdale, NJ: Lawrence Erlbaum.

Heider, F. (1958). *The psychology of interpersonal relations.* New York: John Wiley.

Hewes, D. E. & Planalp, S. C. (1982). There is nothing as useful as a good theory...: The influence of social knowledge on interpersonal communication. In M. E. Roloff & C. R. Berger (Eds.), *Social cognition and communication.* Newbury Park, CA: Sage.

Hewes, D. E., Graham, M. K., Doelger, J., & Pavitt, C. (1985). "Second guessing": Message interpretation in social networks. *Human Communication Research, 11,* 299-334.

Hogarth, R. (1980). *Judgement and choice: The psychology of decision.* New York: John Wiley.

Jablin, F. M., & Krone, K. J. (1987). Organizational assimilation and levels of analysis in organizational communication research. In C. R. Berger & S. H. Chaffee, (Eds.), *Handbook of communication science* (pp. 711-743). Newbury Park, CA: Sage.

Jones, E. E., & Davis, K. E. (1965). From acts to dispositions: The attribution process in person perception. In L. Berkowitz (Ed.), *Advances in experimental social psychology* (Vol. 2, pp. 219-216). New York: Academic Press.

Kahneman, D., Slovic, P., & Tversky, A. (Eds.). (1982). *Judgment under uncertainty: Heuristics and biases.* Cambridge: Cambridge University Press.

Kellermann, K. A., & Berger, C. R. (1984). Affect and the acquisition of social information: Sit back, relax, and tell me about yourself. In R. N. Bostrom (Ed.), *Communication yearbook 8* (pp. 412-445). Newbury Park, CA: Sage.

Kelley, H. H. (1967). Attribution theory in social psychology. In D. Levine (Ed.), *Nebraska Symposium on Motivation* (Vol. 15, pp. 192-237). Lincoln: University of Nebraska Press.

Kelley, H. H. (1971). *Attribution in social interaction.* Morristown, NJ: General Learning Press.

Kelly, G. A. (1955). *The psychology of personal constructs.* New York: Norton.

Lalljee, M., & Cook, M. (1973). Uncertainty in first encounters. *Journal of Personality and Social Psychology, 26,* 137-141.

Lester, R. E. (1987). Organizational culture, uncertainty reduction, and the socialization of new organizational members. In S. Thomas (Ed.), *Culture and communication—methodology, behavior, artifacts and institutions* (pp. 105-113). Norwood, NJ: Ablex.

Livingston, K. R. (1980). Love as a process of reducing uncertainty—cognitive theory. In K. S. Pope et al. (Eds.), *On love and loving* (pp. 133-151). San Francisco: Jossey-Bass.

Mehrabian, A., & Wiener, M. (1966). Non-immediacy between communicator and object of communication in a verbal message. *Journal of Consulting Psychology, 30,* 420-425.

Mehrabian, A., & Williams, M. (1969). Nonverbal concomitants of perceived and intended persuasiveness. *Journal of Personality and Social Psychology, 13,* 37-58.

Miller, G. R., & Steinberg, M. (1975). *Between people: A new analysis of interpersonal communication.* Chicago: Science Research Associates.

Nisbett, R. E., & Ross, L. (1980). *Human inference: Strategies and shortcomings of social judgement.* Englewood Cliffs, NJ: Prentice-Hall.

Orvis, B. R., Kelley, H. H., & Butler, D. (1976). Attributional conflict in young couples. In J. H. Harvey, W. J. Ickes, & R. F. Kidd (Eds.), *New directions in attribution research* (Vol. 1, pp. 353-386). Hillsdale, NJ: Lawrence Erlbaum.

Parks, M. R., & Adelman, M. B. (1983). Communication networks and the development of romantic relationships: An expansion of uncertainty reduction theory. *Human Communication Research, 10,* 55-79.

Parks, M. R., Stan, C. M., & Eggert, L. L. (1983). Romantic involvement and social network involvement. *Social Psychology Quarterly, 46,* 116-131.

Planalp, S., & Honeycutt, J. M. (1985). Events that increase uncertainty in personal relationships. *Human Communication Research 11,* 593-604.

Roloff, M. E. (1981). *Interpersonal communication: The social exchange approach.* Newbury Park, CA: Sage.

Rosenfeld, H. M. (1966). Approval-seeking and approval-inducing functions of verbal and non-verbal responses in the dyad. *Journal of Personality and Social Psychology, 4,* 597-605.

Rubin, R. B. (1977). The role of context in information seeking and impression formation. *Communication Monographs, 44,* 81-90.

Rubin, R. B. (1979). The effect of context on information seeking across the span of initial interactions. *Communication Quarterly, 27,* 13-20.

Schank, R. C. (1982). *Dynamic memory.* Cambridge: Cambridge University Press.

Schank, R. C., & Abelson, R. (1977). *Scripts, goals, plans and understanding.* Hillsdale, NJ: Lawrence Erlbaum.

Scheidel, T. M. (1977). Evidence varies with phases of inquiry. *Western Journal of Speech Communication, 41,* 20-31.

Shannon, C., & Weaver, W. (1949). *The mathematical theory of communication.* Urbana: University of Illinois Press.

Sherblom, J., & Van Rheenen, D. E. (1984). Spoken language indices of uncertainty. *Human Communication Research, 11,* 221-230.

Simard, L. (1981). Cross-cultural interaction. *Journal of Social Psychology, 113,* 171-192.

Sunnafrank, M. (1986). Predicted outcome value during initial interactions: A reformulation of uncertainty reduction theory. *Human Communication, 13,* 3-33.

Thibaut, J. W., & Kelley, H. H. (1959). *The social psychology of groups.* New York: John Wiley.

Wall Street Week. (1985). Program #1514, October 4, 1985.

Waller, W., & Hill, R. (1951). *The family: A dynamic interpretation.* New York: Dryden Press.

Winograd, T. (1980). What does it mean to understand language? *Cognitive Science, 4,* 209-241.

Zajonc, R. B. (1980). Feeling and thinking: Preferences need no inferences. *American Psychologist, 35,* 151-175.

Chapter 3

THE SELF-CONCEPT AND INTERPERSONAL COMMUNICATION

George J. McCall

THE RESURGENCE OF scholarly interest in the self that has developed over the past decade is quite remarkable. Through the dark days of radical behaviorism, the rich American tradition of scholarship regarding the self—stemming from James, Baldwin, Cooley, and Mead—had been kept alive in the scattered camps of phenomenologists, clinicians, and sociologically trained researchers (Scheibe, 1985). The fresh winds of cognitivism sweeping the dreary plain of psychology have fanned those small sparks into a spreading wildfire (Greenwald & Pratkanis, 1984). The self, as a cognitive structure, is again highly fashionable as an explanatory factor in a wide range of social psychological phenomena (Schlenker, 1985).

In fact, social psychology may no longer be big enough to contain the burgeoning research on self cognition. The renewed interest in such matters is so intense as to have spawned among psychologists a new field of investigation—"social cognition"—with its own journals and texts. A lineal descendent of both the earlier work in person perception and cognitive psychology's theory-rich interests in representation and information processing, this emerging field of social cognition seeks to understand the individual's acquisition, organization, and uses of knowledge about persons. Landman and Manis (1983, pp. 51-52), in attempting to distinguish social cognition from its ancestors in social psychology, note that "social psychology has in the past more often addressed issues of cognitive content than process. In contrast, cognitive psychology has from the beginning concentrated on cognitive processes. . . . Social cognition tries to do both."

The phenomena of "social information processing" bear some obvious resemblance to those of interpersonal communication, which I take to be the interpreted exchange of messages between individuals. Indeed, the emerging field of social cognition has already begun to exert serious influence on the study of interpersonal communication (e.g., Berger & Bradac, 1982; Roloff & Berger, 1982a).

Another look at the self-concept and interpersonal communication therefore seems timely indeed. When last I reviewed those matters (McCall, 1976), I took pains to emphasize their mutual interdependence—showing how selves are socially constructed through the interpreted exchange of communicative gestures, on the one hand; and, on the other, how the interpretation of gestures depends on the prior establishment of selves. Those same topics and theme will also serve to organize the present review. But first, we must consider some of the current views about the self in its own right.

SELF, IDENTITY, AND SELF-CONCEPTS

The cognitive approach itself owes much of its newfound popularity to the development of the information-processing perspective, in which the capacities and functions of human intelligence are viewed in the light of what we know about the workings of computers and similar artificial intelligence devices. That perspective emphasizes that, in order to understand what a person does, we must know how that person makes internal representation of the world. These representations are thought to be *schemata,* "cognitive structures of organized prior knowledge, abstracted from experience with specific instances" (Fiske & Linville, 1980, p. 543) that influence the categorization, interpretation, and comprehension of events. From the information-processing perspective,

> the self can be conceptualized as a system of *self-schemata.* . . knowledge structures developed by individuals to understand and explain their own social experiences. . . . A schema integrates all the information known about the self in a given behavioral domain into a systematic framework used during processing. (Markus & Sentis, 1982, p. 45)

This view on the nature of the self is quite consistent with contemporary sociological views (Burke, 1980; McCall, 1987; McCall & Simmons, 1978; Stryker, 1980; Turner, 1978) in which the self is taken to be a system of *role-identities,* or role-specific conceptions of oneself:

> The wealth of concrete detail that is included in these imaginations of self is astounding, ranging in many cases from fantasied heroic accomplishments and encounters right down to how one fancies he should posture and hold his head to communicate exactly the proper affect in a particularly dramatic engagement. . . . In fact, they give the very *meaning* to our daily routine, for they largely determine our interpretations of the situations, events, and other people we encounter. By providing us with plans of action and systems of classification, our role-identities go far to determine the objects of our environment, their identity and meaning. This is particularly true of persons as objects, both ourselves and others. (McCall & Simmons, 1978, pp. 66-68)

Self-schemata, like role-identities, are at once structure and process—"structures of knowledge about the self that engage in a process of ongoing interpretive activity" (Markus & Sentis, 1982, p. 45). After all, the self is both the knower and the known. An important traditional distinction, however, is that between the self and the self-concept (Rosenberg, 1979). In those terms, self corresponds to the *functions* of such knowledge structures, while self-concept may be equated with the *contents* of role-identities (or of self-schemata).

As both theory and empirical research suggest, however, some further distinctions need be drawn within this broad notion of self-cognition. Perhaps the most important of these is a distinction between perceiving the self and conceiving it—a distinction between passing images of the self and the lasting self-conception:

> The picture which the individual sees at a given moment, like the photograph that records one's appearance at an instant of time, will be called a *self-image*. The picture that carries with it the sense of "the real me"—"I-myself as I really am"—will be called the *self-conception*. The self-image may change from moment to moment. There may indeed be multiple self-images simultaneously in effect, when the individual is aware that his behavior at a given moment looks different to his son, his mother, and his wife. Many self-images will be rejected as false, unrepresentative, or unfair. But the self-conception changes more slowly, exhibits a strain toward coherency, and is felt as inescapable fact by the individual. (Turner, 1968, p. 94)

Burke (1980, pp. 20-21) makes the same distinction between *images* and *identity:*

> The easiest way to conceptualize the notion of image in this formulation is as the "current working copy" of the identity. As a "working" copy, it is subject to constant change, revision, editing, and updating as a function of variations in situation, and situational demands. For this reason it cannot really be considered a *copy* of the identity. While identities themselves are not unchanging, relative to an image an identity can be represented as a point while the image is perhaps best represented as a probability density around that point. The probability of a given image point would increase as that point got nearer the location of the identity, and would taper off as it got further away from the location of the identity. Beyond a certain point the probability would be essentially zero, as the individual would (almost) never construct an image departing that much from that individual's identity. This conceptualization suggests that an identity is a kind of idealized picture of the self-in-role which provides the motivation for performance. ... Lack of realization of the idealized picture would thus lie in the contingencies and exigencies of the situation in which the individual was interacting. It is the image, not the identity, which does the work in guiding moment-to-moment interaction. ...
>
> Competent performance in an interactional setting requires a mental model of that setting and of the roles and relationships of the performers. Role/identities

are not good working models because they are too temporally stable and removed from the moment-to-moment interaction and situational demands. The idea proposed here is that the image as constructed in the situation is the working model for constructing interaction. It has the flexibility to act as a map for role-taking or role-performance as well as a guide in role-making or role construction. Performance is thus the externalization of the image in the sense that the meanings of the behaviors in the performance are the meanings of the self contained in the image.

For the purposes of this chapter, then, the distinction will be made between *identity images* and *role-identities* in the sense set forth by Burke, rather than the related but distinct sense employed by Schlenker (1982).

DEVELOPING SELF-CONCEPTS
THROUGH COMMUNICATION

My earlier review (McCall, 1976) of how selves are socially constructed through the interpreted exchange of communicative gestures dealt almost entirely with what we are here calling "identity images." That analysis of the situational negotiation of identity images noted the operation of two *cognitive processes,* imputing a role to other and improvising one's own role, and, correlatively, two *expressive processes,* altercasting and presentation of self. A "working agreement" on identity images is reached when these cognitive processes of each party are in rough accord with the expressive processes of the other parties. An agreement exists, that is, when the altercasting of each party is not greatly inconsistent with the improvised role of the other party and when the presentation of self by each party is not in conflict with the role imputed to one party by the other. In this chapter, then, we will consider the social construction not of identity images, but of role-identities proper. How are those more enduring, less situational pictures of the self shaped through communication with others?

A key idea in the American tradition of scholarship on the self has been that the principal means through which one sees oneself is in the reactions of others to oneself. Developing Adam Smith's metaphor that the reactions of others are a mirror held up to a person, reflecting an image of self that the person might appraise in much the same fashion as another person seen directly would be appraised, Cooley (1902) explicated the concept of "the reflected or looking-glass self." Recent reviews of the voluminous research on the looking-glass self (Felson, 1985; Shrauger & Schoeneman, 1979) suggest that the importance of this reflected appraisal process may have been popularly exaggerated or misunderstood.

Experimental studies do show that, under certain conditions, actual appraisals by experimenter or confederate can be accurately perceived by research participants and can in fact alter the way these participants describe themselves. However, Shrauger and Schoeneman (1979) conclude that there is little convincing evidence that these changes are more than temporary responses to the demand characteristics of the experiments. In our terms, such one-shot appraisal manipulations may exert some effects on identity images but fail to influence role-identities. As Burke (1980, p. 21) suggests, although the identity image does have an influence on role-identity, "this impact is quite small. In this way the image acts as a buffer between the identity and the vicissitudes of normal interaction, though the effects of steady changes in the image over time would have a clear impact."

Survey research studies of the reflected appraisal process in naturally occurring, enduring relationships may thus be more likely to detect its effects. Of course, many of the earlier studies that found strong correlations between self-appraisals and the reflected appraisals from significant others suffered design flaws that barred determination of direction of any causal connection. More recently, Felson (1985) employed both longitudinal designs and simultaneous equation models with cross-sectional data in an attempt to overcome these limitations. Felson found that, in certain domains, the effect of self-appraisals on reflected appraisals was actually far greater than the reciprocal influence. However, he was also able to show that in other domains—especially those self-attributes such as physical attractiveness and popularity—reflected appraisals do causally affect self-appraisals as the model of the looking-glass self would predict.

Also disturbing to these reviewers of recent survey research studies is the finding that the effects of the actual appraisals of others on reflected and self-appraisals are not very strong. Felson (1980) attributes this inaccuracy to the operation of communication barriers that hinder persons in finding out what others actually think of them. In social life, that is, people do not usually communicate their appraisals of others to those others directly. Relationships with significant others are hedged about with tact, discretion, and deference (McCall & Simmons, 1978). These and other such barriers to communication reduce the accuracy of reflected appraisals by distorting the looking-glass process, leading to self-conceptions that are idiosyncratic and idealized.

On the other hand, Felson (1981) concedes that self-appraisal may rest on many social sources of information alternative to (and perhaps more relevant than) reflected appraisals. Indeed, perhaps the most serious limitation of the research on reflected appraisal processes is that these studies have restricted themselves to studying the effects only of direct and explicit appraisals to the exclusion of other, more commonly encountered forms of interpersonal communication.

Turner and Billings (1984) present new evidence that *conversation* is, overwhelmingly, the most frequent locus of a sense of authentic selfhood. Harré (1987) and Backman (1983) contend that conversation with significant others is the locus of selfhood per se. Berger and Kellner (1964) show that it is through implicit, rather than explicit and direct communication that identity is shaped:

> Every individual requires the ongoing validation of his world, including crucially the validation of his identity and place in this world, by those few who are his truly significant others. ... Again in a broad sense, all the actions of the significant others and even their simple presence serve this sustaining function. In everyday life, however, the principal method employed is speech. In this sense, it is proper to view the individual's relationship with his significant others as an ongoing conversation. As the latter occurs, it validates over and over again the fundamental definitions of reality once entered into, not, of course, so much by explicit articulation, but precisely by taking the definitions silently for granted and conversing about all conceivable matters on this taken-for-granted basis. Through the same conversation the individual is also made capable of adjusting to changing and new social contexts in his biography. In a very fundamental sense it can be said that one converses one's way through life. (p. 4)

DEPENDENCE OF COMMUNICATION
ON SELF-CONCEPTS

Thus far I have been concerned with showing how self-concepts are shaped through interpersonal communication. I turn now to the other side of the coin, to examine how the interpreted exchange of gestures depends on established self-concepts. The most cogent framework from within which to do this remains that set forth in Turner (1968), the text of which is followed quite literally here.

Like most symbolic interactionists, Turner follows Mead (1934) in viewing communication as a "conversation of gestures" (vocal and otherwise), in which the meaning or significance of one agent's gesture is to be found in the response of another agent to that gesture. According to Turner,

> Gesture interpretations are normally based in considerable part upon an idea or "picture" of the gesturer. ... The kinds of response gestures and interpretation for which ego is prepared vary according to the kind of person he thinks the potential responder to be. ... Person-conceptions guide behavior by enabling ego to assign the meaning to alter's gesture which ego requires in order to formulate his next gesture. (pp. 96-97)

The self-conception in particular, because it represents the very content of the self, defines the main dimensions of meaning in terms of which the relevance of gestures to the self is appraised. Studies of "social information processing" have already excited considerable interest by documenting the importance of self-schemata in the processing of information about the self (Markus, 1977; Rogers, Kuiper, & Kirker, 1977) and about others (Markus

& Smith, 1981). Reviewing numerous studies of the impact of cognitive self-structures on social information processing, Markus and Sentis (1982, p. 62) summarize the main findings:

> With respect to the *self*, individuals with self-schemata in particular domains: (1) can process information about the self efficiently (make judgments and decisions with relative ease and certainty); (2) are consistent in their responses; (3) have relatively better recognition memory and recall for information relevant to this domain; (4) can predict future behavior in the domain; (5) can resist information that is counter to a prevailing schema; and (6) evaluate new information for its relevance to a given domain. With respect to processing information about *others*, these individuals: (1) make accurate discriminations in the domain in question; (2) categorize or chunk schema-relevant information differentially; (3) are relatively more sensitive to variations in this domain; (4) select and prefer information that is relevant to this domain; and (5) make confident attributions and inferences about behavior in this domain.

Other-conceptions, too, serve as important reference points in the interpretation of gestures. If a person's image of an other is yet tentative, a succession of incongruent gestures by the other will lead the person to modify his or her picture of the other until one is found that adequately prepares him or her to cope with most of other's gestures without constant disruption and revision of the person's own attitude in the course of interaction with other. If, on the other hand, a person already holds an established conception of an other, such a succession of incongruent gestures is much less likely to modify that picture. In the first place, the person will have developed a perceptual bias toward interpreting any gesture by the other as the natural act of a person so characterized. Second, even if the person should perceive the other's gestures as incongruent, he or she is likely to make a separation between an established conception of other and a momentary, situational image of other—an image that expresses a passing mood or an exceptional situation but not the typical individual.

In casual interaction, images and identities of the participants are expressed and negotiated casually through the cycling of gesture and response. Philipsen (1975), for example, shows how a man's talk carries the message that he is a man. Schenkein (1978) demonstrates the subtlety and ubiquity of identity-yielding interchanges even in the most casual of conversations.

Much interaction, however, is not casual but is instead quite purposeful, governed by some specific aim on which one or more participants concentrate throughout the engagement. Gestures are then no longer merely ingenuous expressions of thought and feeling but rather are framed to serve that specific purpose. When interaction is no longer casual but *directed,* the entire process of assigning meanings to gestures becomes organized in relation to that governing purpose.

In *task-directed* interaction there is relatively little attention to the self-image as such; participants are not self-conscious. Once a working agreement on identities has been reached, it ordinarily fades into background and some social task claims the attention of participants unless or until some act or gesture calls into question that working agreement (McCall & Simmons, 1978). Langer (1978) reviews evidence that people prefer to avoid thinking about identities and do so mainly when forced to depart from familiar, ongoing social scripts.

In *identity-directed* interaction, by contrast, the guiding consideration is not coordinated pursuit of some social task but is rather the validation of a particular self-conception. Identities are not background but foreground. Turner identifies several far-reaching consequences of identity-directed interaction, three of which warrant particular consideration here.

The first key consequence of identity-direction is an overwhelming preoccupation with the self-image. Duval and Wicklund (1972) suggest that when attention is directed toward self rather than environment, a state of objective self-awareness arises in which performance comes to be compared against personal and social standards. Such self-awareness may interfere with performance and tends to result in negative feelings about oneself (Buss, 1980). Wicklund (1982) describes how society makes use of self-awareness to increase the correspondence of behavior with relevant internalized standards and to more closely tie self-evaluation to past performance. In reviewing the extensive research on self-awareness and self-consciousness, Berger and Roloff (1980) suggest that during self-focus social cognitions are more than ordinarily related to conduct and individuals are more susceptible to pressures that might lead to attitude change. The bearing of these findings upon the interpersonal communication process is further developed in Berger and Douglas (1982).

A second consequence of identity-direction is that the gesture ceases to be primarily a device for communication and becomes instead an interpersonal technique—"a device employed to create a desired type of relationship between two persons, through ego's implanting in alter the desired person-image of ego" (Turner, 1968, p. 104). These devices have been studied extensively in the research on impression management (Jones & Pittman, 1982; Schlenker, 1980; Snyder, 1979; Tedeschi, 1981). Cheek and Hogan (1983) contrast that sort of self-consciously strategic presentation of a temporary public image in response to situational pressures with that process of self-interpretation characteristic of casual and task-directed interaction. As Turner notes, these contrasting modes are not marked by any surface differences but are distinguishable only by the differing attitude of the gesturer toward his or her own gestures.

Third, identity-directed interaction dictates that participants go beyond the face-value level of interpretation of gestures. Such deeper interpretation may be *empathic,* in which the gesture is taken as concealing or misrepresenting the other's actual feeling or attitude. Such deceptive communication has been studied extensively in recent years. Reviews of these studies (DePaulo, Stone, & Lassiter, 1985; Knapp & Comadena, 1979) show, for example, that accuracy in detecting deception is greatest between intimates (Comadena, 1982). Such a result is not surprising, for intimates are not only permitted but even obliged to engage in a certain amount of empathic interpretation of one another's gestures. As Turner observes, one spouse expects the other not to accept at face value the statement that he or she feels fine but instead to recognize the signs of inner, true feelings. At a still deeper level is *diagnostic* interpretation, in which (like the classic psychiatrist) a person attributes to the other a feeling or attitude that is (a) at variance with the face-value meaning of the other's gesture, and (b) one of which other is assumed to be unaware. Identity-directed interaction, because it dictates empathic and perhaps even diagnostic interpretation of gestures, offends those basic norms of personal privacy and dignity that ordinarily forbid any search for hidden meanings.

At whatever level, the interpretation of gestures requires joint participation in what Mead (1934) called "a universe of discourse"—a body of mutually maintained conventions, understandings, and assumptions. The part played by mutual knowledge of all kinds (Smith, 1982) in the successful interpretation of gestures has been greatly clarified by the rise of theories of pragmatics, such as speech act theory (Bach & Harnish, 1979) and conversational analysis (West & Zimmerman, 1982). Particularly suggestive, I think, is Kreckel's (1981, p. 28) distinction between two varieties of mutual knowledge: "knowledge acquired in mutual interaction between communicants provides the basis for *shared knowledge,* whereas knowledge acquired separately can be at best *common knowledge*" (emphasis added).

The tension between these two varieties of mutual knowledge lies at the very heart of the contention among current theories of interpersonal communication. The so-called rules theories of communication (Cushman & Sanders, 1982; Shimanoff, 1980) place greater weight on the part played by common knowledge, whereas relational theories of communication (Millar & Rogers, 1976; Miller & Steinberg, 1975; Morse & Phelps, 1980) emphasize the contributions made by shared knowledge deriving from a history of previous mutual interaction. In emphasizing the contextual specificity of communication within developing or developed personal relationships, these "relational theories" call attention to the influences of the comparatively stable and detailed conceptions of self and other that constitute the structural heart of such relationships (Backman, 1983; McCall, 1970). Most recently, intriguing attempts to synthesize rule-based and relational views have arisen in the form of rules theories of relationships (Argyle & Henderson, 1985; Cushman, Valentinsen, & Dietrich, 1982; Pearce & Cronen, 1980).

SELF-PROCESS AS COMMUNICATION

A distinctive feature of social cognition is, again, that it takes equal interest in cognitive content and cognitive process. Therefore, even though this chapter deals primarily with self-concept, I would be remiss to omit a few concluding words regarding self as process.

Mead's genius lies in his demonstration (1934) that the "conversation of gestures," analyzed above, is the locus both of mind and of self. Because vocal gestures played a distinctive role in that demonstration, conversational speech—both public and private—has loomed very large in most subsequent analyses of self-cognition and self-regulation. As noted earlier, interpersonal conversation is today thought by many (Backman, 1983; Gergen, 1981; Harré, 1987) to be perhaps the essential locus of selfhood. *Intra*personal conversation, "talking with oneself," is widely viewed (Blumer, 1969; Luria, 1961; Mead, 1934; Vygotsky, 1962; Zivin, 1979) as being derived from but strategically superior to public speech as a medium for both thinking and self-regulation—a view that accords conveniently with the psychologistic bias of many scholars. Thus even sophisticated communication researchers (Roloff & Berger, 1982b; Wenburg & Wilmot, 1973) regard intrapersonal communication as forming the foundation for all other forms of human communication—an assumption that seems inconsistent with the contention that "mindlessness" characterizes a great deal of human interaction (Berger & Douglas, 1982; Berger & Roloff, 1980).

This awkwardness might be avoided through wider recognition of the fact that Mead's theory, though it does give special status to speech communication, actually pivots on *linguistic communication*—that is, the use of "significant symbols," or language. According to Mead (1934, pp. 138-139), "The importance of what we term 'communication' lies in the fact that it provides a form of behavior in which the organism or the individual may become an object to himself" by responding to the individual's own symbolic messages in the same way that others tend to respond. "Language implies organized responses and the value, the implication of these responses is to be found in the community from which this organization of responses is taken over into the nature of the individual" (Mead, 1934, p. 268).

Linguistic communication in any form—even organizational or mass communication—amounts to "the establishment of cooperation in a social activity in which self and other are modified and regulated by the common act" (Pfuetze, 1961, p. 72). Liberated from its overwhelming preoccupation with conversational forms, research on self-cognition and self-regulation might then enter a new era of advancement. Indeed, the work of Felson (1981) on organizational sources of self-appraisals might be regarded as an early exemplar of such new directions in research on self and communication.

REFERENCES

Argyle, M., & Henderson, M. (1985). The rules of relationships. In S. W. Duck & D. Perlman (Eds.), *Understanding personal relationships: An interdisciplinary approach* (pp. 63-84). Newbury Park, CA: Sage.

Bach, K., & Harnish, R. M. (1979). *Linguistic communication and speech acts.* Cambridge: MIT Press.

Backman, C. W. (1983). Toward an interdisciplinary social psychology. In L. Berkowitz (Ed.), *Advances in experimental social psychology* (Vol. 16, pp. 219-261). New York: Academic Press.

Berger, C. R., & Bradac, J. J. (1982). *Language and social knowledge: Uncertainty in interpersonal relations.* London: Edward Arnold.

Berger, C. R., & Douglas, W. (1982). Thought and talk: "Excuse me, but have I been talking to myself?" In F.E.X. Dance (Ed.), *Human communication theory: Comparative essays* (pp. 42-60). New York: Harper & Row.

Berger, C. R., & Roloff, M. E. (1980). Social cognition, self-awareness, and interpersonal communication. In B. Dervin & M. J. Voight (Eds.), *Progress in communication sciences* (Vol. 2, pp. 1-50). Norwood, NJ: Ablex.

Berger, P., & Kellner, H. (1964). Marriage and the construction of reality: An exercise in the microsociology of knowledge. *Diogenes, 54,* 1-24.

Blumer, H. (1969). *Symbolic interactionism: Perspective and method.* Englewood Cliffs, NJ: Prentice-Hall.

Burke, P. J. (1980). The self: Measurement implications from a symbolic interactionist perspective. *Social Psychology Quarterly, 43,* 18-29.

Buss, A. H. (1980). *Self-consciousness and social anxiety.* San Francisco: Freeman.

Comadena, M. E. (1982). Accuracy in detecting deception: Intimate and friendship relationships. In M. Burgoon (Ed.), *Communication yearbook 6* (pp. 446-472). Newbury Park, CA: Sage.

Cheek, J. M., & Hogan, R. (1983). Self-concepts, self-presentations, and moral judgments. In J. Suls & A. G. Greenwald (Eds.), *Psychological perspectives on the self* (Vol. 2, pp. 249-273). Hillsdale, NJ: Lawrence Erlbaum.

Cooley, C. H. (1902). *Human nature and the social order.* New York: Scribners.

Cushman, D. P., & Sanders, R. E. (1982). Rules theories of human communication processes: The structural and functional perspectives. In B. Dervin & M. J. Voigt (Eds.), *Progress in communication sciences* (Vol. 3, pp. 49-83). Norwood, NJ: Ablex.

Cushman, D. P., Valentinsen, B., & Dietrich, D. (1982). A rules theory of interpersonal relationships. In F.E.X. Dance (Ed.), *Human communication theory: Comparative essays* (pp. 90-119). New York: Harper & Row.

DePaulo, B. M., Stone, J. I., & Lassiter, G. D. (1985). Deceiving and detecting deceit. In B. R. Schlenker (Ed.), *The self and social life* (pp. 323-370). New York: McGraw-Hill.

Duval, S., & Wicklund, R. A. (1972). *A theory of objective self-awareness.* New York: Academic Press.

Felson, R. B. (1980). Communication barriers and the reflected appraisal process. *Social Psychology Quarterly, 43,* 223-233.

Felson, R. B. (1981). Social sources of information in the development of self. *Social Psychology Quarterly, 44,* 69-79.

Felson, R. B. (1985). Reflected appraisal and the development of self. *Social Psychology Quarterly, 48,* 71-78.

Fiske, S. T., & Linville, P. W. (1980). What does the schema concept buy us? *Personality and Social Psychology Bulletin, 6,* 543-557.

Gergen, K. J. (1981). The functions and foibles of negotiating self-conception. In M. D. Lynch, A. A. Norem-Hebeisen, & K. J. Gergen (Eds.), *Self-concept: Advances in theory and research* (pp. 59-73). Cambridge, MA: Ballinger.

Greenwald, A. G., & Pratkanis, A. R. (1984). The self. In R. S. Wyer & T. K. Srull (Eds.), *Handbook of social cognition* (Vol. 3, pp. 129-178). Hillsdale, NJ: Lawrence Erlbaum.

Harré, R. (1987) The social construction of selves. In K. Yardley & T. Honess (Eds.) *Self* and *Identity: Psychosocial Perspectives* (pp. 41-52). London: John Wiley.

Jones, E. E., & Pittman, T. S. (1982). Toward a general theory of strategic self-presentation. In J. Suls (Ed.), *Psychological perspectives on the self* (Vol. 1, pp. 231-262). Hillsdale, NJ: Lawrence Erlbaum.

Knapp, M. L., & Comadena, M. E. (1979). Telling it like it isn't: A review of theory and research on deceptive communication. *Human Communication Research, 5,* 270-285.

Kreckel, M. (1981). *Communicative acts and shared knowledge in natural discourse.* London: Academic Press.

Landman, J., & Manis, M. (1983). Social cognition: Some historical and theoretical perspectives. In L. Berkowitz (Ed.), *Advances in experimental social psychology* (Vol. 16, pp. 49-123). New York: Academic Press.

Langer, E. J. (1978). Rethinking the role of thought in social interaction. In J. H. Harvey, W. J. Ickes, & R. F. Kidd (Eds.), *New directions in attribution research* (Vol. 2, pp. 35-58). Hillsdale, NJ: Lawrence Erlbaum.

Luria, A. R. (1961). *The role of speech in the regulation of normal and abnormal behavior.* New York: Liveright.

Markus, H. (1977). Self-schemata and processing information about the self. *Journal of Personality and Social Psychology, 35,* 63-78.

Markus, H., & Sentis, K. (1982). The self in social information processing. In J. Suls (Ed.), *Psychological perspectives on the self* (Vol. 1, pp. 41-70). Hillsdale, NJ: Lawrence Erlbaum.

Markus, H., & Smith, J. (1981). The influence of self-schemas on the perception of others. In N. Cantor & J. Kihlstrom (Eds.), *Personality, cognition, and social interaction* (pp. 233-262). Hillsdale, NJ: Lawrence Erlbaum.

McCall, G. J. (Ed.) (1970). *Social relationships.* Chicago: Aldine.

McCall, G. J. (1976). Communication and negotiated identity. *Communication, 2,* 173-184.

McCall, G. J. (1987). The structure, content, and dynamics of self: Continuities in the study of role-identities. In K. Yardley & T. Honess (Eds.), *Self and identity: Psychosocial perspectives* (pp. 133-145). London: John Wiley.

McCall, G. J., & Simmons, J. L. (1978). *Identities and interactions* (rev. ed.). New York: Free Press.

Mead, G. H. (1934). *Mind, self, and society.* Chicago: University of Chicago Press.

Millar, F. E., & Rogers, L. E. (1976). A relational approach to interpersonal communication. In G. R. Miller (Ed.), *Explorations in interpersonal communication* (pp. 87-103). Newbury Park, CA: Sage.

Miller, G. R., & Steinberg, M. (1975). *Between people: A new analysis of interpersonal communication.* Chicago: Science Research Associates.

Morse, B. W., & Phelps, L. A. (Eds.) (1980). *Interpersonal communication: A relational perspective.* Minneapolis, MN: Burgess.

Pearce, W. B., & Cronen, V. E. (1980). *Communication, action, and meaning: The creation of social realities.* New York: Praeger.

Pfuetze, P. (1961). *Self, society, existence.* New York: Harper & Row.

Philipsen, G. (1975). Speaking "like a man" in Teamsterville: Culture patterns of role enactment in an urban neighborhood. *Quarterly Journal of Speech, 61,* 13-22.

Rogers, T. B., Kuiper, N. A., & Kirker, W. S. (1977). Self-reference and the encoding of personal information. *Journal of Personality and Social Psychology, 35,* 677-688.

Roloff, M. E., & Berger, C. R. (Eds.) (1982a). *Social cognition and communication.* Newbury Park, CA: Sage.

Roloff, M. E., & Berger, C. R. (1982b). Social cognition and communication: An introduction. In M. E. Roloff & C. R. Berger (Eds.), *Social cognition and communication* (pp. 9-32). Newbury Park, CA: Sage.

Rosenberg, M. *Conceiving the self.* (1979). New York: Basic Books.

Scheibe, K. E. (1985). Historical perspectives on the presented self. In B. R. Schlenker (Ed.), *The self and social life* (pp. 33-64). Hillsdale, NJ: Lawrence Erlbaum.

Schenkein, J. (1978). Identity negotiations in conversation. In J. Schenkein (Ed.), *Studies in the organization of conversational interaction* (pp. 57-78). New York: Academic Press.

Schlenker, B. R. (1980). *Impression management: The self-concept, social identity, and interpersonal relations.* Belmont, CA: Brooks/Cole.

Schlenker, B. R. (1982). Translating actions into attitudes: An identity-analytic approach to the explanation of social conduct. In L. Berkowitz (Ed.), *Advances in experimental social psychology* (Vol. 15, pp. 193-247). New York: Academic Press.

Schlenker, B. R. (1985). Introduction: Foundations of the self in social life. In B. R. Schlenker (Ed.), *The self in social life* (pp. 1-28). Hillsdale, NJ: Lawrence Erlbaum.

Shimanoff, S. B. (1980). *Communication rules: Theory and research.* Newbury Park, CA: Sage.

Shrauger, J. S., & Schoeneman, T. J. (1979). Symbolic interactionist view of self: Through the looking glass darkly. *Psychological Bulletin, 86,* 549-573.

Smith, N. V. (Ed.) (1982). *Mutual knowledge.* London: Academic Press.

Snyder, M. (1979). Self-monitoring processes. In L. Berkowitz (Ed.), *Advances in experimental social psychology* (Vol. 12, pp. 86-128). New York: Academic Press.

Stryker, S. (1980). *Symbolic interactionism: A social structural version.* Menlo Park, CA: Benjamin/Cummings.

Tedeschi, J. T. (Ed.) (1981). *Impression management: Theory and social psychological research.* New York: Academic Press.

Turner, R. H. (1968). The self-conception in social interaction. In C. Gordon & K. J. Gergen (Eds.), *The self in social interaction* (Vol. 1, pp. 93-106). New York: John Wiley.

Turner, R. H. (1978). The role and the person. *American Journal of Sociology, 84,* 1-23.

Turner, R. H., & Billings, V. (1984). The social contexts of self-feeling. Paper presented at the International Interdisciplinary Conference on Self and Identity, Cardiff, Wales.

Vygotsky, L. S. (1962). *Thought and language.* New York: MIT Press and John Wiley.

Wenburg, J. J., & Wilmot, W. (1973). *The personal communication process.* New York: John Wiley.

West, C., & Zimmerman, D. H. (1982). Conversation analysis. In K. R. Scherer & P. Ekman (Eds.), *Handbook of methods in nonverbal behavior research* (pp. 506-541). Cambridge: Cambridge University Press.

Wicklund, R. A. (1982). How society uses self-awareness. In J. Suls (Ed.), *Psychological perspectives on the self* (Vol. 1, pp. 209-230). Hillsdale, NJ: Lawrence Erlbaum.

Zivin, G. (Ed.) (1979). *The development of self-regulation through private speech.* New York: John Wiley.

Chapter 4

EMOTION AND INTERPERSONAL COMMUNICATION

Ellen Berscheid

WHAT IS NOW not known about the role emotion plays in interpersonal communication will someday fill books. This chapter is written in the hope that that day will come sooner rather than later. That hope springs, it perhaps need not be said, from a conviction that the emotion-communication interface encompasses a vast, fascinating territory whose systematic exploration cannot fail to benefit importantly our understanding of human emotional phenomena, interpersonal communication, and, in its ultimate practical applications, human relationships.

If the potential benefits are truly so great, there is, of course, the question of why so little theory and research have been directly located within the emotion-communication domain, particularly theory and research inspired by those expert and interested in communication phenomena. With the aim of persuading potential theorists and researchers that illumination of the role emotion plays in interpersonal communication is vital not only to the domain of human emotion but also to the discipline of interpersonal communication, we shall discuss this central question in these few pages. Along the way, we shall argue that the groundwork necessary to approach emotion-communication questions more systematically than ever before now has been laid, and we shall suggest several issues that might be profitably addressed.

INTERPERSONAL COMMUNICATION IN EMOTIONAL VERSUS NONEMOTIONAL STATES

Research along the emotion-interpersonal communication interface is thin and spotty not because communication that takes place between people under emotionally charged conditions is less important in the human scheme of things than symbolic exchanges between people who are not in an emotional state.

To the contrary, consideration of the conditions under which emotion is most likely to be experienced suggests that just the opposite is true.

Emotion theorists such as George Mandler (1975, 1979, 1983, 1984), for example, argue that people are likely to experience emotion when they perceive that important but unexpected changes have occurred in their environment, changes that have altered their circumstances of living, adapting, and surviving. Specifically, and following Schachter's (e.g., Schachter & Singer, 1962) lead, Mandler assumes that physiological arousal is a necessary condition for the experience of emotion. Prediction of the circumstances under which emotion will be experienced thus becomes an important problem in identifying classes of stimulus events associated with arousal. Mandler's "interruption theory" of emotion proposes that

> any event that involves a normal and expected outcome is capable of generating autonomic nervous system arousal if and when the world changes in such a way that that outcome no longer occurs or is no longer possible. More generally, any change in the life of the individual in which the expected no longer happens is potentially stressful. ... [It] is important to note that the relevance of a life event is not defined by how much one likes or dislikes it, or whether one classes a particular event as important or not. The crucial aspect of a life event and its changes is the degree to which the changes are discrepant with one's expectations, the degree to which the new state of the world is subjectively perceived as different from the "normal" modal one. (1983, p. 199)

Mandler's assumption about the survival value of arousal occurring when events disconfirm expectations is compatible with the evolutionary view of human emotion first proposed by Charles Darwin (1899) and now endorsed by virtually all contemporary emotion theorists and researchers. Darwin concluded his landmark dissertation, *Expression of the Emotions in Man and Animals,* with a simple statement of faith that the emotions played and continue to play a vital role in the welfare and survival of *homo sapiens* and, on that basis alone, were worthy of concerted scientific investigation.

Not incidental to the central argument here is the fact that this first systematic empirical investigation of emotion fell squarely into the emotion-communication arena. Darwin was, of course, interested in the manner in which the experience of qualitatively distinct emotions is expressed by man and animal nonverbally, via the facial musculature as well as postural and other nonverbal cues, and whether the different emotional experiences that give rise to these nonverbal displays can be accurately discerned by others of the species. Interest in this question and its many related and subsidiary issues continues to the present day (e.g., Izard, 1971, 1977) and constitutes such an extensive and robust body of literature that it will not be further commented upon here. Rather, the object of our discussion will be human verbal symbolic exchanges, usually but not always made consciously and deliberately and voluntarily, unlike many nonverbal expressions of inner states.

If one agrees with most emotion theorists that the *experience* of emotion promotes our welfare and survival, and if one also agrees with those working directly within the Darwinian tradition that the *expression* of the experienced emotion to another person (whether the expression is verbal or nonverbal) is also vital to our welfare, then it can be argued that the truly important communications that take place between humans—important in terms of their contribution to maintaining and enhancing the individual's welfare—occur when the communicator is experiencing emotion. Following theories such as Mandler's, in fact, it could be further argued that the more emotional the individual, the more critical the consequences of his or her communication at that time will be to him or her and, often, to others with whom the person is associated.

EMOTIONALITY AND COMMUNICATIVE ATTEMPTS

Some will grant that communication under conditions of emotion may be, other things being equal, more important than nonemotional communication when it occurs, but deprecate the centrality of emotion to an understanding of communication processes on the ground that people in emotional states generally do not communicate except by nonverbal displays—that people in emotional states tend to withdraw from others and to become verbally uncommunicative. However, support for Darwin's general hypothesis that people tend to communicate their experiencing of emotions to others is not confined to investigations of the degree to which facial and postural cues transmit information about emotional inner states.

For example, support for the notion that people are genetically wired to attempt to communicate with others when they are experiencing emotion can be seen in the fact that the first responses human infants make to emotional stimuli—both positive and negative, but most especially to those that elicit a strong negative emotion—are vocalization and agitation (see Cairns, 1979). In fact, primitive vocalizations (shrieks, groans, cries, gasps, etc.) continue throughout the life cycle to be a common concomitant of intense emotional states. Even when the individual is capable of highly sophisticated verbal communication, inchoate emotional vocalizations often remain the *first* response an individual makes to emotional stimuli. Moreover, such vocalizations remain for adults, as well as for infants, highly effective in drawing the attention of others to the individual's situation and to environmental elements that may be responsible for the emotional reaction.

It makes good sense that people should instinctively attempt to capture the attention of others when they are experiencing an emotion if the circumstances that prompt emotional experience change the individual's chances for well-being and survival (e.g., for status, comfort, and security), particularly if the change has decreased those chances. An inherited tendency to call our plight to the attention of others who may be willing and able to remove or ameliorate the threatening circumstance that has prompted the emotion would help ensure individual and species survival. One might go so far as to hypothesize that *the* strongest and most frequent reaction to emotional stimuli is to communicate one's situation to others—through involuntary nonverbal (and nonaudible) displays; through audible vocalizations that do not rely on language but nonetheless may be symbolic and informative of emotional state; and, finally, through symbolic language exchange.

With respect to this last, the strong link between emotion and the desire to speak to others was recognized very early within social psychology. Specifically, in proposing his theory of informal social communication, Leon Festinger (1950) outlined the conditions under which people in small groups would attempt to communicate with other group members. One of the three major forces said by Festinger to prompt people to communicate was the existence of an emotional state in the individual. Unfortunately, Festinger proposed this hypothesis at a time when psychology had abandoned the problem of emotion as too difficult for systematic scientific study. Whether for this or other reasons, research generated by social communication theory, as well as research stimulated by Festinger's (1954) theory of social comparison processes (a revision and extension of his communication theory), focused on the other two sources of an individual's tendency to attempt to communicate with others.

Festinger's hypothesis that the experience of emotion prompts active attempts to communicate with others was exhumed a decade later by his student, Stanley Schachter. In his classic studies on the psychology of affiliation, Schachter (1959) found evidence to support the hypothesis that people who are experiencing the emotion of fear will seek the company of others. They do so, Schachter speculated, for a variety of reasons, including a desire to assess the appropriateness of their emotional state, to obtain information about the ways they should deal with the events that precipitated the emotion, and to distract themselves from their situation.

After Schachter's demonstrations that fearful people do often desire to associate with others, especially others whom they perceive to be in the same distressing situation, there was a flurry of research addressed to the emotion-affiliation hypothesis. One of the more influential studies was conducted by Sarnoff and Zimbardo (1961). These investigators replicated Schachter's findings with the induction of the emotion of fear, but they found that anxiety (perhaps more accurately labeled "embarrassment" when their operationalization of "anxiety" is considered) did *not* result in increased desire to interact (and presumably to communicate) with others. An excellent article by Wheeler (1974) reviews the emotion-affiliation literature to that date, after which interest in the subject evaporated.

That researchers lost interest in identifying the circumstances under which people will try to communicate with others when they are experiencing emotion was not surprising; in order to approach systematically the question of emotion as a cause of symbolic exchange, one needs a theory of emotion. But at the time Schachter was conducting his studies on the relationship between emotion and affiliation, the psychology of emotion was still moribund. There was no body of useful emotion theory—nor a zeitgeist within psychology for the development of one—that could fuel further investigation of the links between emotion and communication.

Given the absence of psychological theory and research on emotion, after his affiliation experiments Schachter took the next logical step: He developed a theory of emotion and designed a series of brilliant experiments to test it (Schachter & Singer, 1962). He proposed a two-component theory of emotion, which assumes that for an individual to experience emotion both physiological arousal and an "emotional" cognitive interpretation of that arousal are necessary. This theory sparked the renaissance of interest in emotion that has swept through all areas of psychology in the past decade. (For just a partial listing of the flood of books that appeared on the subject of emotion in 1984 alone, see Berscheid, in press.) The development of more robust theories of emotion now makes it possible to formulate more precise hypotheses about when the experience of emotion will result in attempts to communicate with others and when it will not, and, in addition, the identity of the persons with whom communication will be desired.

Space does not permit extensive development and elaboration of such hypotheses here, but one brief example will be given. If one accepts Mandler's basic tenet that the interruption of the individual's ongoing highly organized activities (and/or higher-order plans) is the major cause of the experience of emotion, and that resumption of the interrupted activities (or completion of the interrupted plans) is the aim of much emotional activity, then it is clear that individuals experiencing emotion should try to communicate with persons whom they perceive to possess both the power to remove the interruption and the willingness to use that power beneficially in this instance (see Berscheid, 1985, for a further discussion of this point). It might be noted that this hypothesis is compatible with Bowlby's (1973) hypothesis, derived from attachment theory, that when an individual is sick, afraid, or otherwise threatened, the individual will seek and maintain proximity with members of the species who are older, stronger, and wiser.

The tendency to want to communicate with others when experiencing a positive emotion as opposed to a negative one is less clear, although the anecdotal and popular literature is rife with speculation that in these cases, too, there is a desire to communicate with others (e.g., in joy to "shout it from the highest hill"). Thus another potentially fruitful area for investigation encompasses the exploration of when, and with whom, individuals who are experiencing positive emotional states will attempt to communicate with others. Positive emotional states often signal that the individual is experiencing altered circumstances of comfort and welfare, but that these events have *enhanced* rather than threatened the probability of survival (see Berscheid, 1983, and Mandler, 1984, for discussions of the antecedents of positive emotion). At the moment, however, it is not clear why an emotionally arousing esthetic experience—such as a beautiful sunset or a spine-tingling musical performance—often leads to attempts to tell others about that experience. In fact, knowledge about the extent to which emotional experiences, both positive and negative, lead to attempts to communicate with others remains largely undeveloped to this day.

INTERPERSONAL COMMUNICATION AS A SOURCE OF HUMAN EMOTION

The relative lack of systematic exploration of the emotion-interpersonal communication interface is surprising not only because many of the most important message exchanges between people occur when one or both are experiencing an emotion, but also because interpersonal communication is an important *source* of human emotional experience. It is, in fact, the most common source. Virtually no one, scholar or layperson alike, disputes the fact that interpersonal relationships are the most frequent context in which people experience emotion. As Albert Ellis and Robert Harper (1977) put it, "other persons are usually the most highly emotogenic stimuli in our civilized environment" (p. 20). It is for this reason, in fact, that Herbert Simon (1967) argued two decades ago "that a theory of emotional behavior, to be satisfactory, must explain this connection of emotion with social interaction" (p. 37).

Berscheid (1983) has proposed a model that attempts to illuminate why other people are emotogenic stimuli and to outline the dynamics of emotion as it occurs in the context of close relationships. This model represents a synthesis of Kelley et al.'s (1983) conceptualization of close relationships and Mandler's interruption theory of emotion.

Specifically, Kelley et al. propose that the extent to which a relationship is close may be profitably conceptualized as the frequency, the strength, and the diversity of the causal interconnections between two individuals' sequences of life events. In other words, a relationship's closeness is represented by the extent to which the activities of one person—e.g., his or her thoughts, internal states, and overt behaviors—influence the activities of the other, and vice versa. Thus close relationships are influential relationships. In close relationships, the partners have a great deal of influence upon each other's activities—whether that influence is for good or for ill and whether it is acknowledged or not are irrelevant to classifying the relationship as close. When the partners' sequences of activities are strongly causally interconnected, such that an action by one is a necessary and sufficient condition for some action on the part of the other, then their organized sequences of behavior are said to be "meshed." Berscheid hypothesizes that when such meshing in a close relationship fails, the activity sequences of one or both people will be interrupted, arousal will result, and an emotional experience (probably, but not necessarily, negative) will follow.

Berscheid differentiates between emotion as it occurs "in" the relationship and emotion that has its source outside the relationship. An emotional event in the relationship is an emotional experience that has been precipitated by a partner-inspired interruption. The partner either has done something he or she was not expected to do or the partner has failed to do something he or she was expected to do. In either case, the individual's sequence of activities is interrupted and an emotional experience will result. Persons and events external to the relationship may also inspire emotional experiences, of course, and these may reverberate to influence all activities within the relationship, including the partners' messages to each other.

The point to be emphasized here is that in performing our own routine activities and fulfilling our own higher-order plans and goals, we are so dependent on the activities of those persons who are near us that those persons have a great deal of *interruptibility* power over us. As a consequence, they also have a great deal of emotional power. Or, as Berscheid (1983) hypothesizes, the extent to which another has interruptibility power over us determines our *emotional investment* in the relationship with him or her. Verbal communication from persons with whom we are close is probably the most frequent source of human emotion simply because people usually *say* what they are going to do before they do it (e.g., "I'm going to get a divorce and run off with Harry") and what they are *not* going to do before they do not do it (e.g., "I'm not going to take you with me to Australia as I promised you earlier"), and thus inform their partner that his or her most cherished activities, plans, and goals are going to be interrupted.

The fact that verbal exchanges between people are undoubtedly the most frequent precipitator of human emotion makes the absence of research exploring emotion-communication phenomena even more striking. Even such basic questions as how the mode of presentation of a piece of interrupting information influences the recipient's reaction is largely unexplored, and this is true even though the primary presenting symptom for psychological therapy is the existence of a negative emotional state that the counselor or clinician will attempt to ameliorate by long sessions of talking to and with the patient (see Berscheid, Gangestad, & Kulakowski, 1984, for a discussion).

It also should be noted that not only is the information conveyed in interpersonal communication *received* from others an important source of emotional experience, recent evidence suggests that the very act of transmitting communication to others may, in itself and regardless of content, prompt an emotional experience. In his book, *The Language of the Heart,* heart researcher James Lynch (1985) presents a great deal of evidence that the simple process of talking and listening to other people affects—sometimes dramatically— the individual's entire cardiovascular system, producing effects not dissimilar to those experienced in intense emotional states.

To recapitulate the discussion so far, I have made the following points:

(1) Interpersonal communication that is transmitted when the individual is experiencing an emotion is, other things being equal, more likely to have important consequences for the welfare and survival of the individual than is communication transmitted under nonemotional conditions.

(2) Persons experiencing emotion are more, rather than less, likely to attempt to communicate with others, although the circumstances under which this is true (and the few circumstances under which it is not true, including individual differences in the tendency to communicate with others when experiencing an emotional state) are in need of elaboration.

(3) Interpersonal communication, especially verbal communication, is an important source of emotional experience, and perhaps the most common source.

None of the above would have the slightest import for investigations of emotion and interpersonal communication phenomena if it were also true that the existence of an emotional state in either the communicator or the message recipient made no difference to the form and content of the message transmitted or to what is received. However, it *does* make a difference. We can begin to sketch the kind of a difference it makes—or, the role of emotion in interpersonal communication—from emerging evidence that the existence of emotional states in individuals influences their attention to certain types of stimuli as well as the subsequent processing and retrieval of information.

INTERPERSONAL COMMUNICATION DIFFERENCES UNDER EMOTIONAL AND NONEMOTIONAL CONDITIONS

Before briefly discussing findings that suggest the effect of emotion on communication, it must be emphasized that the identification of communication differences due to emotion depends heavily upon first distinguishing an *emotional* from an *unemotional* state. This is not as easy as it seems. Since the experience of a specific emotion usually seems to be immediately and directly given, and thus a matter upon which there could be very little controversy, it sometimes comes as a surprise to fledgling students of human emotion that defining what an emotion is has constituted a severe obstacle to the development of theory and research in the area of human emotion (see Berscheid, in press). A great deal of terminological confusion continues to characterize the emotion area, and the problem is exacerbated by a tendency for theorists and researchers to neglect to define their terms, including the central term "emotion," often sharing with laypersons the belief that their own personal conception and definition of emotion will be readily understood and endorsed by others.

This is not the place to discuss the more frequent confusions that prevail within the emotion area today. In this chapter, however, we have been following a terminological convention articulated by Simon (1982) that has been followed to a large extent by Mandler in his theory of emotion (1975, 1984), has been endorsed by Berscheid (1983) after a review of the many vocabularies of emotion in use today, and is gaining widespread use. Simon states,

> I personally prefer to employ *affect* as a generic term, *emotion* to refer to affect that interrupts and redirects attention (usually with accompanying arousal), *mood* to refer to affect that provides context for ongoing thought processes without noticeably interrupting them, and *valuation* to refer to association of cognitive "labels" attributing positive or negative valence to objects or events. (1982, pp. 335-336)

In other words, the term "emotion" increasingly is being reserved for states in which the individual is experiencing physiological arousal, specifically, discharge of the autonomic nervous system—the type of emotion that is experienced may be either positive or negative and of differing varieties, such as fear, anger, joy, elation, or jealousy. Emotion is unlike states of the individual that are affectively toned but in which arousal is not experienced—when, for instance, the individual is in a good or bad mood.

Answers to questions about the role emotion plays in interpersonal communication obviously are going to depend on how emotion is defined. To illustrate, if the term "emotion" is reserved for states in which the individual is experiencing physiological arousal (and not all emotion theorists and researchers endorse this terminological convention) then all available information about the effect of autonomic arousal upon thought processes and consciousness becomes pertinent to the formulation of hypotheses about communication in emotional states. For example, as Mandler (1979) argues, there is less focal conscious attention available for other task-directed and coping activities if it is true that the experience of emotion usually, if not always, involves the perception of the internal events of physiological arousal (pounding heart, sweating palms, etc.); and if it is also true that human attentional capacity is limited, because if the perception of such internal physiological events as arousal symptoms does take up some amount of that finite capacity. One of these "task-directed and coping activities" may be verbal communication to another person about the events that precipitated the aroused emotional state. Thus emerging evidence that physiological arousal affects attentional capacity suggests that interpersonal communication will also be affected under emotional states *when* emotion is defined as a state that is accompanied by autonomic nervous system arousal. If emotion is defined in a different way, then this evidence will, of course, be irrelevant to emotion-communication hypotheses.

To illustrate the point further, some theorists define "emotional state" broadly enough to include "mood." As defined by Isen and her associates (Clark & Isen, 1982; Isen, Means, Patrick, & Nowicki, 1982), mood is simply thinking a series of positive or negative thoughts. Mood has been shown to influence retrieval of information such that persons in a positive mood seem better able to retrieve positively toned information than neutral or negative information (e.g., Isen, Shalker, Clark, & Karp, 1978). The effects of negative mood are less clear. This tendency for mood state to influence the accessibility of stored information is likely to influence the nature of the interpersonal communication the individual engages in when he or she is in that state. In addition, mood states may influence communication differently than states in which arousal is experienced. For example, Clark and her associates have found evidence to suggest that the material people learn when in a high arousal state and the material they learn when in a normal arousal state are best recalled when they are in a *similar* arousal state, suggesting that arousal itself acts as a retrieval cue for arousal-related material in memory (Clark, Milberg, & Ross, 1983). Thus what an individual can retrieve from memory (or how quickly it can be retrieved, how accessible it is) will influence interpersonal communication that takes place when the individual is in an emotional state accompanied by arousal and it also will affect retrieval in mood states, but in somewhat different ways. As a consequence, if communication researchers are not more aware of terminological ambiguities and inconsistencies than theorists and researchers of human emotion have been, the same degree of confusion that has troubled contemporary emotion research can be expected to develop in the emotion-communication area.

CONCLUDING COMMENTS

I have argued in this chapter that one of the most fertile fields for investigation in interpersonal communication lies along the emotion-interpersonal communication interface. Actually, it should now be clear that the term "interface" is not really an accurate one; for, as we have tried to illustrate, the association between the experience of emotion and the tendency to communicate to other people, and the association between interpersonal communication and the experience of emotion are so strong that problems of emotion and of communication are inextricably intertwined and integral to one another; any information about one is likely to benefit understanding of the other. This is particularly true because the experience of emotion ordinarily is not a momentary experience; rather, it is episodic in nature, with the various events that occur in the emotional episode being both the stimulus and response to other events. Thus, interpersonal communication that occurs *during* the episode may be both a response to emotional stimuli and the stimulus for heightened emotion or for lessened emotion depending, of course, upon the information conveyed in that communication and, more interestingly, upon the form and timing of the communication.

REFERENCES

Berscheid, E. (1983). Emotion. In H. H. Kelley, E. Berscheid, A. Christensen, J. Harvey, T. L. Houston, G. Levinger, E. McClintock, L. A. Peplau, & D. R. Peterson (Eds.), *Close relationships* (pp. 110-168). San Francisco: W. H. Freeman.

Berscheid, E. (in press). Vocabularies of emotion. In A. Isen (Ed.), *Affect and social behavior*. Cambridge: Cambridge University Press.

Berscheid, E. (1985). Interpersonal attraction. In G. Lindzey & E. Aronson (Eds.), *The handbook of social psychology* (3rd ed., pp. 413-484). Hillsdale, NJ: Lawrence Erlbaum.

Berscheid, E., Gangestad, S., & Kulakowski, D. (1984). Emotion in close relationships: An overview of theory with implications for counseling. In S. D. Brown & R. W. Lent (Eds.), *Handbook of counseling psychology*. New York: John Wiley.

Bowlby, J. (1973). Affectional bonds: Their nature and origin. In R. W. Weiss (Ed.), *Loneliness: The experience of emotional and social isolation* (pp. 38-52). Cambridge: MIT Press.

Cairns, R. B. (1979). *Social development: The origins and plasticity of interchanges.* San Francisco: W. H. Freeman.

Clark, M. S., & Isen, A. M. (1982). Toward understanding the relationship between feeling states and social behavior. In A. Hastorf & A. M. Isen (Eds.), *Cognitive social psychology* (pp. 73-108). New York: Elsevier.

Clark, M. S., Milberg, S., & Ross, J. (1983). Arousal cues arousal-related material in memory: Implications for understanding effects of mood on memory. *Journal of Verbal Learning and Verbal Behavior, 22,* 633-649.

Darwin, C. (1899). *Expression of the emotions in man and animals.* New York: Appleton.

Ellis, A., & Harper, R. (1977). *A guide to successful marriage.* Los Angeles: Wilshire. (original work published 1961)

Festinger, L. (1950). Informal social communication. *Psychological Review, 57,* 271-282.

Festinger, L. (1954). A theory of social comparison processes. *Human Relations, 7,* 117-140.

Isen, A. M., Means, B., Patrick, R., & Nowicki, G. (1982). Some factors influencing decision-making strategy and risk taking. In M. S. Clark & S. T. Fiske (Eds.), *Affect and cognition: The seventeenth annual Carnegie symposium on cognition* (pp. 243-261). Hillsdale, NJ: Lawrence Erlbaum.

Isen, S. M., Shalker, T., Clark, M., & Karp, L. (1978). Affect accessibility of material in memory and behavior: A cognitive loop? *Journal of Personality and Social Psychology, 36,* 1-12.

Izard, C. E. (1971). *The face of emotion.* New York: Appleton-Century-Crofts.

Izard, C. E. (1977). *Human emotions.* New York: Plenum.

Kelley, H. H., Berscheid, E., Christensen, A., Harvey, J. H., Houston, T. L., Levinger, G., McClintock, E., Peplau, L. A., & Peterson, D. R. (Eds.). (1983). *Close relationships.* San Francisco: W. H. Freeman.

Lynch, J. (1985). *The language of the heart.* New York: Basic Books.

Mandler, G. (1975). *Mind and emotion.* New York: John Wiley.

Mandler, G. (1979). Thought processes, consciousness, and stress. In V. Hamilton & D. M. Warburton (Eds.), *Human stress and cognition: An information processing approach* (pp. 179-201). London: John Wiley.

Mandler, G. (1983). Emotion and stress: A view from cognitive psychology. In L. Temoshok, C. Van Dyke, & L. S. Zegans (Eds.), *Emotions in health and illness: Theoretical and research foundations* (pp. 195-205). New York: Grune & Stratton.

Mandler, G. (1984). *Mind and body: Psychology of emotion and stress.* New York: Norton.

Sarnoff, L., & Zimbardo, P. G. (1961). Anxiety, fear and social affiliation. *Journal of Abnormal and Social Psychology, 62,* 356-363.

Schachter, S. (1959). *The psychology of affiliation.* Stanford, CA: Stanford University Press.

Schachter, S., & Singer, J. E. (1962). Cognitive, social and physiological determinants of emotional state. *Psychological Review, 69,* 379-399.

Simon, H. A. (1967). Motivational and emotional controls of cognition. *Psychological Review, 74,* 29-39.

Simon, H. A. (1982). Affect and cognition: Comments. In M. S. Clark & S. T. Fiske (Eds.), *Affect and cognition: The seventeenth annual Carnegie Symposium on cognition* (pp. 333-342). Hillsdale, NJ: Lawrence Erlbaum.

Wheeler, L. (1974). Social comparison and selective affiliation. In T. L. Huston (Ed.), *Foundations of interpersonal attraction* (pp. 309-329). New York: Academic Press.

Chapter 5

MBRS REKINDLED
Some Thoughts on Compliance Gaining in Interpersonal Settings

Gerald R. Miller, Franklin J. Boster,
Michael E. Roloff, and David R. Seibold

IN RECENT YEARS, a number of communication researchers have underscored the centrality of persuasive communication to interpersonal relationships (e.g., Miller & Burgoon, 1978; Miller, Burgoon, & Burgoon, 1984; Seibold, Cantrill, & Meyers, 1985). At first glance, such pronouncements are hardly earthshaking: Whether the label is "persuasion," "social influence," "compliance gaining," or yet some other process, who could be so naive as to exclude symbolic inducement as part of the warp and weft of people's daily interpersonal transactions? From pleading forgiveness for a social slight to proposing marriage to a romantic partner, persuasive transactions are essential to interpersonal commerce.

Though this fact may be patently obvious, students of communication have only recently commenced to apply terms such as *persuasion* to interpersonal settings. Instead, as Miller and Burgoon (1978) note, face-to-face interactions involving persuasive message exchanges have typically been relegated to conceptual cubbyholes such as "communication and conflict," "person perception," or "interpersonal attraction," thereby creating the illusion that persuasion is something practiced primarily in one-to-many contexts such as the mass media. Consequently, the supposed decline in persuasion research occurring in the 1970s and early 1980s was probably more imagined than real, resulting largely from communication researchers *"falling captive to the limits imposed by their own operational definitions of the area"* (Miller & Burgoon, 1978, p. 31, emphasis in original).

A notable exception to this generalization is the work on compliance-gaining message strategies. In 1977, armed with a list of 16 strategies developed by sociologists Gerald Marwell and David Schmitt (1967a, 1967b), the four of us conducted what we believe to be the maiden communication study on compliance gaining—the authorship order giving birth to the acronym MBRS (Miller, Boster, Roloff, & Seibold, 1977). Respondents in our study were asked to rate the likelihood they would use each of Marwell and Schmitt's 16 strategies in one of four hypothetical scenarios involving face-to-face persuasive exchanges. Though we tried to manipulate the degree of interpersonalness by varying the descriptions of the participants' relational history—relative strangers on the one hand versus close romantic partners on the other— all of the scenarios satisfied situational criteria (Miller, 1978) for defining interpersonal communication. Thus from the outset, communication research on compliance-gaining message strategies has relied heavily on interpersonal settings. Seibold et al. (1985, p. 560) indicated that "this research fuses traditional persuasion concerns and newer interpersonal communication foci," while Wheeless, Barraclough, and Stewart (1983) contend that it has made the study of persuasion in interpersonal situations more viable than in the early and middle 1970s.

Since our initial undertaking, more than 50 published studies and conference papers have probed issues associated with compliance-gaining message strategies; as our title metaphorically suggests, there is much empirical firewood for rekindling MBRS. This chapter considers several recurrent issues that have emerged. Specifically, we first examine some questions relating to attempts to define the concept "compliance-gaining message strategy" and to develop useful strategy typologies; we next focus on approaches and problems associated with the measurement of strategy use; we then discuss several factors influencing the likelihood that self-reports about strategy selection will correlate decently with actual behavior in compliance-gaining situations; and we conclude with a general assessment of the current theoretical status of compliance-gaining work, as well as some capsule recommendations about promising directions for future work.

COMPLIANCE-GAINING MESSAGE STRATEGIES: SOME DEFINITIONAL AND TYPOLOGICAL MATTERS

"Persuasive [compliance-gaining] strategies constitute the symbolic inducements of persuasive messages; they are the linguistic ammunition communicators use to accomplish their persuasive missions" (Miller, 1983, p. 124). As noted earlier, Marwell and Schmitt (1967a, 1967b) generated 16 such strategies (Table 5.1). Their strategies, in turn, were based partially on several shorter lists developed earlier (Etzioni, 1961; French & Raven, 1960; Kelman, 1961).

Perusal of the 16 strategies advanced by Marwell and Schmitt reveals that they rely on several different mechanisms for achieving persuasive force (Miller, 1983). Certain strategies seek to heighten the salience of particular persuadee self-attitudes; for example, the *moral appeal* strategy relies on the assump-

TABLE 5.1
Marwell and Schmitt's 16 Compliance-Gaining Strategies

(1) Promise	(If you comply, I will reward you.) You offer to include another paper by your colleague in a second book you are editing, if he or she completes this chapter promptly.
(2) Threat	(If you do not comply, I will punish you.) You tell your colleague if the chapter is not in your hands promptly, it will be removed from the book's contents.
(3) Expertise (Positive)	(If you comply, you will be rewarded because of "the nature of things.") You tell your colleague that if he or she fulfills writing commitments promptly, he or she will have no trouble finding publishing opportunities.
(4) Expertise (Negative)	(If you do not comply, you will be punished because of "the nature of things.") You tell your colleague that if he or she fails to fulfil writing commitments promptly, publishing opportunities will be few and far between.
(5) Liking	(Actor is friendly and helpful to get target in "good frame of mind" so that he or she will comply with request.) You seek out your colleague for several friendly conversations at a convention, and then ask him or her to be sure to finish the chapter promptly.
(6) Pre-giving	(Actor rewards target before requesting compliance.) In addition to conversing amiably, you buy dinner and drinks for your colleague at the convention, and over an after-dinner brandy ask him or her to be sure to complete the chapter promptly.
(7) Aversive Stimulation	(Actor continuously punishes target making cessation contingent on compliance.) You call and berate your colleague daily at home and at the office, making it clear you will continue to do so until you receive the chapter.
(8) Debt	(You owe me compliance because of past favors.) You point out that you have written forewords for two of your colleague's books for nothing, and that he or she certainly owes you the courtesy of getting the chapter in on time.
(9) Moral Appeal	(You are immoral if you do not comply.) You emphasize to your colleague that others have finished, and that it is unfair and immoral for him or her to delay publication of others' work by tarrying with his or her own chapter.
(10) Self-Feeling (Positive)	(You will feel better about yourself if you comply.) You tell your colleague he or she will feel a real sense of accomplishment if the chapter is done promptly.
(11) Self-Feeling (Negative)	(You will feel worse about yourself if you do not comply.) You tell your colleague he or she will feel very guilty if he or she is late with the chapter.

TABLE 5.1 Continued

(12) Altercasting (Positive)	(A person with "good qualities would comply.) You remind your colleague that since he or she is a mature, committed scholar, he or she will naturally want to complete the chapter promptly.
(13) Altercasting (Negative)	(Only a person with "bad" qualities would not comply.) You tell your colleague that only an immature, uncommitted scholar would fail to finish the chapter on time.
(14) Altruism	(I need your compliance very badly, so do it for me.) You tell your colleague that it is very important to get this book out promptly, and that it would be a personal favor to you if he or she gets the chapter done on schedule.
(15) Esteem (Positive)	(People you value will think better of you if you comply.) You tell your colleague that all the other contributors to the book will respect and admire him or her if the chapter is done promptly.
(16) Esteem (Negative)	(People you value will think worse of you if you do not comply.) You tell your colleague that all the other contributors to the book will think he or she is unreliable and lazy if the chapter is not completed promptly.

NOTE: We have used an example involving a situation where the editor of a book of contributed essays seeks to hasten the work of a tardy, or potentially tardy contributor. The choice of example, of course, is sheer whimsy and is not at all related to any problems the editors have experienced in assembling the chapters of this book (well, hardly at all related, anyway).

tion that people wish to perceive themselves as honest and upright, while the *altruism* strategy assumes people like to be seen as cooperative, helpful, and concerned with the welfare of others. Other strategies rely primarily on conjuring a positive image of the compliance seeker; the persuasive force of *liking,* for example, depends on painting a pleasant, friendly picture of the compliance seeker, while the success of the *expertise* strategies hinges on the perception that the compliance seeker is knowledgeable about the "way things are." Still another group of strategies aims at triggering an appropriate dispositional state in the persuadee—both *threat* and *promise* function this way, with the former seeking to stimulate fear or anxiety and the latter anticipation or appetite. Finally, some of the strategies combine more than one of these intervening outcomes; *pre-giving,* for example, both contributes to a positive image of the compliance seeker as a generous person and sets the stage for subsequent appeals to persuadee self-attitudes regarding fairness and reciprocity. In the last analysis, of course, the persuasive proof of the pudding is in the behavior, for regardless of the precise mediating mechanism, the compliance seeker is hopeful the specific strategy or strategies employed will induce the message target to behave as desired.

In the MBRS study, we sought to develop a more economical typology of strategies than the 16-strategy list offered by Marwell and Schmitt, and we examined whether differences in situational characteristics would affect strategy selection. Since that time, numerous researchers have explored typological issues. Though a review of their research might assist a few readers, we suspect that most interested students of communication have encountered summaries in other sources (e.g., Miller, 1983; Seibold et al., 1985; Wheeless et al., 1983). What follows here, then, is stipulation of a definition of the concept "compliance-gaining message strategies" and a brief consideration of some of the questions implied by the concept, both for communication researchers in general and interpersonal communication researchers in particular.

Borrowing from Seibold et al. (1985, p. 556), we define *compliance-gaining message strategies* as follows: anticipated and actual discourse patterns performed in the service of a personal or interpersonal agenda. Such strategies subsume specific and often multiple message tactics appropriate to the communicator's goal of gaining attitudinal and/or behavioral compliance from the message target.

Implicit in the notion of "strategy" is at least some level of conscious awareness and deliberate choice. Indeed, Seibold et al. (1985) contend that most work on compliance-gaining message strategy selection and use takes the following as given:

(1) conscious awareness of the influence "situation," including all embedded role relationships, salient sociocultural characteristics of the setting, and a clearly identifiable instrumental/interpersonal task;
(2) sufficient time to rationally assess the situation and consider options;
(3) the intention to formulate a plan designed to accomplish a well defined outcome;
(4) a diverse, complex, and differentiated repertoire of strategies and tactics to draw upon;
(5) sufficient awareness and individual perspective-taking ability to weigh the consequences of enacting each strategic alternative; and
(6) an ability to choose some strategies and forego others (that is, all strategies considered acceptable are personally accessible and can be competently enacted, and some strategies—perhaps judged by the actors to be unacceptable or inappropriate under the circumstances—can be eschewed even when they may be habitual modes of response for that actor). (p. 567)

To what extent are these six conditions satisfied in people's daily persuasive transactions? Berger and Douglas (1982), among others, have cautioned against the potential theoretical and methodological pitfalls of viewing most communicative exchanges as very thoughtful and deliberative events. Rather, they opine, many interactions are characterized by their relative "mindlessness"—to use Langer's (1978) term—with the communicators relating in habitual, rigidly scripted routines. In terms of compliance gaining, this possibility underscores the misleading nature of phrases such as *choosing strategies* or *selecting strategies,* expressions implying considerable cognitive activity and volition. Perhaps instead most communicators acquire relatively narrow strategy repertoires by learning and conditioning, and continually use these repertoires regardless of communicative circumstances. Miller (1982) has put the matter this way

> Numerous persuasive compliance-gaining transactions...are characterized by the use of ineffectual persuasive message strategies. Despite the fact that any reasonably objective observer could predict that certain strategies are destined to fail, would-be persuaders often persist in using them. Such persistence suggests that, like other behaviors, message strategy preferences are learned. Moreover, it is likely that during this learning process, persuaders acquire habitual preferences for particular message strategies....Once these patterns are strongly conditioned, persuaders may continue to employ them even though they are ineffective in achieving persuasive goals; and may even, in fact, produce undesirable side effects such as resentment and hostility. (pp. 4-5)

Indeed, it is probably in the daily, face-to-face transactions between acquaintances, friends, and romantic partners—that is, in those settings and relationships typically labeled "interpersonal"—that the majority of mindless, routinized communication occurs. In such circumstances, relational partners are apt to fall into patterns of behavior that minimize the number and types of compliance-gaining strategies employed. By contrast, the painstakingly crafted messages of the mass media usually do involve careful weighing of alternative symbolic inducements, as do important professional and commercial messages exchanged between individuals. The same person who spends hours, or even days, crafting a persuasive message aimed at clinching an important sale or ensuring a prestigious promotion may give little or no thought to the most effective compliance-gaining strategies available for persuading a son or daughter to stay in school rather than dropping out to take a job.

The possibility that communicators are less purposeful in constructing persuasive messages than students of communication have typically assumed does not necessarily impugn the value of the concept of compliance-gaining message strategies, at least in the sense that it is used to refer to actual patterns of persuasive discourse. Rather, what it does suggest is careful scrutiny of the theoretical and mediational baggage associated with the concept. For example, there have been few descriptive attempts to chronicle the range of strategies actually used by persuasive communicators, to determine how consciously persuaders formulate their message plans, or to examine individual differences in strategy usage. We will have occasion to allude to some of these issues in later sections of this chapter. For the moment, we are content to observe that the cognitive and volitional waters engulfing the strategy concept are murky.

A second definitional issue concerns the appropriate level of abstraction for labeling a discourse element a *strategy*. Recall that our definition stipulates a strategy may subsume multiple message *tactics*. Recently, Berger (1985) has argued persuasively that the discourse elements labeled "strategies" by many prior researchers might more usefully be conceived of as "tactics." "There may be numerous tactical variations for a given strategy," he notes, and goes on to say that "any number of verbal messages could be sent to depict threat, and a large number of nonverbal variations could also be used to instantiate the strategy" (p. 485). Though we deem it unnecessary to bring nonverbal behavior to bear on the strategy concept, his point regarding the plethora of verbal discourse elements that can be called into service of a particular compliance-gaining message strategy has much to recommend it.

The scientific desirability of a more economical, abstract typology of compliance-gaining message strategies can best be illustrated by returning to the original list of 16 strategies identified by Marwell and Schmitt (1967a, 1967b). As Miller (1983) has indicated, their relatively cumbersome typology poses both theoretical and methodological difficulties. In the former domain, such an extensive strategy set is all but certain to culminate in empirical generalizations framed at a less-than-optimal level of abstraction. Both intuition and empirical evidence reveal that subsets of the strategies share common symbolic and psychological characteristics:

> To generate separate bodies of generalizations for the strategies of promise, liking, and pre-giving, when all three are clearly reward-oriented strategies [or to put it more precisely in terms of the present discussion, *three message tactics* that can be used when pursuing a *reward-oriented strategy*], is theoretically cumbersome and inelegant; such an approach violates the widely shared scientific value of parsimony. (Miller, 1983, p. 129)

Finally, in terms of the methodological utility of such a complex strategy list, both naive communicators, solicited for self reports about their strategy preferences, and trained raters, asked to code instances of strategy usage by persuasive communicators, face a formidable challenge in classifying the strategies validly and reliably.

To be sure, this point has not escaped prior researchers dealing with compliance-gaining message strategies, as evidenced by the spate of factor analytic and clustering studies aimed at identifying more economical typologies (in addition to Miller et al., 1977, see, for example, Burgoon, Dillard, Doran, & Miller, 1982; Hunter & Boster, 1978; Wiseman & Schenck-Hamlin, 1981). Unfortunately, as Miller (1983) notes and as we shall underscore in later pages of this chapter, these studies have reported about as many varying solutions, as well as interpretations of these solutions, as there have been investigators to report them. Thus researchers seeking to select a set of strategies are faced with a welter of prior procedural approaches and empirical outcomes.

A second possible path to more useful typologies lies in researchers devising schemes from a mixture of existing theory, research, and armchair speculation. For example, Berger (1985, pp. 484-491) outlines a Strategy Attribute Schema (SAS) that holds promise for developing more comprehensive generalizations about strategy selection. Miller and Parks (1982) present a four-category typology of compliance-gaining message strategies based on the two dimensions of reward- versus punishment-oriented strategies and communicator-onus versus communicatee-onus strategies. As can be seen in Figure 5.1, all of Marwell and Schmitt's strategies can be grouped in the four, more abstract strategies generated by the two dimensions Miller and Parks suggest.

Though much more could be said about definitional and typological issues associated with the concept "compliance-gaining message strategies," the preceding discussion has provided a flavor of some of the major problems that must be resolved if the concept is to prove useful in studying interpersonal influence. Since we have also touched on several methodological matters of measurement and observation, it seems sensible to turn next to a more extensive perusal of this topic.

CHECKLISTS, INTERVIEWS,
AND COMMUNICATIVE BEHAVIOR:
SOME PROBLEMS OF
MEASUREMENT AND OBSERVATION

Several procedures have been used to measure compliance-gaining message behavior. The most widely used procedure was devised by Marwell and Schmitt (1967b). In their study, they presented hypothetical compliance-gaining situations to respondents, each situation being followed by 16 brief compliance-gaining messages. These messages were generated using their 16 compliance-gaining strategies to produce messages specific to each of the hypothetical compliance-gaining situations. Respondents were asked to read each situation, imagine themselves in the role of the compliance seeker, and rate how likely they would be to use each of the messages. A slight modification of this procedure was introduced by Williams and Boster (1981). They generated two messages per strategy in order to separate the confounding influences of strategy and message content (Jackson & Backus, 1982). Other researchers have presented respondents with strategy definitions, rather than messages tailored to each compliance-gaining situation (Dillard & Burgoon, 1985).

Investigators have treated these likelihood-of-use responses differently. Some have analyzed responses to each strategy separately, as if each were a separate variable, or factor (e.g., Lustig & King, 1980; Sillars, 1980). As indicated earlier, others have factor analyzed these ratings to assess the dimension, or dimensions, of individual differences underlying them. The mixed results of these analyses are illustrated by the fact that Marwell and Schmitt (1976b) produced a five-factor solution, MBRS (1977) reported an eight-factor solu-

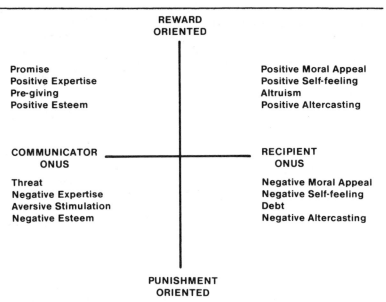

Figure 5.1   Four-Category Typology of Compliance-Gaining Message Strategies

tion, and Roloff and Barnicott (1978, 1979) found a two-factor solution.

These differing outcomes led Hunter and Boster (1978) to reexamine three data sets. Their results indicated that the data could be accounted for by a single factor. Because they had assumed that interitem relationships were linear, prior researchers had concluded erroneously that the ratings were multidimensional; hence a linear algorithm, factor analysis, was employed to analyze the data. Hunter and Boster demonstrated, however, that interitem regressions are nonlinear, the nonlinearity arising from nonlinear item characteristic curves. This nonlinearity produced the spurious factors in earlier analyses.

Although Hunter and Boster show that the judgments are unidimensional, they do not provide validity data concerning the nature of the dimension. They speculate that it is *empathy,* but subsequent research has cast serious doubt on their speculation (Dillard, Hunter, Burgoon, Boster, & Stiff, 1985). Since respondents report they prefer positive strategies, such as positive altercasting, to negative strategies, such as threat, Dillard and Burgoon (1985) argue that the dimension is *verbal aggression.* Specifically, respondents low in verbal aggression generally report they would use only the most positive strategies, while respondents high in verbal aggression indicate they would be likely to use both positive and negative strategies.

It is important for future studies to address this issue. Though the proper index is formed by summing likelihood-of-use judgments for all compliance-gaining strategies, it is unclear what this sum indicates about the respondents. Until that information is available, the meaning of situational difference and individual difference correlates will remain a mystery. For example, Williams and Boster's (1981) finding that as dogmatism increases, persons indicate a willingness to use more strategies could imply that high dogmatics are less empathic than low dogmatics, that high dogmatics are more verbally aggressive than low dogmatics, or that some other individual difference is at work, depending upon what is being measured by responses to the compliance-gaining strategies of Marwell and Schmitt.

Dissatisfaction with Marwell and Schmitt's strategies has led other researchers to develop alternative lists (Clark, 1979; Cody, McLaughlin, & Jordan, 1980; Falbo, 1977; Schenck-Hamlin, Wiseman, & Georgacarakos, 1982). These strategies have been developed inductively, as opposed to Marwell and Schmitt's deductive method. This inductive approach is characterized by Wiseman and Schenck-Hamlin in the following way: "The strategies constructed by subjects for particular persuasive situations are examined, patterns or generalizations among the data are discovered, and these patterns form the basis for the category scheme" (1981, p. 252).

Although proponents of the inductive method argue for the superiority of inductively derived lists, little evidence suggests that such strategy lists are somehow "better" than deductively derived ones. Indeed, the content of the various lists is similar. Boster, Stiff, and Reynolds (1985) recently found that the factor structure of responses to Wiseman and Schenck-Hamlin's (1981) typology is identical to the factor structure of responses obtained for the Marwell and Schmitt list. Moreover, responses to the two lists correlated almost perfectly when corrected for attenuation due to error of measurement. In retrospect, these findings are not surprising. There is no compelling reason to believe that strategies conceived by undergraduate students are superior to those generated by some of the best students of persuasive communication.

These remarks should not be taken as an argument for a moratorium on the generation of additional strategy lists. To the contrary, there are some troublesome gaps in these lists. For example, none of the present lists contains sequential strategies, such as foot-in-the-door or door-in-the-face strategies. Indeed, sequential influence attempts are probably used frequently in interpersonal settings. The addition of such strategies could alter the factor structure of responses to these lists, thereby suggesting other dimensions of individual differences pertinent to the prediction of compliance-gaining behavior.

Not only did Clark (1979) produce an inductively derived list, she also relied on a different method of assessing compliance-gaining strategy use—specifically, an interview approach. In her initial experiment, Clark provided participants with a hypothetical compliance-gaining situation and asked them what they would say to obtain the desired response from the target. Thus the participants' verbal statements, rather than their ratings of a set of messages, provided a measure of compliance-gaining strategy selection and use. In Clark's study, then, the inductive procedure was an end in itself, rather than a means for generating a new list of compliance-gaining strategies.

There is a crucial distinction between this procedure and the checklist approach. In the former, respondents must *generate* strategies, rather than selecting among strategies provided for them. To be sure, respondents in Clark's interviewing procedure may also engage in some kind of selection process. For instance, respondents may mentally generate a list of possible things to say and then edit the list before responding to the interviewer's question. Nevertheless, the distinction remains: No generation process need occur in the checklist procedure, whereas one must take place in Clark's procedure.

The utility of distinguishing between message generation and message selection is of empirical import. The principle of parallelism (Hunter & Gerbing, 1982) asserts that if two measures are alternate indicators of the same underlying trait, they should correlate similarly with other variables. This may not be the case with the checklist procedure and the interview method. For example, self-interest has exerted an impact when using the interviewing method (Clark, 1979), but it has had no effect when employing the checklist procedure (Williams & Boster, 1981). Therefore, these two procedures may well be tapping different dimensions of individual differences, but the evidence pertinent to this issue is limited.

Both the checklist and the interviewing methods rely on role playing, an approach criticized by several writers. For example, Boster et al. (1985) assert:

> While traditional role-playing procedures have produced and may continue to produce useful insights, the external validity of role-playing procedures is limited. . . . Because of this, our primary suggestion for future research is to move in the direction of observational research. We need either to find a natural compliance-gaining situation and observe compliance-gaining message use or to construct a situation which demands that subjects obtain the compliance of another and observe the subjects' use of compliance-gaining messages. (p. 186)

This strategy of using behavioral measures has been employed in three recent studies. Boster and Stiff (1984) had naive participants and confederates engage in a two-person problem-solving task. After the problem-solving period, the confederate was asked to divide the team's points. These points were to be converted into course credit, and the confederate's initially suggested allocation was one the participant was unlikely to accept. Subsequently, the participant was given an opportunity to try to convince the confederate to change the allocation.

Boster and Stiff coded the participant's responses into three categories: (1) give the other (confederate) more points, (2) give self (the participant) more points, or (3) no response. The messages constructed suggest that respondents have a limited repertoire of compliance-gaining strategies, although this conclusion is tempered by the possibility that procedural constraints precluded the articulation of complex compliance-gaining strategies.

Because of this limitation, Boster (1985) attempted to create a less constrained compliance-gaining situation. Research participants were asked to make telephone calls under the guise of soliciting participants for an experiment. These calls actually were made to confederates trained to respond by resisting and denying each compliance-gaining message offered by the participants. If the participant persisted after three denials, then the confederate yielded to the influence attempt.

Several measures were obtained: frequency of talk time, number of reasons provided, number of denials to which the participant responded, and content of the messages. The first three measures correlated highly; moreover, they correlated similarly with other variables. These findings imply that the three measures are alternate indicators of the same underlying construct; therefore, Boster combined them in a single index. While no validity data are currently available, a plausible hypothesis is that *argumentativeness* (Infante, Trebing, Shepherd, & Seeds, 1984) is the dimension underlying this index. Infante et al. (1984, p. 68) define argumentativeness as "a personality trait which predisposes an individual to recognize controversial issues, to advocate positions on them, and to refute other positions." Such a trait would probably affect how frequently one spoke, how many reasons one provided, and how many denials one refuted.

Of interest is the fact that this indeed did not correlate substantially with responses to Marwell and Schmitt's compliance-gaining strategies. This result, in conjunction with the pattern of correlations with other variables, suggests that this index and responses to the Marwell and Schmitt list are measuring different dimensions of individual differences in compliance-gaining behavior.

Boster and Lofthouse (1985) created a situation that enabled participants to argue with their instructors concerning their grade on a paper. In addition to the measures obtained by Boster (1985), Boster and Lofthouse obtained a measure of latency—namely, how long it took the participant to make an appointment to see the instructor—and response strength—whether or not the participant made a second appointment.

Correlations similar to those observed by Boster (1985) were obtained for the measures of speaking time, reasons, and denials. The latency measure and the response strength measure did not, however, correlate substantially with these measures, nor with each other. Moreover, the pattern of correlations with other variables suggested that these measures were not tapping the same underlying dimension of compliance-gaining behavior as the former three measures.

Given the three methods of measuring compliance-gaining message behavior discussed above, the natural question arises as to which measure is "best."

In this context, "best" means which of the methods, if any, is a valid indicator of the strategies communicators would use in actual compliance-gaining situations. We believe this is the wrong question to ask, and we next detail our reasons for this belief.

First, the preceding discussion clearly reveals that people's responses to these measuring techniques indicate something about the respondents. For example, it is plausible that responses to the Marwell and Schmitt strategies indicate something about respondents' verbal aggression. It is also probable that measures of speaking time, reasons, and denials indicate something about respondents' argumentativeness. While we have no hypothesis for Clark's interview measure, it can speculatively be suggested that it is less "pure" than either of the other two measures. Stated differently, by tapping into two processes—message generation and message selection—the interview approach may indicate something about several individual difference traits. Thus such a measure would be problematic because of its multidimensionality. The interview procedure could be modified to separate these processes, making it possible to isolate valid dimensions of individual differences. For example, having respondents list all of the things they thought of to say, and then asking them which of the messages they would send, would provide two measures: The former would be a measure of message generation and the latter a measure of message selection. Like the Boster (1985) and Boster and Lofthouse (1985) measures, the former measure might be an indicator of argumentativeness. Alternatively, this measure might indicate something about respondents' cognitive complexity. The latter measure might well indicate something about respondents' verbal aggressiveness, in much the same way as responses to the Marwell and Schmitt list may provide such an indication. But since the preceding discussion is largely speculative, future research needs to address this issue. Validity studies should aim at uncovering the dimensions of individual differences that underlie responses to these various measures.

Given this pespective on measures of compliance-gaining message behavior, the question of the "best" measure is clearly irrelevant. If the goal of scholarly inquiry is to predict compliance-gaining behavior, then *all* of these measures are potentially useful. For example, assume that the results of validation studies are consistent with our speculation: that responses to the Marwell and Schmitt list do indicate something about people's verbal aggressiveness and that responses to the Boster indices do reveal something about people's argumentativeness. The claim is that knowledge of these two variables can improve prediction of compliance-gaining message behavior.

Consider an individual high both in verbal aggression and argumentativeness. In a compliance-gaining situation, such a person probably would advance numerous arguments, since she or he is highly argumentative, and those arguments would likely be both positive and negative, since the person is high in verbal aggressiveness and has no qualms about using negative messages. Others may see such a person as *contentious*. Contrast such an individual with one high in verbal aggression but low in argumentativeness. This individual would advance few arguments but would be willing to transmit negative messages to obtain the listener's compliance. Such a communicator might send one message, a threat, and be perceived by others as *hostile*. On the other hand, a communicator low in verbal aggression but high in argumentativeness would be likely to send numerous messages, all or most of which would be positive. Since these messages would not vary much on affectiveness, observers might attribute the qualities *extremely rational* and *persistent* to the communicator. Finally, an individual who is low in both traits would be likely to say very little. Such a person might simply request compliance, and if it were not forthcoming, stop sending compliance-gaining messages. Others might see such a person as *timid* or *shy*.

In this hypothetical case, knowledge of two variables helped to narrow down the kinds of strategies communicators would be *likely* to use in actual compliance-gaining situations. Conceivably, knowledge of additional traits would permit exact prediction of the strategies communicators *will* use in compliance-gaining situations. While such a goal may be overly optimistic, it is clearly premature to search for the "most valid" indicator of compliance-gaining message behavior and to discard all other measures. There may well be multiple causes of compliance-gaining message behavior that require many different kinds of measuring instruments to estimate them. Moreover, these multiple causes may differ for noninterpersonal and interpersonal settings. Further complicating matters is the fact that procedures used in many prior compliance-gaining studies fail to capture the interactive nature of persuasive transactions in interpersonal settings. We turn next to a discussion of this problem.

FROM LAB TO LIVING ROOM: ON THE INTERACTIVE NATURE OF COMPLIANCE GAINING

In the majority of cases, interpersonal compliance gaining involves dyadic interaction, with each of the relational partners responding to the communication behaviors of the other. At a minimum, responsiveness may only involve monitoring cues to determine when it is appropriate to take a speaking turn. In such cases, the interaction is merely a sequenced monologue. In other situations, relational partners are responsive not only to turn-taking cues, they also monitor their own and their partner's intentions and feelings and adapt the content of their communication accordingly. A partner may engage in communicative behaviors that seek to refute or to reciprocate the other's communication, and may even try to preempt likely arguments. Thus interpersonal compliance-gaining requires, at bare minimum, at least one stimulus-response sequence.

Most previous research on the selection of compliance-gaining strategies has used procedures that do not capture the interactive nature of compliance gaining. As noted earlier, these studies typically have three phases. First, respondents are presented with the compliance-gaining situation. They may read a written description of a particular situation, or they may be asked to recall a situation having certain communicative characteristics. Second, after considering the situation, respondents indicate the likelihood that they would use a number of strategies within the situation, or they are asked to compose a message they would present to the target person. Finally, respondents complete questionnaire items measuring variables such as individual differences, perceptions of the compliance-gaining situation, and/or anticipated effects of a compliance-gaining strategy.

Although researchers have not claimed that such procedures are generalizable to all interactions, it seems useful to highlight how they may constrain knowledge about the interactive nature of compliance gaining. Specifically, these procedures may create an experience for the compliance seeker or the message target that differs markedly from those of communicators in actual interactions. We next consider several of these potential differences.

First, as discussed briefly earlier, participants in compliance-gaining studies may be more mindful or reflective about the nature of compliance-gaining than are interactants in situated encounters. Participants are presented with, or asked to imagine, situations with certain characteristics. In some cases, questions are asked about characteristics the situation may possess or outcomes that may accrue from using a particular strategy. Such procedures virtually ensure that respondents will focus their attention on certain cues when making the selection: In other words, they will *deliberate*. We have already argued that while conscious consideration of cues may be a part of some compliance-gaining situations, it is not common to all of them. Perhaps study procedures have stimulated the formation of conscious plans where such planning would not have normally occurred. In addition to Langer's (1978) earlier noted contention that a great deal of human behavior is mindlessly enacted, Hinde (1979) has acknowledged that many interactions may be entirely "ballistic," or unconsciously directed. Since research by Tesser (1978) reveals that simply asking people to think about something can change their judgments, it seems reckless to generalize the results of most prior compliance-gaining research beyond those types of interactions that are typically planned.

Second, information-processing demands are less formidable for research participants than for actual interactions. Participants in most studies are presented with fixed, static situations rather than dynamic, fluid ones. To provide a clean manipulation of situational cues, only a few factors may be highlighted. In addition, there are seldom demands for an immediate response, which might be found within an actual interaction. The person may reread the description of the situation or ponder a variety of actions before selecting a compliance-gaining strategy. All of these circumstances point to the likelihood that uncertainty levels about hypothetical research situations are lower than in many actual interactions.

Third, research participants who select and/or compose compliance-gaining strategies may do so relatively unemotionally or may experience feelings unrelated to the communicative context described in the manipulation. Often, respondents are asked not only to imagine what they would think or do, but also the kinds of feelings they would have toward a target person, topic, or relationship. In essence, the research relies on the cognitive skills of respondents to produce affective reactions. If they can imagine themselves within the situation, respondents can also produce appropriate emotions. However, this cognitive manipulation may not generate the desired affect, or it may not create an emotional reaction of similar or sufficient intensity to accurately model an actual interaction. Though manipulation checks may demonstrate that respondents *understand* the emotion they are supposed to feel in the situation, it is uncertain whether they are *actually feeling* it. Indeed, the research setting frequently does not lend itself to much emotional involvement. Often, class time is used to distribute compliance-gaining questionnaires. Though convenient, such a setting may include a number of cognitive and affective distractions that reduce the emotional impact of the manipulation. In addition, the use of written descriptions and responses may not adequately tap the arousal that is experienced when communicating orally in the presence of another person.

Fourth, when evaluating lists of alternative strategies, respondents may report a preference for some they would not ordinarily enact. This problem should not be confused with the earlier discussed argument that deductively derived lists of strategies are inferior to inductively derived taxonomies. Instead, the present argument is that providing persons with *any* list of strategies may force them to consider alternatives they might not have otherwise contemplated. In actual persuasive exchanges, time constraints may prohibit serious consideration of many alternatives. People may enact strategies habitually, preventing consideration of alternatives. Finally, people simply may not be sophisticated persuaders. As noted above, Boster and Stiff (1984) discovered only two rather simple strategies in their analysis of compliance-gaining interactions. Thus lists of compliance-gaining strategies may provide respondents with more, and perhaps better options than they normally would consider.

Fifth, research respondents select their strategies in persuasive *vacuo*; they do not expect to engage in actual persuasive transactions. Absence of anticipated interaction could influence both the quality and type of strategy selected. Davis and Wicklund (1972) reported that descriptive essays were more integrated when written under conditions of anticipated interaction than when not. Also, bargaining research indicates that negotiators select more cooperative strategies when they anticipate meeting a soft bargainer, and more competitive strategies when anticipating a tough one, than when anticipating no interaction at all (Marlowe, Gergen, & Doob, 1986). Thus a more realistic procedure that requires respondents to carry out their strategies may profoundly impact strategy selection and composition.

Sixth, the methods used in prior studies have largely ignored the pattern and structure of compliance-gaining strategies. Though most strategies are relatively simple, under certain conditions they may be quite complex. Hinde (1979) suggests that much interaction behavior is actually part of a larger master plan that involves a particular pattern of behaviors. For example, a *low-ball* strategy involves gaining the commitment of the message target to perform an ambiguous task followed by a message indicating the actual high costs associated with the task the target has agreed to perform (Cialdini, Cacioppo, Bassett, & Miller, 1978). Similarly, sequential messages are used with foot-in-the-door and door-in-the-face strategies (Dillard, Hunter, & Burgoon, 1984). As noted above, present research methods largely ignore such sequential strategies. When participants are asked to write out what they would say to gain compliance, the message product is only an initial compliance attempt. When indicating the probability that a set of strategies will be used, time order may enter into the estimates but the sequence remains hidden. Consequently, prior research on compliance gaining is largely limited to opening strategies, or "lines."

Finally, because there is no interaction, potential influences on strategy selection are limited to entry variables. Research has focused on initial perceptions of the situation, preliminary assessments of the impact of particular strategies, and individual difference variables as predictors of strategy selection. This focus ignores the importance of the target's response on the subsequent selection of strategies. Spector's (1977) bargaining model implies that individual differences, perceptions of the situation, and expectations are primarily predictors of *initial* plans of action. Once the bargaining begins, negotiators react to each other's behavior. Indeed, bargaining research indicates that individuals reciprocate concessions (Esser & Komorita, 1975; Pruitt, 1968), integrative strategies (Putnam & Jones, 1982), and, in some cases, threats (Putnam & Jones, 1982). This research suggests that initially unplanned strategies emerge or that certain strategies are not enacted because the target's response renders them inappropriate.

In light of the preceding comments, the reader well may have concluded: (1) A method that relies upon self-reports of strategy usage provides *no valid* insights into persuasive interactions, and (2) such a method makes *no unique* contribution to our understanding of interpersonal influence. We hasten to add that these two conclusions seem to us to be as wrongheaded as assuming that the self-report approach provides an all-encompassing portrait of compliance-gaining interactions. Instead, we advocate a more moderate position.

It should be remembered that methods requiring respondents to select or to compose compliance-gaining strategies produce data that are equivalent to behavioral intentions. Indeed, research indicates that message selection is predictable from two variables correlated with intentions in other behavioral domains: attitude toward the use of a particular strategy, and subjective norms about strategy use (Chmielewski, 1982; Roloff, 1981). Consequently, self-reports should be highly correlated with the intentional portions of an interaction.

Since prior research has assessed strategy selection or message composition prior to the interaction, it can be arued that the intentions tapped are most reflective of communication early rather than later in the interaction. After interaction begins, new factors may emerge that cause alteration in the initial intentions, and may even prompt new ones. Consequently, the list of strategies may be reduced or expanded depending upon the success of initially employed strategies or the strategies that were selected by the other person.

Moreover, message selection and composition may embrace a greater portion of some interactions than others. Jones and Gerard (1967) propose a taxonomy of four differing interactions that provides insight into how much behavior in a given interaction is related to behavioral intentions.

The first type of interaction, *pseudocontingency,* occurs when "each individual's responses are...largely determined by his preestablished plan, but semblance of interaction is maintained in that responses are alternated and the timing of the alternation requires that each read certain signs emitted by the other" (pp. 506-507). This type of interaction is similar to what we previously called sequenced monologues, since the content of the partner's communication is largely ignored. To some extent, prior research on compliance gaining fits this prototype well, for the plans selected are carried out rather rigidly.

The second type, *asymmetrical contingency,* involves one person responding to the other's communication while the other enacts a plan. Such an interaction may result from a "surprise attack": One party wants something and has a plan to achieve it while the other has no advanced warning. Prior research on compliance gaining adequately describes some of the behavior, but it fails to describe the responses of the other. Even research concerned with resistance to compliance-gaining strategies has ignored the responses of the target to the compliance seeker's enacted strategies.

The third type, *reactive contingency,* is characterized by the initial absence or subsequent abandonment of plans, thus resulting in total mutual adaptation. Previous compliance-gaining research has little to say about this type of interaction. The strategies emerge from cues presented during the interaction rather than from entry plans of action.

The final type, *mutual contingency,* consists of a situation in which communication is jointly determined by preliminary plans of action and ongoing reactions to the partner's behavior. As it has typically been conducted, compliance-gaining research adequately describes at least some of the plans, but it misses the emergent behavior. Since under some conditions strategy selection and composition are related to interaction behaviors, future research needs to determine when and how much they are related.

Self-report methods that focus on strategy selection and composition may also provide unique insights into interaction. Typically, research centered on interaction uses coders to classify interaction behaviors into a priori categories and the behaviors are then analyzed to identify pattern and sequence. This approach provides little insight into the goals sought by the interactants or the strategies they *thought* they employed to achieve these goals. Indeed, the actual patterns and sequences of behaviors may seem foreign to the interactants, who may perceive their own behavior as patterned in a totally different way.

Finally, research on strategy selection and composition can provide useful information about the cognitive representation of the behaviors enacted when seeking compliance. As mentioned earlier, some writers have argued that persuasive strategies may be used with such regularity that they become scripted (e.g., Miller, 1982; Roloff, 1980; Schank & Abelson, 1977). This possibility implies that many communicators form expectations about the behavioral sequences they enact to gain compliance from certain others about specific topics. Recently, Rule, Bisanz, and Kohn (1985) presented self-report data that, on a preliminary basis, suggest such cognitive structures exist. If the existence of these persuasion schema is supported in future research, they may eventually reveal how information within the interaction is organized, processed, and retained. Furthermore, these cognitive structures could be influential even if analysis of the interaction behavior provides little evidence of their occurrence. Thus research on strategy selection and composition may reveal a great deal about what persuasive communicators want to do or what they think will happen. By comparing their expectation with what happened in the interaction, the fit between cognition and subsequent behavior can be determined.

Obviously, previous investigational methods can provide useful information about some questions but not about others. On the other hand, an exclusive focus on actual interaction is equally restrictive. As long as researchers are aware of the limitations of a method and that method satisfies the demands of the question, various approaches, including joint use of self-reports and actual interaction, are appropriate for studying compliance-gaining strategies. No matter what the method, the acid test of the eventual utility of strategy research lies in the extent to which it eventuates in a coherent, scientifically robust theory, or theories, of social influence, both in noninterpersonal and interpersonal settings. The final major section of this chapter examines some theoretical problems and promises of strategy research.

TOWARD THEORETICAL EXTENSION:
PRESENT LIMITATIONS AND
PROMISING DIRECTIONS

Although prior research on compliance-gaining message strategies has yielded reliable findings concerning situational and individual effects on strategy selection and usage, reviewers and critics have correctly noted that, in terms of theory, the area has been allowed to lie fallow (Clark, 1979; Cody & McLaughlin, 1985; Seibold et al., 1985; Tracy, Craig, Smith, & Spisak, 1984; Wheeless et al., 1983). Rarely has theory been used to guide the choice of factors that may affect strategy selection and to derive predictions about the strategies selected, nor have findings been interpreted within accepted theoretical perspectives. When coupled with the earlier discussed diversity and limitations of methods used to investigate message choices, the potpourri of individual and situational variables studied, and the above-noted immoderate concern with taxonomic classification of compliance-gaining strategies, it is not surprising that more than 50 prior studies have less advanced the area than repeated each other.

The roots of these problems rest at least partly in the original work of Marwell and Schmitt (1967a, 1967b), as well as the way in which MBRS (1977) approached and extended it. Viewed historically, social psychologists Marwell and Schmitt sought to move beyond the hundreds of theoretical and empirical studies offering explanations of why people are persuaded or comply (see Miller et al.'s 1984 survey of these positions) and to break new ground by describing *behavioral techniques* people use to gain others' compliance. Neither their goals nor their approach were the best *theoretical* bets for communication researchers, since Marwell and Schmitt's concern was "mapping any individual's behavioral repertoire" (1967a, p. 322) and their focus was on "variables which differentiate among individuals with regard to compliance-gaining techniques they use" (pp. 318-319). They were only incidentally interested in persons' preferences for *communication*-related strategies and techniques; indeed, they listed many techniques that either do not necessitate communication for their enactment (e.g., *murder, fines, confinement,* proper *dress*) or, when communication is likely, mask how the tactic would be implemented in discourse (e.g., *liking*) or obscure perhaps significant variations in its enactment (e.g., *aversive stimulation*). And since Marwell and Schmitt believed that "the number of more or less discrete techniques at [actors'] disposal is enormous" (1967a, p. 322), their approach was very *reductionistic*: They were indifferent to interactional complexities such as actors' multiple goals in interactions, bases for selection of one tactic over others related to the same strategy, variations in influence settings and in the relationships between actors and targets, and differences in the compliance outcomes sought. Finally, although critics may too broadly charge that their work was atheoretical because Marwell and Schmitt heuristically derived their conceptual strategy taxonomy (1967a) and the empirically grounded 16 compliance-gaining techniques (1967b) from a variety of social influence perspectives, it certainly is true that there is *little theoretical coherence and integration* within their work, and neither the strategies (1967a) nor the techniques (1967b) are *theoretically exhaustive or exclusive.*

Several of these problems were continued and compounded in the MBRS study. We relied heavily on the taxonomy of Marwell and Schmitt in our research program aimed at (1) identifying and grouping communication "control strategies available to potential persuaders," (2) examining the effects of situational differences on choice of control strategies, and (3) linking "individual differences of potential persuaders" to their choice of messages (1977, p. 38). Though we recognized and sought to remedy a number of limitations in the work of Marwell and Schmitt (especially sample, data-analytic, and situational stimuli problems), our failure to deal explicitly with theoretical weaknesses in the Marwell and Schmitt scheme and to ground our research questions on firm theoretical footings, our own reductionistic "major goal" of developing "a smaller, more abstract typology of compliance-gaining strategies which could...replace the rather cumbersome set of sixteen strategies developed by Marwell and Schmitt" (1977, p. 48), and our reliance on checklist and content analytic methods (that precluded learning whether the compliance-gaining messages actually could secure compliant *outcomes*) probably all contributed to the present theoretical void in strategy research.

Absent strong a priori theory and because of methodological expedience, typical compliance-gaining strategy studies evidence an *implicit theory* of message selection that Seibold et al. (1985) term the "Strategic Choice Model," a model grounded in the assumptions of conscious volition and mindfulness underscored earlier in our discussion of definitional and conceptual problems. Such a concern with conscious awareness veils the interactional, adaptive, and partially nonreflective character of communicative influence by emphasizing rational, purposive, self-aware, and competent communicators. There is considerable evidence that interactants often have multiple goals and intentions that they simultaneously pursue, only some of which are explicitly directed toward interpersonal influence (Winograd, 1977); that the relative importance of these goals affects actors' strategic choices in influence situations (Clark, 1979; McLaughlin, Cody, & O'Hair, 1983); that persons may not be consciously aware of all the goal-oriented objectives embedded in their communication routines (Brown & Levinson, 1978; Langer, Blank, & Chanowitz, 1978); that agents are differentially competent at recognizing and adapting to requirements of various influence situations (Applegate & Delia, 1980); that communicative influence often is the manifestation of tacitly accepted conventions rather than instrumental goal attainment (Duncan, 1981; Jacobs & Jackson, 1983; Lewis, 1969); and that even apparently "rational" message strategies may be less the result of introspection and conscious calculation than of actors' cognitive schemes for monitoring how events unfold (Cody & McLaughlin, 1985; Goody, 1978).

Researchers increasingly are recognizing the theoretical gap in compliance-gaining strategy investigations; in their own studies, they are acknowledging the interactional, multifunctional, adaptive character of communicative influence. Progress has been particularly evident on two fronts. First, some researchers have utilized the compliance-gaining perspective to describe particular kinds of discourse. Tracy et al. (1984), for example, demonstrated the value of the compliance-gaining approach in describing the discourse of requests and, based on their attempts to deal with the "face wants" of interactants, urged that future research be "redirected fruitfully toward a study of ways in which speakers design their messages to seek, balance, and resolve conflicts among multiple goals" (p. 535). Second, researchers are explicitly couching their studies of compliance-gaining messages in theoretical terms. Several have developed their own perspectives, including inductive (Hunter & Boster, 1978, 1979, 1981) and deductive (Clark, 1979, 1984; Schenk-Hamlin et al., 1982; Smith, 1984) frameworks for interpreting empirical findings concerning message choices, plus there have been broader attempts at theory building, such as the Wheeless et al. synthesis of "relevant *power* literature into a conceptual framework" (1983, p. 188) for better understanding the nature, bases, and types of compliance-gaining strategies. Others have treated compliance-gaining message issues by recourse to established perspectives such as constructivism (O'Keefe & Delia, 1982), Brown and Levinson's (1978) theory of politeness (Baxter, 1984), and subjective utility predictions (Sillars, 1980).

Though each and all of these advances should fill the theoretical void in previous strategy research, future work must sooner or later address a larger theoretical issue facing compliance-gaining strategy research in particular and the study of interpersonal influence in general: whether priorities are better given to what Tedeschi and Bonoma (1972) term *divergent* or to *convergent* lines of theorizing. On one hand, most prior conceptual and empirical work on both communicative and interpersonal influence has *diverged* into particularistic studies of influence tactics (see the review by Seibold et al., 1985) and diverse minitheories of altercasting (Weinstein & Deutschberger, 1963), disclosure (Chelune, 1979), ingratiation (Jones, 1964; Jones & Wortman, 1973), and impression management (Goffman, 1969; Schlenker, 1980) among others. Not surprisingly, our knowledge of communicative influence is grounded in interesting but unintegrated studies of children's strategic communication (O'Keefe & Benoit, 1982) and the influence tactics of parents, teachers, and other authority figures (Applegate, 1980a, 1980b; Smith, 1983); gender and influence tactics (Eagly, 1983; Kramerae, 1981); communicative strategies in game contexts (Seibold & Steinfatt, 1979) and in therapy (Dorn, 1984; Haley, 1977) among many, many areas of studying symbolic influence.

On the other hand, when systematic studies of social processes occasionally have *converged* to suggest grand theories of power and influence (Dahl, 1957; French, 1956; Homans, 1961; March, 1955; Parsons, 1963; Weber, 1947), they usually have been too general to yield precise predictions concerning communicative influence. The most difficult part of convergent theory building, for those committed to this path, will be maintaining both explanatory generality and specificity concerning message choices while still surmounting what Grimshaw (1980) summarily calls "intractabilities" in understanding communication and interpersonal influence: "While 'everybody' may 'do it,' different people do it in quite different ways and with quite different effectiveness, in quite different situations with quite different constraints and available resources" (p. 204). Theoretical perspectives that surmount these intractabilities, yet still yield explanatory generality and predictive specificity concerning compliance-gaining messages, must minimally and simultaneously (1) articulate the interaction of motivation and cognition in communicators' perceptions of, and responses to, salient features of influence encounters; (2) treat relevant instrumental, relational, and identity goals and the ways in which actors reconcile them in designing their messages; (3) deal with individual differences among influencers and in characteristics of their targets; (4) adequately describe the breadth and variation in compliance-gaining messages utilized; (5) reliably link message choices to influence outcomes in ways that yield knowledge of the relative efficacy of particular compliance-gaining strategies; and (6) locate communicative influence in streams of interaction, including attention to sequential strategies and reciprocal influence. Several of these six requirements have been examined in earlier portions of this chapter.

Our emphasis on the need for deeper theoretical spadework is not intended to suggest disillusionment with previous compliance-gaining strategy research. Prior studies have significantly increased our knowledge of the message choices that specifiable types of persons say they would make in specifiable situations. Notwithstanding, we believe that enhanced theoretical development in the area—especially fresh and coherent conceptualizations, and application of existing powerful theoretical perspectives to the dynamics of communicative influence—will vouchsafe the value of research on compliance-gaining message choices and, eventually, ensure its contribution to our understanding of symbolic influence in interpersonal settings.

REFERENCES

Applegate, J. L. (1980a). Adaptive communication in educational contexts: A study of teachers' communicative strategies. *Communication Education, 29,* 158-170.

Applegate, J. L. (1980b). Person and position-centered teacher communication in a daycare center. In N. K. Denzin (Ed.), *Studies in symbolic interaction* (Vol. 3, pp. 59-96). Greenwich, CT: JAI Press.

Applegate, J. L., & Delia, J. G., (1980). Person-centered speech, psychological development, and the contexts of language usage. In R. St. Clair & H. Giles (Eds.), *The social and psychological contexts of language* (pp. 245-282). Hillsdale, NJ: Lawrence Erlbaum.

Baxter, L. A. (1984). An investigation of compliance-gaining as politeness. *Human Communication Research, 10,* 427-456.

Berger, C. R. (1985). Social power and interpersonal communication. In M. L. Knapp & G. R. Miller (Eds.), *Handbook of interpersonal communication* (pp. 439-499). Newbury Park, CA: Sage.

Berger, C. R., & Douglas, W. (1982). Thought and talk: "Excuse me, but have I been talking to myself?" In F.E.X. Dance (Ed.), *Human communication theory* (pp. 42-60). New York: Harper & Row.

Boster, F. J. (1985). *The impact of self interest, other interest, and relevant personality traits on indicators of argumentativeness.* Unpublished manuscript, Department of Communication, Arizona State University, Tempe.

Boster, F. J., & Lofthouse, L. J. (1985). *Not just another investigation into compliance-gaining.* Unpublished manuscript, Department of Communication, Arizona State University, Tempe.

Boster, F. J., & Stiff, J. B. (1984). Compliance-gaining message selection behavior. *Human Communication Research, 10,* 539-556.

Boster, F. J., Stiff, J. B., & Reynolds, R. A. (1985). Do persons respond differently to inductively-derived lists of compliance-gaining message strategies? A reply to Wiseman and Schenck-Hamlin. *Western Journal of Speech Communication, 49,* 177-187.

Brown, P., & Levinson, S. (1978). Universals in language usage: Politeness phenomena. In E. N. Goody (Ed.), *Questions and politeness: Strategies in social interaction* (pp. 56-289). New York: Cambridge University Press.

Burgoon, M., Dillard, J. P., Doran, N. E., & Miller, M. D. (1982). Cultural and situational influences on the process of persuasive strategy selection. *International Journal of Intercultural Relations, 6,* 85-100.

Chelune, G. J. (Ed.). (1979). *Self-disclosure.* San Francisco: Jossey-Bass.

Chmielewski, T. (1982). A test of a model for predicting strategy choice. *Central States Speech Journal, 33,* 505-518.

Cialdini, R. B., Cacioppo, J. T., Bassett, R., & Miller, J. A. (1978). Low-ball procedure for producing compliance: Commitment then cost. *Journal of Personality and Social Psychology, 36,* 463-476.

Clark, R. A. (1979). The impact of self-interest and desired liking on selection of persuasive strategies. *Communication Monographs, 46,* 257-273.

Clark, R. A. (1984). *Persuasive messages.* New York: Harper & Row.

Cody, M. J., & McLaughlin, M. L. (1985). The situation as a construct in communication research. In M. L. Knapp & G. R. Miller (Eds.), *Handbook of interpersonal communication* (pp. 263-312). Newbury Park, CA: Sage.

Cody, M. J., McLaughlin, M. L., & Jordan, W. (1980). A multidimensional scaling of three sets of compliance-gaining strategies. *Communication Quarterly, 28,* 34-46.

Dahl, R. A. (1957). The concept of power. *Behavorial Science, 2,* 201-218.

Davis, D., & Wicklund, R. A. (1972). An objective self-awareness analysis of communication sets. In S. Duval & R. Wicklund (Eds.), *A theory of objective self-awareness* (pp. 180-184). Orlando, FL: Academic Press.

Dillard, J. P., & Burgoon, M. (1985). Situational influences on the selection of compliance-gaining messages: Two tests of the predicted utility of the Cody-McLaughlin typology. *Communication Monographs, 52,* 289-304.

Dillard, J. P., Hunter, J. E., & Burgoon, M. (1984). Sequential-request persuasive strategies: Meta-analysis of foot-in-the-door and door-in-the-face. *Human Communication Research, 10,* 461-488.

Dillard, J. P., Hunter, J. E., Burgoon, M., Boster, F. J., & Stiff, J. B. (1985). *An empirical test of the empathy model of compliance-gaining message selection.* Paper presented at the annual meeting of the International Communication Association, Honolulu, HI.

Dorn, F. J. (1984). *Counseling as applied social psychology: An introduction to the social influence model.* Springfield, IL: Charles C Thomas.

Duncan, J., Jr. (1981). Conversational strategies. In T. A. Sebeok & R. Rosenthal (Eds.), *The Clever Hans phenomenon: Communication with horses, whales, apes, and people* (pp. 144-151). New York: New York Academy of Sciences.

Eagly, A. H. (1983). Gender and social influence. *American Psychologist, 38,* 971-981.

Esser, J. K., & Komorita, S. S. (1975). Reciprocity and concession making in bargaining. *Journal of Personality and Social Psychology, 31,* 864-872.

Etzioni, A. (1961). *A comparative analysis of complex organizations.* New York: Free Press.

Falbo, T. (1977). Multidimensional scaling of power strategies. *Journal of Personality and Social Psychology, 35,* 537-547.

French, J.R.P., Jr. (1956). A formal theory of social power. *Psychological Review, 63,* 181-194.

French, J.R.P., Jr., & Raven, B. (1960). The basis of social power. In D. Cartwright & A. Zander (Eds.), *Group dynamics* (2nd ed., pp. 607-623). Evanston, IL: Row, Peterson.

Goffman, E. (1969). *Strategic interaction.* Philadelphia: University of Pennsylvania Press.

Goody, E. N. (1978). Introduction. In E. N. Goody (Ed.), *Questions and politeness: Strategies in social interaction* (pp. 1-16). New York: Cambridge University Press.

Grimshaw, A. D. (1980). Selection and labeling of instrumentalities of verbal manipulation. *Discourse Processes, 3,* 203-229.

Haley, J. (1977). *Problem-solving therapy: New strategies for effective family therapy.* San Francisco: Jossey-Bass.

Hinde, R. A. (1979). *Toward understanding relationships.* Orlando, FL: Academic Press.

Homans, G. C. (1961). *Social behavior: Its elementary forms:* New York: Harcourt Brace Jovanovich.

Hunter, J. E., & Boster, F. J. (1978). *An empathy model of compliance-gaining message selection.* Paper presented at the annual meeting of the Speech Communication Association, Minneapolis, MN.

Hunter, J. E., & Boster, F. J. (1979). *Situational differences in the selection of compliance-gaining messages.* Paper presented at the annual meeting of the Speech Communication Association, San Antonio, TX.

Hunter, J. E., & Boster, F. J. (1981). *Compliance-gaining message experiments: Some evidence for an empathy model.* Unpublished manuscript, Department of Communication, Arizona State University.

Hunter, J. E., & Gerbing, D. W. (1982). Unidimensional measurement, second order factor analysis and causal models. In B. M. Straw & L. L. Cummings (Eds.), *Research in organizational behavior* (Vol. 4, pp. 267-320). Greenwich, CT: JAI Press.

Infante, D. A., Trebing, J. D., Shepherd, P. E., & Seeds, D. E. (1984). The relationship of argumentativeness to verbal aggression. *Southern Speech Communication Journal, 50,* 67-77.

Jackson, S., & Backus, D. (1982). Are compliance-gaining strategies dependent on situational variables? *Central States Speech Journal, 33,* 469-479.

Jacobs, S., & Jackson, S. (1983). Strategy and structure in conversational influence attempts. *Communication Monographs, 50,* 285-304.

Jones, E. E. (1964). *Ingratiation: A social psychological analysis.* New York: Meredith.

Jones, E. E., & Gerard, H. B. (1967). *Foundations of social psychology.* New York: John Wiley.

Jones, E. E., & Wortman, C. (1973). *Ingratiation: An attributional approach.* Morristown, NJ: General Learning Press.

Kelman, H. C. (1961). Processes of opinion change. *Public Opinion Quarterly, 25,* 57-78.

Kramarae, C. (1981). *Women and men speaking.* Rowley, MA: Newbury House.

Langer, E. J. (1978). Rethinking the role of thought in social interaction. In H. Harvey, W. Ickes, & R. Kidd (Eds.), *New directions in attribution research* (Vol. 2, pp. 35-58). Hillsdale, NJ: Lawrence Erlbaum.

Langer, E. J., Blank, A., & Chanowitz, B. (1978). The mindlessness of ostensibly thoughtful action: The role of "placebic" information in interpersonal interaction. *Journal of Personality and Social Psychology, 36,* 635-642.

Lewis, D. K. (1969). *Convention: A philosophical study.* Cambridge, MA: Harvard University Press.

Lustig, M. W., & King, S. W. (1980). The effect of communication apprehension and situation on communication strategy choices. *Human Communication Research, 7,* 74-82.

March, J. G. (1955). An introduction to the theory and measurement of influence. *American Political Science Review, 49,* 431-451.

Marlowe, E. D., Gergen, K. J., & Doob, A. N. (1966). Opponent's personality, expectation of social interaction, and interpersonal bargaining. *Journal of Personality and Social Psychology, 3,* 206-213.

Marwell, G., & Schmitt, D. R. (1967a). Compliance-gaining behavior: A synthesis and model. *Sociological Quarterly, 8,* 317-328.

Marwell, G., & Schmitt, D. R. (1967b). Dimensions of compliance-gaining behavior: An empirical analysis. *Sociometry, 30,* 350-364.

McLaughlin, M. L., Cody, M. L., & O'Hair, H. D. (1983). The management of failure events: Some contextual determinants of accounting behavior. *Human Communication Research, 9,* 208-224.

Miller, G., Boster, F., Roloff, M., & Seibold, D. (1977). Compliance-gaining message strategies: A typology and some findings concerning effects of situational differences. *Communication Monographs, 44,* 37-51.

Miller, G. R. (1978). The current status of theory and research in interpersonal communication. *Human Communication Research, 54,* 164-178.

Miller, G. R. (1982). *Effects of persuasive message strategy selection on family members' attitudes toward the family.* Unpublished manuscript, Department of Communication, Michigan State University, East Lansing.

Miller, G. R. (1983). On various ways of skinning symbolic cats: Recent research on persuasive message strategies. *Journal of Language and Social Psychology, 2,* 123-140.

Miller, G. R., & Burgoon, M. (1978). Persuasion research: Review and commentary. In B. Ruben (Ed.), *Communication yearbook 2* (pp. 29-47). New Brunswick, NJ: Transaction Books.

Miller, G. R., Burgoon, M., & Burgoon, J. K. (1984). The functions of human communication in changing attitudes and gaining compliance. In C. C. Arnold & J. W. Bowers (Eds.), *Handbook of rhetorical and communication theory* (pp. 400-474). Boston: Allyn & Bacon.

Miller, G. R., & Parks, M. R. (1982). Communication in dissolving relationships. In S. Duck (Ed.), *Personal relationships 4: Dissolving personal relationships* (pp. 127-154). Orlando, FL: Academic Press.

O'Keefe, B. J., & Benoit, P. J. (1982). Children's arguments. In R. Cox & C. Willard (Eds.), *Advances in argumentation theory* (pp. 154-183). Carbondale: Southern Illinois University Press.

O'Keefe, B. J., & Delia, J. G. (1982). Impression formation and message production. In M. E. Roloff & C. R. Berger (Eds.), *Social cognition and communication* (pp. 33-72). Newbury Park, CA: Sage.

Parsons, T. (1963). On the concept of influence. *Public Opinion Quarterly, 27,* 35-62.

Pruitt, D. G. (1968). Reciprocity and credit building in dyads. *Journal of Personality and Social Psychology, 8,* 143-147.

Putnam, L. L., & Jones, T. S. (1982). Reciprocity in negotiations: An analysis of bargaining interaction. *Communication Monographs, 49,* 171-191.

Roloff, M. E. (1980). Self-awareness and the persuasion process: Do we really *know* what we are doing? In M. Roloff & G. Miller (Eds.), *Persuasion: New directions in theory and research* (pp. 29-66). Newbury Park, CA: Sage.

Roloff, M. E. (1981). *Individual differences in communication: Where are they?* Paper presented at the annual convention of the International Communication Association, Minneapolis, MN.

Roloff, M. E., & Barnicott, E. F., Jr. (1978). The situational use of pro- and anti-social compliance-gaining strategies by high and low Machiavellians. In B. D. Ruben (Ed.), *Communication yearbook 2* (pp. 193-205). New Brunswick, NJ: Transaction Books.

Roloff, M. E., & Barnicott, E. F., Jr. (1979). The influence of dogmatism on the situational use of pro- and anti-social compliance-gaining strategies. *Southern Speech Communication Journal, 45,* 37-54.

Rule, B. G., Bisanz, G. L., & Kohn, M. (1985). Anatomy of a persuasion schema: Targets, goals, and strategies. *Journal of Personality and Social Psychology, 48,* 1127-1140.

Schank, R. C., & Abelson, R. P. (1977). *Scripts, plans, goals and understanding.* Hillsdale, NJ: Lawrence Erlbaum.

Schenck-Hamlin, W. J., Wiseman, R. L., & Georgacarakos, G. N. (1982). A model of properties of compliance-gaining strategies. *Communication Quarterly, 30,* 92-100.

Schlenker, B. R. (1980). *Impression management: The self-concept, social identity, and interpersonal relations.* Belmont, CA: Wadsworth.

Seibold, D. R., Cantrill, J. G., & Meyers, R. A. (1985). Communication and interpersonal influence. In M. L. Knapp & G. R. Miller (Eds.), *Handbook of interpersonal communication* (pp. 551-611). Newbury Park, CA: Sage.

Seibold, D. R., & Steinfatt, T. M. (1979). The creative alternative game: Exploring interpersonal influence processes. *Simulation & Games, 10,* 429-457.

Sillars, A. (1980). The stranger and the spouse as target persons for compliance-gaining strategies: A subjective utility model. *Human Communication Research, 6,* 265-279.

Smith, M. J. (1984). Contingency rules theory, context, and compliance behaviors. *Human Communication Research, 4,* 489-512.

Smith, T. E. (1983). Parental influence: A review of the evidence of influence and a theoretical model of the parental influence process. *Research in Sociology of Education and Socialization, 4,* 13-45.

Spector, B. I. (1977). Negotiation as a psychological process. *Journal of Conflict Resolution, 21,* 607-618.

Tesser, A. (1978). Self-generated attitude change. In L. Berkowitz (Ed.), *Advances in experimental social psychology* (Vol. 11, pp. 290-338). Orlando, FL: Academic Press.

Tedeschi, J. T., & Bonoma, T. V. (1972). Power and influence: An introduction. In J. T. Tedeschi (Ed.), *The social influence processes* (pp. 1-49). Chicago: Aldine.

Tracy, K., Craig, R. T., Smith, M., & Spisak, F. (1984). The discourse of requests: Assessment of a compliance-gaining approach. *Human Communication Research, 10,* 513-538.

Weber, M. (1947). *The theory of social and economic organization.* New York: Oxford University Press.

Weinstein, E. A., & Deutschberger, P. (1963). Some dimensions of altercasting. *Sociometry, 26,* 454-466.

Wheeless, L. R., Barraclough, R., & Stewart, R. (1983). Compliance-gaining and power in persuasion. In R. Bostrom (Ed.), *Communication yearbook 7* (pp. 105-145). Newbury Park, CA: Sage.

Williams, D. L., & Boster, F. J. (1981). *The effect of beneficial situational characteristics, negativism, and dogmatism on compliance-gaining message selection.* Paper presented at the annual convention of the International Communication Association, Minneapolis, MN.

Winograd, T. (1977). A framework for understanding discourse. In M. A. Just & P. A. Carpenter (Eds.), *Cognitive processes in comprehension* (pp. 63-88). Hillsdale, NJ: Lawrence Erlbaum.

Wiseman, R. L., & Schenck-Hamlin, W. (1981). A multidimensional scaling validation of an inductively-derived set of compliance-gaining strategies. *Communication Monographs, 48,* 251-270.

Chapter 6

RELATIONAL DIMENSIONS OF INTERPERSONAL DYNAMICS

Frank E. Millar and L. Edna Rogers

FOR SEVERAL YEARS we have been concerned with how to conceive of interpersonal dynamics in ways that take "social interaction seriously" (Blumer, 1969: p. 53)—where *seriously* means that the organizing communication processes per se are considered as determinant of interactional consequences as are personal attributes and sociostructural prescriptions. Like others (Hahlweg & Jacobson, 1984; Helmersen, 1983; Kantor & Lehr, 1975; Lennard & Bernstein, 1969; Mishler & Waxler, 1968; Penman, 1980), we believe that a central quest in current social science is the "search for a scientific language for describing" interpersonal relationships (Gottman, 1982a, p. 943). We (Giddens, 1983; Hinde, 1979; Jackson, 1965; McCall & Simmons, 1966; Simmel, 1950; Weick, 1979) also agree that "there is little reason to expect that new insights into the structure of social behavior" will result from the exclusive study of interpersonal perceptions and cognitions; cognitive and behavioral data are undoubtedly related, "but researching their interdependencies requires separate measurements of social behavior and social perceptions" (Stiles, 1980, p. 373). Further, if an individual's meanings are necessarily retrospective (Schutz, 1967; Weick, 1979), then intrapersonal cognitions and perceptions are more accurately thought of as "post hoc commentaries on the ongoing events" (Scheflen, 1974, p. 194) of interpersonal dynamics and not as causes of behavior in face-to-face situations. Regardless of whether cognitions are thought of as causes or as effects, they are known about and knowable only through behavioral interactions with others.

Interaction has been one of the most talked about and least studied phenomena in the social sciences. The position we take, a relational communication approach, focuses directly on interaction. We assume that interpersonal processes are formative in their own right (Blumer, 1969), that people relate through talk (Duncan, 1967, 1968), that the structuring of relationships is immanent in copresent message performances (Bateson, 1972; Ellis, 1982).

Simply, a relational approach assumes that interpersonal relationships are emergent patterns; they are redundant, interlocked cycles of messages, continually negotiated and co-defined rather than unilaterally caused by personal qualities and/or social role prescriptions.

Given the above thoughts and assumptions, this chapter is a brief report of our role in the quest to develop a dynamic language of interpersonal relationships. Our empirical findings are meager compared with our discoveries about the paradoxical nature of human interactions (Bochner, 1984; Foss, 1980; Millar, Rogers, & Bavelas, 1984; Sprey, 1971). As we have investigated communicative patterns, we have become painfully aware of the limitations of our efforts and humbled by the enormity of the task.

We began our quest by grappling with the following question: What are basic dimensions describing all social relationships? This chapter outlines our attempt to answer that question. First, three dimensions of control, trust, and intimacy are delineated from a relational point of view; second, selected results from our studies of the control dimension in husband-wife interactions are summarized.

THREE DIMENSIONS OF
INTERPERSONAL RELATIONS

Various classifications have been offered for social relationships. These include an enumeration of characteristics from sociologically based role-pairs (husband-wife, teacher-student, employer-employee, doctor-nurse) to psychologically oriented conceptual pairings (bold-timid, friendly-hostile, dominant-submissive, managerial-self-effacing, distressed-nondistressed, introverted-extroverted), and from supposedly unidimensional categories (instrumental-expressive, primary-secondary, voluntary-involuntary, fleeting-repetitious) to macro-level typologies (*Gemeinshaft-Gesellshaft,* sacred-secular, mechanical solidarity-organic solidarity). Though several insights and guides for studying interpersonal dynamics are contained within these schemes, comparatively little work has used characteristics of communication processes to classify relationships. The writings of Simmel (1950), McCall and Simmons (1966), and Kantor and Lehr (1975) have particularly influenced our thoughts on delineating basic relational dimensions immanent in patterned message performances.

Simmel pioneered the notion that interpersonal relationships reside partially in members' cognitions and partially in behavioral performances, yet are reducible to neither data type. Interpersonal relationships "develop upon the basis of reciprocal knowledge, and this knowledge upon the basis of the actual relations. Both are inextricably interwoven" (Simmel, 1950, p. 309). The simultaneous occurrence of these aspects reveals that interactions are events "where being and conceiving make their mysterious unity empirically felt" (Simmel, 1950, p. 309). The work of McCall and Simmons (1966) and Kantor and Lehr (1975) builds upon Simmel's insights into the reflexive, recursive nature of interpersonal dynamics.

Kantor and Lehr rely on a spatial metaphor in their conceptual model of the family, assuming that the family, like any interpersonal system, is "primarily an information-processing system and the information it processes is *distance regulation* in nature" (1975, p. 222; emphasis added). They emphasize that social systems are "continually informing their members what constitutes a proper or optimal distance" (1975, p. 222) between themselves or between themselves and external objects and events. They further assume that family systems are goal-oriented or purposeful[1] and propose three inclusive goals that organize the appropriate relational "distances" between members—power, affect, and meaning (Kantor & Lehr, 1975, pp. 46-52).[2]

McCall and Simmons (1966) emphasize that an individual's identity is created and sustained through repetitive interactions with others. Individuals are also assumed to be symbolic and purposeful in developing situational plans of action (1966, p. 60). The most basic object to be identified in any interaction is the person him- or herself (1966, p. 61). An individual's identity is not a personal, idiosyncratic construction, but a "social object" (1966, p. 62) constructed and maintained in interactions with particular others who become inherent parts of one's view of self (1966, p. 69). The socialness of self-identity prompts people to seek out dependable sources of role-identity support.[3] Thus McCall and Simmons assert that reward dependability is the most fundamental of their five suggested "interpersonal ties"—reward dependability, ascription, commitment, investment, and attachment (1966, pp. 170-172).[4]

Based on the above works, as well as other literature, the following picture of interpersonal relationships is offered: Interpersonal relationships are self-organizing "holons" (Koestler, 1978) that are continually structuring themselves and their members in and through distancing ties manifested in communicative performances. Three generic "distances" characterizing this structuring process are *control, trust,* and *intimacy.* Though not intended as an exhaustive list of relational dimensions, they are conceived of as basic distancing dimensions immanent in message patternings. In explicating them, we will begin with a general conceptual overview of each dimension, then offer a structural identification, discuss its temporal and functional relevance, suggest felicity criteria of phenomenological importance to the interactants, and posit possible measures for the dimension.[5] These issues are outlined in Table 6.1.

CONTROL

In an ongoing interaction, presentations of self are continually "given off" (Goffman, 1959) and simultaneously imply particular actions for other through "altercasting" (McCall & Simmons, 1966) imputations. These definitions vis-à-vis the interactants concern their "expected acts of deference and demeanor" (Denzin, 1970, p. 71) and collectively make up the patterns of constraint within the interpersonal system. Concern for the control implications of messages is frequently heard in such utterances as "You can't talk to me like that"; "She lets him boss her around too much"; "You don't have the right to tell me what to do"; "Listen to me when I talk to you"; "I'm in charge here"; and "I have a right to say what I think."

Conceptually, the control dimension represents the vertical distance between participants and refers to the process of establishing the right to define, direct, and delimit the actions of the dyad at the current moment. The temporal relevance of the control dimension is the *present*, since the right to define the system's actions varies with topic and context. In the temporal sense, the control dimension is the most basic and dynamic of the three, for the issue of definitional rights must be continually negotiated according to changing conditions.

Given the assumptions that one cannot *not* behave and that in any interaction every behavior has possible relational implications (Bateson, 1951; Watzlawick, Beavin, & Jackson, 1967), it follows that every message constrains and is constrained by all other messages. The structure of the control dimension, then, is the diachronic pattern of constraints, the shape of the relationship. Functionally, control patterns affect the "constructive efficacy" (Kantor & Lehr, 1975, p. 49) of the system's capacity to accomplish desired goals.

The felicity judgments about control patterns are encapsulated in the notions of freedom and equity. The subjective assessment of freedom is based on the "simple fact that the individual is tied by others and ties others"; it presumes that one is bound in power relations with others and concerns the "possibility of making oneself count within a given relationship" (Simmel, 1950, p. 122). But individuals not only assess whether their actions count, they also estimate whether their contributions have been respected and equitably rewarded. Equity, stemming from Homan's (1961) concept of "distributive justice," is necessarily a subjective comparison between ego's and alter's rewards for fulfilling the obligations of the relationship in just proportion to one's contributions.

There are at least three possible measures of the control dimension: redundancy, dominance, and power. *Redundancy* refers to the amount of alteration in the participants' patterns of constraint; or, stated another way, to the variability in their negotiation over definitional rights.[6] The more redundant the system's interactions within and across topics and contexts, the more rigid the control pattern; the more variable, the more flexible the control pattern; and when there is little stochastic regularity, the control pattern is said to be chaotic.

Dominance is indexed by complementary transacts in which the assertion of definitions by one person is accepted by the other (e.g., A says "Let's go to a movie tonight" and B responds "Okay"). Dominance, then, is a momentary outcome within the ongoing pattern of constraints. The frequency with which participants have been dominant in a given conversation can be compared by dividing ego's score by alter's. The closer the dominance ratio is to one, the more equivalency in the negotiation of definitional rights; conversely, the greater the divergence from one in either direction, the more one person is said to dominate the dyad's interactions.

A third index of the control dimension, *power,* is a perceptual measure[7] referring to the potential to influence or constrain another's behaviors (French & Raven, 1959; Olson & Cromwell, 1975; Rogers-Millar & Millar, 1979; Rollins & Bahr, 1976). This potential is based in alter's perceptions of ego's resources (e.g., money, education, title, territorial ownership) and/or qualities (e.g., intelligence, attractiveness, expertise, strength) that increase alter's expectations of deferring or submitting to ego's assertions. A power ratio, created by dividing ego's estimated potential by alter's, indicates the degree of interdependence in the expectations about who *is likely to* and who *should* be dominant in the dyad's interactions.

TRUST

Relational dynamics are continually in flux; their "temporal form" (Gottman, 1982a) is evolving, emergent. Participants do not simply act out their assigned parts, but spontaneously write, direct, produce, and act in their own jointly created historical script. There is an inherent fragility to relational

TABLE 6.1
Summary of Relational Dimensions

	Control	*Trust*	*Intimacy*
Spatial Distance	height	width	depth
Temporal Relevance	present	future	past
Structure	pattern of constraints	pattern of predictions	pattern of sentiments
Function	regulation of structuring definitions and constructive efficacy	regulation of commitments and uncertainty	regulation of exclusive identities and enmeshment
Felicity Judgments	freedom and equity	sincerity and empirical veracity	affection and understanding
Possible Measures	redundancy dominance power	vulnerability reward dependability confidence	transferability attachment knowledge

dramas, and the price of casting is paid with uncertainty and vulnerability. The trust dimension concerns the inherent uncertainty of purposeful systems and metaphorically represents the horizontal distance between persons. By definition system members are interdependent; their actions mutually influence one another such that ego's outcomes are contingent upon alter's actions. Participants, therefore, are concerned with the predictability of the other's behavior since there is no certainty that the other will behave properly or competently. The best to be hoped for is to establish limitations on alter's choices (e.g., commitments, norms, rules, promises, threats, codiciles, contracts, argeements) and to make probability estimates that alter will behave congruently with those restraints. As Simmel (1950) asserts, "Confidence...is one of the most important synthetic forces within society" (p. 318). Every acknowledged limitation on choice also implies an obligation to live up to the "confidence" implicit in that agreement.[8]

Conceptually, then, trust involves the predictability and obligatory nature of limitations on future choices; it concerns the individuals' attempts to seek and develop dependable sources of rewards (McCall & Simmons, 1966, p. 170). Structurally, trust is identified by the pattern of predictions made by ego and alter about the other's probable actions relative to themselves. Functionally, these predictions produce a sense of certainty about future actions and outcomes that permits present decisions and commitments to be made. Our everyday concern for trust is observed in such remarks as "He's reliable"; "I can count on her"; "She can be trusted"; "You can't depend on him"; "He is a man of his word"; "Somehow, whatever she says I just don't believe"; "You could tell him anything"; and "Don't take her into your confidence for she'll use it to her advantage."

The temporal relevance of trust is the *future,* although probability estimates about alter's actions are obviously based on previous experiences and/or external factors. The proposed criteria of felicity are sincerity and empirical veracity. Sincerity refers to ego's judgment about alter's intentions relative to ego; specifically, sincerity judgments concern whether or not alter is planning to harm, injure, or exploit ego. Empirical veracity refers to ego's assessment of alter's competence in a given situation; it is an estimate of the accuracy of alter's knowledge and skills.

Three possible useful indices for describing and differentiating the degree of trust in an interpersonal system are vulnerability, reward dependability, and confidence. The *vulnerability* measure indicates the frequency, weighted by the difference between subjective cost and reward values, with which ego has accepted a vulnerable position relative to alter. A vulnerable position is one where ego's desired outcome, which is a function of alter's actions, is less rewarding to ego than the potential cost. For instance, self-disclosing to another may be rewarding, but the costs may be devastating if alter publicizes ego's disclosure. Similarly, loaning money to help a friend is rewarding, but the cost of not having the money returned may outweigh the benefit of help-ing. If neither person has been in a vulnerable position relative to other (i.e., in a trusting position) there is no basis for the development of trust even though each may believe the other is trustworthy. Dividing ego's score by alter's score yields the vulnerability ratio. The closer this ratio is to one, the more trust in the relationship; the farther away from one, the more caution, suspicion, and strategic maneuvering characterize the interpersonal system.

Another measure of relational trust is *reward dependability*. This score is based on the frequencies, weighted by the difference between subjective cost and reward values of each occurrence, with which ego has been rewarded for assuming positions of vulnerability. Again, the closer the comparative ratio is to one, the more trust in the relationship; the farther away from one, the more one person is said to be dependent upon the other and the more poten-tially exploitative the relationship.

A third index of trust is *confidence;* it assesses ego's subjective probability estimate of nonbetrayal by alter, weighted by the vulnerability score. This in-dex becomes a relationship descriptor by dividing ego's score by alter's. The closer the ratio is to one, the more mutual confidence, and the more trust in the relationship. The larger or smaller the ratio, the more unilateral the relationship, the more potential for exploitation, and the less trust.

INTIMACY

Within relational encounters "good" and "bad" feelings about ourselves and others arise. Our moods lighten, our pulse quickens, our spirits soar as we experience the joys of connectedness; conversely, our bodies feel heavy, our movements sluggish, our spirits deaden when we experience the pains of separateness. Intimacy, the third dimension proposed, concerns the sentiments associated with connectedness and separateness; it refers to the depth of our "attachments" (McCall & Simmons, 1966, p. 172). Metaphorically intimacy represents the depth vector of our "sentient experiences" (Kantor & Lehr, 1975, p. 46) with one another.

While the larger society is more concerned with ascriptions and com-mitments, "individuals are most preoccupied with their attachments" (McCall & Simmons, 1966, p. 174). This dimension is the key to differentiating inter-personal from other social relationships. "An *interpersonal* relationship must be defined as one that necessarily involves each participant as a personal entity" (McCall & Simmons, 1966, p. 169; emphasis in original; see also Miller & Steinberg, 1975). In such relationships, each person must view the other as a unique, subjective center of experience; or, in Simmel's (1950, p. 320) words, interpersonal relations are based on the "what" (individuality) of the other and not the "that" (physical and/or social existence) of the other. The "what" of the other is based on the amount and type of knowledge ego claims to know about the other's subjective self. Such knowledge is never complete; "one can never know another person *absolutely,* which would involve knowledge of every single thought and mood" (Simmel, 1950, p. 308; emphasis in original).

Intimacy is not based on the content of the interactional behaviors (Simmel, 1950)—there is no such event as an intimate behavior although some actions (e.g., touch, self-disclosure, openness, sexual contact) are assumed necessary for the development of intimacy. Rather, intimacy is based upon the degree to which each uses the other as a source of self-confirmation and the affective evaluation of the subjective self confirmed.[9]

Structurally, the intimacy dimension refers to the pattern of sentiments characterizing a relationship's history. This pattern functions to define the exclusivity or uniqueness of the relationship and the self-identities known within its boundaries. The temporal relevance of intimacy is therefore the *past,* since judgments about uniqueness are necessarily based on what has been shared. Clearly these result in expectations about the continuation of sharing uniquely with other; these expectations, in turn, result in concerns for the relationship's termination such that a "feeling tone" of endangeredness and irreplaceability characterizes intimate dyads (Simmel, 1950, p. 124). This "tone" is readily observed in such comments as "I couldn't live without him"; "No one understands me the way you do"; "Only you know the real me"; "Life is unbearable now that my wife's gone"; and "I wouldn't last a moment without you." Most love songs reify the exclusivity of such feelings and concern the joys and pains of feeling endangered and irreplaceable.

These illustrative utterances also suggest that the primary felicity criteria of the intimacy dimension are affection and understanding. Affection concerns the belief that the other likes or loves us as we are, while understanding concerns the belief that other understands or knows us from our own point of view. Of course, we do not know ourselves completely anymore than other does. Rather, who we are as unique, subjective selves develops in, is sustained by, and is changed through interacting with particular others. In that sense, an intimate relationship is characterized by the implicit promise to create aspects of self previously unknown. That promise may or may not be fulfilled, and may lead either to an enriching togetherness or a stagnating, debilitating sense of "triviality" (Simmel, 1950, p. 125).[10] The seeds of triviality are sown in intimacy and develop from a lack of optimal distancing between self and other; or, in Sprey's (1971) words, "Intimacy, to be viable, . . . requires an awareness and acceptance of the stranger in the other" (p. 724).

The following measures are possible indices of the degree of intimacy characterizing any given interpersonal relationship. *Transferability* refers to the number of others in ego's environment who can confirm ego's desired self. The larger the number, the more transferable the relation, the less dependent ego is on a particular alter, and the less confirmatory the relationship for ego. Conversely, the smaller the number of particular alters, the more non-transferable, the more irreplacable, endangered, and intense the relationship is for ego. The transferability ratio, then, compares ego's and alter's transferability scores weighted by ego's importance of the self experienced with alter. The greater the inequality of this ratio, the more ego "needs" alter more than alter "needs" ego, the more potentially exploitative the relationship, and the less intimate.

The measure of *attachment* refers to ego's evaluation of alter's ego. The more strongly ego evaluates the self that she or he perceives alter confirming, weighted by ego's importance of the self experienced with alter, the more attached ego is to alter. When the evaluation is positive, we say we like or love the other; when negative, we say we dislike or hate the other. Either a positive or negative evaluation, when used to confirm ego's identity, portends a degree of attachment. The attachment ratio indicates the degree of equality in the affections characterizing the interpersonal system.

Finally, the *knowledge* index compares the accuracy of alter's ego with ego's alter's ego—what Laing, Phillipson, and Lee (1966) call realization or failure to realize understanding or misunderstanding. The more frequently each understands and realizes that he or she has been understood by other, the more knowledge characterizing the relationship. Put another way, the more frequently two persons have attained "communication-states" (Millar, 1979) times the number of topics on which these have occurred, the more knowledge characterizing the relationship, the more each is said to "know" the other as a unique person, and the more intimate the relationship. Again, comparing the frequency times the number of topics which ego has realized she or he has been understood by alter plus the frequency times the number of topics that ego has understood alter yields the knowledge ratio. The closer this ratio is to one, the more the mutual knowledge, the more intimate the dyad; conversely, the greater the divergence of this ratio from one, the more ego knows alter more than ego is known by alter, the less intimacy, and the more potentially exploitative the relationship.

In sum, the three dimensions of control, trust, and intimacy are assumed to be mutually causal or interdependently related (Zetterberg, 1965). Based on the measures presented, the following are a small set of possible hypotheses selected as guides for investigation. Space limitations do not allow a thorough discussion of their rationale; however, readers are encouraged to assess the utility of these hypotheses against their own research and interpersonal experiences and to generate their own hypotheses:

(1) The larger the dominance ratio, the smaller the reward dependability ratio and the smaller the knowledge ratio characterizing the interpersonal system.
(2) The greater the confidence scores, the more flexible the control system and the more mutual knowledge characterizing the dyadic system.
(3) The greater ego's transferability score relative to alter's and the more attached alter is to ego, the more ego is in a dominant position with alter and the more redundant the control pattern.

(4) The more equal the attachment ratio, the more equal the reward dependability and confidence ratios and the more flexible the control pattern.

(5) The smaller ego's transferability score relative to alter, the greater ego's vulnerability and the greater alter's power.

These hypotheses will undoubtedly be refined and more precise ones will be generated. But their empirical investigation requires the development of reliable descriptions of interactive dynamics and will, therefore, further the construction of communication theories of interpersonal relationships—the purpose of this book.

RELATIONAL CONTROL FINDINGS

The theoretical conceptualizations underlying our method for studying the control dimension stem from the cumulative efforts of Bateson (1972) and the "Palo Alto" group (Jackson, 1965; Sluzki & Beavin, 1965; Sluzki & Ransom, 1976; Watzlawick et al., 1967; Watzlawick & Weakland, 1977; Wilder, 1979). In 1937, Bateson proposed that social interaction could be described as symmetrical or complementary, thereby introducing a monothetic terminology of relationships based upon message patternings. A coding scheme was developed by Rogers and Farace (1975) that refined those of Sluzki and Beavin (1965) and Mark (1971) in the attempt to operationalize these fundamental concepts (Rogers, 1982). This scheme, like the earlier ones, assumes that the meanings of messages are multileveled and attempts to describe the control implications of the "command" (Bateson, 1951) or "relational" (Millar & Rogers, 1976; Watzlawick et al., 1967) level of verbal messages. On the basis of their grammatical form and response mode, verbalizations are classified as one-up ($\uparrow$), an attempt to assert definitional rights; one-down ($\downarrow$), a request or an acceptance of the other's definition; or one-across ($\rightarrow$), a nonaccepting but nonasserting leveling maneuver.[11] We have used the Rogers and Farace coding scheme to operationalize the control indices of redundancy and dominance.[12] The findings reported below primarily focus on dominance (a relational outcome measure) and domineeringness (a measure of an individual's control movements) derived from this coding procedure. These variables were the principal focus in a set of analyses of two samples of husband-wife conversations (Courtright, Millar, & Rogers, 1979; Millar, Rogers, & Courtright, 1979; Rogers-Millar & Millar, 1979).

DOMINEERINGNESS AND DOMINANCE

Domineeringness is a monadic measure operationally defined by the number of one-up moves made by an individual during an ongoing conversation (domineeringness = $1/$ total number of maneuvers). *Dominance* characterizes the dyad's control structure and is a momentary outcome within the ongoing conversation; it is operationally defined by the number of one-up moves responded to with a one-down maneuver (dominance = given $1/\%\downarrow$). Dividing one spouse's score by the other's provides domineeringness and dominance ratios assumed to be relationally specific control characteristics.[13] The use of these measures provides information about both an individual's verbal behavior with the other (i.e., domineeringness) as well as relationally specific structures immanent in verbal behavior (i.e., dominance).

As expected, domineeringness and dominance are *independent* measures. Whether or not ego will be relatively more dominant when compared to alter *cannot* be predicted from the frequency of ego's domineering movements. However, the more domineering a given interactant, the less likely the other is to occupy a dominant position. Therefore, these correlations are assumed to evidence the conceptual distinction between individual and relational measures and remind us that dyadic structures cannot be additively reconstructed from monadic measures.

In the first sample (N = 45 dyads), husband and wife domineeringness were unrelated. In the second, larger study (N = 86 dyads), these measures were moderately correlated indicating a tendency for one spouse's domineeringness to be matched by the other. When there are inconsistencies in the findings across these two data sets, this correlation seems to account for these differences. We now turn to some specific results associated with the dominance and domineeringness measures.

Message type. The number of talkovers manifested during the husband and wife conversation is positively correlated with domineeringness. This correlation was stronger for wives than for husbands in both samples, suggesting that domineering wives interrupt more than domineering husbands. Notably, dominance *is not* related to talkover behavior in these intimate relations. Since interruptions are frequently used in the literature as a sign of dominance, we again urge that individual behaviors not be confused with dyadic structures and patterns.

The more domineering the wife, the fewer the number of support statements she gives her husband. This inverse relation was observed for husbands in the second sample; in the first sample, husband domineeringness was, instead, positively related to the transmission of support statements. Thus the more the wife attempts to define their activities, the less she verbally supports her husband; but the same cannot be said for him.

Contrary to expectations, domineeringness is *not consistently* related to nonsupport statements. These variables were positively related for both husbands and wives in the first sample, but not the second. In combination, the correlations of domineeringness with support and nonsupport statements imply that, in husband-wife pairs, the withholding of support and not the transmission of nonsupportive messages is related to the degree of domineeringness. These findings suggest a style of marital negotiation in which agreement is not manifested rather than disagreements being actively pursued. What is not made overt cannot be tested, though it can be assumed known. Put another way, husbands and wives seem to be more oriented toward "not rocking the relational boat" than risking open negotiation. This interpretation is also evidenced by the positive correlations between the number of support statements made by one spouse and the other's frequency of occupying the dominant position.

Apparently, husbands and wives resist discussing and/or avoid perceiving disagreements; instead, they emphasize supporting and agreeing with other. Coser's (1956, pp. 67-78) proposition that intimate relations suppress conflicts seems relevant here. If long-term relationships involving more of the "whole person" (i.e., low transferability and high affection scores) do tend to suppress conflicts, then one way of achieving an illusion of harmony is to place a greater emphasis on the giving and receiving of support rather than on isolating and discussing differences to be resolved (Millar et al., 1984). Such an emphasis would be associated with relatively low knowledge scores and infrequent communication states.

McCall and Simmons propose that people do not have to agree on all topics relevant to their interaction; "all that is needed is a *sufficient lack of disagreement* about another for each to proceed in some degree with his own plans of actions" (1966, p. 127; emphasis added). They assert that a "working agreement" between persons "can be said to exist when the cognitive processes of one person, with respect to social identities, are not in gross conflict with the expressive processes of the other person" (1966, p. 142). Such a working agreement, precariously balanced by several behavioral and perceptual processes, would be easily upset by the frequent expression of nonsupport statements that would force the dyad to search for mutual understandings that may never have existed.

Message intensity. The investigation of the intensity values is in the initial stages of development and has only been conducted on the second data set. Nonetheless, some preliminary findings seem worth reporting in this review. Interestingly, the proportion of domineering statements is *not* related to their average intensity values for either husbands or wives (Courtright, Millar, & Rogers, 1980; Rogers, Courtright, & Millar, 1980). The frequency of transmitting one-up statements is, however, positively related to the average intensity level of one-down statements and to less distancing one-up responses from the spouse. To restate these findings, a domineering style by either husband or wife suggests a less "submissive" or less "supportive" posture from the other.

The more frequently the husband is in a dominant position, the lower the average intensity of his one-down statements. Wife dominance, on the other hand, is positively related to the intensity of husband one-up statements and the distancing of his one-up responses. This second finding suggests a "frustration" image of the husband "shouting" his infrequent one-up moves in order to be "heard" by his more dominant wife. There was a slight indication of this frustration picture for the wives also, but the image was more clearly descriptive of the husbands' behaviors.

Transactional redundancy. Transactional redundancy decreases as the husband makes more one-up statements; thus a more flexible control pattern is observed when the husband is more domineering. There was a positive correlation in the second sample between husband dominance and redundancy, but not at a sufficient level to be considered an unequivocal finding. (*Transactional redundancy* refers to the amount of alternation or oscillation in the couple's control structurings and was operationally defined as the sum of the absolute deviation from random use of the nine transactional configurations comprising the Rogers-Farace coding scheme.)[14]

The correlation between redundancy and husband domineeringness appears to complement Gottman's (1982b; see also Gottman, 1979) observations of distressed couples. Gottman reports that distressed marriages are characterized by less emotional responsiveness and more withdrawal on the part of the husband, and more argumentative behaviors by the wife. The frequent assertion of one-up statements by the husband characterizing flexible patterns implies more involvement and less withdrawal from interspousal conversations; when this involvement is accompanied by frequent supportive statements, as in the first sample, it may be considered a "positive" emotional response. But when the wife makes frequent one-up statements, she provides fewer supportive comments and interrupts more often, which is suggestive of an argumentative stance. These results suggest a degree of functionality to husband domineeringness and a degree of dysfunctionality to wife domineeringness—suggestions that are further evidenced by the satisfaction correlations reported next.

Role strain. In the first sample, but not the second, wife domineeringness was positively related to the couple's reported role strain, while husband dominance was negatively related. (*Role strain* refers to the degree of perceived inequity reported by the marriage pair and was operationalized as the discrepancy between who does and who should do a variety of household tasks.) The findings of the first study are consistent with the sociological literature on the family (Centers, Raven, & Rodrigues, 1971; Kolb & Straus, 1974; Sprenkle & Olson, 1978) and were expected to be replicated. The lack of replication is a bit puzzling, but appears to be related to the positive correlation between husband and wife domineeringness found only in the second sample.

Marital satisfaction. The more domineering the wife, the less marital satisfaction she reports. Furthermore, her frequency of occupying a dominant position is unrelated to her reported level of marital satisfaction. Husband domineeringness was not consistently related to either spouse's reported level of marital satisfaction. Husband dominance, however, is slightly related to his reported level of marital satisfaction as well as how often he reports discussing various topics with his wife (which may be an index of involvement).

Speaking loosely, the more the wife attempts to "take charge" of the relationship, the less satisfied she feels (perhaps the result of an argumentative stance). This dissatisfaction is attenuated by her husband's acceptance of her "take charge" attempts, but his acceptance does *not* increase her reported satisfaction. Conversely, the husband's attempts to "take charge" and define their activities are not consistently related to his reported marital satisfaction, but his wife's acceptance of his attempts is satisfying. Please notice these subtle differences; for wives, the frequent doing of one-up statements appears to be dissatisfying, while for husbands, the frequent outcome of dominance appears to be satisfying.

One wonders where the wife's conversational satisfiers are. Perhaps these correlations are another indicant of the oft-cited finding that married men are happier than single men while the reverse is true for women. Our own data, some of which are reported here, definition evidence the notions of a "his marriage" and a "her marriage" discussed by Bernard (1972). The fact of a "his" and "her" marriage further substantiates our claim that the relationship per se is not reducible to individual measures or their sum; it must be studied in its own right.

Communication satisfaction. The more domineering the wife, the less satisfaction both she and her husband report with their interspousal communication. This same inverse relationship was found for husband domineeringness in the second sample, but not in the first.

Some clues about how the spouses interpret their conversations can be gleaned by looking at correlations with the individual items in the communication satisfaction index. Factor analyzing 15 statements about interspousal communication resulted in a principal factor of six items, labeled *communication satisfaction*. The correlations mentioned below concern these six.

The more domineering the wife, the less satisfaction the husband reports with (a) their ability to talk things out together, (b) the ease with which they discuss problems and complaints, and (c) the less frequently he feels understood by his wife. Conversely, the more domineering the husband, the less satisfaction the wife reports with (a) their ability to talk things out together, (b) her husband's ability to express his own emotions and feelings, (c) the ease with which they discuss problems and complaints, (d) the encouragement she receives about expressing her own concerns, (e) the less frequently she feels understood by her husband, and (f) the more likely she is to report that others are more interesting to talk to than her husband.

None of these items were related to either the husband's or wife's dominance scores. The couple's dominance ratio, however, was related to the husband's responses to five of these items, but to none of the wife's responses. These correlations indicate a positive evaluation of their interspousal communication from the husband's point of view. The larger the couple's dominance ratio (e.g., the more the husband is in a dominant position more than his wife, the greater the inequality of the dominance ratio) the more satisfaction the husband reports with (a) their ability to talk things out together, (b) the frequency with which he feels understood by his wife, (c) the ease with which problems and complaints are discussed, (d) his wife's ability to express her emotions and feelings, and (e) the less likely he is to find others more interesting to talk to than his wife.

Level of understanding. The more either spouse is clearly dominant or domineering relative to the other, the less each understands the other (Millar et al., 1979).[15] Put another way, the more equivalency in the pure dominance and domineeringness ratios, the more accurate both spouses' knowledge claims about other; the less equivalency, the less accuracy and the less mutual knowledge. Juxtaposing this finding with the self-reported satisfactions listed above evidences an incongruency, at least for husbands. On the one hand, the greater the dominance ratio, the more likely the husband is to report feeling understood by his wife. On the other hand, the greater the inequality of this ratio, the less likely he is to actually understand or be understood by his wife. These results again stress the importance of recognizing the different interpretations evidenced by perceptual and behavioral data.

CONCLUSION: LOOKING BACK
AND LOOKING FORWARD

As we have reflected on these findings, several issues have surfaced. First, the range constituting a "sufficient lack of disagreement" of a viable "working agreement" (McCall & Simmons, 1966) is apparently fairly broad. But how broad is broad? When does too much disagreement (recognized or unrecognized) pose problems for the couple? Further, is an insufficient lack of disagreement also dysfunctional or undesirable? Several studies (Dymond, 1954; Ferguson & Allen, 1978; Luckey, 1960; Taylor, 1965) have evidenced a positive, linear relationship between understanding and marital satisfaction. But rephrasing the issue in terms of sufficient lack of disagreement suggests that too little disagreement might also be dysfunctional by instituting too much informational similarity (assumed or actual) and arresting the growth and

dynamism of the marriage. The relationship stagnates from too little disagreement, from too much understanding and "togetherness" so that the
"feeling tone" of triviality may become "desperate and fatal" (Simmel, 1950,
p. 126). Not risking "rocking the relational boat" may preserve the illusion
of harmony and sustain the collusion of mutual self-confirmations characterizing nexal units (Laing, 1967, pp. 87-89), but the price paid is lives of
quiet desperation.

Second, in interpersonal systems it is often what is absent rather than
present, what did not or is not happening rather than what did or is, that
provides a sense of understanding about interpersonal dynamics. For example,
not remembering an anniversary with a gift may result in a "gross conflict"
between one spouse's behaviors and the other's cognitions, thus violating their
"working agreement" and explaining hurt feelings and deafening silences. Or,
as reported earlier, it is not the presence of nonsupporting statements that
is associated with domineeringness but the lack of support statements. The
point is that "not-doing" is an explanatory principle in human interactions
that compounds the difficulty of developing precise theoretical predictions.

Third, if both not-doing and doing are explanatory notions in human relationships, then researchers must study multiple behavior patterns and their
interpretations *in context* if useful predictive models of interpersonal relations
are to result. Recognition of contextual limitations and relational specificities
encourages the use of comparative measures (e.g., difference scores and ratios
that index the "distance" between interactants) rather than noncontextual,
nonrelational individual measures. Contextual, relationally specific, comparative measures are necessary for describing *how* it is that "the pattern which
connects is a metapattern" (Bateson, 1979, p. 13). These metapatterns, in turn,
should differentiate qualitatively different types of relationships.

Fourth, contemplation of the notions of pattern and metapattern raises
a question about studying the cognitive and behavioral dynamics of human
interactions. Because "mind is a necessary explanatory principle" (Bateson,
1977, p. 239) in interpersonal communication and humans are symbolic animals
(Burke, 1966), our relationships are intrinsically reflexive (Cronen, Johnson,
& Lannaman, 1982). "Reflexiveness...is the essential condition, within the
social process, for the development of mind" (Mead, 1934, p. 134). However,
it is "absurd" to conceive of mind solely or "simply from the standpoint of
the individual human organism"; rather, mind or consciousness must be
regarded as "arising and developing within...the matrix of social interactions"
(Mead, 1934, p. 133). Our pragmatic approach has begun to describe the recursive, behavioral loops of interpersonal control structures and patterns. A
cognitive approach, similarly, must attempt to describe the reflexive, hierar-
chical loops of interpretive structures and patterns (Cronen et al., 1982; Cronen
& Pearce, 1981; Cronen, Pearce, & Harris, 1982; Pearce, 1976). At a minimum,
perceptual measures must be combined for characterizations of relationship

types (Fitzpatrick, 1977, 1981, 1983, 1984). The conjoint use of methods describing the behavioral and cognitive dynamics of interpersonal relationships is necessary for the construction of adequate communication theories of human patterns and metapatterns regulating the distance between persons. We hope that the three proposed dimensions of control, trust, and intimacy and the reported findings on the control dimension will spur such investigations. Much empirical and conceptual work awaits us. We have only the seedlings of a useful language of interpersonal relationships that is both social and scientific.

NOTES

1. A purposeful system is one that can change its goals as well as the means for attaining them in constant environmental conditions (Ackoff & Emery, 1972, p. 31). As Simmel (1950) asserts, it is impossible to conceive of human interactions and relationships—or societies for that matter—which are not characterized by selected, edited, and "teleologically directed" message performances (p. 312).

2. We believe that meaning is either an aspect of the intimacy dimension (a knowledge index) or an emergent gestalt that incorporates aspects of all three dimensions.

3. As Cushman and Craig (1976) posited, the "unique function" of participation in interpersonal communication processes is the regulation of "consensus regarding individual self-conceptions" (p. 46). The construction of individual identities and of the world around the interpersonal system "occurs principally in the course of conversation" and "the implicit problem of this conversation is how to match" differing conceptions of themselves and their realities (Berger & Kellner, 1964, p. 61).

4. Ascription (e.g., kinship ties) is assumed to be imposed upon individuals rather than interactively achieved by them. Therefore, although we agree that ascriptive ties are a significant contextual variable for describing and differentiating interpersonal relationships, they are not included in our focus on communicative dynamics. The attachment tie of McCall and Simmons (1966) is part of our intimacy dimension, and reward dependability, commitment, and investment are explicitly or implicitly included in our trust and control dimensions.

5. Since every message serves to regulate the distance between interactants and to support or fail to support their presented identities, felicity judgments are the primary criteria used by individuals to evaluate message performances. Felicity assessments are not made by comparing the content of utterances against some presupposed external reality, but by evaluating the objective experiences of the communicants in the context of their evolving relationship (Pearce & Cronen, 1980).

6. Lag sequential and Markov chain analyses are frequent techniques for measuring redundancy (Manderscheid, Rae, McCarrick, & Silbergeld, 1982; Rogers, Millar, & Bavelas, 1985). Although descriptive of conversational regularities, these procedures are somewhat awkward for comparative purposes. Recently Courtright (1984) introduced the "GSK" approach, which overcomes this difficulty and will prove useful in comparing the stochastic differences in two or more subsamples of conversations.

7. As a perceptual variable, power is relatively more static than redundancy and dominance; in this sense, power is consistent with the assumption that the form of the relationship is predetermined by the resources or qualities each person is perceived to bring to or accumulate within interpersonal interactions. But just because ego has previously acquired the potential to influence does not necessarily mean that potential will be exercised or accepted in any given conversation. If it did, the only way the shape of a relationship could be changed is by the acquisition of resources or qualities valued by alter—a conclusion inconsistent with the open systems characteristics of emergence and equifinality assumed here (Fisher, 1978; Watzlawick et al., 1967).

8. Trust may seem to be a subset of intimacy, but we believe that objectified, modern culture has effectively differentiated these dimensions (Simmel, 1950). Many modern encounters are not between persons as subjective centers of experience, but between objects, between abstract categories—for example, customer-clerk, buyer-seller, producer-consumer, client-lawyer, doctor-patient, bureaucrat-citizen. All that is required in these interactions is some minimal knowledge of external facts about the other—the doctor is licensed to practice, the patient can pay the bill, the product is safe because it is properly sealed, the IRS auditor is a representative of the government—in order for interdependent action to proceed. The "regulation" of such encounters has "become so objectified that confidence no longer needs any properly personal knowledge" (Simmel, 1950, p. 319). Although we assume that trust and intimacy are positively related, we are contending that trust is an analytically distinct dimension—at least within modern American culture.

9. An overconcern with this dimension, because it is the key in distinguishing interpersonal from the other social relations, has led to the "ideology of intimacy" (Parks, 1982) in interpersonal communication. The "ideology of intimacy" assumes the closer the better; the more knowledge and love shared, the more glorious or perfect or excellent the relationship. But, as Kantor and Lehr's (1975) discussion of "affect fusion," Minuchin's (1974) notion of "enmeshment," and Laing's (1967) almost cynical characterization of "nexus" indicate, too much intimacy is toxic for the interpersonal system and its members.

10. Simmel (1950) defines *triviality* as the frequency "of the consciousness that a content of life is repeated, while the value of this content depends on its very opposite—a certain measure of rarity" (p. 125). Further, "dyads alone are susceptible to the peculiar coloration or discoloration" (p. 125) called triviality because "the dyad is inseparable from the immediacy of interaction" (p. 126).

11. The conceptualization of one-across maneuvers is a continuing source of debate in the relational control literature (Rogers & Millar, 1982). The debate is important because these movements are the most frequently observed and because they are central to establishing and maintaining a conversation's "set point" around which control patterns oscillate (Courtright, Millar, & Rogers, 1983; Rogers et al., 1980). Parks and Dindia-Webb (1979) suggest that one-across movements may have no control implications, or have such minimal control implications that they can be discarded from analyses; or, these movements may be so subtle and the coding procedures used so gross that their control implications cannot be adequately classified without the addition of nonverbal measures (pp. 42-45). Our position states that one-across movements are multifunctional maneuvers of a different logical type than the other two such that one-across messages contain one-up and one-down elements yet subsume these more unifunctional

maneuvers (Rogers et al., 1980). However, we agree with Parks and Dindia-Webb when they assert that "the original reasons for restricting coding to the verbal band may not be as good now as they once were" (p. 47). They contend that the development of nonverbal measures to augment or even supplant verbal schemes is "of central importance" to relational researchers. The "temptation to classify" verbalizations as "the central message" and to contend that nonverbal (or contextual) components serve "only as modifiers rests upon untested assumptions" about communication processes (Birdwhistell, 1970, p. 86). We concur with these assessments.

12. Reliability coefficients ranged from .68 to 1.00, with an average of .86 across all comparisons in the initial study using the Rogers-Farace (1975) procedures. In the second data set, reliability estimates ranged from .79 to 1.00 with an average of .89 across all possible comparisons. In an unpublished study of couples in counseling, the estimates ranged from .75 to 1.00 with an average of .85. The coding scheme, then, represents a workable, reliable instrument for describing the control implications of verbalizations. Its predictive validity has been evidenced by Ayers and Miura (1981).

13. Various domineeringness and dominance measures have been investigated. Those defined here were labeled *domineeringness* and *pure dominance* (Rogers-Millar & Millar, 1979, p. 241). Submissiveness and pure submission are the exact structural opposites of domineeringness and dominance; they are based on the number of one-downs manifested and the proportion of one-downs followed by a one-up from other. Although potentially useful descriptors of conversational dynamics, submissive and submission measures have not been consistent predictors or correlates of other control movements and/or interspousal perceptions.

14. A more global measure of the amount of oscillation around the dyad's homeostatic "set point" manifested in a conversation is called the "coefficient of variation" (Courtright et al., 1983). This measure is based on the message intensity weights and provides a single quantitative index of the variation around the average control "distance" maintained during conversation.

15. In Millar et al. (1979), understanding was measured by comparing a person's predictions about her or his spouse's answers to the role strain items. An index of understanding was created for each spouse by summing the absolute size of the "errors" in these predictions. The index, therefore, is more accurately described as an index of misunderstanding; but, for stylistic reasons, the absence of misunderstanding—a score of zero—is referred to as *understanding*.

REFERENCES

Ackoff, R. L., & Emery, F. E. (1972). *On purposeful systems.* Chicago: Aldine-Atherton.

Ayers, J., & Miura, S. Y. (1981). Construct and predictive validity of instruments for coding relational control. *Western Journal of Speech Communication, 45,* 159-171.

Bateson, G. (1937). *Naven.* Cambridge: Cambridge University Press.

Bateson, G. (1951). Information and codification: A philosophical approach. In J. Ruesch & G. Bateson, (Eds.), *Communication: The social matrix of psychiatry* (pp. 168-211). New York: Norton.

Bateson, G. (1972). *Steps to an ecology of mind.* New York: Ballantine.

Bateson, G. (1977). Afterword. In J. Brockman (Ed.), *About Bateson* (pp. 235-247). New York: E. P. Dutton.

Bateson, G. (1979). *Mind and nature: A necessary unit.* New York: E. P. Dutton.

Berger, P., & Kellner, H. (1964). Marriage and the construction of reality. *Diogenes, 46,* 1-25.

Bernard, J. (1972). *The future of marriage.* New York: Bantam Books.

Birdwhistell, R. L. (1970). *Kinesics and context: Essays on body motion communication.* Philadelphia: University of Pennsylvania Press.

Blumer, H. (1969). *Symbolic interactionism: Perspective and method.* Englewood Cliffs, NJ: Prentice-Hall.

Bochner, A. P. (1984). The functions of human communicating in interpersonal bonding. In C. C. Arnold & J. W. Bowers (Eds.), *Handbook of rhetorical and communication theory* (pp. 544-621). Boston: Allyn & Bacon.

Burke, K. (1966). *Language as symbolic action.* Berkeley: University of California Press.

Centers, R., Raven, B. H., & Rodrigues, A. (1971). Conjugal power structures: A re-examination. *America Sociological Review, 36,* 264-278.

Coser, L. A. (1956). *The functions of social conflict.* New York: Free Press.

Courtright, J. A. (1984). Methods for integrating observational and traditional data analysis. *Communication Quarterly, 32,* 197-206.

Courtright, J. A., Millar, F. E., & Rogers, L. E. (1979). Domineeringness and dominance: Replication and expansion. *Communication Monographs, 46,* 179-192.

Courtright, J. A., Millar, F. E., & Rogers, L. E. (1980). Message control intensity as a predictor of transactional redundancy. In D. Nimmo (Ed.), *Communication yearbook 4* (pp. 199-216). New Brunswick, NJ: Transaction Books.

Courtright, J. A., Millar, F. E., & Rogers, L. E. (1983). A new measure of interactional control patterns. *Communication, 12,* 47-68.

Cronen, V. E., Johnson, K. M., & Lannaman, J. W. (1982). Paradoxes, double binds, and reflexive loops: An alternative theoretical perspective. *Family Process, 20,* 91-112.

Cronen, V. E., & Pearce, W. B. (1981). Logical force in interpersonal communication: A new concept of necessity in social behavior. *Communication, 6,* 5-67.

Cronen, V. E., Pearce, W. B., & Harris, L. M. (1982). The coordinated management of meaning. In F.E.X. Dance (Ed.), *Human communication theory* (pp. 61-89). New York: Harper & Row.

Cushman, D. P., & Craig, R. T. (1976). Communication systems: Interpersonal implications. In G. R. Miller (Ed.), *Explorations in interpersonal communication* (pp. 37-58). Newbury Park, CA: Sage.

Denzin, N. K. (1970). Rules of conduct and the study of deviant behavior: Some notes on the social relationship. In G. J. McCall, M. M. McCall, N. K. Denzin, G. D. Suttles, & S. B. Kurth (Eds.), *Social relationships* (pp. 62-94). Chicago: Aldine.

Duncan, H. D. (1967). The search for a social theory of communication in American sociology. In F.E.X. Dance (Ed.), *Human communication theory* (pp. 236-263). New York: Holt, Rinehart & Winston.

Duncan, H. D. (1968). *Symbols in society.* London: Oxford University Press.

Dymond, R. (1954). Interpersonal perception and marital happiness. *Canadian Journal of Psychology, 8,* 164-171.

Ellis, D. G. (1982). The epistemology of form. In C. Wilder-Mott & J. H. Weakland (Eds.), *Rigor and imagination: Essays from the legacy of Gregory Bateson* (pp. 215-230). New York: Praeger.

Ferguson, L. R., & Allen, D. R. (1978). Congruence of parental perception, marital satisfaction and child adjustment. *Journal of Consulting and Clinical Psychology, 46,* 345-356.

Fisher, B. A. (1978). *Perspectives on human communication.* New York: Macmillan.

Fitzpatrick, M. A. (1977). A typological approach to communication in relationships. In B. D. Ruben (Ed.), *Communication yearbook 1* (pp. 263-275). New Brunswick, NJ: Transaction Books.

Fitzpatrick, M. A. (1981). A typological approach to enduring relationships: Children as audience to the parental relationships. *Journal of Comparative Family Studies, 12,* 81-94.

Fitzpatrick, M. A. (1983). Predicting couple's communication from couple's self-reports. In R. Bostrom (Ed.), *Communication yearbook 7* (pp. 41-54). Newbury Park, CA: Sage.

Fitzpatrick, M. A. (1984) A typological approach to marital interaction: Recent theory and research. In L. Berkowitz (Ed.), *Advances in experimental social psychology* (Vol. 18, pp. 1-47). Orlando, FL: Academic Press.

Foss, J. E. (1980). The paradoxical nature of family relationships and family conflict. In M. A. Straus & G. T. Hotaling (Eds.), *The social causes of husband-wife violence* (pp. 115-135). Minneapolis: University of Minnesota Press.

French, J. P., & Raven, B. H. (1959). The bases of social power. In D. Cartwright (Ed.), *Studies in social power* (pp. 150-167). Ann Arbor: University of Michigan Press.

Giddens, A. (1983). *Central problems in social theory.* Berkeley: University of California Press.

Goffman, E. (1959). *The presentation of self in everyday life.* Garden City, NY: Doubleday.

Gottman, J. M. (1979). *Marital interaction: Experimental investigations.* New York: Academic Press.

Gottman, J. M. (1982a). Temporal form: Toward a new language for describing relationships. *Journal of Marriage and the Family, 44,* 943-962.

Gottman, J. M. (1982b). Emotional responsiveness in marital conversations. *Journal of Communication, 32,* 108-120.

Hahlweg, K., & Jacobson, N. S. (1984). *Marital interaction.* New York: Guilford Press.

Helmersen, P. (1983). *Family interaction and communication in psychology.* London: Academic Press.

Hinde, R. A. (1979). *Towards understanding relationships.* London: Academic Press.

Homans, G. C. (1961). *Social behavior: Its elementary forms.* New York: Harcourt Brace Jovanovich.

Jackson, D. D. (1965). The study of the family. *Family Process, 4,* 1-20.

Kantor, D., & Lehr, W. (1975). *Inside the family.* San Francisco: Jossey-Bass.

Koestler, A. (1978). *Janus: A summing up.* New York: Vintage Books.

Kolb, T. M., & Straus, M. A. (1974). Marital power and marital happiness in relation to problem-solving ability. *Journal of Marriage and the Family, 36,* 756-766.

Laing, R. D. (1967). *The politics of experience.* New York: Ballantine.

Laing, R. D., Phillipson, H., & Lee, A. R. (1966). *Interpersonal perception: A theory and a method of research.* New York: Harper & Row.

Lennard, H. L., & Bernstein, A. (1969). *Patterns in human interaction.* San Francisco: Jossey-Bass.

Luckey, E. G. (1960). Marital satisfaction and congruent self-spouse concepts. *Social Forces, 39,* 153-157.

Manderscheid, D. W., Rae, D. S., McCarrick, A. K., & Silbergeld, S. (1982). A stochastic model of relational control in dyadic interaction. *American Sociological Review, 47,* 62-75.

Mark, R. A. (1971). Coding communication at the relationship level. *Journal of Communication, 21,* 221-232.

McCall, G. J., & Simmons, J. L. (1966). *Identities and interactions.* New York: Free Press.

Mead, G. H. (1934). *Mind, self and society.* Chicago: University of Chicago Press.

Millar, F. E. (1979). Communication: Discipline, process, event. *The Communicator, 9,* 52-68.

Millar, F. E., & Rogers, L. E. (1976). A relational approach to interpersonal communication. Pp. 87-103. In G. R. Miller (Ed.), *Explorations in interpersonal communication* (pp. 87-103). Newbury Park, CA: Sage.

Millar, F. E., Rogers, L. E., & Bavelas, J. (1984). Identifying patterns of verbal conflict in interpersonal dynamics. *Western Journal of Speech Communication, 48,* 231-246.

Millar, F. E., Rogers, L. E., & Courtright, J. A. (1979). Relational control and dyadic understanding: An exploratory predictive regression model. In D. Nimmo (Ed.), *Communication yearbook 3* (pp. 213-224). New Brunswick, NJ: Transaction Books.

Miller, G. R., & Steinberg, M. (1975). *Between people: A new analysis of interpersonal communication.* Chicago: Science Research Associates.

Minuchin, S. (1974). *Families and family therapy.* Cambridge, MA: Harvard University Press.

Mishler, E. G., & Waxler, N. E. (1968). *Interaction in families.* New York: John Wiley.

Olson, D. H., & Cromwell, R. E. (1975). Power in families. In R. E. Cromwell & D. H. Olson (Eds.), *Power in families* (pp.3-11). New York: Halsted.

Parks, M. R. (1982). Ideology of interpersonal communication: Off the couch and into the world. In M. Burgoon (Ed.), *Communication yearbook 5* (pp. 79-107). New Brunswick, NJ: Transaction Books.

Parks, M. R., & Dindia-Webb, K. (1979). *Recent developments in relational communication research.* Paper presented at the annual meeting of the International Communication Association, Philadelphia.

Pearce, W. B. (1976). The coordinated management of meaning: A rules-based theory of interpersonal communication. In G. R. Miller (Ed.), *Explorations in interpersonal communication* (pp. 17-35). Newbury Park, CA: Sage.

Pearce, W. B., & Cronen, V. E. (1980). *Communication, action, and meaning: The creation of social realities.* New York: Praeger.

Penman, R. (1980). *Communication processes and relationships.* London: Academic Press.

Rogers, L. E. (1982). Symmetry and complementarity: Evolution and evaluation of an idea. In C. Wilder-Mott & J. H. Weakland (Eds.), *Rigor and imagination: Essays from the legacy of Gregory Bateson* (pp. 231-251). New York: Praeger.

Rogers, L. E., Courtright, J. A., & Millar, F. E. (1980). Message control intensity: Rationale and preliminary findings. *Communication Monographs, 47,* 201-219.

Rogers, L. E., & Farace, R. V. (1975). Analysis of relational communication in dyads: New measurement procedures. *Human Communication Research, 1,* 222-239.

Rogers, L. E., & Millar, F. E. (1982). The question of validity: A pragmatic answer. In M. Burgoon (Ed.), *Communication yearbook 5* (pp. 249-257). New Brunswick, NJ: Transaction Books.

Rogers, L. E., Millar, F. E., & Bavelas, J. B. (1985). Methods for analyzing marital conflict discourse: Implications of a systems approach. *Family Process, 24,* 53-72.

Rogers-Millar, L. E., & Millar, F. E. (1979). Domineeringness and dominance: A transactional view. *Human Communication Research, 5,* 238-246.

Rollins, B. C., & Bahr, S. J. (1976). A theory of power relationships in marriage. *Journal of Marriage and the Family, 38,* 619-626.

Scheflen, A. E. (1974). *How behavior means.* Garden City, NY: Doubleday.

Schutz, A. (1967). *The phenomenology of the social world.* Evanston, IL: Northwestern University Press.

Simmel, G. (1950). *The sociology of Georg Simmel* (K. H. Wolff, Trans.). New York: Free Press.

Sluzki, C., & Beavin, J. (1965). Simetria y complementaridad: Una definicion operacional y una tipologia de parejas. *Acta Psiquiatrica y Psicologia de America Latina, 11,* 321-330.

Sluzki, C., & Ransom, D. C. (1976). *Double bind: The foundation of the communication approach to the family.* New York: Grune & Stratton.

Sprenkle, D. H., & Olson, D. H. (1978). Circumplex model of marital systems: An empirical study of clinic and nonclinic couples. *Journal of Marriage and Family Counseling, 4,* 59-74.

Sprey, J. (1971). On the management of conflict in families. *Journal of Marriage and the Family, 33,* 722-732.

Stiles, W. B. (1980). Comparison of dimensions derived from rating versus coding of dialogue. *Journal of Personality and Social Psychology, 38,* 359-374.

Taylor, A. B. (1965). Role perception, empathy, and marriage adjustment. *Sociology and Social Research, 22,* 22-31.

Watzlawick, P., Beavin, J., & Jackson, D. D. (1967). *Pragmatics of human communication.* New York: Norton.

Watzlawick, P., & Weakland, J. H. (1977). *The interactional view: Studies at the mental research institute, Palo Alto, 1965-1974.* New York: Norton.

Weick, K. E. (1979). *The social psychology of organizing* (2nd ed.). Reading, MA: Addison-Wesley.

Wilder, C. (1979). The Palo Alto group: Difficulties and directions of the interactional view for human communication research. *Human Communication Research, 5,* 171-186.

Zetterberg, H. L. (1965). *On theory and verification in sociology* (3rd ed.). Totowa, NJ: Bedminster Press.

Chapter 7

CONFLICT AS A SOCIAL SKILL

Alan L. Sillars and Judith Weisberg

SLIGHTLY OVER A DECADE ago the state of research on interpersonal conflict was severely criticized for relying on games played by strangers to simulate conflict (most notably, the Prisoner's Dilemma game). The game format simply did not capture the intensity or drama associated with actual conflicts, and the role of interpersonal communication was necessarily quite limited and superficial (Johnson, 1974; Nemeth, 1972). Subsequently a great deal has changed. Studies of unacquainted college students simulating cooperation and competition are passé, and there are many more studies of the kinds of conflicts that really count; for example, conflicts at home, in the workplace, and in the classroom. However, there is still something antiseptic about this area of study, only now it seems that the issue goes deeper than research design. Something seems to be missing, a failure sometimes to call attention to the more disorderly and emotional side of interpersonal conflict.

A bitter personal conflict is very messy to behold and quite perplexing to study. Lines of argument are diffuse and disorganized; issues and motives are hard to pin down; perceptions are fraught with ambiguity, and conversational rules are tortured. Serious personal conflicts may represent nothing less than the dissolution of consensus about the core issues and basic ground rules of a relationship. Yet the implication often drawn from conflict research is that a relationship could be set back on its proper course if a few simple changes in communication were instituted. Communication is implicitly seen as a simple, almost mechanical process of giving information or expressing agreement, not as a complex process of meaning creation, with all its potential for ambiguity and confusion.

The way we look at interpersonal conflict has been influenced less by any single intellectual tradition than it has by a general cultural interpretation of interpersonal relationships. Americans and similar cultural groups are

AUTHORS' NOTE: The authors would like to thank Professors Donald Cegala, Joseph Folger, and William Wilmot for their comments on an earlier draft of this chapter.

characteristically introspective about their personal relationships (Gudykunst & Kim, 1984), and they regard relationships as something to be analyzed, understood, and tinkered with—that is, as something that can be done well or done poorly (see Deetz, 1981). Although it is not our intention to discuss the general implications of such a perspective (the writing of this book presupposes it), we are concerned with a major corollary, which we shall call the *social skill* metaphor for interpersonal communication. "Skill" is used as a metaphor for communication when people speak of effective communication as a set of techniques. The metaphor invites comparisons with other activities that involve talent or proficiency at mastering behaviors and strategies—e.g., tennis, mathematics, and salesmanship. These are activities that generally have clear goals (to score points, solve equations, or sell shoes) and definite ground rules (to keep the ball in play, make all squared numbers positive, and preserve the profit margin). When applied to communication during conflict, the social skill metaphor suggests that conflicts also have clear goals and definite ground rules, and conflicts can thus be managed or resolved by application of the appropriate behavioral skills. Conversely, a lack of effective communication is the reason why friendships break up, businesses fail, and marriages end in divorce.

The social skill metaphor is found in both popular literature and academic books on communication and conflict. For example, popular magazines advise young couples to acquire "negotiation skills" consisting primarily of open, expressive communication and direct engagement over conflict issues (Kidd, 1975). According to the historian Gadlin (1977), an obsession with technique most characterizes the contemporary American vision of intimate relationships. In the social sciences, the skill metaphor is reflected in the use of expressions such as "effective communication," "communication skill," and "communication competence" to explain why people do or do not get along. The skill metaphor is explicitly embraced by numerous textbooks on communication (see Parks, 1981) and by communication-based approaches to marital and family intervention, such as behavioral marriage therapy, negotiation training, and marital enrichment (see Birchler, 1979). The metaphor is implicitly a point of reference for many studies comparing the communication patterns of happy and unhappy couples to reveal communication-related causes of relationship dissatisfaction.

Under close evaluation, the skill metaphor is subject to several criticisms. For one thing, it presupposes that people are rational social actors whose communication is designed to achieve well-defined goals. In many conflicts, goals are quite complex and ephemeral. They may seem clear and transparent only in retrospect (Hawes & Smith, 1973). Further, much communication is expressive, rather than instrumental. People may communicate (or withhold communication) to satisfy an emotional urge, not to achieve some future goal state. Second, human relationships are not plastic and malleable, like a chunk of clay that can be reshaped at will. There is a strong undercurrent of conservatism in human interaction. In particular, people may experience excruciating difficulty generating fundamental change in established relationship rules, because such change presupposes a totally new outlook or "reframing" of the situation (Watzlawick, Weakland, & Fisch, 1974). And people may not necessarily be able to control external forces affecting the relationship (work schedules and the like), although they may exercise some control through their response to external pressures.

Third, the view of effective communication associated with the skill metaphor is often rigid and simplistic. Effective communication is mostly construed as a pattern of communication that is clear, consistent, direct, supportive, focused, and reciprocal. To be sure, these are some of the characteristics of communication commonly observed in happy or well-adjusted relationships. However, it would be misleading to use the qualities of communication in harmonious relationships to define effective communication without showing sensitivity to the special complexities of conflictful relationships. Occasionally people's best efforts to reconcile conflicts are frustrating and self-defeating, despite the fact that they possess good intentions and exercise an ordinary amount of common sense (Folger & Poole, 1984). Thus communication in the ideal relationship does not always provide an easy model to emulate.

Fourth, it is often hard to say what represents effective communication, because of lack of a strong consensus about what one should expect or hope will occur during interpersonal communication. Interpersonal relationships are characterized by equifinality—that is, different styles of interaction may lead to essentially the same outcome. The example comes to mind of a couple who fights habitually but seems, nonetheless, content with the arrangement. As Morton, Alexander, and Altman (1976) suggest, people may seem to disagree on just about every issue and still have a viable relationship if they mutually agree on the definition of their relationship (in this case, they agree to bicker). It is very difficult to accommodate the skill metaphor with the open-ended nature of communication effects and outcomes.

Throughout this chapter, we will examine areas in which communication "skill," in the usual sense of open, direct, confirming, and relevant communication, does and does not account for the complexities of interpersonal conflict. We have tried not to overstate our argument. There are numerous occasions when a solution to conflict could be found if people were only more direct, clear, or positive. On the other hand, the most difficult conflicts are often those that resist straightforward explanation and do not mesh with simple, formulaic expositions of communication. Further, alternative cultural interpretations of interpersonal relationships are obviously difficult to explain from a culturally fixed view of social skill. Thus a straightforward definition of effective communication may fit some examples of interpersonal conflict but may be ill-suited to many others. It is often as important to address the difficult, noncompliant examples that tax a research model as it is to account for the larger set of cases that are "easy marks" for the social scientist.

The first section of the chapter is designed to acquaint the reader with existing literature. We have focused our attention mostly on conflict within family and intimate relationships, both because there is a concentration of research in these areas and because both of us have a keen interest in personal relationships. Later we discuss two alternative ways of looking at interpersonal conflict, either of which is inconsistent with the skill metaphor. First, conflict may be seen as a relational event, with an ambiguous, disorderly, and improvisational structure. This image is suggested by the inherently problematic and occasionally chaotic nature of conflict over abstract relationship issues. Second, conflict may be seen as a culturally defined and regulated event. A cultural view of conflict is suggested by the great diversity of values and expectations for conflict held by different groups and dyads. Finally, in the last section we reassess the value of a social skills approach to communication and conflict in light of the points raised by our discussion of disorganization, ambiguity, and cultural diversity.

A BRIEF OVERVIEW OF EXISTING TRENDS IN CONFLICT RESEARCH

Most studies of conflict in personal relationships pertain to two particular dimensions of communication. The first dimension is affect, referring to messages that express positive or negative feelings about another person—for example, supportiveness, hostility, confirmation, coercion, sarcasm, or global positiveness or negativeness. The second dimension is engagement, which is the tendency to confront or avoid conflict (see Raush, Barry, Hertel, & Swain, 1974). Engagement is reflected in direct discussion of conflict, whereas conflict avoidance is reflected in circumscribed, irrelevant, or ambiguous communication (see Sillars, Coletti, Parry, & Rogers, 1982).

AFFECT

There are many indications that the communication of less compatible individuals is less happy, friendly, humorous, affectionate, or supportive, and more negative, threatening, abusive, or critical in comparison to more compatible individuals. For example, less compatible married couples are more negative and less positive in their tone of voice (Gottman, 1979; Pike & Sillars, 1985; Rubin, 1983); they show less nonverbal immediacy by sitting further apart, looking at one another less, holding their legs in a more closed position, touching one another less, and by engaging in more body-focused gestures and fewer open gestures (Beier & Steinberg, 1977); they express less agreement or approval and more disagreement (Gottman, 1979; Riskin & Faunce, 1972; Vincent, Friedman, Nugent, & Messerly, 1979); they make more competitive or coercive statements (Pike & Sillars, 1985; Raush et al., 1974); they make more domineering statements (Millar & Rogers, 1976), and they engage in less nonhostile joking and laughter (Mishler & Waxler, 1968; Riskin & Faunce, 1970).

The most common explanation for the negative style of communication found in incompatible relationships is based on social learning and systems theories. Both perspectives suggest that the sequence of communication is the most telling factor in the way two people resolve conflict. Systems theory suggests that a message is simultaneously a stimulus, response, and reinforcer, such that interpersonal communication represents a chain of overlapping and interdependent links (Bateson, 1951; Watzlawick, Beavin, & Jackson, 1967). The sequences that occur repeatedly presumably reflect implicit, underlying rules of the relationship, which are difficult to change. When coupled with systems theory, the social learning tradition suggests that the interpersonal communication process represents interdependent patterns of reinforcement behavior. Troubled relationships are thought to have destructive, self-perpetuating patterns. In fact, several schools of family intervention have evolved from efforts to modify the inadvertent reinforcement behaviors of couples and families (Azrin, Naster, & Jones, 1973; Jacobson & Martin, 1976; Lederer & Jackson, 1968; Weiss, Birchler, & Vincent, 1974).

Patterson's work is one of the prominent applications of social learning theory to interpersonal conflict. Patterson's (1976) *coercion hypothesis* suggests that coercion becomes the dominant method for resolving conflict in some relationships because individuals reinforce coercive messages and fail to reinforce more positive forms of conflict resolution. For example, children will often exhaust an entire repertoire of persuasive strategies to win a favor from adults. Furthermore, they may begin with relatively mild strategies (for example, simple requests, persuasive arguments, and promises) and then shift to increasingly punishing strategies (for example, threats, tantrums, and "sit-down strikes") when the first attempts fail and no alternatives are offered by the adult. If the adult gives in only after his or her will to resist has been exceeded by the child's coercive behavior, then coercion is reinforced as a method of conflict resolution.

Modeling may also be involved in the development of coercive patterns. Patterson points out that the roles of coercive agent and target shift back and forth from one person to the other as individuals imitate successful compliance-gaining behavior. As the partners become more skillful at coercion and counter-coercion, extended patterns of coercive exchange may increasingly dominate the relationship (Patterson, 1976; Patterson & Reid, 1970). In support of this framework, some studies have found that the rates of rewarding and punishing behaviors by different family members are correlated (Alexander, 1973; Birchler, 1972; Wills, Weiss, & Patterson, 1974). Moreover, reinforcement training appears to have some beneficial effects on marital, parent-child, and teacher-student relationships (Jacobson & Martin, 1976; Patterson, 1971), although the efficacy of behavioral approaches to marriage therapy has been vigorously disputed (Gurman & Kniskern, 1978; Gurman & Knudson, 1978).

Gottman (1979, 1982), who is best known for his research with married couples, is another author with a social learning foundation. Gottman suggests that distressed spouses reinforce a negative style of communication by reciprocating one another's negative messages and by failing to reciprocate positive messages. Research partially supports this idea. Gottman (1979) and Ting-Toomey (1983) found that incompatible couples are more likely than compatible couples to follow complaints with countercomplaints or defensive comments. Also, less compatible couples have been found to reciprocate hostile-dominant remarks (Billings, 1979) and negative utterances (Gottman, 1979; Gottman, Markman, & Notarius, 1977; Margolin & Wampold, 1981; Mettatal & Gottman, 1980; Pike & Sillars, 1985; Rubin, 1983) to a greater extent than more compatible couples. Each of these studies statistically controlled the effects of base rates in communication to ensure that the differences in reciprocity were over and above the tendency of distressed couples to be more negative in general. However, positive reciprocity has not been a consistent discriminator of compatible and incompatible couples. A few studies have even indicated that distressed couples had somewhat greater immediate reciprocity of positive affect (Gottman, 1979; Rubin, 1983), although nondistressed couples were more likely to reciprocate positive affect several acts later.

The research on affect is hard to interpret because causality is very ambiguous in most studies. Authors appear to assume that relationships become dissatisfying because a punishing, abusive style of communication permeates the conversation. However, the opposite interpretation—that communication patterns are caused by (not the cause of) relationship satisfaction—cannot be dismissed: People who are unhappy about their relationships are likely to be grim in their style of communication. Although causality is a thorny issue, it does seem safe to conclude that a process of "contagion" characterizes communication within incompatible relationships. In other words, complaints and bad feelings tend to elicit reciprocal behavior, therefore leading to escalation of conflict.

ENGAGEMENT AND AVOIDANCE

To repeat an earlier point, there is a strong cultural bias about openness in human relationships. Openness is presumed to be one of the cornerstones of personal and intimate relationships in contemporary American society (Katriel & Philipsen, 1981; Kidd, 1975). Widespread commitment to this view of close relationships makes it difficult to discuss conflict engagement and avoidance with the emotional detachment of, say, a soil scientist studying the chemical composition of nitrogen-based fertilizers. However, a social scientist must strive for some impartiality lest social science becomes merely a drab version of popular culture.

Academic publications tend to lean in one of two directions. Many follow the lead of the "classic" conflict theorists (Boulding, 1962; Coser, 1956; Deutsch, 1973; Simmel, 1955), who suggested that overt expression of conflict has many positive functions. For example, conflict may lead to adaptation, change, and revitalization; whereas suppression of conflict may cause an accumulation of tensions and make the eventual expression of conflict more explosive. At the opposite end of the spectrum, several authors have expressed skepticism about the unequivocal need for open communication in personal relationships (Aldous, 1977; Bochner, 1981; Gilbert, 1976; Kursh, 1971; Parks, 1981; Rawlins, 1983). For example, Parks (1981) refers to the persistent call for open communication as the "ideology of intimacy," suggesting that academics and professionals in the human relations disciplines have allowed their own personal and cultural preference for open communication to erode objectivity. The skeptics point out that the ideology of intimacy presents an unbalanced picture of personal relationships, one which stresses the importance of companionship, understanding, and sharing without emphasizing corresponding needs for privacy, mystery, and the occasional need to "let sleeping dogs lie."

Quite obviously there is a strong element of truth both in the classic theorists' admonitions about conflict avoidance and in the skeptics' criticisms of openness carried to an ideological extreme. Most conflicts are not resolved unless addressed at some point. However, some conflicts do go away eventually if left alone, and there are also subtle and indirect ways of working through conflicts, such as hinting and joking (see Sillars, 1980). Moreover, conflict engagement sometimes creates as many problems as it solves. Thus direct verbal disclosure is not prima facie the optimal pattern of conflict; the best method will be determined by such factors as the nature of the issue and the beliefs and values of individuals.

The relevant research literature has proceeded along two different paths. Many studies have examined complaints and satisfactions within relationships based on participants' self-reports, while a smaller number have directly observed the communication of couples engaging in conflict. The self-report studies are unequivocal. They indicate that a perceived lack of direct or clear communication is associated with general dissatisfaction in relationships. For example, complaints about the clarity and expressivity of the partner are among the most frequent expressed by married and cohabiting couples (Birchler, 1979; Cunningham, Braiker, & Kelley, 1982; Snyder, 1979). Distressed couples most often voice these complaints (Birchler, 1979). Further, marital satisfaction and adjustment are positively associated with reported self-disclosure and overall communication in the relationship (Burke, Weir, & Harrison, 1976; Hendrick, 1981; Levinger & Senn, 1967; Locke, Sabagh, & Thomas, 1957; Naravan, 1967; Snyder, 1979; see Gilbert, 1976; Waterman, 1979 for reviews). More compatible college roommates and married couples also report less avoidance of conflicts (Rands, Levinger, & Mellinger, 1981; Sillars, 1980).

Observational studies are not quite so clear. In these studies couples were recorded as they discussed relationship issues or acted out conflicts. Although satisfied married couples sometimes enact a *problem-solving* style of discussion, characterized by strings of descriptive and task-oriented remarks (Ting-Toomey, 1983), in some contexts they are more likely to adopt an avoidance style, consisting of topic shifts, jokes, denial of conflict, and abstract, ambivalent, or irrelevant comments (Pike & Sillars, 1985; Raush et al., 1974). Different subgroups appear to have their own preferred patterns for managing conflicts. Among satisfied couples there is at least one subgroup that manages conflict through an engagement style consisting of direct, noninflammatory disclosures and questions. Another subgroup of satisfied couples responds to conflict with avoidance (Raush et al., 1974; Sillars, Pike, Jones, & Redmon, 1983). These subgroups may be distinguished by their personal values. The engagement couples endorse an ideal of interdependence, openness, and sharing in marriage (according to self-report attitude measures), whereas the avoiding couples prefer greater autonomy and discretion (Sillars et al., 1983; see also Fitzpatrick, 1983).

Observational and self-report studies may not be as inconsistent as they initially appear because the two types of research evaluate different domains of conflict behavior. Self-report studies evaluate how people account for their relationships. These studies unequivocally show that most people regard open communication as an important aspect of healthy relationships and that people often attribute relationship problems to a lack of open or clear communication. On the other hand, behavioral studies evaluate how people perform conflict in the presence of an observer—the researcher, tape-recorder, or video camera. These studies present a more muddled picture of compatible relationships, in which maintenance of harmony may at least occasionally supersede the desire to confront and resolve conflicts.

SUMMARY

If we were to offer a definition of effective communication based on the preceding discussion of affect and engagement, it would go something like this: More competent individuals and dyads engage in reciprocal patterns of positive communication and avoid reciprocal patterns of negative and coercive communication; they utilize conflict when it arises as an opportunity for revitalization, problem solving, and reaffirmation of their relationship; however, they balance engagement and avoidance of conflict according to situational needs as well as their own personal standards and expectations.

As a summary of broad regularities in communication, our statement about effective communication is innocuous; however, as a blueprint for people to follow in conflict situations, it has objectionable qualities. For one thing, the phrase "situational needs as well as...personal standards" is exceedingly vague. Much work would be needed to give substance to this expression, particularly since most research on interpersonal communication has not considered alternative personal and cultural orientations to human relationships. In addition, any statement about competent or effective communication is implicitly a causal statement. Undoubtedly, communication has a causal impact on relationship satisfaction, but we doubt that causality is nearly as simple as it may seem from conflict research—that is, that more positive people have more positive relationships. Even simpleminded people should discern that critical, blaming, sarcastic, or coercive messages poison relationships, but nonetheless, people often fail to exercise appropriate control over patterns of communication. Reinforcement principles may provide some explanation for such seemingly irrational behavior; however, as Patterson (1971) points out, reinforcement is neither a necessary nor sufficient condition for the development of behavioral patterns, although it is a significant variable. Reinforcement principles may explain some aspects of spontaneous behavior in conflict, but unless we assume that people are ultimately blind and thoughtless, it is not apparent from reinforcement principles alone why individuals fail to recognize and to modify aversive patterns of communication.

To put the discussion of social skill in proper perspective, it is necessary to augment this discussion with a much greater appreciation of the factors that contextualize or "frame" a particular pattern of communication. When contextualizing influences are complex, communication skills are not as straightforward and self-evident as they may seem to a casual observer. We have mentioned culturally and socially based expectations as one type of contextualizing influence, and we take up the subject of cultural patterns later in the chapter. In addition, the level of ambiguity and confusion that often accompanies conflict helps to explain exactly why communication about conflict can be such a difficult event to manage. Conflict simply cannot be fully appreciated from a highly rational view of human behavior. Sometimes people lose control over conflict—not because they are naive, but because the process itself has disorderly and irrational elements.

THE ROLE OF AMBIGUITY, DISORDER, AND CONFUSION IN CONFLICT

The characteristic of conflict that is most difficult to capture in research is the chaos that pervades a heated argument or long-simmering conflict.

Private arguments do not necessarily conform to public standards of reasonableness, consistency, or relevance in argumentation because a dyad defines its own sense of "correct" or "appropriate" argument. Neither do conflicts necessarily follow conversational rules of topicality and order, because arguers are not required, like college debaters, to respond directly, specifically, and relevantly to the points raised by another person. In fact, a striking feature of intense interpersonal conflict is the disintegration of conventional patterns of conversation. As conflicts intensify, conversations become increasingly less orderly, clear, relevant, and goal-directed, and increasingly impulsive, emotional, and improvisational. Thus to the extent that conflicts are deep-seated and volatile, it is less useful to regard communication as an instrumental act designed to resolve focused issues and more appropriate to view communication as an expressive and relational event with ambiguous goals and consequences. Though any number of specific factors may account for the sense of ambiguity and disorder that occurs in conflict, we have focused on three: (1) the source of conflict, (2) the organizational complexity of conflict patterns, and (3) the embeddedness of conflict in daily activities.

CONFUSION OVER THE SOURCE OF CONFLICT

In some instances of interpersonal conflict a single focused issue is the source of conflict and both individuals have a clear understanding of their own goals. Presuming that both persons are somewhat flexible and their goals are reconcilable, the solution to this type of conflict is straightfoward. If the individuals openly discuss their motives, *integrative* solutions probably will emerge that satisfy both people and preserve the relationship (Pruitt & Lewis, 1977; Walton & McKersie, 1965). Pruitt and Lewis (p. 162) cite the following example:

> A married couple is trying to decide where to spend the husband's two weeks of vacation time. The husband prefers the mountains, and his wife the seashore. A possible compromise would be to divide the available time down the middle and spend one week in the mountains and one at the seashore. But there may be other, more integrative solutions. For example, with a little discussion, they may decide that two extra weeks of vacation is worth the income that would be lost if the husband took a leave of absence from his work. With four weeks, each can have the kind of vacation he (or she) wanted. Alternatively, in discussing the needs and values underlying their preferences, they may discover that the husband's main interest is fresh-water fishing while the wife's is swimming and sunbathing. This might lead them to search for a mountain resort on a lake or a seashore near a well-stocked stream.

Although the preceding example resembles many conflicts, it would be a mistake to think that all conflicts have such a clear structure. Serious relationship conflicts often do not focus on clear issues that can be isolated and deliberated (like an agenda item before the board of directors of a corporation). Relationship conflicts are more entangled, difficult to isolate, and impossible to define objectively. In many instances, two people will not share the same perception of the critical issue driving the conflict and this, itself, is a further cause of conflict. In fact, there are several potential areas of confusion: Both people may not perceive that a conflict exists; the individuals may perceive the conflict to be about two different matters; the individuals may attribute conflict to different causes; or the individuals may assign a different meaning to either person's behavior, including his or her attempts to communicate about the conflict.

One reason why people define issues differently is simply that relationships can embrace an enormous number and variety of issues, and people selectively focus on issues that are personally salient. One of the distinctive characteristics of close, personal relationships is that the breadth of potential topics is nearly exhaustive (Altman & Taylor, 1973; Knapp, 1984). A relationship may involve issues of work, money, family life, vacation time, sex, self-image, communication, affection, and so on. Invariably some topics are of greater concern to one individual than to another. For example, wives tend to report more problem areas in marriage and they report different types of problems than do husbands (Barry, 1970; Harvey, Wells, & Alvarez, 1978; Hicks & Platt, 1970; Scanzoni & Fox, 1980). Furthermore, neither husbands nor wives are generally aware of this discrepancy (Harvey et al., 1978). As a second illustration of the unequal salience of issues, divorced and separated individuals tend to provide simple, story-like accounts of their marriage that greatly oversimplify the likely causes of marital dissolution (Weiss, 1975). In some cases, husbands and wives from the same marriage construct accounts that do not even overlap (Weiss, 1975). Thus conflicts may begin on unequal footing, where the items on one person's agenda are entirely different from those on another's. Conflicts may even be fought merely to establish an issue on the agenda of a relationship.

A further reason for the ambiguity of conflict issues is the fact that different issues exist simultaneously at different levels of abstraction. Conflicts involving relatively focused "surface" issues may also implicitly involve abstract relationship issues (e.g., trust, mutuality, respect, or authority; see Miller & Steinberg, 1975). Following Watzlawick et al. (1967), messages have both content and relationship levels, with the latter being metacommunicative and therefore at a higher level of abstraction than the literal content of a message. Thus the relational level indicates how the rest of the message should be taken— for example, as an insult, command, or show of disrespect. In mild conflicts, there is a consensus about core relationship issues and the focus of conflict is primarily on content issues. There is a strong basis for resolution of such conflicts because the basic premises of each person are shared. More bitter and destructive conflicts, on the other hand, involve core relationship issues

(Altman & Taylor, 1973). Bitter relationship conflicts are especially complex because a vague sense of dissatisfaction over core relationship issues may have a rippling effect, creating conflict over many peripheral issues (Altman & Taylor, 1973). Thus conflicts over abstract relational issues, such as dominance, affection, or trust, are often acted out through explicit discussion of more concrete content issues (Hocker & Wilmot, 1985). For example, two people who argue in public about the choice of dinners at a Chinese restaurant may be implicitly arguing about who has the right to make decisions for the couple.

Relationship struggles are particularly insidious because people may lack the ability to metacommunicate effectively about their relationship. An inability to metacommunicate can result from two considerations discussed by Watzlawick et al. (1967). First, direct, verbal metacommunication is not always an adequate means for resolving relational conflicts, because the more trusted relational messages are analogic, nonverbal ones. This obervation is supported by Gottman's (1979) finding that distressed married couples spend much of their discussions verbally metacommunicating about their relationship without establishing agreement. Second, analogic forms of metacommunication are mostly imprecise. A particular tone of voice, for example, often admits many interpretations of a speaker's intent. Consequently, the same utterance may be variously seen as a compliment, verbal "jab," or good-natured joke.

The ambiguity of relational communication is readily illustrated by research. For example, the sender and receiver of messages tend to form different perceptions of relational communication because of their emotional involvement with the message, their respective focus of attention, and other factors (see Sillars & Scott, 1983). Specifically, relational communication tends to be seen more favorably (i.e., as more affectionate, disclosing, egalitarian, or cooperative)—by the source than by the receiver of messages (Dalusio, 1972; Fichten, 1978; Hawkins, Weisberg, & Ray, 1980; Sypher & Sypher, 1982; Thomas & Pondy, 1977; Zucker & Barron, 1971). Further, distressed married couples are particularly incongruent in their perceptions of messages, whereas satisfied couples are relatively congruent (Gottman et al., 1976; Kahn, 1970; Noller, 1980).

Thus serious relational conflicts are not comparable to conflicts over focused content issues. When there is a basic consensus at the relationship level and the source of conflict is focused and mutually understood, then communication is likely to have a straightforward, positive role in conflict. However, in important relational conflicts, the source of conflict is diffuse and selectively perceived. Attempts to communicate are therefore frustrated by a failure to agree on the definition of the conflict and by an inability to metacommunicate. In this respect, it can be misleading to generalize about effective communication from observations of highly compatible individuals, because communication is inherently easier when there is a strong foundation of consensus on fundamental perceptions of the relationship.

ORGANIZATIONAL COMPLEXITY

The ambiguity brought about by dissensus on fundamental relationship perceptions also affects conversational organization. Because relational conflicts involve abstract and relatively intangible issues, which are not easily isolated or objectified, it naturally follows that relational conflicts are difficult to discuss in an orderly and cooperative manner. Indeed, there is no transparent rule structure for carrying out relational conflict and this contributes to the sense of disorientation one gets from either being in or observing a personal argument.

Although conversation is described by many academics as an orderly, rule-governed activity (e.g., Craig & Tracy, 1983), it is far easier to describe the rule structure of casual conversation than to characterize the rules people follow to air disaffections or have an argument. Casual conversation is characterized by adherence to a set of cooperative principles that make the conversation intelligible and lend it a sense of coherence. Four such principles suggested by Grice (1975) are the maxims of quality ("be truthful"), quantity ("be succinct yet complete"), relation ("be relevant"), and manner ("be clear and orderly"). In competitive interactions these maxims are repeatedly violated because it may not be in each individual's self-interest to be truthful, complete, relevant, and clear. Ambiguous, incomplete, and irrelevant comments may be spoken to avoid incriminating oneself in a difficult situation (Bavelas, 1983; Eisenberg, 1984) or to disrupt another speaker's argument. Speakers may repeatedly shift the topic of conversation in a struggle to redefine the issue (Gottman, 1979). Comments from another person may also be ignored if the speaker does not want to state outright acceptance or rejection of the earlier message (Watzlawick et al., 1967). For all of these various reasons, interpersonal conflicts can assume disorderly properties bordering on the pathological. In fact, there have been frequent speculations that disorderly, unclear, and paradoxical communication is a characteristic of disturbed relationships (Riskin & Faunce, 1972; Watzlawick et al., 1967). On the other hand, "devious" communication can also be a natural human response to difficult, stressful, or paradoxical circumstances (Bavelas, 1983).

While it would be incorrect to say that relational conflicts have no structure, the structure is often difficult to discern. Recurring patterns may emerge in repeated episodes of conflict, but these patterns may be so variable and subtle that the participants themselves cannot easily or accurately describe them. This variable and dynamic quality of conflict can be seen in at least two areas: the presence of nonreciprocal patterns in more competitive conflicts, and shifting patterns of topical contingency.

Reciprocal and nonreciprocal patterns of conflict. Most research on the temporal organization of conflict treats conflict as a first-order process; that is, the basic unit of analysis is the relationship between an act and the preceding act within a conversation (Fisher, Glover, & Ellis, 1977; Hewes, 1979), as in the research on affect cited earlier. Further, conversations show substantial evidence of first-order structure, which is mostly of a reciprocal nature. For example, if a wife or husband begins a conversation with a message that avoids conflict, the spouse is most likely to follow with another avoidance message. Similarly, hostile or competitive statements tend to evoke a hostile or competitive response, supportive statements tend to evoke a supportive response, and so forth (Pike & Sillars, 1985).

However, the rule of reciprocity does not operate equally in all contexts. More hostile and expressive conflicts often have a dynamic quality characterized by oscillation between aggression and withdrawal, rather than the chaining of reciprocal exchanges as we would see in a mutually confirming interaction or a long, drawn-out relationship struggle. Nonreciprocal patterns are documented by at least three studies reporting alternating patterns of verbal aggression and withdrawal in less satisfied or harmonious marriages (Peterson, 1979; Pike & Sillars, 1985; Raush et al., 1974). For example, Pike and Sillars found that less satisfied couples were more likely to utter hostile and competitive remarks in all circumstances except when the spouse's preceding remark was verbally competitive, in which case they shifted to a conciliatory or avoidance style of conflict. This type of "hit-and-run" pattern may result from an underlying approach-avoidance conflict in which individuals experience simultaneous desires to lash out at the other person and, at the same time, to retain composure. The resulting pattern is "binding" for the individual actor because the prior buildup of bad feelings may cancel the positive impact that conciliatory messages might otherwise have. Further, since conciliatory behavior evokes hostility, each person must either become the abuser or the abused.

Variable patterns of topical contingency. The usual description of conflict as a first-order process assumes that each person's statement is a direct response to the preceding message. First-order structure is a simplifying assumption used by researchers who study conflict to render the description of conversation manageable. In some cases the assumption of first-order structure is a useful abstraction (e.g., when one wants to describe the reciprocity of positive and negative statements). On the other hand, the assumption of first-order structure, if viewed rigidly, can also blind observers to complex variations in conflict patterns. For example, the development of different topical issues in a conversation is often characterized more by variations in structure than by adherence to a particular first-order pattern. Speakers are likely to initiate, expand, terminate, and recycle issues without great regularity, in contrast to the continuity we would expect if people merely reacted to the preceding message. Variations in topical structure occur because reactions to another person are tempered and occasionally nullified by the speaker's own internal agenda, consisting of global or localized plans of argument. A plan may take the form of an internalized monologue that the individual wants to verbalize or an interactive "script," such as a series of questions and answers that are designed to confirm a premise of the initial speaker. Several different patterns of contingency may result from the interplay of individual plans and contingent reactions. Because the process can be exceedingly variable and either person only partly controls the flow of conversation, it is not necessarily easy for an individual to predict or control where a discussion will lead.

To illustrate the various forms of contingency occurring in conflicts, we have compiled a list of different ways a speaker may respond to the topical focus of earlier messages. The illustrations are from transcripts of marital conversations edited to increase anonymity and intelligibility. Some of these patterns are briefly described in another source (Trower, Bryant, & Argyle, 1978).

(1) *Reactive contingency* occurs when a speaker's message prompts a direct and immediate reaction, without significant change in the focus of conversation. Reactive contingency is present, for example, in simple request-refusal, assertion-denial, or assertion-support sequences. An extended example of reactive contingency may take the form of "primitive argument" (Jackson & Jacobs, 1980; Piaget, 1959), which is a process of simple alternation between opposing statements. For example:

A1:   You come home depressed every night.
B1:   I'm not depressed much.
A2:   You're depressed because you're unhappy with your boss.
B2:   I may be unhappy but I'm not depressed.
A3:   Well, it seems like you're depressed to me.

(2) *Mutual contingency* refers to a sequence in which each person reacts to the other but also attempts to carry out a plan, giving rise to a partial, first-order process. An extended, mutually contingent pattern will reflect a series of "progressive holding moves" (Goldberg, 1983), which refer directly to the preceding statement but expand the focus of conversation,[1] as in the following example:

A1:   We're not ever together.
B1:   Well, in the evenings, working the shift I work, we can't be together; I think we spend more time now than when we were first married.
A2:   Yes, but during the week, if I want to go somewhere we can't go together.
B2:   I have to work nights. I can't be there.
A3:   You didn't have to work nights. That was your own decision.
B3:   I did it for a reason. I get a better job, a raise. and more security. We're both better off.
A4:   Does that mean that you like not seeing me anymore?
B4:   No, I don't like it! But until some things change, that's the way it has to be.

(3) *Asymmetric contingency* occurs when one speaker carries out a plan while the other speaker reacts. Asymmetric contingency patterns often involve

interactive scripts controlled and disguised by the initial speaker. For example, Jackson and Jacobs (1980) describe "presequences" in arguments, in which an initial question or request is used to "set up" the listener by lowering anticipated objections to a later argument or request. In the discussion that follows, Person A's ultimate point is not explicitly stated until the last utterance, after a series of leading questions:

A1: Do you want to go back to gambling?
B1: No. I like it but I'm not going back to it.
A2: Why?
B2: Well, I have obligations now.
A3: And you see those obligations as more important than gambling?
B3: Right.
A4: You don't think there's anything that could cause you to go back to that again?
B4: I don't think so.
A5: You're not sure, are you?
B5: I'm pretty sure. As a matter of fact I'll say I am sure.
A6: I don't want you going to horse races anymore.

(4) *Pseudo-contingency* occurs when the remarks of two speakers are coordinated primarily in terms of timing and "licensing" behaviors that acknowledge the preceding message in order to show topic coherence, although the speech is mostly preplanned. For example, in the following conversation, the first statement by Person B and the second statement by Person A begin with a reference to the preceding statement, but then the focus of the statement shifts dramatically:

A1. We've never ever really gone to bed mad. But I've got a temper, and when I get mad, I get mad. Once I get it all out I forget it.
B1. Your temper is not as bad as your pouting. Sometimes if something's wrong I have to drag it out of you. You just don't want to talk about it, or you just would rather sit and not discuss it.
A2. I don't like to talk sometimes and maybe I should. Once in awhile I don't like some of your ideas because you take more time to think about things. I think I'm freer because when I get the idea that I'm going to do something I just pursue it. I don't really think about it as much as you do.

(5) *Noncontingent reactions* consist of alternating preplanned comments (a zero-order process). Statements do not acknowledge preceding statements, although there may be continuity in the general topic of conversation. Noncontingent patterns may take the form of *disconfirmation* messages, where a speaker ignores the preceding message rather than expressing outright disagreement (see Cissna & Sieburg, 1981). For example, the second speaker disconfirms the first in the following exchange:

A1: You come home from work and you're all upset. You take it all out on me. You just turn away from me and...

B1:   [interrupts] There's a lot of pressure anymore. No wonder people are not living to be very old. They start worrying as soon as they get old enough to walk and they worry until the day that they die.

A2:   They worry but they don't take it out on...

B2:   [interrupts] It's always been that way. You're always going to have worries about whether you have enough money to do this, to go there, or the house payment's due, the electric bill is due. There's always something. Money for this! Money for that! Always something.

(6) *Delayed contingency* occurs when a speaker reacts to a message or event that took place several speaking turns or more earlier. In some cases the time element involved in delayed contingency can take on ridiculous proportions, thereby adding to the ambiguity of the sequence. A statement may be a response to something that was said an hour ago, yesterday, last week, or even earlier. The following example is from the same couple who spoke of gambling (see the conversation illustrating asymmetric contingency). About 60 speaking turns later the discussion returns to the earlier topic:

A1:   I feel like you're ignoring the real issue.

B1:   I'm not ignoring anything.

A2:   Can't we just give our marriage a fresh start? I mean, I could get really upset thinking about the money you threw away at the race tracks. I could think of a lot better things to do with money than throw it away.

A regular, first-order process is a characteristic of more predictable conversations. Predictability of the response enables each speaker, in his or her own turn, to exercise greater control over the path of the conversation because the partner's response may be anticipated. However, the sequence may become rigid (i.e., overly predictable), as is the case when one critical or domineering message invariably leads to a similar message and sets off a struggle for control in the relationship (Rogers & Millar, 1980; Watzlawick et al., 1967). Conversely, the sequence may become chaotic or difficult to predict because the individuals do not abide by the cooperative maxims and protocols of polite conversation. Intense relationship conflicts appear to be characterized by both rigid and chaotic patterns (see Olson & McCubbin, 1983), but rigidity in communication is the more frequently discussed topic in the communication literature.

A chaotic sequence is present when the pattern of contingency shifts throughout a conversation. Our intuitive sense from studying interpersonal and marital conflicts is that a rapid alternation of message patterns is often found in intense arguments, whereas mild conversations tend to be more regular and predictable. When the plans of two speakers conflict there is often a struggle to redefine the focus of conversation on each individual's own terms, and this may result in frequent phasic shifts between different patterns of contingency. Thus more intense conflicts naturally tend to be less coherent or predictable and less easily controlled.

EMBEDDEDNESS OF CONFLICT

Disorganization of conflict is also related to disorganization in the context of conflict. The context of interpersonal conflict is quite chaotic by comparison with formal means of interacting, such as formal negotiation and decision making. In formal bargaining, a time and place is set aside for conflicts to be resolved, and formal notice of demands, concessions, and conditions is provided by individuals who are specifically recognized as negotiators, mediators, or arbitrators. This version of conflict, which is self-conscious, highly controlled, and explicitly announced, is very uncharacteristic of conflicts occurring in personal relationships. Interpersonal conflicts generally do not have such a formal structure until they reach a desperate stage at which the services of therapists, mediators, or legal representatives are sought.

There are, in fact, no definite boundaries on interpersonal conflict. Conflicts occur at all hours of day and night, on any occasion, during any activity, for any number of different reasons. There is often a large surprise element in conflict for both parties involved; neither person necessarily anticipates having conflict at a particular moment and conflict may not be recognized as such until after it has occurred. Interpersonal conflict, therefore, is often a retrospective activity, something that is not anticipated and that may seem to be understandable and predictable only after the fact (Hawes & Smith, 1973).

The "surprise" factor in conflict is accounted for by the embeddedness of conflict in daily activities (Weick, 1971). People usually do not set aside a special time on their schedule for airing grievances; families who subscribe to the concept of the "family council" are an exception. Rather, conflicts hitchhike on other events. People have conflict over dinner, while on vacation, and when trying to get the kids off to school in the morning. Further, grievances are more likely to be felt when events in the situation are absorbing and stressful—for example, when the car repeatedly stalls or the checkbook doesn't balance—rather than during a lull in the action. Because conflicts tend to be initiated and terminated according to the flow of other activities, there is a carry-over factor. An issue may come up repeatedly but never be discussed at length on a single occasion, thereby adding to a backlog of unfinished business (Weick, 1971).

SUMMARY

To say that ambiguity and disorder play an important role in interpersonal conflict is not to say that the process is entirely irrational or that people utterly lack control over their destinies. Nonetheless, some conflicts are inherently more difficult to manage than others; and, in this respect, the communication "skills" demonstrated by extremely compatible individuals are not necessarily illuminating. When people have a high degree of congruence in their perceptions and expectations of a relationship, then the process of communication is naturally more orderly and transparent. This is a qualitatively different type of situation than that which occurs when people have important disagreements about core issues and basic perceptions of a relationship. The latter type of situation is not easily rectified by simple, formulaic prescriptive models of communication because conflict becomes a difficult thing for two people to mutually define, label, and predict.

ALTERNATIVE CULTURAL VIEWS OF RELATIONSHIPS

It goes without saying that all individuals cannot be understood from a single cultural frame of reference. As Hocker and Wilmot (1985) point out, conflict management often requires an appreciation of different logical systems. Yet, when individuals speak of exercising communication skills, they invariably have an American, middle-class, white-collar, mainstream cultural view of interpersonal relationships in mind. Even individuals who study cultural differences in family and interpersonal relationships often have their own cultural ax to grind—for example, one gets the impression that there are no healthy or happy blue-collar families.

In this section we explore two main characteristics of interpersonal relationships that help to differentiate the interpretations of conflict held by various cultural and subcultural groups. These characteristics are, first, the emphasis placed on expressive communication, and second, the interrelated concerns of privacy and individuality. The purpose of this section is not to stereotype any particular cultural group but rather to illustrate the diversity of culturally based expectations for interpersonal and family conflict that exists in society. Failure to recognize social and cultural diversity can easily lead to the assumption that subcultural groups are inept at managing interpersonal conflict.

EXPRESSIVITY

Few distinctive subcultural groups existing in American society match the emphasis placed on explicit negotiation of conflict that is characteristic of mainstream American culture. An exception to this may be the Jewish family. Jews often place such a high value on discussion and analysis of problems that they can appear argumentative by mainstream cultural standards. In fact, McGoldrick (1982) reports that the preferred Jewish style of communication is sometimes taken for verbal aggression by non-Jewish family therapists. Other ethnic, social, and national groups appear indirect or evasive when compared with the mainstream American ideal. To give just a few examples, Native American and Black American males may regard deep personal feelings as too personal to express openly (Attneave, 1982; McGoldrick, 1982; Pinderhughes, 1982). Studies of working-class families also describe the inexpressive male (Komarovsky, 1962; Rubin, 1976; Safilio-Rothschild, 1969). Comparing British, Australian, and American clients, three international therapists (Breulin, Cornwall, & Cade, 1983) describe the British as the most reserved, least disclosive, and least expressive of affect, although both British and Australian clients maintain emotional distance and avoid public displays of affect. Irish-Americans, on the other hand, are thought to emphasize expressivity of a different sort. McGoldrick (1982), in commenting about Irish clients seen during family therapy, suggests that Irish families avoid direct verbal confrontation, preferring instead to deal with conflicts indirectly, through sarcasm, innuendo, and allusion. Finally, a comparative study (Kumagai & Straus, 1983) of marital conflict tactics in three countries revealed that Americans were the most expressive, Japanese the most reserved, and Indians the least violent. Much has been made of the limited expression of conflict in Japanese society in comparison with Western countries, although the norms of harmony appear to operate much more strongly in public situations than in private interactions involving family members or close friends (Krauss, Rohlen, & Steinhoff, 1984; Lebra, 1984; Nishiyama, 1971; Niyekawa, 1984; Saito, 1982).

The mainstream American expressive ideal cannot be transplanted to other cultural and subcultural contexts for at least two reasons. First, the values of some groups are incongruent with individualistic disclosures. For example, less expressive groups may hold a stoic attitude that life's problems are to be met with a certain degree of resignation and endurance. This seems to be true of West Indians (Brice, 1982), Scandinavians (McGoldrick, 1982), Irish-Americans (McGoldrick, 1982), and Blacks (Hines & Boyd-Franklin, 1982). Blue-collar families also exhibit this stoicism and resignation. Problems experienced in working-class families are often perceived as lying outside the family and within the realm of natural economic, social, and biological conditions that are futile for the family to address (Komarovsky, 1962; Rubin, 1976). Thus working-class families may adopt a passive problem-solving style that emphasizes family cohesion over active problem solving (McCleod & Chaffee, 1972; Reiss, 1971).

Although the passive or stoic attitude of working-class and ethnic families is sometimes seen as a negative trait, we found in two recent studies that satisfied married couples often demonstrated an attitude of stoicism in their discussion of marital conflict issues, whereas less satisfied couples were more likely to become mired in extended conversations about individual personalities and marital roles (Sillars, Weisberg, Burggraf, & Wilson, in press). Thus the stoic values of some groups may facilitate conflict management, even though these values mitigate against explicit discussion and negotiation of conflict issues.

A second reason why the expressive ideal is inappropriate in some cultural contexts is that cultures differ generally in their relative emphasis on explicit verbal codification of information. In so called high-context cultures, including many of the Mediterranean, African, Asian, Native American, and South American cultures, subtle and implicit elements of the physical, historical, and social context are assigned a great deal of communicative significance (Hall, 1977; Ting-Toomey, 1985). Relatively less information is explicitly codified in the form of spoken or written messages within high-context cultures, as opposed to low-context cultures such as the United States, Canada, and northern Europe. Gudykunst and Kim (1984) note a similar tendency for blue-collar families to emphasize implicit meaning, whereas white-collar families are more verbal (see also Bernstein, 1971). Because low-context cultures derive important meaning from subtle and implicit cues, indirect and nonconfrontational messages about conflict may have a transparent meaning within the culture. For example, Lebra (1984) found that the Japanese use a number of nondirect and nonexplicit conflict tactics (e.g., anticipatory management of conflict before it arises, silence, and communication through a third party) that are clearly understood within the culture as conflict management maneuvers. Similarly, Ouchi (1981) observed that techniques of management control within Japanese companies may be so subtle as to appear nonexistent to Westerners. Explicit communication about conflict is avoided within high-context cultures because conflicts are seen as intrinsically personal and emotional rather than as instrumental issues that can be intellectually separated from the relationship existing between the principal parties (Ting-Toomey, 1985). Consequently, the emphasis on indirectness and discretion normally found in high-context cultures is necessary to maintain harmony and preserve interpersonal relationships.

PRIVACY AND INDIVIDUALITY

Privacy and individuality are closely linked. Relationships that are more private (i.e., autonomous from friends, relatives, and the larger society), also tend to emphasize individuality. Conversely, when there is extensive participation in intimate relationships from extended family or other members of the community, relationships reflect communal standards promoting harmony and preserving tradition (Bott, 1971; Gadlin, 1977). In the mainstream American ideal, intimate relationships are highly autonomous from the community (Swidler, 1980). The dyad (or immediate family) jealously protects its sovereignty over relationship issues. Unsolicited advice from outsiders, even grandparents, may be seen as interference with the private affairs of a relationship. Privacy is emphasized mostly among the middle class and among residents of highly mobile communities (Bott, 1971). On the other hand, extensive kin and friendship networks are maintained in working-class families, many ethnic families, and in stable communities with low population mobility, such as rural communities (Bott, 1971; Brice, 1982; Hines & Boyd-Franklin, 1982; Lee, 1980; McGoldrick, 1982; Niyekawa, 1984; Richards, 1980).

Both private and extended network relationships have tradeoffs. Because of the public nature of relationships in extended families, individual spouses have less opportunity to influence each other uniquely (Richards, 1980). Therefore, extended families are more likely to be conformist (Cohler & Geyer, 1982) and to encourage traditional sex-role segregation (Bott, 1971; Richards, 1980; Spiegel, 1982), and they are less companionate and less introspective about family and interpersonal relationships (Bott, 1971; Komarovsky, 1982; Richards, 1980). Although most readers will see these characteristics as undesirable, the homogenizing influence of the extended network also has a functional side. Extended network families are likely to have greater agreement about attitudes and values (Cohler & Geyer, 1982), and their relationships are often more stable and subjectively satisfying (Hicks & Platt, 1970; Lewis & Spanier, 1979). Because extended networks promote communal and traditional norms, there are more definite guidelines for resolving conflicts. Also, in extended network families, the social and kinship network is an important source of intimate companionship (Argyle & Furnham, 1983), guidance, protection (Falicov, 1982), and instrumental support; for example, family members may provide occasional child care and lend support during crises.

Whereas conflicts in private relationships are resolved through interpersonal communication, extended network families may utilize forms of third-party mediation. The influence of the extended network as a third-party mediator helps to stabilize and moderate perceptions, thereby counteracting the usual erosion of consensus in conflict situations. For example, in Japanese families, interpersonal problems are often resolved by the intervention of friends and relatives rather than by the action of the parties themselves (Niyekawa, 1984).

Extended families may also diffuse conflicts by emphasizing the well-being of the larger group over individual self-interests. In contrast to the middle-class, mainstream emphasis on self-fulfillment, many ethnic and working-class families stress the communal aspects of life at the expense of the individual. Groups such as Native Americans (Attneave, 1982), West Indians (Brice, 1982), Africans (Pinderhughes, 1982), Asians (Kumgai & Straus, 1983; Staples & Mirande, 1980), Mexicans (Falicov, 1982), Japanese (Niyekawa, 1984), and Catholics and Mormons (Fisher, Giblin, & Hoopes, 1982) stress interdependence, cooperation, and affiliation. Unique individual needs, preferences, or complaints may be less a focus of these groups than in cultural groups with a greater emphasis on individuality. For example, Attneave (1982) describes the reliance of Native American and Native Alaskan groups on true consensus as a decision-making style. In tribal meetings, discussion is expected to lead to absolute consensus, a method that assumes limited conflict and subordination of individual to group goals. Members who continually refuse to agree with others are eventually ostracized (Attneave, 1982). In the Japanese business community, consensus marks the final decision to emerge from a group. Proposals are circulated and discussed until everyone concerned is willing to sign on to accept both the praise and the blame (Nishiyama, 1971). In contrast, the mainstream American cultural ideal is that people should "agree to disagree" (Miller, Nunnally, & Wackman, 1975) because absolute consensus is seen as an impractical and even undesirable goal.

SUMMARY

When a single cultural standard is used to evaluate interpersonal communication, many cultural groups are made to appear inadequate in one respect or another. Jews may seem argumentative; West Indians, Native Americans, and Scandanavians inexpressive; and the Irish or Japanese indirect and unclear. Blue-collar families and many ethnic families may seem to lack true intimacy because of the intrusion of extended family and friends into the private affairs of a relationship. These relationships may also appear rigid because of a reliance on tradition and a passive problem-solving style. However, from alternative value orientations, working-class and ethnic relationships do not seem nearly so dreary. Some interpersonal conflicts are minimized by the value structure and support system of ethnic, religious, and working-class groups, and other conflicts may be worked through indirectly, without explicit confrontation. The diversity of social and cultural orientations toward interpersonal conflict is an especially thorny matter for a behavioral skills approach to interpersonal communication. Conflict management strategies are implicitly seen from such a perspective as having the same functional impact in different cultural contexts. Clearly, the number of different conflict strategies that are functional in some context is considerably more varied than the social skills metaphor suggests.

SOCIAL SKILL RECONSIDERED

Scientists in every discipline employ metaphors or analogies that help to conceptualize an area and that focus attention on specific research questions (Hawes, 1975; Kaplan, 1964). In the literature on interpersonal communication and conflict, social scientists have largely relied on a skill metaphor: Interpersonal communication is viewed as behavioral techniques and strategies that either enhance or diminish the quality of interpersonal relationships. Specific "skills" include clear, consistent, direct, supportive, focused, and reciprocal communication. Interpersonal relationships plagued by destructive conflict are thought to reflect deficits in one or more of the important communication skills. The skill metaphor has tremendous intuitive appeal, for it is also a dominant cultural interpretation of interpersonal relationships. Also, the skill metaphor has an appealing, pragmatic quality because it appears to target concrete ways of improving communication and managing interpersonal conflict productively.

Nevertheless, the skill metaphor may not be the most useful heuristic for research on interpersonal conflict. Research modeled on the skill metaphor has focused substantially on the behavioral differences of communication in compatible and incompatible relationships. This research has been carried out in the interests of identifying communication skills demonstrated by compatible individuals and skill deficits shown by incompatible parties. A major limitation is that it treats communication about conflict as if it were qualitatively the same phenomenon in compatible and incompatible relationships. In many cases it is not, because the intense relationship conflicts of incompatible relations are inherently more difficult to discuss and resolve than conflicts over focused content issues, the latter being more characteristic of conflicts in very compatible relationships. The research literature on compatible and incompatible relationships also fosters the impression that both relationship types are homogeneous subgroups. Much more attention is directed toward the normal or average tendencies of these groups than to the range of variation among either compatible or incompatible individuals. Consequently, the research does not call attention to the various alternative conflict strategies used by compatible individuals in accordance with their own personal values and expectations. Because of both limitations, research stemming from a skills perspective generally appears to suggest absolute standards for effective communication that are applicable only to idealized and culturally homogeneous examples of conflict.

In our discussion, we have proposed two alternative ways of looking at conflict: First, conflict may be seen as a relational process with an ambiguous and improvisational structure; second, conflict may be seen as a culturally defined and regulated event. Although we have discussed both ideas in the context of criticizing a skills perspective on conflict, the alternatives are not intrinsically opposed to a skills approach. It is possible to reconcile both relational and cultural perspectives on conflict with a social skills model, given that social skill is not identified with an absolute standard for behavior. Social skill is best indicated by a person's adaptation to his or her situation, not by the ability to produce "competent" messages in some absolute sense. This suggests that more attention should be paid to the full range of alternative strategies used to manage conflicts (including implicit, indirect, and noncommunicative strategies) and to the factors that contextualize the use of a given strategy. For example, scant attention has been devoted to such basic human tendencies as joking and equivocation in the face of conflict, although both represent important management strategies (see Eisenberg, 1984; Weick, 1971).

The inherent ambiguities of relational communication and the corresponding difficulties of mutually defining and discussing abstract relationship issues are widely noted topics in the conflict literature, but researchers have not seriously wrestled with the significance of these concepts for studying the effects of interpersonal communication. A relational perspective calls for more attention to the role of implicit communication and to the complex organizational qualities of hostile and expressive conflicts. Finally, there is also little mention in the conflict literature of the significance attributed to explicit communication about conflict by individuals of various social or ethnic groups or to other important subjective dimensions of conflict, including: (1) the extent to which a particular group or dyad legitimizes an impulsive style of conflict over a more deliberate, carefully controlled process; (2) the extent to which conflict is seen as expressive or cathartic versus instrumental; or (3) the tolerance of expressive conflict within different dyads, families, organizations, and cultures. These norms may largely determine what type and level of conflict engagement is desirable or practical in a given social context.

NOTE

1. Goldberg (1983, p. 34) defines a progressive holding move as an utterance that "shares some of the referents as its prior locution while expanding or adding new referents not contained therein." Given this definition, many examples of reactive contingency and noncontingent patterns also represent progressive holding moves; however, in these examples there is only minimal expansion or overlap with the preceding message.

REFERENCES

Aldous, J. (1977). Family interaction patterns. *Annual Review of Sociology, 3,* 105-135.
Alexander, J. F. (1973). Defensive and supportive communication in family systems. *Journal of Marriage and the Family, 35,* 223-231.
Altman, I., & Taylor, D. (1973). *Social penetration.* New York: Holt, Rinehart & Winston.
Argyle, N., & Furnham, A. (1983). Sources of satisfaction and conflict in long-term relationships. *Journal of Marriage and the Family, 45,* 481-493.
Attneave, C. (1982). American Indians and Alaska native families: Emigrants in their own homeland. In M. McGoldrick, J. K. Pearce, & J. Giordano (Eds.), *Ethnicity and family therapy* (pp. 55-83). New York: Guilford Press.
Azrin, N. H., Naster, B. J., & Jones, R. (1973). Reciprocity counseling. *Behavior Research and Therapy, 11,* 365-382.
Barry, W. A. (1970). Marriage research and conflict: An integrative review. *Psychological Bulletin, 73,* 41-54.
Bateson, G. (1951). Information and codification. In J. Reusch & G. Bateson, *Communication: The social matrix of psychiatry* (pp. 168-211). New York: Norton.

Bavelas, J. B. (1983). Situations that lead to disqualification. *Human Communication Research, 9,* 130-145.

Beier, E. G., & Steinberg, D. P. (1977). Subtle cues between newlyweds. *Journal of Communication, 27,* 92-97.

Bernstein, B. (1971). *Class, codes and control.* Boston: Routledge & Kegan Paul.

Billings, A. (1979). Conflict resolution in distressed and nondistressed married couples. *Journal of Consulting and Clinical Psychology, 47,* 368-376.

Birchler, G. R. (1972). *Differential patterns of instrumental affiliative behavior as a function of degree of marital distress and level of intimacy.* Unpublished doctoral dissertation, University of Oregon.

Birchler, G. R. (1979). Communication skills in married couples. In A.S. Bellack & M. Hersen (Eds.), *Research and practice in social skills training* (pp. 273-315). New York: Plenum Press.

Bochner, A. P. (1981). On the efficacy of openness in close relationships. In M. Burgoon (Ed.), *Communication yearbook 5* (pp. 109-124). New Brunswick, NJ: Transaction Books.

Bott, E. (1971). *Family and social network.* New York: Free Press.

Boulding, K. E. (1962). *Conflict and defense: A general theory.* New York: Harper & Row.

Breulin, D., Cornwall, M., & Cade, B. (1983). International trade in family therapy: Parallels between societal and therapeutic values. In C. J. Falicov (Ed.), *Cultural perspectives in family therapy* (pp. 91-107). Rockville, MD: Aspen Publications.

Brice, J. (1982). West Indian families. In M. McGoldrick, J. K. Pearce, & J. Giordano (Eds.), *Ethnicity and family therapy* (pp. 123-133). New York: Guilford Press.

Burke, R. J., Weir, T., & Harrison, D. (1976). Disclosure of problems and tensions experienced by marital partners. *Psychological Reports, 2,* 531-542.

Cissna, K.N.L., & Sieburg, E. (1981). Patterns of interactional confirmation and disconfirmation. In C. Wilder-Mott & J. H. Weakland (Eds.), *Rigor and imagination: Essays from the legacy of Gregory Bateson* (pp. 253-282). New York: Praeger.

Cohler, B., & Geyer, S. (1982). Psychological autonomy and interdependence within the family. In F. Walsh (Ed.), *Normal family processes* (pp. 186-228). New York: Guidion.

Coser, L. A. (1956). *The functions of social conflict.* London: Free Press.

Craig, R. T., & Tracy, K. (Eds.). (1983). *Conversational coherence: Form, structure, and strategy.* Newbury Park, CA: Sage.

Cunningham, J., Braiker, H., & Kelley, H. (1982). Marital status and sex differences in problems reported by married and cohabiting couples. *Psychology of Women Quarterly, 6,* 415-427.

Cushman, D., & Whiting, G. (1972). An approach to communication theory: Toward consensus on rules. *Journal of Communication, 22,* 217-238.

Dalusio, V. E. (1972). *Self-disclosure and perceptions of that self-disclosure between parents and their teenage children.* Unpublished doctoral dissertation, American International University.

Deetz, S. (1981). *Interpretive research in intercultural communication: Metaphor analysis as an example.* Paper presented at the annual meeting of the Speech Communication Association, Anaheim, CA.

Deutsch, M. (1973). *The resolution of conflict: Constructive and destructive processes.* New Haven, CT: Yale University Press.

Eisenberg, E. M. (1984). Ambiguity as strategy in organizational communication. *Communication Monographs, 51,* 227-242.

Falicov, C. J. (1982). Mexican families. In M. McGoldrick, J.K. Pearce, & J. Giordano (Eds.), *Ethnicity and family therapy* (pp. 134-163). New York: Guilford Press.

Fichten, C. M. (1978). *Videotape and verbal feedback: Effects on behavior and attributions in distressed couples.* Unpublished doctoral dissertation, McGill University, Toronto.

Fisher, B.A., Glover, T. & Ellis, D. G. (1977). The nature of complex communication systems. *Communication Monographs, 44,* 230-240.

Fisher, B. L., Giblin, P. R., & Hoopes, M. H. (1982). Healthy family functioning: What therapists say and what families want. *Journal of Marital and Family Therapy, 8,* 273-284.

Fitzpatrick, M.A. (1983). Predicting couples' communication from couples' self-reports. In R. Bostrom (Ed.), *Communication yearbook 7* (pp. 49-82). Newbury Park, CA: Sage.

Folger, J. P., & Poole, M. S. (1984). *Working through conflict: A communication perspective.* Glenview, IL: Scott, Foresman.

Gadlin, H. (1977). Private lives and public order: A critical view of the history of intimate relations in the United States. In G. Levinger & H. Raush (Eds.), *Close relationships: Perspectives on the meaning of intimacy* (pp. 33-72). Amherst: University of Massachusetts Press.

Gilbert, S. (1976). Self disclosure, intimacy, and communication in families. *Family Coordinator, 25,* 197-215.

Goldberg, J. A. (1983). A move toward describing conversational coherence. In R. T. Craig & K. Tracy (Eds.), *Conversational coherence: Form, structure and strategy* (pp. 25-45). Newbury Park, CA: Sage.

Gottman, J. (1979). *Marital interaction: Experimental investigations.* New York: Academic Press.

Gottman, J. (1982). Temporal form: Toward a new language for describing relationships. *Journal of Marriage and the Family, 44,* 943-962.

Gottman, J., Markman, H., & Notarius, C. (1977). The topography of marital conflict: A study of verbal and nonverbal behavior. *Journal of Marriage and the Family, 39,* 461-477.

Gottman, J., Notarius, C., Markman H., Bank, S., Yoppi, B., & Rubin, M. E. (1976). Behavior exchange theory and marital decision making. *Journal of Personality and Social Psychology, 34,* 14-23.

Grice, H. P. (1975). Logic and conversation. In. P. Cole & J. L. Morgan (Eds.), *Syntax and semantics, vol. 3: Speech acts* (pp. 41-58). New York: Academic Press.

Gudykunst, W. B., & Kim, Y. Y. (Eds.). (1984). *Communicating with strangers: An approach to intercultural communication.* Reading, MA: Addison-Wesley.

Gurman, A. S., & Kniskern, D. P. (1978). Behavioral marriage therapy: II. Empirical perspective. *Family Process, 17,* 139-148.

Gurman, A. S., & Knudson, R. M. (1978). Behavioral marriage therapy: I. A psychodynamic systems analysis and critique. *Family Process, 17,* 121-138.

Hall, E. T. (1977). *Beyond culture.* Garden City, NY: Anchor.

Harvey, J. H., Wells, G. L., & Alvarez, M. D. (1978) Attribution in the context of conflict and separation in close relationships. In J. H. Harvey, W. J. Ickes, & R. F. Kidd (Eds.), *New directions in attribution research* (Vol. 2, pp. 236-260). Hillsdale, NJ: Lawrence Erlbaum.

Hawes, L. C. (1975). *Pragmatics of analoguing: Theory and model construction in communication.* Reading, MA: Addison-Wesley.

Hawes, L. C., & Smith, D. (1973). A critique of assumptions underlying the study of communication in conflict. *Quarterly Journal of Speech, 59,* 423-435.

Hawkins, J. L., Weisberg, C., & Ray, D. W. (1980). Spouse differences in communication style: Preference, perception, and behavior. *Journal of Marriage and the Family, 42,* 585-593.

Hendrick, S. S. (1981). Self-disclosure and marital satisfaction. *Journal of Personality and Social Psychology, 40,* 1150-1159.

Hewes, D. E. (1979). The sequential analysis of social interaction. *Quarterly Journal of Speech, 65,* 56-73.

Hicks, M. W., & Platt, M. (1970). Marital happiness and stability: A review of research in the sixties. *Journal of Marriage and the Family, 32,* 553-574.

Hines, P. M., & Boyd-Franklin, N. (1982). Black families. In M. McGoldrick, J. K. Pearce, & J. Giordano (Eds.), *Ethnicity and family therapy* (pp. 84-107). New York: Guilford Press.

Hocker, J. L., & Wilmot, W. W. (1985). *Interpersonal conflict* (2nd ed.). Dubuque, IA: William C. Brown.

Jackson, S., & Jacobs, S. (1980). Structure of conversational argument: Pragmatic bases for the enthymeme. *Quarterly Journal of Speech, 66,* 251-265.

Jacobson, N. S., & Martin, B. (1976). Behavioral marriage therapy: Current status. *Psychological Bulletin, 83,* 540-556.

Johnson, D. W. (1974). Communication and the inducement of cooperative behavior in conflicts: A critical review. *Speech Monographs, 41,* 64-78.

Kahn, M. (1970). Nonverbal communication and marital satisfaction. *Family Process, 9,* 449-456.

Kaplan, A. (1964). *The conduct of inquiry: Methodology for behavioral science.* San Francisco: Chandler.

Katriel, T., & Philipsen, G. (1981). "What we need is communication": "Communication" as a cultural category in some American speech. *Communication Monographs, 48,* 301-317.

Kidd, V. (1975). Happily ever after and other relationship styles: Advice on interpersonal relations in popular magazines, 1951-1973. *Quarterly Journal of Speech, 61,* 31-39.

Knapp, M. L. (1984). *Interpersonal communication and human relationships.* Newton, MA: Allyn and Bacon.

Komarovsky, M. (1962). *Blue-collar marriage.* New York: Random House.

Krauss, E. S., Rohlen, T. P., & Steinhoff, P. G. (1984). Conflict: An approach to the study of Japan. In E. S. Krauss, T. P. Rohlen, & P. G. Steinhoff (Eds.), *Conflict in Japan* (pp. 3-15). Honolulu: University of Hawaii Press.

Kumagai, F., & Straus, M. A. (1983). Conflict resolution tactics in Japan, India and the U.S.A. *Journal of Comparative Family Studies, 14,* 377-392.

Kursh, C. O. (1971). The benefits of poor communication. *Psychoanalytic Review, 58,* 189-208.

Lebra, T. S. (1984). Nonconfrontational strategies for management of interpersonal conflicts. In E. S. Krauss, T. P. Rohlen, & P. G. Steinhoff (Eds.), *Conflict in Japan* (pp. 41-60). Honolulu: University of Hawaii Press.

Lederer, W. J., & Jackson, D. D. (1968). *The mirages of marriage.* New York: Norton.

Lee, G. R. (1980). Kinship in the seventies: A decade review of research and theory. *Journal of Marriage and the Family, 42,* 923-934.

Levinger, G., & Senn, D. J. (1967). Disclosure of feelings in marriage. *Merrill Palmer Quarterly, 13,* 237-249.

Lewis, R. S., & Spanier, G. B. (1979). Theorizing about the quality and stability of marriage. In W. R. Burr, R. Hill, F. I. Nye, & I. L. Reiss (Eds.), *Contemporary theories about the family* (Vol. 1, pp. 268-294). New York: Free Press.

Locke, H. J., Sabagh, G., & Thomas, M. M. (1957). Interfaith marriages. *Social Problems, 4,* 319-333.

Margolin, G., & Wampold, B. E. (1981). Sequential analysis of conflict and accord in distressed and nondistressed marital partners. *Journal of Consulting and Clinical Psychology, 49,* 554-567.

McGoldrick, M. (1982). Normal families: An ethnic perspective. In F. Walsh (Ed.), *Normal family processes* (pp. 399-424). New York: Guilford Press.

McLeod, J. M., & Chaffee, S. H. (1972). The construction of social reality. In J. T. Tedeschi (Ed.), *The social influence processes* (pp. 50-99). Chicago: Aldine-Atherton.

Mettatal, G., & Gottman, J. M. (1980). *Affective responsiveness in spouses: Investigating the relationship between communication behavior and marital satisfaction.* Paper presented at the annual meeting of the Speech Communication Association, New York.

Millar, F. E., & Rogers, L. E. (1976). A relational approach to interpersonal communication. In G. R. Miller (Ed.), *Explorations in interpersonal communication* (pp. 87-103). Newbury Park, CA: Sage.

Miller, G. R., & Steinberg, M. (1975). *Between people: A new analysis of interpersonal communication.* Chicago: Science Research Associates.

Miller, S., Nunnally, E. W., & Wackman, D. B. (1975). *Alive and aware: How to improve your relationship through better communication.* Minneapolis, MN: Interpersonal Communication Programs.

Mishler, E. G., & Waxler, N. E. (1968). *Interaction in families: An experimental study of family process in schizophrenia.* New York: John Wiley.

Morton, T. L., Alexander, J. F., & Altman, I. (1976). Communication and relationship definition. In G. R. Miller (Ed.), *Explorations in interpersonal communication* (pp. 105-125). Newbury Park, CA: Sage.

Naravan, L. Z. (1967). Communication and adjustment in marriage. *Family Process, 6,* 173-184.

Nemeth, C. (1972). A critical analysis of research utilizing the prisoner's dilemma paradigm for the study of bargaining. In L. Berkowitz (Ed.), *Advances in experimental social psychology* (Vol. 6, pp. 203-234). New York: Academic Press.

Nishiyama, K. (1971). Interpersonal persuasion in a vertical society—the case of Japan. *Speech Monographs, 38,* 148-154.

Niyekawa, A. M. (1984). Analysis of conflict in a television home drama. In E. S. Krauss, T. P. Rohlen, & P. G. Steinhoff (Eds.), *Conflict in Japan* (pp. 61-84). Honolulu: University of Hawaii Press.

Noller, P. (1980). Misunderstandings in marital communication: A study of couples' nonverbal communication. *Journal of Personality and Social Psychology, 39:* 1135-1148.

Olson, D. H., & McCubbin, H. I. (1983). *Families: What makes them work*. Newbury Park, CA: Sage.

Ouchi, W. (1981). *Theory Z*. Reading, MA: Addison-Wesley.

Parks, M. R. (1981). Ideology in interpersonal communication: Off the couch and into the world. In M. Burgoon (Ed.), *Communication yearbook 5* (Vol. 5, pp. 79-107). New Brunswick, NJ: Transaction Books.

Patterson, G. R. (1971). Behavioral intervention procedures in the classroom and in the home. In A. E. Bergin & S. L. Garfield (Eds.), *Handbook of psychotherapy and behavior change: An empirical analysis* (pp. 751-775). New York: John Wiley.

Patterson, G. R. (1976). The aggressive child: Victim and architect of a coercive system. In E. Mash, L. Hamerlynck, & L. Handy (Eds.), *Behavior modification and families* (pp. 267-316). New York: Brunner/Mazel.

Patterson, G. R., & Reid, J. B. (1970). Reciprocity and coercion: Two facets of social systems. In C. Neuringer & J. L. Michael (Eds.), *Behavior modification in clinical psychology* (pp. 133-177). New York: Appleton-Century-Crofts.

Peterson, D. R. (1979). Assessing interpersonal relationships by means of interaction records. *Behavioral Assessment, 1,* 221-236.

Piaget, J. (1959). *The language and thought of the child* (3rd ed.). London: Routledge & Kegan Paul.

Pike, G. R., & Sillars, A. L. (1985). Reciprocity of marital communication. *Journal of Social and Personal Relationships, 2,* 303-324.

Pinderhughes, E. (1982). Afro-American families and the victim system. In M. McGoldrick, J. K. Pearce, & J. Giordano (Eds.), *Ethnicity and family therapy* (pp. 108-122). New York: Guilford Press.

Pruitt, D. G., & Lewis, S. A. (1977). The psychology of integrative bargaining. In D. Druckman (Ed.), *Negotiations: Social-psychological perspectives* (pp. 161-192). Newbury Park, CA: Sage.

Rands, M., Levinger, G., & Mellinger, G. D. (1981). Patterns of conflict resolution and marital satisfaction. *Journal of Family Issues, 2,* 297-321.

Raush, H. L., Barry, W. A., Hertel, R. K., & Swain, M. A. (1974). *Communication, conflict and marrige*. San Francisco: Jossey-Bass.

Rawlins, W. K. (1983). Openness as problematic in ongoing friendships: Two conversational dilemmas. *Communication Monographs, 50,* 1-13.

Reiss, D. (1971). Varieties of consensual family experience 1. *Family Process, 10,* 1-27.

Richards, E. F. (1980). Network ties, kin ties, and marital role organization: Bott's hypothesis reconsidered. *Journal of Comparative Family Studies, 11,* 139-151.

Riskin, J., & Faunce, E.E. (1970). Family interaction scales, III. Discussion of methodology and substantive findings. *Archives of General Psychiatry, 22,* 527-537.

Riskin, J., & Faunce, E. E. (1972). An evaluative review of family interaction research. *Family Process, 11,* 365-455.

Rogers, L. E., & Millar, F. E. (1980). *A holistic description of transactional patterns in marital dyads: Focus on redundancy*. Paper presented at the annual meeting of the Speech Communication Association, New York.

Rubin, L. B. (1976). *Worlds of pain: Life in the working class family*. New York: Basic Books.

Rubin, M. E. (1983). *Differences between distressed and nondistressed couples in verbal and nonverbal communication codes*. Unpublished doctoral dissertation, Indiana University.

Safilio-Rothschild, C. (1969). Patterns of familial power and influence. *Sociological Focus, 2,* 7-19.

Saito, M. (1982). Nemawashi: A Japanese form of interpersonal communication. *Et Cetera, 39,* 205-214.

Scanzoni, J., & Fox, G. L. (1980). Sex roles, family and society: The seventies and beyond. *Journal of Marriage and the Family, 42,* 743-756.

Sillars, A. L. (1980). Attributions and communication in roommate conflicts. *Communication Monographs, 47,* 180-200.

Sillars, A. L., Coletti, S. F., Parry, D., & Rogers, M. A. (1982). Coding verbal conflict tactics: Nonverbal and perceptual correlates of the "avoidance-distributive-integrative" distinction. *Human Communication Research, 9,* 83-95.

Sillars, A. L., Pike, G. R., Jones, T. S., & Redmon, K. (1983). Communication and conflict in marriage. In R. Bostrom (Ed.), *Communication yearbook 7* (pp. 414-429). Newbury Park, CA: Sage.

Sillars, A. L., & Scott, M. D. (1983). Interpersonal perception between intimates: An integrative review. *Human Communication Research, 10,* 153-176.

Sillars, A. L., Weisberg, J., Burggraf, C., & Wilson, E. (in press). Content themes in marital conversations. *Human Communication Research.*

Simmel, G. (1955). *Conflict.* New York: Free Press.

Snyder, D. K. (1979). Multi-dimensional assessment of marital satisfaction. *Journal of Marriage and the Family, 41,* 813-823.

Spiegel, J. (1982). An ecological model of ethnic families. In M. McGoldrick, J.K. Pearce & J. Giordano (Eds.), *Ethnicity and family therapy* (pp. 31-51). New York: Guilford Press.

Staples, R., & Mirande, A. (1980). Racial and cultural variations among American families: A decennial review of the literature on minority families. *Journal of Marriage and the Family, 42,* 157-173.

Swidler, A. (1980). Love and adulthood in American culture. In N. J. Smelser & E. Erikson (Eds.), *Themes of work and love in adulthood* (pp. 120-147). Cambridge, MA: Harvard University Press.

Sypher, B. D., & Sypher, H. E. (1982) *Seeing ourselves as others see us: Convergence and divergence in assessments of communication behavior.* Paper presented at the annual meeting of the Speech Communication Association, Louisville, KY.

Thomas, K. W., & Pondy, L. R. (1977). Toward an "intent" model of conflict management among principal parties. *Human Relations, 30,* 1089-1102.

Ting-Toomey, S. (1983). An analysis of verbal communication patterns in high and low marital adjustment groups. *Human Communication Research, 9,* 306-319.

Ting-Toomey, S. (1985). Toward a theory of conflict and culture. In W. Gudykunst, L. Stewart & S. Ting-Toomey (Eds.), *Culture and organizational processes: Conflict, negotiation and decision-making* (pp. 71-86). Newbury Park, CA: Sage.

Trower, P., Bryant, B., & Argyle, M. (1978). *Social skills and mental health.* London: Methuen.

Vincent, J. P., Friedman, L., Nugent, J., & Messerly, L. (1979). Demand characteristics in the observation of marital interaction. *Journal of Consulting and Clinical Psychology, 47,* 557-566.

Walton, R. E., & McKersie, R. B. (1965). *A behavioral theory of labor negotiation.* New York: McGraw-Hill.

Waterman, J. (1979). Family patterns of self disclosure. In G. J. Chelune et al. (Eds.), *Self disclosure* (pp. 225-242). San Francisco: Jossey-Bass.

Watzlawick, P., Beavin, J., & Jackson, D. D. (1967). *Pragmatics of human communication: A study of interactional patterns, pathologies and paradoxes.* New York: Norton.

Watzlawick, P., Weakland, J. H., & Fisch, R. (1974). *Change: Principles of problem formation and problem resolution.* New York: Norton.

Weick, K. E. (1971). Group processes, family processes, and problem solving. In J. Aldous et al. (Eds.), *Family problem solving: A symposium of theoretical, methodological and substantive concerns* (pp. 3-39). Hinsdale, IL: Dryden Press.

Weiss, R. S. (1975). *Marital separation.* New York: Basic Books.

Weiss, R. S., Birchler, G., & Vincent, J. (1974). Contractual models for negotiation training in marital dyads. *Journal of Marriage and the Family, 36,* 1-11.

Wills, T. A., Weiss, R. L., & Patterson, G. R. (1974). A behavioral analysis of the determinants of marital satisfaction. *Journal of Consulting and Clinical Psychology, 42,* 802-811.

Zucker, R. A., & Barron, F. H. (1971). *Toward a systematic family mythology: The relationship of parents' and adolescents' reports of parental behavior during childhood.* Paper presented at the annual meeting of the Eastern Psychological Association, New York.

Chapter 8

SELF-DISCLOSURE AND RELATIONSHIP DEVELOPMENT
An Attributional Analysis

Valerian J. Derlega, Barbara A. Winstead, Paul T. P. Wong, and Michael Greenspan

CONSIDERABLE RESEARCH ON personal relationships has embraced the perspective of theory and research on self-disclosure processes (see Derlega, 1984, for a review). The importance of attributions in relationships has also received increasing attention (e.g., Kelley, 1977; Newman, 1981). Unfortunately, not much is known about how disclosure input affects attributions, and how attributions determine one's own self-disclosure. We will argue that the types of attributions for disclosure input, particularly those emphasizing positive characteristics of the self and the relationship, may increase self-disclosure. Consider the following examples:

John and Michael both work for an air freight company. They have gone to lunch together a number of times and their jobs as supervisors require that they spend considerable time together. Their conversations usually deal with work, sports, or their children. One morning, however, John asks Michael if he can share something that was on his mind. He tells Michael that his daughter has leukemia and he feels under enormous pressure at home that is also affecting his work. John says that he does not feel comfortable telling these things to anyone else at the office except Michael. Michael is shaken emotionally by the information John has divulged. He also perceives that the personal information was revealed because John trusts him and that they have a close relationship. At lunch the next day, Michael shares with John how he reacted to his mother's death a few years ago.

Peggy is a computer programmer for a consulting company in Washington, D.C. After work, she is at a street corner waiting for a bus that is already 20 minutes late. Another woman, who has been standing next to her, is attempting to start a conversation. The woman is describing some problems she is having with her children at home. Peggy does not say anything. She thinks that the woman is obviously disclosing so much because of her personal problems, but that she is too forward. Peggy hopes the bus will come quickly so that they do not have to stand together any longer.

These two anecdotes deal with one person's self-disclosure and another person's reactions. The listener's reactions to the disclosure input, including his or her own self-disclosure, may depend on the causal explanations or attributions the listener makes for the initial discloser's behavior. The causal explanations the listener makes for the disclosure input reflect his or her assessment of the other person, of the other person's interest in developing a closer relationship, and of his or her own position in the relationship. Attributions for disclosure input that reflect favorably on the recipient and the relationship may lead to greater self-disclosure by the recipient, in order to make the relationship more intimate or perhaps as a reward for the other's openness. Believing that the disclosure reflects favorably on one's self (e.g., "I am a good listener, a nice person"), the recipient feels rewarded and is more likely to reward the other with a personal self-disclosure. A belief that characteristics of the relationship led to the other's disclosure suggests an involvement in the relationship; and if it is a desired relationship, a wish to maintain it by, for example, reciprocating the self-disclosure. Finally, if the disclosure is attributed to positive characteristics of the other, the recipient's behavior is more difficult to predict. Positive other attributions suggest liking for the other but yield no information about the value of self to the other person or the value of the relationship to self or other. However, if the circumstances were favorable for starting a relationship—for example, if the recipient and the discloser were interested and available—then positive other attributions might increase self-disclosure.

EXCHANGE OF SELF-DISCLOSURE

Self-disclosure refers to the process by which one person lets himself or herself be known by another person. According to Derlega and Grzelak,

> *Self-disclosure includes any information exchange that refers to the self, including personal states, dispositions, events in the past, and plans for the future.* It can be objectively defined as any verbal message that formally begins with the word "I" (for instance, "I think," "I feel") or any other verbal message about the self. (1979, p. 152)

Self-disclosure can play a major role in the development of personal relationships. In Altman and Taylor's (1973) theory of social penetration processes, relationships are predicted to move from superficial to more intimate areas of interpersonal exchange as individuals get to know one another. Individuals are expected to react positively to others' self-disclosure; and, in turn, people are willing to disclose personal information about themselves to these others. Little by little, in a spiraling fashion, the bonds of intimacy are expected to build as the individuals take turns exchanging increasingly more intimate information about themselves to one another.

A number of experiments have examined how individuals react to being recipients of disclosure input. Many studies have found support for disclosure reciprocity, what Sidney Jourard (1971) called the "dyadic effect." One person's intimate disclosure encourages intimate disclosure by the listener, and superficial disclosure encourages superficial disclosure in return (Altman, 1973; Archer, 1979; Kleinke, 1979).

ATTRIBUTIONS FOR DISCLOSURE

Despite the apparent support for the dyadic effect and its importance for relationship development, there are circumstances when disclosure recipients may not react positively to others who offer intimate self-disclosures. Our view is that the recipient generates subjective reasons to account for the disclosure input, using an assessment of the discloser's and the recipient's contributions. These subjective reasons, or *attributions,* mediate the recipient's own self-disclosure and evaluations of the other person. The anecdotes at the beginning of this chapter illustrate the role of attributions in mediating recipients' reactions to disclosure input. Michael inferred that the disclosure input was based on John's trust for him and that they have a close relationship—emphasizing positive personal characteristics about Michael and their relationship. These positive attributions make the interaction rewarding for Michael and he, in turn, shares personal information about himself. Michael believes that he has a good relationship going with John and that they can be fairly open. Peggy, on the other hand, attributed the other woman's disclosure to personal problems she is having—emphasizing negative personal characteristics of the othe person. These negative attributions about the woman make the interaction unrewarding for Peggy, and she sees no reason to be open about herself or to continue the interaction (see Worthy, Gary, & Kahn, 1969).

Considerable research on self-disclosure confirms the critical role of attributions. A study by Town and Harvey (1981) shows how the tendency to make attributions per se in response to a disclosure input influences behavior. These authors arranged for participants to watch a videotape in which a stimulus person revealed highly intimate information about having homosexual tendencies. Some participants were provided an opportunity to make attributions about the stimulus person's behavior while others were not. Participants subsequently interacted with the stimulus person whom they had seen on the videotape. With this high disclosure input, participants reacted more negatively to the stimulus person in the attribution than in the nonattribution condition, including less eye contact, shorter speech duration, more anxiety, and lower reported comfort. There was also a correlation between the number of attributions generated by the participants and their behavioral tendency to *withdraw* during the interaction (e.g., decreased eye contact, proximity, and speech duration). The disclosure of the homosexual information may have evoked negative attributions about the stimulus person's characteristics. Hence, the more negative attributions generated, the more behavioral withdrawal that occurred.

Town and Harvey (1981) also ran a low disclosure input condition in which the stimulus person conveyed a neutral attitude on gay rights but also revealed information about new job responsibilities. There was no effect of the attribution manipulation on behavioral reactions in the low disclosure input condition. In the attribution condition, there was a strong correlation between the number of attributions generated by the low disclosure input and the participants' behavioral tendency to *get closer* during the interaction (i.e., increased eye contact, proximity, and speech duration). The disclosure of the nonintimate information over the videotape may have evoked positive attributions about the stimulus person's characteristics. Hence, the more positive attributions generated, the more behavioral approach that occurred.

An attributional explanation has also been used to explain the effects of timing of disclosure input on the recipient's reactions. For instance, Wortman, Adesman, Herman, and Greenberg (1976) speculated that timing affects whether a person's reaction to a high-disclosing other is negative or positive. These authors reasoned that

> if an individual [a stranger] makes a highly personal remark to us early in a conversation, we may conclude that this remark has little to do with his or her feelings for us. Instead, we may infer that he or she is the kind of person who is disclosing to everyone. If someone makes a disclosing remark after he or she has been talking to us for a while, we may be more likely to take the remark personally and infer that it has positive implications for the relationship. (p. 185)

In their experiment, Wortman et al. (1976) arranged for a confederate to reveal personal information either at the beginning or near the end of a 10-minute conversation with a participant. Results indicated, in support of the attributional explanation, that the early discloser was liked less than the late discloser and that the early discloser was seen as more maladjusted and immature. Also, participants perceived that the late discloser liked them more and wanted to get to know them more than did the early discloser.

Reactions to intimate self-disclosure may also depend on whether or not recipients perceive that they have been singled out or "personalistically chosen" (Jones & Archer, 1976) as a disclosure recipient. Being singled out for disclosure may lead to the inference that one is liked and trusted, which could serve as a reward, leading in turn to greater liking for and self-disclosure to the other person.

Evidence for the mediating role of attributions in reacting to personalistic disclosure was obtained by Taylor, Gould, and Brounstein (1981). They manipulated the recipient's perception of the attributions a discloser made concerning the reasons for the disclosure. Participants listened to a partner who made either highly intimate or nonintimate disclosures. Then participants were shown a questionnaire (ostensibly filled out by the partner) indicating that the level of disclosure was determined by the discloser's dispositional characteristics, the recipient's characteristics, or the situation. The discloser was liked more when she disclosed intimately and attributed her behavior to the characteristics of the participant than when she disclosed nonintimately and attributed her behavior to the characteristics of the participant. The Taylor et al. findings suggest that being singled out as a target for disclosure may have positive or negative effects depending on the attributions that are generated. Consider the participants selected to receive intimate disclosure because of their own characteristics. These persons probably attributed the other's disclosure input to positive personal attributes (e.g., "He thinks I am a trustworthy individual"; "I am likable"). On the other hand, participants who were selected to receive a nonintimate disclosure because of their own characteristics probably attributed the other's disclosure input to negative or unfavorable personal attributes ("She doesn't think I am trustworthy"; "I am unlikable").

Attributions are a strong conceptual tool in understanding the results of studies on the effects of timing and personalistic feedback. These studies have not focused directly, however, on the relationship between type of attributions generated by disclosure recipients themselves for others' disclosure and their behavior toward these others. The Town and Harvey (1981) study is an important exception, but that research did not examine the effects of particular types of attributions generated by the recipient on behavioral reactions.

Attributions can vary along two dimensions: content and valence. Content refers to what or to whom the disclosure is attributed (e.g., self, other, or relationship). Valence refers to whether the causal statement says something positive, neutral, or negative about the self, other, or relationship. Attributions to self suggest that the other's disclosure reflects on one's own personal characteristics; and, if this reflection is positive, then the event is rewarding. This is the point made by research on "personalism"; but as demonstrated in the Taylor et al. study, self-attributions lead to liking only when they are assumed to be positive. Relationship attributions indicate a perception of connectedness (or lack of connectedness) to the other person and ought to have a fairly strong correlation with relationship behavior, such as self-disclosure. Other attributions reflect the recipient's appraisal of the discloser. They indicate focus on the other rather than on self or relationship.

What might the relationship between type of attributions for disclosure and a person's behavior toward the other person be? In general, positive attributions ought to be associated with greater self-disclosure. Positively valenced attributions for the disclosure input (e.g., "He thinks I am trustworthy") are a favorable sign of initiating, maintaining, or enhancing the relationship. Making negative or neutral attributions should not be positively associated with self-disclosure. Negatively valenced attributions may, in fact, be inversely associated with self-disclosure.

Given the rewarding nature of positive self attributions and the favorable involvement in a relationship implied by positive relationship attributions, these ought to have stronger correlations with behavioral responsiveness to another's disclosure than positive other attributions. Positive other attributions suggest a good impression of other but do not indicate how personally rewarding the relationship might be for the disclosure recipient.

In emphasizing the special role of type of attributions in mediating the effects of disclosure input, a caveat should be added at this point: Positive self and relationship attributions for another's disclosure input may not inevitably induce self-disclosure by the recipient. The recipient's reaction also depends on his or her interest in beginning or sustaining a relationship as well as on his or her capacity to self-disclose. Hence, a person who has "enough" friends may not respond intimately to a disclosure input provided by a stranger; a lonely person who does not have good social skills may be inhibited about self-disclosing (Derlega & Margulis, 1982); or a passive person may not feel that it is appropriate to follow-up the other's disclosure input by divulging personal information (Margulis, Derlega, & Winstead, 1984).

STUDY 1: EFFECTS OF FRIENDSHIP ON ATTRIBUTIONS FOR DISCLOSURE INPUT

How are attributions used by recipients in deciding whether or not to self-disclose in response to a disclosure input? Assuming that people find it more rewarding to interact with a friend than a stranger, persons who make friend-type attributions for someone's disclosure may be more likely to self-disclose. On the other hand, people who make stranger-type attributions for someone's disclosure may not be more likely to self-disclose. Our first task is to identify differences in the types of attributions persons would make for a friend's versus a stranger's disclosure input. Then we can predict more confidently what attributions lead to self-disclosing behavior.

We expect that persons will generate attributions for a friend's disclosure that reflect positively on themselves and their relationship. Attributions for a stranger's disclosure, on the other hand, will focus more on neutral or negative characteristics of the partner, since the other person presumably has no information about the recipient and no relationship history exists. If individuals generate different attributions for a friend's versus a stranger's disclosure input, similar differences in attributions may occur in individuals' thinking about ongoing or potential relationships that are desired or less desired. The type of attributions generated for a disclosure input may affect the recipient's own willingness to self-disclose, and hence influence how likely one is to develop further the opportunities for a close relationship.

METHOD

Participants and design. Study 1 involved 50 male and 50 female participants. The design was a 2 × 2 × 2 × 2 analysis of variance with repeated measures on the last two factors. The between-participants factors were disclosure content (marital problem or going to psychotherapy) and participant sex. The within-participants factors were the degree of relationship between discloser and recipient (stranger versus friend) and discloser sex. Each participant was exposed to four situations involving a male friend, a female friend, a male stranger, and a female stranger. The order of presentation of these four conditions was randomized for each participant.

Perceived causes for stimulus person's willingness to disclose. Participants were asked why the stimulus person was willing to disclose. Based on their open-ended responses, frequencies of attributions in six major categories were computed. These attributional dependent measures were: (1) *positive self,* based on positive personal characteristics of the participant (e.g., "I am friendly"; "I am a good listener"); (2) *neutral or negative self,* based on neutral (e.g., "I am a male") or negtive (e.g., "I must look like an idiot") personal characteristics of the participant; (3) *positive relationship,* based on a positive relationship shared by individuals (e.g., "We are good friends") or a benefit that one can provide for the other ("She knows that I can help her"); (4) *neutral or negative relationship,* based on a neutral (e.g., "We have met before") or a negative relationship shared by the individuals (e.g., "We are both ugly ducklings") or concerns about being used or taken advantage of (e.g., "Needs to embroil others in problems," "Somehow trying to take advantage of me"); (5) *positive other,* based on positive personal characteristics of the disclosing partner (e.g., "She is being nice"; "He is a trusting person"); and (6) *neutral or negative other,* based on neutral (e.g., "She is open") or negative personal characteristics ("She is emotionally disturbed," "in despair") of the disclosing partner. Two judges agreed 95% in scoring the content into the self, other, and relationship categories. They agreed 89% in scoring the valence.

RESULTS AND DISCUSSION

We examined the results of Study 1 to see how participants generate different types of attributions for a friend's versus a stranger's disclosure input. In this role-playing situation, participants generated more positive self-attributions (F = 34.56, p < .001) and fewer neutral-negative other attributions (F = 77.06, p < .001) for a friend's than a stranger's disclosure input. Participants also generated more positive relationship (F = 15.24, p < .001) *and* more neutral-negative relationship attributions (F = 6.71, p < .02) for a friend's than a stranger's disclosure. (For these effects, df = 1, 96.)

If we assume that friendships are generally found to be rewarding, it is understandable that recipients attribute positive characteristics of themselves as well as to their relationship for the disclosure input. The disclosure input derives from both the favorable impression the other has for the recipient and the good qualities attributed to the relationship. Participants might also be expected to generate more neutral or negative other attributions for the stranger's than the friend's disclosure input given the inappropriateness of disclosing intimate information to a stranger (Chaikin & Derlega, 1974). We did not expect that neutral-negative relationship attributions would occur more frequently in the friend than the stranger condition. Still, when individuals have a relational history, it is perhaps reasonable for participants to account for disclosure input in terms of neutral (e.g., "We know one another") and certain kinds of negative relationship attributions (e.g., "We have common problems"). It may not make sense to use relationship attributions to account for a stranger's disclosure input unless there is an assumption of an ulterior motive or a desire to exploit the disclosure recipient, which would be examples of negative relationship attributions according to our scoring system.

STUDY 2: EFFECTS OF ATTRIBUTIONS ON SELF-DISCLOSURE TO A FRIEND AND TO A STRANGER

Study 1 showed how participants generated different attributions for a friend's versus a stranger's disclosure in a role-playing situation. The role-playing undoubtedly encourages participants to rely on their expectations about how friends and strangers behave in generating their attributions for disclosure input. Also, participants were not presented with self-disclosure inputs but only with a topic that the stimulus person ostensibly talked about. It may be that an *in vivo* social interaction with a friend or stranger produces findings different from those of Study 1. Hence, it is important to replicate Study 1 to examine whether persons generate different attributions for disclosure input as a function of level of relationship. More important, we wanted to test directly whether the types of attributions made for a friend's versus a stranger's disclosure input in Study 1 predict self-disclosure in a social encounter.

How might different types of attributions for disclosure input influence self-disclosure? If the recipient generates positive self and relationship attributions about the disclosure input (e.g., "He trusts me," "We get along") he or she feels rewarded. The recipient in turn might self-disclose to provide a reward to the initial discloser. It may also occur that *any* relationship attributions that emphasize the bonds or links between the initial discloser and the listener lead to greater self-disclosure as the parties sample and assess what it is like to interact together. Given that participants made more positive self and fewer negative other attributions for a friend's disclosure, and that they made more relationship attributions (positive as well as neutral-negative) for a friend's disclosure, we expected this pattern of attributions would be highly correlated with participants' disclosure tendencies. Participants will self-disclose more to a friend and perhaps a stranger if they make this pattern of friend-type attributions. Study 2 provided an opportunity to test these ideas as participants were provided with self-disclosure inputs by either a friend or a stranger and were asked to prepare open-ended attributions for the input as well as to prepare a self-disclosure for the other.

METHOD

Participants and design. Study 2 involved 33 males and 33 females. Participants were asked to bring a close friend of the same sex to the experiment. The design was a 2 × 2 factorial. The independent variables were the participant's gender and whether his or her partner was a friend or a stranger (i.e., a friend brought by another participant). Participants were randomly assigned to the friend or stranger conditions. The major dependent measures were based on participants' attributions for their partner's disclosure input and judges' ratings of the intimacy of the participants' self-disclosure.

Procedure. Two pairs of individuals (either all males or all females) participated per session, and they sat together in a waiting room for several minutes before the study officially began. Participants were told the study was about communication and involved passing information back and forth by notes. Then each participant was placed in a separate cubicle where they waited for the study to begin.

The participants were told that their partner for the session (either their friend or a stranger) was randomly selected to send the first note. They were soon given the partner's note, which was a self-disclosure of high intimacy. The participant then wrote a self-description for the partner. Following this, participants were asked why their partner was willing to disclose personal information to them. Next, they filled out an impression questionnaire that asked them to rate the partner.

Relationship manipulation. Although all participants brought a friend to the experiment, the friend participated in the study only half the time. In the *friend condition,* after participants entered their individual cubicles, the friends who came with them were taken to a separate room. The experimenter explained the true nature of the study, and the friends were asked to serve as "confederates" by writing a highly intimate note to their friends. These persons also expected that their notes would be copied and shown to at least one other participant in the experiment. No one refused the request to write the note and they quickly became involved in the task.

In the *stranger condition,* the participants, after waiting with their friends for a few minutes, were also placed in individual cubicles. They were told their assigned partner was one of the individuals whom they had just met (a stranger). The participants were each given a note prepared by a person in a preceding session. The procedure allowed us to yoke participants in the friend and stranger conditions who were run in different sessions; both received the identical note. Male participants in the stranger condition received only notes prepared by another male; females received only notes prepared by another female.

The friends who accompanied participants in the stranger condition had no particular role to play in the experiment, except to insure that comparable participants were recruited for the friend and stranger conditions.

Creation of the high disclosure input. Friends were asked to write a highly intimate note emphasizing personal feelings or problems the individual had experienced. To give the friends a feeling for high intimacy, they were shown the scale used by the authors for scoring intimacy (Chaikin, Derlega, Bayma, & Shaw, 1975). In writing the notes, friends were encouraged to use their own words, drawing on past experiences as much as possible.

Dependent measures. These were the dependent measures:

(1) Attributions for the partner's willingness to self-disclose: Participants were asked why their partner was willing to reveal personal information to them. Based on their open-ended responses, frequencies of attributions in the following major categories were computed: positive self, neutral or negative self, positive relationship, neutral relationship, positive other, and neutral or negative other. We also coded negative relationship attributions but this category was never used by participants. The causal attributions were coded by two judges who were blind to the treatment conditions. The interjudge agreement in scoring attributions was 84% for the valence and 87% for the self, other, and relationship categories.

(2) Self-disclosure intimacy: After participants read their partner's disclosure input, they were asked to prepare a self-description of the partner. Participants expected that their self-disclosure would be passed to the partner before the end of the experimental session.

To obtain the intimacy measure, two judges rated independently each disclosure along a nine-point scale (1 = not at all intimate, 9 = extremely intimate information, see Chaikin et al., 1975, for information about the scoring system). The average for the two raters was used as the disclosure intimacy measure (Pearson r = .78). To check the intimacy input, the same two judges who scored the participant's self-disclosure rated the partner's self-disclosure on a nine-point scale.

RESULTS

Manipulation check. Participants were asked to indicate on a nine-point scale the level of relationship with the partner. Participants in the friend condition indicated having a closer relationship with their partner than did their counterparts in the stranger condition (F = 554.13, p < .001).

The results of a t-test for independent groups indicated that the partner's disclosure inputs did not significantly differ in the female (M = 6.09, SD = 1.60) and the male (M = 6.06, SD = 1.01) conditions, based on judges' ratings (t < 1). There was also no significant difference in the number of words used by the partner in the female (M = 162.41, SD = 58.45) and the male (M = 173.35, SD = 76.85) conditions (t < 1). The intimacy and word length of the partner's disclosure inputs were used jointly as covariates for the analyses of covariance computed on the attribution and self-disclosure measures.

Effects of friendship. The attribution and disclosure data were analyzed using a 2 (relationship) × 2 (participant sex) analysis of covariance. The covariates were the disclosure intimacy and word length of the disclosure inputs read by the participants. For all effects reported below, df = 1,60.

(1) Attributions: Several ANCOVAs were performed on participants' attributions for the partner's disclosure input. None of the relationship effects were significant at the .05 level (two-tailed tests), but there were trends for positive self attributions (F = 3.09, p < .09) and positive relationship attributions (F = 2.85, p < .10) to be cited more frequently in the friend than in the stranger condition. Also, there was a trend for neutral-negative other attributions (F = 3.34, p < .08) to be cited more frequently in the stranger than in the friend condition.

(2) Self-disclosure: To address whether self-disclosure differed as a function of friendship, the level of intimacy of participants' self-disclosures was analyzed. Participants disclosed significantly more intimately when they were communicating with a friend (M = 4.47) than a stranger (M = 3.78, F = 4.67, p < .05). Also, as might be expected, females (M = 4.73) disclosed more intimately than males (M = 3.54, F = 13.62, p < .001).

Effects of type of attributions on self-disclosure. Multiple regressions were computed separately for participants in the friend and stranger conditions to predict disclosure intimacy as a function of the attribution measures as well as the intimacy and word length of the disclosure input. (The last two measures were included to control for individual differences in the disclosure input given to each participant.) The predictor variables were entered into the regression equations simultaneously (see Table 8.1).

The regression equation for the friend condition indicated that positive self and positive other attributions were significant predictors of disclosure intimacy. Positive relationship and neutral relationship attributions were also positively related to disclosure intimacy, although the beta weights were only

TABLE 8.1
Multiple Regressions to Predict Self-Disclosure Intimacy in the Friend and Stranger Conditions for Study 2

Predictors	Disclosure Intimacy in Friend Condition Beta Weight	Disclosure Intimacy in Stranger Condition Beta Weight
Word Count Input	.040	.397*
Intimacy Input	.027	.153
Positive Self	.465**	.069
Neutral/Negative Self	.277	−.076
Positive Other	.470***	−.117
Neutral/Negative Other	.073	.087
Positive Relationship	.300*	—
Neutral Relationship	.290*	.290
Multiple R	.680	.496
Adjusted R²	.291	.027
F value for regression equation	2.692**	1.123

NOTE: The positive relationship attribution category did not enter the multiple regression equation for the stranger condition because this category was not used by participants in the stranger condition.
*p < .10.
**p < .05.
***p < .01.

marginally significant. On the other hand, none of the attribution measures were significant predictors of disclosure intimacy in the stranger condition.

GENERAL DISCUSSION

The results of Study 2 support the view that attributions generated by the disclosure recipient influence self-disclosing behavior. Moreover, the positivity of the attribution had major impact. When persons in the friend condition made positive self, other, and (albeit marginally) relationship attributions, self-disclosure increased. There was one exception to this finding: Positive as well as neutral relationship attributions predicted self-disclosure at a marginally significant level. Relationship attributions, which are either positive or neutral, may highlight the linkage and involvement between individuals and hence may contribute to self-disclosure intimacy.

Why did positively valenced attributions increase self-disclosure? Favorable self and other attributions probably make the recipient feel good (serving as a reward), which in turn increases the likelihood of rewarding the initial discloser through self-disclosure. Also, the positive other attribution suggests that the recipient feels good about the other person. The disclosure recipient then discloses to explore the possibility of sustaining or intensifying the relationship. If positively valenced self and other attributions contributed significantly to self-disclosure among friends, why was there no similar effect among strangers? The disclosure recipient's interest in sustaining or initiating a relationship with the initial discloser may be the critical factor. Individuals in the friend condition have a commitment to sustaining a relationship with their partner; no such commitment exists in the stranger condition. In fact, persons in the stranger condition may have little interest in developing a same-sex friendship with someone whom they have just met, particularly since they had come to the session with a friend in the first place.

If the disclosure recipient had an interest in initiating a *new* relationship, then attributions could well affect one's own self-disclosing behavior. Derlega, Winstead, Wong, and Hunter (1985) found that males paired with a female partner showed a strong, positive relationship between frequency of self-attributions for a partner's willingness to disclose to them (which were generally positively valenced) and self-disclosure. Assuming that some males had an interest in developing an opposite-sex relationship, the self-attributions may have served as a measure, from the participant's point of view, of the woman's interest in him. Curiously, self-attributions did not correlate with self-disclosure for female participants who believed they had an opposite-sex partner in the Derlega et al. (1985) study. Sex differences in participants' perceptions about how much control or responsibility they can exercise in initiating a relationship may have influenced these results. Thus if a male thinks a woman is interested in disclosing to him, he takes the initiative to disclose. If a woman thinks a man is interested in disclosing to her, she may not take the initiative to disclose fearing that she will be perceived as "taking control."

This chapter is based on the following model: disclosure input → attributions → disclosure output (Town & Harvey, 1981). The finding that attributions, particularly positive self and other, and (marginally) positive relationship attributions as well as neutral relationship attributions, enhance self-disclosing behavior documents how this model might operate in a social encounter in which interactants have a commitment to sustaining an interest in or initiating a relationship. There are, however, numerous questions about how social and personality processes affect attributions and self-disclosure that might be examined. We have suggested, for instance, how one's personal commitment (based on being in an ongoing relationship or taking an active role in initiating a relationship) may determine whether or not generating certain types of atributions leads to self-disclosure. Indeed, personality variables may affect the attribution process itself in a way that inhibits or enhances self-disclosure. For instance, chronically lonely persons suffering from low self-esteem may generate negatively valenced self attributions for another's disclosure input, and these negative attributions may inhibit their own self-disclosing behavior. Lonely persons may say, for instance, "He probably doesn't know what a bad listener I am" (Young, 1982). These attributions are not ego-enhancing nor do they make one feel good about the other person. Hence the lonely person has no reason to believe that good outcomes will derive from self-disclosing to the other person. Persons who are not lonely and have relatively high self-esteem may be more likely to generate positively valenced self attributions that enhance their self-disclosing behavior.

The finding that women disclosed more than men in Study 2 is also consistent with the view that individual differences in thought processes, such as attributions, may be associated with individual differences in behavior. Compared to males, females used a greater number of positive self (F = 4.36, p < .05) and neutral relationship (F = 5.00, p < .03) attributions to explain the disclosure input. Females also tended to use, albeit marginally significantly, a greater number of positive relationship attributions (F = 2.85, p < .10). To the extent that women are "relationship experts" they would be more likely to perceive themselves as having contributed to the other's self-disclosing behavior and to be thinking in terms of the relationship when making attributions. Thus females in comparison to males also disclosed more intimately and were more likely to use the types of attributions that predicted self-disclosure among friends. Perhaps sex differences in attributions contribute to sex differences in self-disclosure.

What do we know about the connection between attribution content and self-disclosure? Certainly positive attributions can be expected and have been shown in our studies to predict approach behavior in relationships. But will self, other, and relationship attributions predict different sorts of behavior? Positive self attributions indicate that the other's self-disclosure is rewarding. We have suggested that reciprocal self-disclosures may be viewed as an exchange of rewards. Might the disclosure recipient making positive self attributions reward the discloser in other ways if they were available? Positive relationship attributions may indicate involvement in the relationship and, presumably, a wish to maintain it. In some cases this may mean reciprocating the disclosure; in others it may not (see Berg & Clark, 1986, about the effects of communal versus exchange relationships on self-disclosure). Positive relationship attributions should predict whatever behavior maintains or enhances the relationship. The effects of positive other attributions should depend on appraisals of the potential for a relationship. These attributions suggest liking for the other, but an individual's response will depend both on his or her interest in pursuing a relationship and perceptions of the other's willingness to pursue it. Thus we predict that the content of attributions (i.e., self, other, or relationship) will predict behavior. Research investigating attributions and relationship behavior in various situations can test these hypotheses.

In summary, numerous questions about attributions and self-disclosing behavior are fair game for future research. Certain attributions, which tend to be made more often for a friend's than a stranger's self-disclosure, foster self-disclosure in situations where one has a commitment to developing, sustaining, or intensifying a relationship. It is our hope that the discussion of the phenomenology of people's responses to a disclosure input will serve to stimulate further work on this topic as well as to expand the attribution model for understanding reactions to disclosure input.

REFERENCES

Altman, I. (1973). Reciprocity of interpersonal exchange. *Journal for the Theory of Social Behavior, 3,* 249-261.

Altman, I., & Taylor, D. A. (1973). *Social penetration: The development of interpersonal relationships.* New York: Holt, Rinehart and Winston.

Archer, R. L. (1979). Role of personality and the social situation. In G. J. Chelune & Associates, *Self-disclosure* (pp. 28-58). San Francisco: Jossey-Bass.

Berg, J. H., & Clark, M. S. (1986). Differences in social exchange between intimate and other relationships. Gradually evolving or quickly apparent? In V. J. Derlega & B. A. Winstead (Eds.), *Friendship and social interaction* (pp. 101-128). New York: Springer-Verlag.

Chaikin, A. L., & Derlega, V. J. (1974). Variables affecting the appropriateness of self-disclosure. *Journal of Consulting and Clinical Psychology, 42,* 588-593.

Chaikin, A. L., Derlega, V. J., Bayma, B., & Shaw, J. (1975). Neuroticism and disclosure reciprocity. *Journal of Consulting and Clinical Psychology, 43,* 13-19.

Derlega, V. J. (1984). Self-disclosure and intimate relationships. In V. J. Derlega (Ed.), *Communication, intimacy, and close relationships* (pp. 1-9). Orlando, FL: Academic Press.

Derlega, V. J., & Grzelak, J. (1979). Appropriateness of self-disclosure. In G. J. Chelune & Associates, *Self-disclosure* (pp. 151-176). San Francisco: Jossey-Bass.

Derlega, V. J., & Margulis, S. T. (1982). Why loneliness occurs: The interrelationship of social psychological and privacy concepts. In L. A. Peplau & D. Perlman (Eds.), *Loneliness* (pp. 152-165). New York: John Wiley.

Derlega, V. J., Winstead, B. A., Wong, P. T. P., & Hunter, S. (1985). Gender effects in an initial encounter: A case where men exceed women in disclosure. *Journal of Social and Personal Relationships, 2,* 25-44.

Jones, E. E., & Archer, R. L. (1976). Are there special effects of personalistic self-disclosure? *Journal of Experimental Social Psychology, 12,* 180-193.

Jourard, S. M. (1971). *Self-disclosure: An experimental analysis of the transparent self.* New York: John Wiley.

Kelley, H. H. (1977). An application of attribution theory to research methodology for close relationships. In G. Levinger & H. L. Raush (Eds.), *Close relationships: Perspectives on the meaning of intimacy* (pp. 87-113). Amherst: University of Massachusetts Press.

Kleinke, C. L. (1979). Effects of personal evaluations. In G. J. Chelune & Associates, *Self-disclosure* (pp. 59-79). San Francisco: Jossey-Bass.

Margulis, S. T., Derlega, V. J., & Winstead, B. A. (1984). Implications of social psychological concepts for a theory of loneliness. In V. J. Derlega (Ed.), *Communication, intimacy, and close relationships* (pp. 133-160). Orlando, FL: Academic Press.

Newman, H. (1981). Communication within ongoing intimate relationships: An attributional perspective. *Personality and Social Psychology Bulletin, 7,* 59-70.

Taylor, D. A., Gould, R. J., & Brounstein, P. J. (1981). Effects of personalistic self-disclosure. *Personality and Social Psychology Bulletin, 7,* 487-492.

Town, J. P., & Harvey, J. H. (1981). Self-disclosure, attribution, and social interaction. *Social Psychology Quarterly, 44,* 291-300.

Wortman, C. B., Adesman, P., Herman, E., & Greenberg, R. (1976). Self-disclosure: An attributional perspective. *Journal of Personality and Social Psychology, 33,* 184-191.

Worthy, M., Gary, A., & Kahn, G. (1969). Self-disclosure as an exchange process. *Journal of Personality and Social Psychology, 13,* 59-64.

Young, J. E. (1982). Loneliness, depression and cognitive therapy: Theory and application. In L. A. Peplau & D. Perlman (Eds.), *Loneliness* (pp. 379-405). New York: John Wiley.

Chapter 9

INFORMATION EXCHANGE
IN SOCIAL INTERACTION

Kathy Kellermann

SOCIAL INTERACTION DEPENDS on communication. The form, the purpose, the outcome, and the participants in social interaction may vary; communication remains the vehicle. Conversation is the form of communication occurring most frequently in social interaction: One-half to three-fourths of our interactions, with others occur in a dyadic conversational context (James, 1951; Wheeler & Nezlek, 1977). Still, the question of the nature of conversation remains. Is conversation to be viewed in linguistic terms of sentence production and grammar, in physiological terms of sound production by the vocal chords, or in electrical engineering terms of signal and noise ratios? None of these approaches, nor a series of others that could be employed, characterize conversation as an interactive phenomenon, a joint product of two or more persons. Furthermore, these approaches fail to model conversation as a psychological process. Few individuals perceive conversation as a transformational grammar, a physiological method of sound production, or a sequence of electronic signals. Rather, conversation is perceived by participants as an exchange of information (Berger & Kellermann, 1983; Douglas, 1983, 1984; Kellermann & Berger, 1984). The information may already be known to the participants; the exchange may be short; the conversation may be "superficial"; nonetheless, what constitutes conversation is the exchange of information. Social interaction devoid of information exchange is social interaction sans conversation. This chapter describes a formal model of conversation that treats it as a process of information exchange.

The perspective that information exchange defines the nature of conversation is not new except, perhaps, in the degree to which it has been made explicit. Acts of self-disclosure (Davis & Perkowitz, 1979; Emler & Fisher, 1981; Gilbert, 1976; Tognoli, 1969), bargaining/negotiation sessions (Pruitt, 1981), and psychotherapeutic interviews (Siegman & Pope, 1972) have all been referred to, at least in passing, as information exchange processes. Chang (1982) has recently developed a model of interaction in which conversation is defined as the "process of information exchange between two agents" (p. 314). Taylor (1979) argues that social penetration occurs via information exchange, and Duck (1976) explicitly identifies relationship development as an information-based process. Simply put, conversation is the foundation for self-disclosure, bargaining, psychotherapy, and relationship development, and it is essentially an information exchange process.

> Conversation constitutes a reciprocal and rhythmic interchange of verbal emissions. . . . The core of the conversational dyad consists of the mutual transfer of information between partners. . . . The vital process of information transfer is implicit in the record of verbal intercourse. . . . Information transfer is a simple essential of all social operations regardless of language or culture. It is the essential outcome of every conversational relation. . . . Information is the universal element of all conversational contacts and it constitutes the only substantive base for face-to-face conversation. (Allen & Guy, 1974, pp. 11, 17-18, 57, 240, 251)

This chapter explores conversation as a process of information exchange by formally modeling the components and changes in the process over time. To undertake formal modeling, the boundaries of the model and its assumptions must first be identified. Based on these boundaries and assumptions, the components, process, and implications of the model are explored.

BOUNDARIES

Given a model that treats conversation as a process of information exchange, the question immediately arises as to how the terms "information" and "exchange" are to be defined. Is information only that which reduces uncertainty, as suggested by information theory? To specify arbitrarily that everything redundant or irrelevant to reducing uncertainty is not information promotes an unmanageable view of information—constantly shifting, contextually bound, impossible to isolate. Whether or not an individual is aware my name is "Kathy" is irrelevant to the fact that my name constitutes information about me. If an individual is ignorant of my name, uncertainty about my identity may not be reduced but my name is still information—information that has not been *exchanged*. In essence, information can only be defined in terms of *exchange*, for information, by itself, is an infinite set containing all past, present, and future cognitions and behaviors. Information exchange, on the other hand, involves the transmission of some finite amount of the set. Information exchange focuses on what is said, done, or perceived in a given interaction regardless of whether it is detected, regardless of its accuracy, and regardless of its purpose. Information exchange involves realization of the process of emitting, detecting, and perceiving behavior. In conversation, the interactants' streams of verbal and nonverbal behavior and/or the detection and perception of those streams are defined as the information exchanged.

For ease of discussion, conversation will be restricted to dyadic exchanges. Such a restriction does not greatly limit the utility of the model. Cherry (1971) argues that the two-person conversational encounter is the fundamental unit of human behavior; indeed, much of our lives is spent in dyadic interaction (Allen & Guy, 1974; O'Mara, 1973). Furthermore, the decision to restrict conversation to two participants stems from the twin motives of parsimony and convenience. The model could theoretically be extended to any number of participants.

The conversational dyad begins when two persons in face-to-face contact direct their verbal and nonverbal behavior toward each other. The conversational dyad terminates when both individuals' behavior shifts so as to be aimed at persons or objects other than the conversational partner. The conversational dyad is a system composed of two actors who are face-to-face and who are emitting, detecting, and perceiving the stream of verbal and nonverbal behaviors constituting the conversation.

During the conversation, each participant is assumed to engage in three operations: (1) emitting verbal and/or nonverbal behavior, (2) detecting and perceiving one's own emissions, and (3) detecting and perceiving the conversational partner's emissions. Not all emissions will be detected and perceived (Allen & Guy, 1974) nor will the two actors necessarily agree in their perceptions (Ross, 1977). The stream of behavior is assumed to be segmented into discrete acts (Atkinson & Allen, 1979; Massad, Hubbard, & Newtson, 1979; Newtson, 1973, 1976; Newtson & Engquist, 1976; Newtson, Engquist, & Bois, 1977). While interlocutors are capable of segmenting the stream of verbal and nonverbal behavior differently, marked unanimity in the "chunking" of the ongoing behavioral stream exists (Newtson, 1973; Newtson & Engquist, 1976). Each chunk is called an "act" and the participant producing the act is called the "actor." Thus conversation is represented as a stream of information chunked into discrete acts, each produced by an actor. In other words, conversation is a linear ordering of discrete units of information wherein actors produce turns composed of acts.

Two potential problems with this conceptualization of conversation must be addressed. First, each actor constantly emits verbal and nonverbal behaviors; consequently, segmentation and assignment of an act to an actor ignores the other actor's information stream for that time period. Basically, the nonproducing actor is in a state of "nonacting," or listening, throughout the producing actor's turn (Miller, 1963). The turn is a natural unit of conversation (Gallois & Markel, 1975) that has repeatedly been used to describe the linear sequencing of conversations (Allen & Guy, 1974; Argyle, 1969; Duncan, 1974; Goffman, 1964; Jaffe & Feldstein, 1970; Sacks, Schegloff, & Jefferson, 1978). The turn "can be seen by participants as following or coming after another

speaker's turn. A conversation gets built by means of the flow of turns"
(Speier, 1973, p. 77). The turn segments and orders the stream of verbal and
nonverbal behaviors at a level attended to both actors. Such simultaneous
(Schegloff, 1968). As a result, actors perceive conversations as turns composed
of acts where acts are produced by one and only one actor. The nonproducing
actor still emits behavior, but at a level both actors ignore in their perception
of the information exchange process.

The second concern centers on the exclusion of simultaneous acts of any
form. Sometimes in conversations the nonproducing actor emits verbal and/or
nonverbal behaviors at a level attended to both actors. Such simultaneous
acts are infrequent (Duncan & Fiske, 1977) and of short duration (Bein, 1974;
Jaffe & Feldstein, 1970). When simultaneity occurs, the model handles it by
chunking separate acts and linearly sequencing the acts in order of their
initiation. Thus conversation is modeled as a linear sequence of acts produced
by actors; each act is a chunk from the stream of verbal and nonverbal
behaviors emitted, detected, and/or perceived.

Conversations do not occur in spatial or chronological vacuums; they occur
in a context. The context includes aspects of both the interactional setting and
the relationship of the interactants. The conversational history of a dyad defines
the nature of the interactants' interpersonal relationship. Hinde (1979) defined
an interpersonal relationship as "some sort of intermittent interaction between
two people, involving interchanges over an extended period of time" (p. 14).
Thus any model of interpersonal relationships rests on the foundation of a
model of conversational encounters. Furthermore, many dyads do not persist
beyond the first encounter; beginning exchanges are a critical determinant of
relational history (if there is to be a history). The model presented here focuses
solely on initial interaction—conversations between persons meeting for the
first time. This limitation can, over time, be removed as components tracking
relational history are added to the model.

ASSUMPTIONS

Defining communication as an information exchange process requires
specification of important influences on the realizations of the process. A process is a system that changes over time; changes are recognized because the
realizations do not remain stable. The issue is one of modeling the sources
of influence to describe and explain changes in the realizations over time. For
conversation, the issue concerns how information exchange is initiated and
tracked over time. This section identifies influences on information exchanged
in dyadic encounters; it focuses on those influences that guide and direct the
realizations of the process over time.

THE INFLUENCE OF PAST EXPERIENCE

Though relationship development research focuses on relational history, the influence of *past experience* on dyadic interaction is rarely considered. Stated differently, individuals bring past experiences to encounters in the form of knowledge and behavior patterns, but these are often ignored in favor of knowledge and behavior patterns that develop in the dyad. Interpersonal communication must assume that past experiences of individuals affect their present and future conversational encounters. People converse in the context of a history of past encounters. Over the course of their lives, people engage in many social encounters and experience many different outcomes from these encounters. This rich experiential fabric affects the behaviors and cognitions exhibited by individuals in particular conversational encounters: A dyad's history occurs in the context of the histories of its members.

An individual's history can be summarized in different ways, and the manner chosen mirrors the influence it is presumed to have on present activities. Personality theorists represent an individual's history in terms of traits that guide behavior, presuming a consistent and a significant impact of the past on the present. By contrast, situational theorists argue that *only* present cues direct behavior; past history has no significant impact on the production of behavior. Interactionists compromise these two apparently polarized alternatives by arguing that behavior is the joint product of personality and present situation. While each perspective can marshal evidence that supports its point of view, none taken alone is sufficient to explain the production of behavior. Critical issues have been submerged by polarized argument.

Though personality theorists must grant that behavior is not always cross-situationally consistent, situational theorists must accept the occurrence of cross-situational consistency in radically different situations for some individuals and/or some behaviors. Furthermore, all perspectives ignore the influence of past situations on present behavior. Situations differ on numerous dimensions (Berger & Douglas, 1981; Berger & Perkins, 1978, 1979; Forgas, 1982) and behavior appropriate to these differing situations can be abstracted and stored in memory (Schank, 1982; Schank & Abelson, 1977). In other words, past experiences bounded by situational definition can guide future behavior.

Two major assumptions concerning the influence of past experience must, therefore, be recognized. First, past experience varies in the degree to which it produces consistency in present behavior. The range of past experience and the number of situationally differentiated knowledge structures affect the range of present behavior. Thus variance in behavior is a necessary ingredient of any model of information exchange. This variance occurs in two ways: (1) for a given individual, some behaviors exhibit more consistency than others; (2) for a given behavior, individuals differ in the amount of variance exhibited.

Thus both within individuals (across behaviors) and within behaviors (across individuals) the past influences the present to produce behavioral variability. Second, past experience influences the level of behavioral response. The mean response of an individual can be high or low for some behavior. This mean response can also vary across behaviors (within individuals) or across individuals (within behaviors). Thus past experience affects both the mean and variance of present behavioral responses.

Modeling individuals distributionally incorporates both of these principles. For example, consider Person A just prior to commencing an initial interaction. Person A has engaged in, heard of, or observed many initial interactions, and has been attracted in varying degrees to others. Person A's attraction to others can be represented as a frequency distribution of responses ranging from hatred to love. Suppose Person A usually likes others, though not strongly: Person A would have a slightly skewed distribution for liking of others, with the mean of the distribution being greater than the value representing the neutral point. The variance of the distribution represents A's response repertoire in terms of A's liking of others; the less the variance, the greater A's affectional consistency toward others. Now consider Person B, who also has a somewhat positive affectional stance toward others. Suppose, however, that B has a wider response repertoire (larger variance) than A; in other words, B is more likely than A to strongly dislike and/or strongly like others. In such a case, B's affectional stance would be less consistent than A's. Figure 9.1 depicts hypothetical distributions for A and B such that both distributions have similar means but B's has greater variance. Notice that if the variance of A's distribution approaches zero, A will be considered "trait-oriented" in terms of liking others. By contrast, consider Person C, whose mean liking response is quite negative (Figure 9.1). C is typically low, while both A and B are moderately high, in their liking of others. Note that Person C may have a large or small response repertoire, indicating situationally inconsistent or consistent behavior, respectively. Thus across individuals (within behaviors) a distributional model permits the influence of past experience to vary in degree and level.

A distributional model also permits variation in the influence of past experience across behaviors for a given individual. For example, not only may Person A have a skewed frequency distribution with a mean liking for others that is slightly positive, A may also have a frequency distribution that is skewed in the opposite direction for A's desire to exchange intimate information in initial encounters. Furthermore, A may have a wider or narrower response repertoire (variance) for the exchange of intimate information than for liking others. A distributional model permits these ranges of influence in past experience by modeling both the "typical" (mean) response as well as the repertoire (variance) of responses. Modeling individuals distributionally allows both trait and situationally differentiated influences of past experience to guide future behavior.

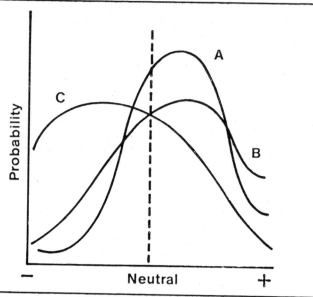

Figure 9.1   Representing Actors with Tendencies

To formalize these assumptions about past experience, let each actor in an initial dyadic conversation be represented as a set of *predispositional tendencies*. Each predispositional tendency is a probability distribution abstracted from past experience. The set of probability distributions identifies the range of potential past influences on conversation. Conceptually, predispositional tendencies represent actors' desires prior to entering a conversation; they suggest what actors typically want to have happen in conversations. The mean of each predispositional tendency is the *characteristic tendency*, which defines the typical desire of actors to enact a given behavior. The variance of each distribution describes the extent of actors' *cross-situational consistency*; the smaller the variance, the greater the cross-situational consistency. Consequently, a uniform distribution describes a situationally inconsistent tendency while a distribution with variance approaching zero describes a behavioral trait. Figure 9.2 graphs these two extremes.

Distributional modeling has the advantage of permitting individual differences without simultaneously restricting variance. Generally, a trait requires different characteristic tendencies across *and* minimal variance within individuals. A distributional model allows individuals to differ in terms of characteristic tendencies while still manifesting response variance across situations. For example, Persons B and C (Figure 9.1) manifest quite different characteristic tendencies in their liking of others though both also show considerable

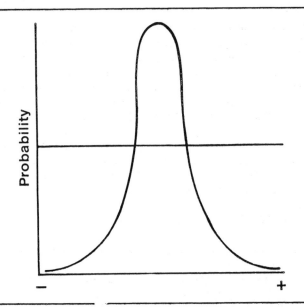

Figure 9.2 Trait and Situation Representations

response variance. Thus a distributional approach considers individual differences in the context of situational variance; the influence of past experience is incorporated with great ease and flexibility.

THE INFLUENCE OF THE PRESENT SITUATION

Predispositional tendencies describe how individuals generally approach conversational encounters. When faced with a specific encounter, however, the present situation often exerts a strong influence on behavior. Situational stimuli include the physical environment, the conversational partner, and time constraints. A specific desire for the conversation at hand will be based on assessment of situational cues in the context of a predispositional tendency. If the specific desire for a given behavior were measured for many encounters, the distribution formed by plotting the frequency of each level of the specific desire would be the predispositional tendency. As predispositional tendencies are representations of experiences, the distributions of specific desires over many encounters would be the probability distributions corresponding to those specific desires.

Each predispositional tendency is *instantiated* before conversation begins. The instantiation reflects the influence of the present situation on the actor's desires for a particular interaction. For example, Person A might have a positively skewed predispositional tendency for desire for elaboration, but for a given interaction instantiate the tendency at a point far from the mean of the distribution. Person A may decide that for this interaction he or she *wants* to elaborate only to X degree. Similar instantiations across multiple situations would imply that the actor does not differentiate those situations, yielding a consistent influence of past experience on present behavior. The unique influence of situations surfaces in varying instantiations across multiple situations and/or a consistent pattern of instantiations across actors with differing predispositional tendencies. Thus modeling individuals distributionally permits representation of varying degrees of influence of past experiences, situational differentiation, and present situational cues.

THE INFLUENCE OF CONVERSATIONAL HISTORY

Students of conversational modeling and relationship development have generally restricted "historical" influence to prior encounters and/or prior conversational acts in the present encounter. Clearly conversational history importantly influences conversational behavior; interlocutors do exert mutual behavioral effects during encounters (see, e.g., Cappella, 1981). Conversational history affects not only what *actually* occurs but also what individuals *want* to occur. Conversational history affects information exchange by influencing *desire for* as well as *actualization of* behavior.

When a predispositional tendency is instantiated, a *global desire* results, representing how an actor wants to behave in the present, specific encounter. This global desire can change during a conversation in response to previously occurring acts. For example, while awaiting a bus, an individual may initiate a conversation with a stranger. Initially, the global desire for exchanging important information may be instantiated at a low level. Nevertheless, the sequence of conversational acts may heighten the individual's desire to exchange more important information. In other words, the global desire can respond to conversational history by tracking realizations of what one *wants* in a conversation, permitting *changes* in the desire as the encounter progresses. Changes in the global desire represent changes in an actor's goals for the conversation.

Actors not only have global desires for a conversation, they also have *local desires* reflecting momentary fluctuations resulting from prior conversational utterances. Whereas global desires represent actors' goals for a *conversation*, local desires represent their goals for *acts* in a conversation. In other words, local desires reflect the influence of prior conversational acts on actors' goals for subsequent acts; they represent the constraints of prior acts on actors' subsequent behaviors. For example, assume an actor has a low *global* desire to provide information to the partner. If the partner asks numerous questions, however, the actor may have a high *local* desire to provide information because prior conversational acts constrain the actor's motives. To be polite, the actor may answer immediate questions even though the global desire to provide information is low. Thus the local desire fluctuates in response to momentary influences of conversational history, whereas the global desire changes in response to one's overall desire for the conversation. The necessary assumption here is that actors respond not only in accordance with what they personally want but also in accordance with interactional constraints.

Not only do an actor's global and local desires influence the nature of future conversational acts, but what has actually occurred also affects what is likely to occur. Each act is, therefore, represented as a set of *characteristics* corresponding to the set of tendencies. For example, an actor not only globally desires to seek X amount of information during the conversation and is locally constrained in pursuing that desire; the conversation is also segmented into acts, and each act is characterized by the amount of information actually sought. Characteristics represent what actually occurs in the conversation while desires represent what actors want to have occur. Characteristics specify the values of acts on dimensions that correspond conceptually to the set of predispositional tendencies.

Characteristics are assessed at both global and local levels. *Local characteristics* describe a particular act produced; *global characteristics* describe the history of acts up to the present moment. For example, an actor may produce an act that seeks considerable information (local characteristic) but may have sought little information if all acts up to the present are considered (global characteristic). Acts are assessed in terms of what has happened so far in the conversation (global characteristics) as well as what is happening now (local characteristics).

The first act in a conversation is based solely on global desires. Thereafter, local desires develop and place constraints on actualization of global desires. Thus all subsequent acts are influenced by both local and global desires. However, all acts after the first are also influenced by characteristics of prior acts. Various forms of reciprocity, matching, compensation, and spiraling occur in conversational behavior (Cappella, 1981; Chelune & Associates, 1979), indicating that *actualization* as well as *desire* determines the course of conversations. Global characteristics permit actors to assess the extent to which global desires are being actualized, as well as to compare relative conversational "inputs" by the participants. Global and local desires in conjunction with global and local characteristics determine the local characteristics of subsequent acts. Each act is a function of global desires, local desires, global characteristics, and the prior act's local characteristics.

This model of conversation implies that actors "track" the conversation at multiple levels. Actors track what they want to do (desires) and what they actually do (characteristics). Furthermore, desires and actualizations are tracked for the conversation (globally) as well as for the act (locally). Each actor is represented by a set of predispositional tendencies, each of which is instantiated prior to the conversation. These instantiations are the initial values of the global desires, which can change over the course of the conversation. While global desires represent what an actor wants for the conversation, local desires reflect moment-to-moment tracking of what the actor wants for an act. Conversational history influences desire for, as well as actualization of, behavior. Each act is thus represented by a set of characteristics that correspond conceptually to the set of desires. Conversational actors respond to global and local desires. An individual's life history, the present situation, and the conversational history all influence the information exchange process and are represented by predispositional tendencies, initial instantiations (initial global desires), and global and local desires and characteristics, respectively.

COMPONENTS AND PROCESS

The previous section described the sources of influence on the information exchange process. This section explores the exact composition of these sources of influence by specifying the structural components of the tendencies, desires, and characteristics. Furthermore, the relationships among these components will be described.

COMPONENTS

Given the interrelationship between tendencies, desires, and characteristics, specification of one implies specification of the components of all three. For example, desires are instantiated from the predispositional tendencies, since they are simply point estimates for a particular encounter along the same dimensions as the tendencies. Thus an actor has a predispositional tendency in the form of a probability distribution for liking of others, but in a given conversation this actor has a specific liking expectation for the partner. As predispositional tendencies are formed from initial instantiations across many encounters, specification of predispositional tendencies provides specification of global and local desires. Similarly, specification of predispositional tendencies provides specification of characteristics. Though characteristics define conversational acts, they nonetheless correspond conceptually to predispositional tendencies. Instead of having a probability distribution representing desire, characteristics have dimensions representing actuality. For example, assume my predispositional tendency for desiring to exchange intimate information is a negative exponential distribution (an "inverted-J" curve). Then, an intimacy dimension (from "not at all intimate" to "very intimate") is used to assess the characteristic of any act. The characteristic is the specific level of intimacy actualized in a given act or history of acts. Specification of predispositional tendencies provides specification of the dimensions of characteristics. In essence, the model posits structural correspondence between actors' desires and their behaviors; that is, actors track desire for and actualization of information exchange along similar dimensions.

Given this conceptual correspondence in components, component specification will be discussed in terms of predispositional tendencies. Keep in mind the following distinctions: Predispositional tendencies describe the distribution of an actor's desires across a lifetime of initial encounters; desires (global and local) describe an actor's wants in the present encounter; and characteristics (global and local) describe what actually occurs along the same dimensions. For example, my desire to seek information from others in initial encounters may be a normal distribution; my initially instantiated desire may be quite high, indicating I want to seek considerable information from my present partner; and my first few acts may not involve any information seeking at all. Thus for each component specified for predispositional tendencies, similar components exist in the model for desires (global and local) and characteristics (global and local).

Each conversational actor is represented by a set of predispositional tendencies related to *form, content, and value.* Form tendencies describe the manner in which an actor desires to emit verbal and nonverbal behavior; content tendencies describe the type of information an actor wants to emit; and value tendencies reflect judgments made of, by, and about the actors in the conversation. In other words, form tendencies define the actors' style, content tendencies define the actors' information desires, and value tendencies describe the actors' cognitions.

Form tendencies. The manner in which an actor wishes to emit verbal and nonverbal behavior can be conceptualized using two groups of related form predispositional tendencies. The first group reflects goals for outcomes of the interaction, while the second reflects goals for behaviors in the interaction. Put differently, abstract goals for conversational outcomes and for behaviors achieving those outcomes make up the form predispositional tendencies. Table 9.1 lists and defines each of the form predispositional tendencies.

Four form predispositional tendencies relate to goals for outcomes: seeking information, providing information, anticipating future interaction, and desiring to be polite. Seeking and providing information are essential aspects of conversational information exchange. In the most fundamental sense, actors either seek or provide information (or both) when they converse. Moreover, both desires are important determinants of conversational behavior during initial encounters (Berger & Kellermann, 1983, 1985; Kellermann & Berger, 1984). Generally, individuals have a greater desire to seek than to provide information (Kellermann, 1984b). Since both actors cannot achieve these desires simultaneously, the tension between seeking and provision must be resolved.

TABLE 9.1
Form Tendencies

Tendency	Definition
Outcome Goal	
Desire to seek information	Distribution describing the extent an actor wishes to solicit information about or from conversational partners, about factual or procedural matters, or about any information such partners may have or exhibit including information that is verbal or nonverbal, direct or indirect, and implicit or explicit.
Desire to provide information	Distribution representing an actor's wishes to engage in acts that emit information about or by the actor, about factual or procedural matters, or about any information the actor may have or exhibit.
Anticipation of future interaction	Distribution perceived by an actor that conversations other than those immediately involving the actor and conversational partners will occur.
Desire to be polite	Distribution representing the extent the actor wishes to adhere to socially appropriate behavior in accordance with courtesy or social norms.
Behavior Goal	
Desire to interrogate	Distribution reflecting an actor's wishes to ask conversational partners questions for or about any matter (regardless of the purpose for which interrogation is desired).
Desire to disclose	Distribution reflecting an actor's wishes to engage in the transfer of information that *because* of its transfer creates some perceived risk for the actor (i.e., transfer of information is the locus of perceived risk not type of information).
Desire to demonstrate affect	Distribution reflecting an actor's wishes to emit verbal or nonverbal behaviors over the range of strongly positive to strongly negative emotions.
Desire to be involved	Distribution reflecting an actor's wishes to be engaged in, partake of, or participate in the conversation.
Desire to elaborate	Distribution reflecting the extent to which an actor will emit verbal or nonverbal behavior to maintain conversational dyads by amplification or extension.

The typical resolution appears to under-actualize the information-seeking desire while over-actualizing the information-provision desire (Kellermann, 1984b). Both desires can be represented as probability distributions since their instantiations do vary across initial interactions (Kellermann, 1984b).

The remaining form predispositional tendencies related to outcomes are anticipating future interaction and desiring to be polite. Both desires regulate information exchange in conversational encounters. As anticipation of future interaction with others increases, attention to and recall of information about them increases (Berscheid, Graziano, Monson, & Dermer, 1976; Harvey, Yarkin, Lightner, & Town, 1980). Furthermore, people are more attracted to and more willing to make inferences about persons they expect to meet again (Kiesler, Kiesler, & Pallak, 1967; Knight & Vallacher, 1981; Miller, Norman, & Wright, 1978; Tyler & Sears, 1977). Berger and Roloff (1982) have suggested that anticipating future interaction with others also alters the extent to which information about them is sought.

As with anticipation of future interaction, the desire to be polite is important in initial interactions. The social appropriateness of disclosure (Chaikin & Derlega, 1974; Derlega & Grzelak, 1979) and politeness forms (Brown & Levinson, 1978; Ferguson, 1976) regulate information flow in interactions. Indeed, information seeking and provision are at least partially regulated by social appropriateness (Berger & Kellermann, 1983, 1985; Kellermann & Berger, 1984).

These four form tendencies concerned with outcomes are related to a second group of form tendencies that more directly concern the behavior of actors. This second group represents various behavioral goals actors have for the conversation. There are five behavioral-goal form predispositional tendencies: desire to interrogate, desire to disclose, desire to demonstrate affect, desire to be involved, and desire to elaborate. Desire to question (Berger & Kellermann, 1983), disclose information (Chelune & Associates, 1979), exhibit positive or negative emotions (Harper, Wiens, & Matarazzo, 1978; Kellermann & Berger, 1984), actively converse (Cappella, 1983; Cegala, 1978, 1981; Cegala, Savage, Brunner, & Conrad, 1982), and amplify or extend utterances (Berger & Kellermann, 1985) all vary across conversational encounters. Furthermore, the instantiation of these five tendencies defines the nature of strategies of information exchange. For example, the interrogation strategy isolated by Berger and Kellermann (1983) requires more than instantiation of a strong desire to interrogate; it also generally results in a low instantiation of the disclosure tendency, a medium-high (positive) instantiation of the affect tendency, a relatively high instantiation of the involvement tendency, and a medium-low instantiation of the elaboration tendency (Kellermann, 1983). Similarly, the relaxation strategy (Kellermann & Berger, 1984) is not only defined by a very high positive instantiation of the affect tendency; but also a medium-low instantiation of the interrogation tendency, a medium instantiation of the disclosure tendency, a very high instantiation of the involvement tendency, and a medium instantiation of the elaboration tendency. Instantiations of these five tendencies describe the strategies individuals attempt to actualize when seeking information. Moreover, instantiations of these five tendencies describe strategies individuals may employ to avoid seeking information. Persons avoiding information seeking often refrain from asking questions, disclose a great deal about the self, display medium-high positive affect, medium levels of involvement, and very high levels of elaboration (Berger & Kellermann, 1983; Kellermann & Berger, 1984).

The two groups of form predispositional tendencies—outcome goals and behavioral goals—describe how actors regulate the transfer of information in conversation. Depending upon the instantiations of these nine predispositional tendencies, actors will vary their desire to seek or provide information, expect or not expect to converse with their partner again, want to act in a socially appropriate manner, or ask questions, disclose information, demonstrate affect, be involved, and maintain or extend utterances.

Content tendencies. Content predispositional tendencies refer to the attributes of information an actor may wish to emit. These predispositional tendencies imply that the information exchanged in conversations can and should be represented dimensionally rather than categorically. Thus this model suggests that categorical schemes, based on such features as topics or facts versus opinions, inadequately represent the concept of information. Since any topic can be discussed in various ways, it has a range of values along any dimension of interest. For example, while "the weather" is often deemed a superficial and general topic, it is certainly possible to discuss specific, exact details of the weather given the desire and opportunity. Moreover, the weather need not be a boring topic; in times of floods, hurricanes, tornados, and blizzards, the weather is a critically important and interesting topic of discussion. A dimensional approach that includes such concepts as "specificity," "interest value," and "importance," would detect differences that occur in the discussion of any topic while a categorical scheme would ignore such variance. The present model is dimensionally based, suggesting that actors are less concerned with tracking the exact topic than they are with how they are doing so or how they want the topic to progress.

The nature of the information exchanged in conversations is described by 13 content tendencies. These tendencies are defined by the endpoints of the dimensions underlying the distribution. For ease of discussion, however, each will be referred to by only one of its two defined endpoints. Table 9.2 summarizes these 13 content tendencies: clarity, generality, personalness, importance, similarity, knowledge base, interest level, accuracy, opinionation, explanatory, typicality, positivity, and informativeness.

These 13 content predispositional tendencies provide a basis for understanding information strategies interlocutors may employ. For example, the "stranger-on-the-train" phenomenon can be described by examining the instantiations of content tendencies. The stranger desires to be high in information clarity, very particular, very personal, very important, somewhat to very dissimilar, high in knowledge, high in interest, somewhat to very accurate, moderately explanatory, a mixture of facts and opinions, very atypical, neutral to positive in affective reaction, and highly informative. By contrast, the

TABLE 9.2
Content Tendencies

Tendency	Definition
Ambiguity/Clarity	Distribution of an actor's wishes concerning the extent to which the meanings of conversational acts are open to many or few interpretations.
General/Specific	Distribution indicating the extent an actor wishes conversational acts to contain particular information.
Nonpersonal/Personal	Distribution referring to the actual or perceived intimacy of the information an actor wishes conversational acts to contain.
Unimportant/Important	Distribution of the extent an actor wishes conversational acts to contain information of consequence or significance.
Dissimilarities/Similarities	Distribution of the extent an actor wishes conversational acts to contain information that concerns differences or communalities between the actors.
Nonknowledgeable/ Knowledgeable	Distribution of the extent an actor wishes conversational acts to contain information about which the actor has (or does not have) an internal store of associated information (i.e., the extent of the knowledge base an actor can bring to bear on conversational acts).
Uninteresting/Interesting	Distribution of the extent an actor wishes conversational acts to contain information that excites or engages attention.
Inaccurate/Accurate	Distribution of the extent an actor wishes conversational acts to contain information that is exact, truthful, or correct (i.e., the reliability and validity of the information).
Fact/Opinion	Distribution of the extent an actor wishes conversational acts to contain information that reflects a given state of events, ranging from actuality to beliefs of or about actuality.
Description/Explanation	Distribution of the extent an actor wishes conversational acts to contain information that characterizes persons or objects, ranging from characteristic presentation to interpretation.
Atypical/Typical	Distribution of the extent an actor wishes conversational acts to contain information that ranges in the degree to which it is expected (i.e., frequent).
Negative/Positive	Distribution of the emotional reaction an actor wishes the information in conversational acts to produce.
Uninformative/Informative	Distribution of the extent the actor wishes conversational acts to permit the making of inferences about the actor's self.

recipient of the stranger's woes desires less specific, particular, personal, and important information. Regardless of the specific topic, individuals desire to regulate the information transferred along these dimensions.

Each of these dimensions is tracked by actors during conversations, both in terms of desire and behavior. Ambiguity (Eisenberg, 1984; Siegman & Pope, 1972) often eases conversational strains, permitting actors to restrict information flow or signal the undesirablility of particular conversational acts. While actors can desire to exchange clear information, they can also desire to keep the information exchanged general. Most categorical schemes for information implicitly assume that information varies in its generality. The personalness dimension reflects the importance of informational intimacy in initial encounters—long the subject of much self-disclosure research (for a review, see Chelune & Associates, 1979). Actors also vary in their instantiated desire to exchange important information, with differences often reflecting the purpose of a particular encounter. For example, encounters concerning the proper style for typing a dissertation have actors instantiating a high desire for important information. By contrast, the jolly exchanges that frequently occur in the hallway outside my office usually create instantiations of a low desire for exchange of important information.

The desire to exchange information about similarities conforms with the common observation that conversants in initial encounters often search for common ground. Having a knowledge base about information exchanged during initial interaction relates to the degree to which the interaction can be labeled "scripted" and "mindless" (Langer, 1978; Schank & Abelson, 1977) as opposed to "nonscripted" and "mindful." Though individuals prefer familiar to unfamiliar topics, a "knowledge information differential" often spurs conversations onward (Allen & Guy, 1974). While the information in most initial interactions is relatively superficial, this does not mean it is necessarily uninteresting. When engagement and/or continuation of a conversation is not preferred, the desire to exchange interesting information likely will be low. The accuracy of the information exchanged in a conversation may reflect both a reporting bias and a knowledge bias (Higgins, 1981). Hewes and Planalp (1982) indicate that social actors believe a considerable portion of information exchanged is inaccurate. The desire to exchange opinion information cannot only be instantiated at differing levels by actors, it can change during the course of initial encounters. Initial interactions typically commence with factual exchanges and move progressively to opinion exchanges (Berger, Gardner, Clatterbuck, & Schulman, 1976). The desire to exchange explanatory information also varies depending on actors' goals in initial encounters (Berger & Kellermann, 1983). The desire to exchange typical, positive, and informative information has been examined in the context of the negativity effect (Fiske, 1980; Kanouse & Hanson, 1972; Kellermann, 1984b). In general, movement away from neutral affective reactions decreases typicality and increases informativeness. As a whole, these 13 content tendencies emphasize that actors consider numerous dimensions when regulating the information exchanged in initial encounters.

Value tendencies. Value predispositional tendencies refer to the cognitions and judgments actors have of themselves and others that influence the information exchange process. Because of the nature of such judgments, value desires and value characteristics are viewed as equivalent.

There are 13 value predispositional tendencies, and these can be grouped into five categories (Table 9.3). The liking category includes both one's liking of the other and the perception of the other's liking of self. The importance of attraction to initial interaction is well documented, with research indicating that liking is an important cognitive appraisal of affective orientation (Berscheid & Walster, 1978).

Perceived similarity defines the second category of value tendencies, which can occur at demographic, experience, attitude, goal, or value levels. Though similarity and liking are often positively related, recent evidence suggests that these judgments are made independently in initial encounters (Sunnafrank, 1983; Sunnafrank & Miller, 1981).

The uncertainty category of value tendencies embraces uncertainty about self as well as the partner. Berger (1979, 1987; Berger & Calabrese, 1975) has assigned to uncertainty the role of a central explanatory construct in understanding initial interactions, and judgments of uncertainty clearly are made and do vary across conversational encounters (Kellermann, 1984b). Operating in conjunction with these uncertainty tendencies are important value tendencies. While Berger generally assumes that uncertainty reduction is important in initial encounters, instances clearly exist when its reduction is irrelevant. For example, service encounters (e.g., visiting with the gas station attendant or the McDonald's clerk) rarely reduce actors' uncertainty about each other nor do the actors care to do so.

The outcome category of value tendencies reflects actors' judgments about the "end result" of the conversational encounter. Actors not only track their own outcome valence and the importance of that outcome, they also consider the outcome valence and outcome importance for the partner. The actor category of value tendencies includes judgments of the expected importance of the conversational partners to each other. Actors consider both their importance to their partners and their partners' importance to themselves. While outcomes in a given conversation may be trivial, many initial interactions often take place where, for some reason, at least one of the two actors is perceived to be important to the other.

These 13 value tendencies all concern an actor's cognitions about self and about conversational partners. Considerable research indicates the importance of such judgments in initial encounters. Although there are many possible judgments that actors may make in conversations, these 13 are most relevant. Furthermore, other judgments are determinants of these distributions but *not* determinants of behavior in initial interactions. For example, status differences between individuals in initial interactions often affect the social behavior of

TABLE 9.3
Value Tendencies

Tendency	Definition
Liking	
Liking of other	Distribution reflecting an actor's affective orientation toward others.
Perception of liking of self	Distribution reflecting an actor's appraisal of others' effective orientation toward the actor.
Perceived Similarity	Distribution of an actor's beliefs about the extent of correspondence between conversational partners and the actor.
Uncertainty	
Uncertainty about self	Distribution reflecting an actor's knowledge of performance of behaviors (behavioral uncertainty).
Uncertainty about other	Distribution reflecting an actor's ability to describe, predict, and understand others' behavior (cognitive uncertainty).
Importance of self uncertainty	Distribution reflecting an actor's assessment of the relevance of the uncertainty about self.
Importance of other uncertainty	Distribution reflecting an actor's assessment of the relevance of uncertainty about others.
Outcome	
Outcome valence for self	Distribution of perceived conversational outcomes, ranging from very negative to very positive, that an actor expects to experience.
Outcome valence for other	Distribution of an actor's perceptions of others' expected outcomes.
Importance of self outcome	Distribution of an actor's perceptions of the consequence or significance of conversational outcomes for the actor.
Importance of other outcome	Distribution of an actor's perceptions of the consequence or significance of conversational outcomes for conversational partners.
Actor	
Importance of self to other	Distribution of an actor's beliefs about his or her significance to conversational partners for achieving some goal, material or non-material, at present or in the future.
Importance of other to self	Distribution of an actor's perceptions of his or her partner's significance of the actor for achieving some goal, material or non-material, at present or in the future.

interactants. Nevertheless, status differences are reflected in the predispositional tendencies (based on experience) and the initial instantiation (due to the conversational partner); status differences alter what instantiations will occur in form, content, and value tendencies.

PROCESSUAL THESIS

While this model of information exchange in initial interaction appears complex, its workings are conceptually simple. Actors converse after instantiating form, content, and value predispositional tendencies. Actors' global desires may change during the conversation for any of these tendencies. Furthermore, local desires develop in response to preceding conversational acts. Actors track both desire and actualization of each form, content, and value dimension. This section addresses how these desires and characteristics (actualizations) affect each other during the conversation by examining the process that relates the structural components.

The model focuses on movement from act to act in conversations. In other words, the model assumes the characteristics of acts need not remain stable and that changes in characteristics can be described and predicted. Furthermore, the model posits that global and local desires interact with global and local characteristics of previous acts in the production of subsequent acts. Thus the model aims at predicting changes in desires and characteristics from act to act during the course of a conversation.

The first act in the conversation is completely determined by initial instantiations (initial global desires). All following acts are determined by local and global desires and characteristics. Given an act, the actor's and partner's perceptions of it set or reset their global and local desires. The perception of the act sets its local characteristics in the context of past experience, including previous conversational history. Global characteristics associated with each act indicate the extent to which each dimension has been actualized. Changes in global desires reflect changes in the desire to act in a particular way for the conversation, while changes in local desires reflect changes in act-by-act demands. Given a dyadic conversation, it is assumed that actors have predispositional tendencies that are instantiated, that acts can be assigned to an actor, that acts have characteristics, and that the instantiations and characteristics change in particular ways over the course of the conversation. Actors track both their own desires and characteristics and the characteristics of their partner's acts. In addition, actors infer the desires of conversational partners from the partner's acts.

Though the exact relationships specifying change have been modeled with recursive equations (Kellermann, 1983), only the more abstract, conceptual underpinnings of the modeling of change will be discussed here. Three principles underlie the recursive equations. First, each desire and characteristic following the first act is weighted in the context of the previous value for that desire or characteristic. Thus each form, content, and value global desire is used to predict the next value of that desire after each act. Second, each form and content desire or characteristic can influence other (though not all) desires and characteristics within its own type. In other words, both form and content desires and characteristics affect other form and content desires and characteristics. For example, the desire to seek information (a form global desire) influences the desire to interrogate (among others), though it does not serve as a causal determinant of anticipation of future interaction. Third, content characteristics are the sole determinants of changes in value desires. Value and content components can both influence subsequent form components; similarly, value and form components can influence subsequent content components. In the absence of any new information, however, the initial value desires remain stable. These three principles are diagrammed in Figure 9.3.

A value desire (judgment) does not arise in a vacuum; it stems from information. Although perceived similarity and liking sometimes have been linked in a mutually causal relationship, and liking another and perceiving the other's liking of self have been interpreted similarly, these "relationships" arise through the influence of information. Studies examining such relationships typically provide individuals with similar or dissimilar *information* or negative or positive evaluations (also *information*), and the relationships are measured and attributed solely to similarity or liking. Nevertheless, the information is the crucial determinant of these judgments. The correlation of judgments after receiving information relates to how actors use the information rather than direct causal linkages between judgments.

This view of information exchange in the alteration of instantiations of value desires is similar to views proposed by Ajzen (1974, 1977) and Anderson (1981). The information processing approach to such judgments as attraction assumes:

> The attraction of one person (P) toward another person (O) is determined by P's information about O. If the information is generally favorable, P will be attracted to O; if the information is unfavorable, P's evaluation of O will be negative. ... The only direct and immediate determinant of attraction is the information that is available to P. Any other factor can influence attraction only to the extent that it has an effect on this information. (Ajzen, 1977, p.53)

Though Ajzen's and Anderson's approaches are somewhat different, both assume that information is the immediate determinant of change in such value judgments as attraction. Such an approach holds that information drives changes in inferences and judgments. Kellermann (1983) demonstrated that for the value desires of liking other, other's liking of self, perceived similarity, outcome valence, and outcome importance, changes occurred as a function of the information exchanged in the conversation. Thus information plays a central role in this model of conversation, since only information produces changes in value tendencies.

The model also assumes that actors track each form and content characteristic of every conversational act and then revise global and local desires for form, content, and value. Furthermore, the model posits that actors' perceptions and judgments are anchored in previous ones, that the desires and

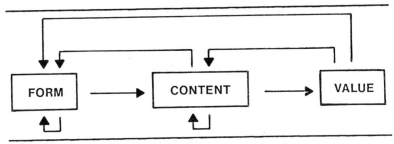

Figure 9.3 Processual Relationships

characteristics related to each act are perceived in the context of previous values of those desires and characteristics. Spirals of intimacy (for a review, see Chelune & Associates, 1979), movement from factual to opinion information (Berger et al., 1976), and movement from descriptive to explanatory information (Ayres, 1979) are modeled using assumptions about the nature of the information exchange process. The primary assumptions are that such spirals will occur when information is perceived to be typical, somewhat positive, and somewhat informative (Kellermann, 1984b) and when individuals are at least somewhat attracted to their conversational partners (Sears & Whitney, 1973). Both of these assumptions have been extensively supported in prior research. Moreover, the two assumptions define the "typical" initial encounter. The model also suggests that spirals are not necessary in initial encounters and specifies conditions when such information characteristics are not expected. For example, negative evaluations of the partner, low desire for involvement, and atypical information exchange inhibit such spirals. Thus the model sees information as the fundamental determinant of changes in judgment and suggests the information exchanged is determined by desires and characteristics of prior conversational acts. The processual thesis is thus quite simple: *Information exchange is the only basis for alteration of desires or characteristics; without information, stasis occurs.*

PROCESSUAL RESEARCH

The form, content, and value desires and characteristics are related to each other by recursive equations too lengthy to describe in this chapter. Research examining some of these linkages will be explored in this section; particularly, research that examines these linkages in terms of the influence *of* components on other components and the influence *by* components on other components. Only selected form, content, and value components will be examined.

Form component research. Form components influence other form components and content components. When desire to seek information is high, both the desire to provide information and actualization of elaboration tend to be low (Berger & Kellermann, 1983). A strong desire to seek information does not necessarily produce increases in the desire or actualization of question asking. The desire to seek information in conjunction with the desire to provide information determines levels of question asking, disclosure, and affect (Kellermann, 1983). A strong desire to seek information and a weak desire to provide information create a strong desire to ask questions; however, if both information seeking and provision desires are strong, disclosure and affect are actualized at a higher level than interrogation. In a similar vein, a low desire to provide information decreases the desire to interrogate (Berger & Kellermann, 1985). In other words, information provision and information seeking desires jointly influence the desires to ask questions, demonstrate affect, disclose, and elaborate. Still, the actualization of these desires is often attenuated by the desire to be polite. Since it is socially inappropriate to ask too few (Berger & Kellermann, 1983) or too many questions (Berger, 1979), a strong desire to be polite fosters a local desire to interrogate that attenuates the actualization of extreme interrogation desires. Similarly a strong desire to be polite limits the actualization of disclosure. Chaikin and Derlega (1974) found that nonreciprocal disclosure, either too much or too little, was viewed as less appropriate than reciprocal disclosure.

Anticipation of future interaction also influences other form components. As the expectation of future encounters decreases, positive affect displays are inhibited and the desire to be involved decreases (Kellermann, 1983). From a social exchange perspective, the investment in exchanging more positive affect is not warranted by the potential costs of such an exchange when the expectation of future contact is low. Form desires causally influence other form desires and characteristics.

Form desires also influence information desires and characteristics. As the desire to seek information increases, individuals exchange more opinion and explanatory information (Berger & Kellermann, 1983). As the desire to provide information decreases, specificity and interest value of the exchanged information decrease (Berger & Kellermann, 1985). As the desire to exchange affect decreases—that is, as the desire to exchange negative affect increases—individuals exchange more negative information (Kellermann & Berger, 1984). Anticipation of future interaction relates parabolically (U-shaped) to information personalness. When anticipation of future interaction is either high or low, the global desire to exchange personal information is strong (Davis, 1976; Murdoch, Chenowith, & Rissman, 1969; Thibaut & Kelley, 1959). The stranger-on-the-train phenomenon occurs because of a lack of constraints imposed by the improbability of future interaction. The anticipation of future interaction also increases the desire to exchange important information, since information is valued because of its potential future utility (Roloff & Miller, in press). The desire to be involved is directly related to the clarity of exchanged information: the more involved, the more clear (Siegman & Pope, 1972). Similarly, as the desire to be involved increases, information specificity (Baxter, 1979b), personalness (Baxter, 1979a; Cappella, 1983; Cegala, 1981), and positivity (Archer & Berg, 1978) increase. The desire to be polite is positively correlated with the desire to exchange positive information (Gilbert & Whiteneck, 1976). A strong desire to be polite promotes information ambiguity when prior conversational acts are negatively received (Bavelas, 1983). Though surely not comprehensive, these results provide some idea of the influence of form components on information components and on other form components.

Content and value components research. While content desires and characteristics influence form, content, and value components, this section will mainly explore the content to value component linkage. As mentioned earlier, this content to value linkage is the core of the model, with changes in judgments occurring only as a function of the information being exchanged.

For liking the conversational partner, information alters the initial instantiation as a function of its informativeness and negativity: The more informative and negative the information, the less the actor will like the partner (Kellermann, 1983, 1984b). Significantly, information similarity does not play a role in the judgment of attraction. Ajzen (1974, 1977) has argued that similarity in information leads to the perception of positivity or negativity. By contrast, other researchers (Byrne & Rhamey, 1965; Clore, 1977; Clore & Baldridge, 1970) argue Ajzen's studies have insufficient power to detect the influence of similarity information on judgments of liking. Nonetheless, in a study reporting high power, Kellermann (1983) found that only the interaction of positivity and informativeness significantly predicted change in initial values of liking. Moreover, Kellermann found that similarity information was not significantly related to alterations in liking when the positivity and informativeness of the information were controlled. Sunnafrank (1983; Sunnafrank & Miller, 1981) has recently reported equivalent inability to produce attraction effects from similarity in initial interactions.

By contrast, the value judgment of perceived similarity changes in response to information similarity (Kellermann, 1983). Furthermore, the more important (Banikotes, Russel, & Linder, 1972; Lamberth, Rataj, & Padd, 1974) and opinion based (Shrauger & Jones, 1968) the similarity, the greater its impact on judgment. Consequently, changes in perceived similarity are a function of the interactive product of information similarity, importance, and opinionation (Kellermann, 1983). Individuals can, therefore, perceive themselves to be dissimilar from others while simultaneously liking them, just as others perceived to be similar can be disliked. Interlocutors may perceive themselves to be similar to others and may like others if the information exchanged is equivalently positive, informative, similar, important, and opinionated. Indeed, given the somewhat positive and informative information typically exchanged in initial interactions (Kellermann, 1983, 1984b) and the moderately similar, somewhat important, and somewhat opinionated information exchanged (Kellermann, 1983), these judgments could be correlated but not causally related. Kellermann (1983) found that while the interaction of negative and informative information formed a basis for the liking judgment, the interaction of similar, important, and opinion-based information formed a basis for the similarity judgment.

It is significant that uncertainty reduction did not occur as a function of the informativeness of information exchanged in Kellermann's (1983) research. Berger (1979) has argued that atypical information reduces uncertainty more than typical information. Given that atypical information is more informative than typical information (Fiske, 1980; Kanouse & Hanson, 1972; Kellermann, 1984b), uncertainty reduction theory predicts that informativeness permits the formation of proactive and retroactive attributions and, consequently, the reduction of uncertainty. Nonetheless, uncertainty did not vary in relation to the informativeness of information even though uncertainty did decrease over the course of the conversation. The role of information in the reduction of uncertainty clearly requires further examination.

While the model suggests information should be examined dimensionally, much content analysis of conversations focuses on topics as a fundamental feature (Crow, 1983; Haas & Sherman, 1982; Planalp & Tracy, 1980). Similarly, much social cognition work presumes that the "unit" of content analysis should be the topic. Researchers in psychology (Abelson, 1976, 1981; Bower, Black, & Turner, 1979; Schank, 1982; Schank & Abelson, 1977) have suggested that knowledge about behavior in social interaction is extracted and stored in the form of cognitive scripts. Scripts are cognitive structures that provide conceptual representations of routine event sequences for specific situations. Scripts involve knowledge about action sequences, provide a summary of information about one type of situation across many different dimensions, vary in abstractness and internal coherence, and support a body of inferences (Kellermann, 1984a). The initial interaction script consists of a "topic bank" and a "procedural routine" for handling topic development. The topic bank puts conversational topics in sequences within three main areas—initiation, maintenance, and termination—though within each area, the topics are only loosely ordered. The procedural routine orders talk about a given topic, proceeding through a fact acquisition phase, a discussion phase, an evaluation phase, a direction phase (i.e., goals), and an enabling condition phase (Kellermann & Broetzmann, 1984). The choice of topic, as well as how far interlocutors will move through the procedural routine for any topic, seems to depend on such variables as intimacy, liking, and information-seeking desire. Thus form, content, and value components drive the employment of the initial interaction script. Content components are tracked by actors and in conjunction with form and value components, determine topic selection and development.

Viewing conversation as an information exchange process rests on the thesis that information exchange regulates changes in cognitions; content components completely determine value components. While the form and content components each influence other components within their category, the value components change strictly as a function of content components. By necessity, the form components influence the value components only through the mediation of content, that is, information exchange.

IMPLICATIONS

Five main implications of this model of conversation as a process of information exchange are apparent. First, cognition both guides and is influenced by the exchange of information. The model suggests that conversational behavior is a function not only of talk but of thought; in other words, information exchange is a cognitive as well as a behavioral process. However, no presumption is made that individuals are consciously aware of the information processing that is occurring. Desires can be instantiated without cognitive awareness just as they may change in response to the conversational history without awareness. Nonetheless, the process of information exchange involves cognitive and behavioral components. Second, affect guides and is responsive to information exchange. The form predispositional tendency of desire to exchange affect, the information characteristic of positivity, and the liking value tendencies all reflect the role of affect in conversational interaction. Thus this model views conversation not only as a behavioral and cognitive process, but as an affective process as well. Third, the cognitive, behavioral, and affective interface in the information exchange process occurs in the context of conversational history as well as the history of people's lives. The information exchange process suggests that context is critical to understanding interpersonal communication. However, this context must include more than just the history that develops as the conversation progresses. Individuals come to conversations with life histories that shape the context of specific interactions. Fourth, modeling conversation as an information exchange process provides a comprehensive and thorough approach to examining conversational behavior. Including verbal and nonverbal components as well as affective, behavioral, and cognitive components results in a holistic view of interpersonal interaction. Finally, communication is clearly the heart of social interaction. Information is the critical link in the model, and the generation, production, and comprehension of information rest on communicative exchanges.

REFERENCES

Abelson, R. P. (1976). Script processing in attitude formation and decision making. In J. S. Carroll & J. W. Payne (Eds.), *Cognition and social behavior* (pp. 33-45). Hilldale, NJ: Lawrence Erlbaum.

Abelson, R. P. (1981). Psychological status of the script concept. *American Psychologist, 36,* 715-729.

Ajzen, I. (1974). Effects of information on interpersonal attraction: Similarity versus affective value. *Journal of Personality and Social Psychology, 29,* 374-380.

Ajzen, I. (1977). Information processing approaches to interpersonal attraction. In S. W. Duck (Ed.), *Theory and practice of interpersonal attraction* (pp. 51-78). London: Academic Press.

Allen, D. E., & Guy, R. F. (1974). *Conversation analysis: The sociology of talk.* The Hague: Mouton.

Anderson, N. H. (1981). *Foundations of information integration theory.* New York: Academic Press.

Archer, R. L., & Berg, J. H. (1978). Disclosure reciprocity and its limits: A reactance analysis. *Journal of Experimental Social Psychology, 14,* 527-540.

Argyle, M. (1969). *Social interaction.* Chicago: Aldine.

Atkinson, M. L., & Allen, V. L. (1979). Level of analysis as a determinant of meaning of nonverbal behavior. *Social Psychology Quarterly, 42,* 270-274.

Ayres, J. (1979). Uncertainty and social penetration theory expectations about relationship communication: A comparative test. *Western Journal of Speech Communication, 43,* 192-200.

Banikotes, P. G., Russel, J. M., & Linden, J. D. (1972). Interpersonal attraction in real and simulated interactions. *Journal of Personality and Social Psychology, 23,* 1-7.

Bavelas, J. B. (1983). Situations that lead to disqualification. *Human Communication Research, 9,* 130-145.

Baxter, L. (1979a). Self-disclosure as a relationship disengagement strategy: An exploratory investigation. *Human Communication Research, 5,* 215-222.

Baxter, L. (1979b). *Self-reported disengagement strategies in friendship relationships.* Paper presented at the annual meeting of the Western Speech Communication Association, Los Angeles.

Bein, M. F. (1974). *Temporal factors of talk in unconstrained conversation: Personal and situational relationships.* Unpublished doctoral dissertation, University of Florida.

Berger, C. R. (1979). Beyond initial interaction: Uncertainty, understanding, and the development of interpersonal relationships. In H. Giles & R. St. Clair (Eds.), *Language and social psychology* (pp. 122-144). Oxford: Basil Blackwell.

Berger, C. R. (1987). Communicating under uncertainty. In M. Roloff & G.R. Miller (Eds.), *Interpersonal Processes* (pp. 39-62). Newbury Park, CA: Sage.

Berger, C. R., & Calabrese, R. J. (1975). Some explorations in initial interaction and beyond: Toward a developmental theory of interpersonal communication. *Human Communication Research, 1,* 99-112.

Berger, C. R., & Douglas, W. (1981). Studies in interpersonal epistemology: III. Anticipated interaction, self-monitoring, and observational context selection. *Communication Monographs, 48,* 183-196.

Berger, C. R., Gardner, R. R., Clatterbuck, G. W., & Schulman, L. S. (1976). Perceptions of information sequencing in relationship development. *Human Communication Research, 3* 29-46.

Berger, C. R., & Kellermann, K. (1983). To ask or not to ask: Is that a question? In R. Bostrom (Ed.), *Communication yearbook 7* (pp. 342-368). Newbury Park, CA: Sage.

Berger, C. R., & Kellermann, K. (1985). *Personal opacity and social information acquisition: Seek, but ye may not find.* Paper presented at the annual meeting of the International Communication Association, Honolulu, HI.

Berger, C. R., & Perkins, J. W. (1978). Studies in interpersonal epistemology: I. Situational attributes in observational context selection. In B. D. Ruben (Ed.), *Communication yearbook 2* (pp. 171-184). New Brunswick, NJ: Transaction Books.

Berger, C. R., & Perkins, J. W. (1979). *Studies in interpersonal epistemology: II. Self-monitoring, involvement, facial affect, similarity, and observational context selection.* Paper presented at the annual meeting of the Speech Communication Association, San Antonio, TX.

Berger, C. R., & Roloff, M. E. (1982). Thinking about friends and lovers: Social cognition and relational trajectories. In M. E. Roloff & C. R. Berger (Eds.), *Social cognition and communication* (pp. 151-192). Newbury Park, CA: Sage.

Berscheid, E., Graziano, W., Monson, T.O., & Dermer, M. (1976). Outcome dependency: Attention, attribution, and attraction. *Journal of Personality and Social Psychology, 34,* 978-989.

Berscheid, E., & Walster, E. H. (1978). *Interpersonal attraction* (2nd ed.). Reading, MA: Addison-Wesley.

Bower, G. H., Black, J. B., & Turner, J. T. (1979). Scripts in text comprehension and memory. *Cognitive Psychology, 11,* 177-220.

Brown, P., & Levinson, S. (1978). Universals in language usage: Politeness phenomena. In E. N. Goody (Ed.), *Questions and politeness: Strategies in social interaction* (pp.74-289). Cambridge: Cambridge University Press.

Byrne, D., & Rhamey, R. (1965). Magnitude of positive and negative reinforcements as a determinant of attraction. *Journal of Personality and Social Psychology, 2,* 884-889.

Cappella, J. N. (1981). Mutual influence in expressive behavior: Adult-adult and infant-adult dyadic interaction. *Psychological Bulletin, 89,* 101-132.

Cappella, J. N. (1983). Conversational involvement: Approaching and avoiding others. In J. M. Wiemann & R. P. Harrison (Eds.), *Nonverbal interaction* (pp. 113-148). Newbury Park, CA: Sage.

Cegala, D. J. (1978). *Interaction involvement: A necessary dimension of communicative competence.* Paper presented at the annual meeting of the Speech Communication Association, Minneapolis, MN.

Cegala, D. J. (1981). Interaction involvement: A cognitive dimension of communicative competence. *Communication Education, 30,* 109-121.

Cegala, D. J., Savage, G. T., Brunner, C. C., & Conrad, A. B. (1982). An elaboration of the meaning of interaction involvement: Toward the development of a theoretical concept. *Communication Monographs, 49,* 229-248.

Chaikin, A. L., & Derlega, V. J. (1974). *Self-disclosure.* Morristown, NJ: General Learning Press.

Chang, S. K. (1982). On a theory of information exchange. In R. Trappl, L. Ricciardi, & G. Pask (Eds.), *Progress in cybernetics and systems research* (Vol. 9, pp. 313-323). Washington, DC: Hemisphere.

Chelune, G. J., & Associates (1979). *Self-disclosure: Origins, patterns, and implications of openness in interpersonal relationships.* San Francisco: Jossey-Bass.

Cherry, C. (1971). *World communication: Threat or promise? A socio-technical approach.* London: John Wiley.

Clore, G. L. (1977). Reinforcement and affect in attraction. In S. W. Duck (Ed.), *Theory and practice in interpersonal attraction* (pp. 23-30). London: Academic Press.

Clore, G. L., & Baldridge, B. (1970). The behavior of item weights in attitude-attraction research. *Journal of Experimental Social Psychology, 6,* 177-186.

Crow, B. K. (1983). Topic shifts in couples' conversations. In R. T. Craig & K. Tracy (Eds.), *Conversational coherence: form, structure, and strategy* (pp. 136-156). Newbury Park, CA: Sage.

Davis, D., & Perkowitz, W. T. (1979). Consequences of responsiveness in dyadic interaction: Effects of probability of response and proportion of content-related responses on interpersonal attraction. *Journal of Personality and Social Psychology, 37,* 534-550.

Davis, J. (1976). Self-disclosure in an acquaintance exercise: Responsibility for level of intimacy. *Journal of Personality and Social Psychology, 33,* 787-792.

Derlega, V. J., & Grzelak, J. (1979). Appropriateness of self-disclosure. In G. J. Chelune & Associates, *Self-disclosure: Origins, patterns, and implications of openness in interpersonal relationships* (pp. 151-176). San Francisco: Jossey-Bass.

Douglas, W. (1983). Scripts and self-monitoring: When does being a high self-monitor really make a difference? *Human Communication Research, 10,* 81-96.

Douglas, W. (1984). *Initial interaction scripts: When knowing is behaving.* Paper presented at the annual meeting of the International Communication Association, San Francisco.

Duck, S. W. (1976). Interpersonal communication in developing acquaintance. In G. R. Miller (Ed.), *Explorations in interpersonal communication* (pp. 127-147). Newbury Park, CA: Sage.

Duncan, S. D. (1974). On the structure of speaker-auditor interaction during speaking turns. *Language in Society, 2,* 161-180.

Duncan, S. D., & Fiske, D. (1977). *Face-to-face interaction: Research, methods, and theory.* Hillsdale, NJ: Lawrence Erlbaum.

Eisenberg, E. M. (1984). Ambiguity as strategy in organizational communication. *Communication Monographs, 51,* 227-242.

Emler, N., & Fisher, S. (1981). *Conversation as a medium of personal information exchange.* Paper presented at the annual meeting of the British Psychological Societies, Oxford.

Ferguson, C. A. (1976). The structure and use of politeness formulas. *Language in Society, 5,* 137-151.

Fiske, S. T. (1980). Attention and weight in person perception: The impact of negative and extreme behavior. *Journal of Personality and Social Psychology, 38,* 889-908.

Forgas, J. P. (1982). Episode cognition: Internal representations of interaction routines. In L. Berkowitz (Ed.), *Advances in experimental social psychology* (Vol. 15, pp. 59-101). New York: Academic Press.

Gallois, C., & Markel, N. N. (1975). Turn-taking: Social personality and conversational style. *Journal of Personality and Social Psychology, 31,* 1134-1140.

Gilbert, S. J. (1976). Empirical and theoretical extensions of self-disclosure. In G. R. Miller (Ed.), *Explorations in interpersonal communication* (pp. 197-215). Newbury Park, CA: Sage.

Gilbert, S. J., & Whiteneck, G. G. (1976). Toward a multidimensional approach to the study of self-disclosure. *Human Communication Research, 2,* 347-355.

Goffman, E. (1964). The neglected situation. In J. Gumperz & D. Hymes (Eds.), *The ethnography of communication* (pp. 133-136). Special publication of the *American Anthropologist, 66*(6) (Part II).

Haas, A., & Sherman, M. A. (1982). Reported topics of conversation among same-sex adults. *Communication Quarterly, 30,* 332-342.

Harper, R. G., Wiens, H. N., & Matarazzo, J. D. (1978). *Nonverbal communication: The state of the art.* New York: John Wiley.

Harvey, J. H., Yarkin, K. L., Lightner, J. M., & Town, J. P. (1980). Unsolicited interpretation and recall of interpersonal events. *Journal of Personality and Social Psychology, 38,* 551-568.

Hewes, D. E., & Planalp, S. (1982). There is nothing as useful as a good theory...: The influence of social knowledge on interpersonal communication. In M. Roloff & C. Berger (Ed.), *Social cognition and communication* (pp. 107-130). Newbury Park, CA: Sage.

Higgins, E. T. (1981). The "communication game": Implications for social cognition and persuasion. In E. T. Higgins, C. P. Herman, & M. P. Zanna (Eds.), *Social cognition: The Ontario symposium* (Vol. 1, pp. 343-392). Hillsdale, NJ: Lawrence Erlbaum.

Hinde, R. A. (1979). *Towards understanding relationships.* London: Academic Press.

Jaffe, J., & Feldstein, S. (1970). *Rhythms of dialogue.* New York: Academic Press.

James, J. (1951). A preliminary study of the size determinant in small group interaction. *American Sociological Review, 16,* 474-477.

Kanouse, D. E., & Hanson, L. R., Jr. (1972). Negativity in evaluations. In E. E. Jones, D. E. Kanouse, H. H. Kelley, R. E. Nisbett, S. Valins, & B. Weiner (Eds.), *Attribution: Perceiving the causes of behavior* (pp. 47-62). Morristown, NJ: General Learning Press.

Kellermann, K. (1983). *A formal model of information exchange in social interaction.* Unpublished doctoral dissertation, Northwestern University.

Kellermann, K. (1984a). *Scripts: What are they; how do you know; and why should you care?* Paper presented at the annual meeting of the Speech Communication Association, Chicago.

Kellermann, K. (1984b). The negativity effect and its implications for initial interaction. *Communication Monographs, 51,* 37-55.

Kellermann, K., & Berger, C. R. (1984). Affect and the acquisition of social information: Sit back, relax, and tell me about yourself. In R. Bostrom (Ed.), *Communication yearbook 8* (pp. 412-445). Newbury Park, CA: Sage.

Kellermann, K., & Broetzmann, S. (1984). *Scripts in initial communicative encounters.* Paper presented at the annual meeting of the Speech Communication Association, Chicago.

Kiesler, C. A., & Kiesler, S. B., & Pallak, M. S. (1967). The effect of commitment to future interaction on reactions to norm violations. *Journal of Personality, 35,* 585-599.

Knight, J. A., & Vallacher, R. R. (1981). Interpersonal engagement in social perception: The consequences of getting into the action. *Journal of Personality and Social Psychology, 40,* 990-999.

Lamberth, J., Rataj, G. W., & Padd, W. (1974). An evaluation of differential topic importance, population homogeneity, and relatedness of attitudinal stimuli in attraction research. *Representations to the Research Society in Psychology, 5,* 89-91.

Langer, E. J. (1978). Rethinking the role of thought in social interaction. In J. H. Harvey, W. J. Ickes, & R. F. Kidd (Eds.), *New directions in attribution research:* (Vol. 2, pp. 35-58). Hillsdale, NJ: Lawrence Erlbaum.

Massad, C. M., Hubbard, M., & Newtson, D. (1979). Selective perception of events. *Journal of Experimental Social Psychology, 15,* 513-532.

Miller, D. T., Norman, S. A., & Wright, E. (1978). Distortion in person perception as a consequence of effective control. *Journal of Personality and Social Psychology, 36,* 598-607.

Miller, G. A. (1963). Speaking in general: Review of J. H. Greenberg (Ed.), "Universals of Language." *Contemporary Psychology, 8,* 417-418.

Murdoch, P., Chenowith, R., & Rissman, K. (1969). *Eligibility and intimacy effects of self-disclosure.* Paper presented at the annual meeting of the Society of Experimental Social Psychology, Madison, WI.

Newtson, D. (1973). Attribution and the unit of perception of ongoing behavior. *Journal of Personality and Social Psychology, 28,* 28-38.

Newtson, D. (1976). Foundations of attribution: The perception of ongoing behavior. In J. H. Harvey, W. J. Ickes, & R. R. Kidd (Eds.), *New directions in attribution research* (Vol. 1, pp. 223-247). Hillsdale, NJ: Lawrence Erlbaum.

Newtson, D., & Engquist, G. (1976). The perceptual organization of ongoing behavior. *Journal of Experimental Social Psychology, 12,* 436-450.

Newtson, D., Engquist, G., & Bois, J. (1977). The objective basis of behavior units. *Journal of Personality and Social Psychology, 35,* 847-862.

O'Mara, J. J. (1973). *Characteristics of dyadic conversation: An ecological approach.* Unpublished doctoral dissertation, Duquesne University.

Planalp, S., & Tracy, K. (1980). Not to change the topic but...A cognitive approach to the management of conversation. In D. Nimmo (Ed.), *Communication yearbook 4* (pp. 237-260). New Brunswick, NJ: Transaction Books.

Pruitt, D. G. (1981). *Negotiation behavior.* New York: Academic Press.

Roloff, M., & Miller, G. R. (in press). *Communicating and negotiating.* Orlando, FL: Academic Press.

Ross, L. (1977). The intuitive psychologist and his shortcomings: Distortions in the attribution process. In L. Berkowitz (Ed.), *Advances in experimental social psychology* (Vol. 10, pp. 173-220). New York: Academic Press.

Sacks, H., Schegloff, E. A., & Jefferson, G. (1978). A simplest systematics for the organization of turn taking for conversation. In J. Schenkein (Ed.), *Studies in the organization of conversational interaction* (pp. 7-56). New York: Academic Press.

Schank, R. (1982). *Dynamic memory: A theory of reminding and learning in computers and people.* New York: Cambridge University Press.

Schank, R., & Abelson, R. (1977). *Scripts, plans, goals and understanding: An inquiry into human knowledge structures.* Hillsdale, NJ: Lawrence Erlbaum.

Schegloff, E. A. (1968). Sequencing in conversational openings. *American Anthropologist, 70,* 1075-1095.

Sears, D. O., & Whitney, R. (1973). Political persuasion. In I. Pool, W. Schramm, N. Maccoby, & E. B. Parker (Eds.), *Handbook of communication* (pp. 253-289). Chicago: Rand-McNally.

Shrauger, J. S., & Jones, S. C. (1968). Social validation and interpersonal evaluations. *Journal of Experimental Social Psychology, 4,* 315-323.

Siegman, A. W., & Pope, B. (1972). The effects of ambiguity and anxiety on interviewee verbal behavior. In A. W. Siegman & B. Pope (Eds.), *Studies in dyadic communication* (pp. 29-68). New York: Pergamon.

Speier, M. (1973). *How to observe face-to-face communication: A sociological introduction.* Pacific Palisades, CA: Goodyear Publishing.

Sunnafrank, M. (1983). Attitude similarity and interpersonal attraction in communication processes: In pursuit of an ephemeral influence. *Communication Monographs, 50,* 273-284.

Sunnafrank, M. J., & Miller, G. R. (1981). The role of initial conversations in determining attraction to similar and dissimilar strangers. *Human Communication Research, 8,* 16-25.

Taylor, D. A. (1979). Motivational bases. In G. J. Chelune & Associates, *Self-disclosure: Origins, patterns, and implications of openness in interpersonal relationships* (pp. 110-150). San Francisco: Jossey-Bass.

Thibaut, J. W., & Kelley, H. H. (1959). *The social psychology of groups.* New York: John Wiley.

Tognoli, J. (1969). Response matching in interpersonal information exchange. *British Journal of Social and Clinical Psychology, 8,* 116-123.

Tyler, T. R., & Sears, D. O. (1977). Coming to like obnoxious people when we must live with them. *Journal of Personality and Social Psychology, 35,* 200-211.

Wheeler, L., & Nezlek, J. (1977). Sex differences in social participation. *Journal of Personality and Social Psychology, 35,* 742-754.

Chapter 10

ANALYZING INTERPERSONAL INTERACTION

Marshall Scott Poole, Joseph P. Folger, and Dean E. Hewes

COMMUNICATION RESEARCHERS HAVE given considerable attention to the role of messages in structuring social exchanges and in defining interpersonal relationships. Interaction research has examined message exchange and its consequences for social relationships in small group, organizational, family, conflict, doctor-patient, courtroom, and educational settings. These efforts have prompted the development and use of diverse methods for analyzing interaction. Included among these methods are interaction coding, ethnographic observation, conversational analysis as well as more specific techniques such as critical incident and stimulated recall procedures.

These analytical methods share a common objective of providing systematic ways of studying and understanding social interaction. Despite this underlying similarity, they differ in many important respects. These investigative tools reflect both quantitative and qualitative approaches to the study of messages in face-to-face settings. They are founded on different assumptions about how to support interpretive claims and reflect different decisions about which features of interaction need to be studied in order to understand behavior in social contexts. These and other differences raise important questions about which investigative approaches are suited to researchers' epistemological dispositions and specific research aims.

This analysis provides researchers with a basis for raising key questions about methodological options for studying social interaction. We shall outline the key features of interaction that various methods could analyze and then map the various methods for studying social interaction according to these key features.

ON THE NATURE OF INTERACTION

It is easy to assume that what is accessible to available research methods is all that is there (or, at least, all that is important) in the study of social interaction. Since methods are our eyes and ears on social interaction, they must be designed, selected, and judged with respect to the phenomena they attempt to represent. To understand methods we must first gain a broad view of interaction.

Taking a broad view of interaction has at least two benefits. First, it helps clarify the relationships among various techniques. A rather astonishing array of methods has been developed over the past 40 years, and a good way to keep them straight is to identify the features of interaction on which particular techniques are focused. This view reveals the relationships among techniques. In some cases, techniques purported to be competitors turn out to be focused on entirely different features or domains. A broad view also helps us identify the limitations of our methods. Some methods are better than others for studying a given feature, and the claims that can be supported by any given method are inherently limited.

Several key features of social interaction are displayed in Table 10.1. This set serves as a reference point for our discussion of methods. The universe distinguishes two major characteristics of social interaction, each with its own cluster of distinctive features. Interaction is, first, *structured*

TABLE 10.1
A Set of Features of Interaction Amenable to Research

I.   STRUCTURE
　　A.　Global structure
　　　　1.　Sequential
　　　　2.　Syntagmatic
　　B.　Local structure
　　　　1.　Sequential
　　　　2.　Syntagmatic

II.　MEANING
　　A.　Domain
　　　　1.　Observer-privileged meaning
　　　　　　a. Generalized
　　　　　　b. Restricted
　　　　2.　Subject-privileged meaning
　　　　　　a. Generalized
　　　　　　b. Restricted
　　B.　Intersubjectivity
　　　　1.　Stage
　　　　　　a. Fixed outcome
　　　　　　b. Variable property
　　　　2.　Process

and, second, *meaningful* in some respect. Of course, these two features may be interdependent.

STRUCTURE

Social interaction is ordered, and order derives from and is depicted in its structure. People perceive both *local* and *global* structure. Local structures are relations among individual discourse units, which include words, sentences, utterances, and turns. Localized structures are the building blocks of interaction, the immediate source of coherence and order. Global structures represent extended interaction sequences, patterned according to the purposes or issues they address. Global structures serve as an organizing framework for local units. Global structures vary in generality and extent, depending on the units they subsume; examples include topics or themes (Planalp & Tracy, 1980), social episodes such as arguments or conversations (Forgas, 1979), and long-term interaction structures in relationships (Knapp, 1984). Global structures tie into social life and social institutions as sensible units of social action. Our ability to engage in and comprehend interaction depends on the cyclical interdependence of local and global structures. The parts make sense only in the context of the whole, but the whole is understood only in terms of its parts (Gadamer, 1975; Mosenthal & Tierney, 1984).

Social interaction structure also has both temporal and time-independent aspects. People use their knowledge and expectations of *temporal sequences* to understand and engage in interaction, as shown by research in such divergent areas as mother-infant communication (Cappella, 1981) and script processing (Bower, Black, & Turner, 1979). In addition, people apprehend time-independent or *syntagmatic* structure. Syntagmatic structure may be generated through cumulation of events (for example, when a group member decides who talks the most and "hogs" the floor) or through synthesis of events subject to a guiding principle (for example, when someone makes judgments about who controls or dominates a marriage). In ongoing interaction, temporal and syntagmatic structures are cyclically interdependent, as is the case for global and local structures. Understanding either one presupposes the other (Garfinkel, 1967). Both temporal and syntagmatic structures exist at local as well as global levels.

MEANING

Meaning has been defined in terms of function, intent, and signification, to name just a few constructions, and for present purposes we will treat them as though they were equivalent. A whole field of debate surrounds these definitions, but the distinctions developed here should hold for all. Two aspects of meaning are important: the domain of meaning and the degree of intersubjectivity created by the interaction.

Several different domains of meaning may be distinguished, depending upon the interpreter's vantage point. Most fundamental is a division into *observer-privileged* and *subject-privileged* perspectives. Observer-privileged meanings (which we will shorten to "observer meanings") are those accessible to outside observers of interaction. They represent the judgments about interaction an uninvolved and uninitiated onlooker might have. These can be further subdivided into observer meanings available to every observer (*generalized* observer meanings) and those available only to observers versed in a particular theory or interpretive scheme (*restricted* observer meanings). One example of a generalized observer meaning is a concrete event that can be recognized by anyone, such as a vocalized pause. Restricted observer meanings are defined by a theory without reference to participants' point of view. Many coding systems are used to generate restricted observer meanings; for example, Longabough (1963) developed a system for coding exchange behaviors in interpersonal interaction. It is, of course, possible, though not essential, for participants' interpretations to be consistent with observer meanings.

Subject-privileged meanings (which we will term "subject meanings") are those implicated by participants' interpretive schemes. They represent the meaning of interaction for those involved. Like observer meanings, subject meanings can be subdivided into two sorts—subject meanings accessible to all members of the subject's cultural or subcultural group (*generalized* subject meanings) and those meanings available only to the actual participants in the interaction (*restricted* subject meanings). Generalized subject meanings are cultural constructs shared to some extent by others similar to the participants, such as the characteristics of "talking like a man" that Philipsen (1975) found in his study of "Teamsterville." All members of the culture would have a sense of the meaning of such a transaction. Relationships may also develop unique meanings and codes, whose import no outsider, even of the same culture, can grasp fully. These restricted subject meanings can be ascertained only by going directly to the participants themselves.

These differentiations parallel several previous distinctions. In their work on coding validity, Folger, Hewes, and Poole (1984; Poole & Folger, 1981a) distinguish three modes of observation, each of which generates claims about a particular domain of meaning. Their *experienced* mode corresponds to the restricted observer domain, the *experiencing* mode to the generalized subject domain, and the *experiencer* mode to the restricted subject domain. In the study of relational development, Olson (1978) draws a line between "outsider" and "insider" perspectives. The anthropological dichotomy of "emic" and "etic" indexes generalized and restricted subject perspectives, respectively.

A final point with respect to domains of meaning: A single utterance, not to mention an entire sequence or episode, may be *multifunctional* (Hewes, 1979); that is, it may carry multiple meanings. These meanings may be associated with different channels, such as verbal and nonverbal channels, or with different pragmatic impacts, such as content and relational levels (Watzlawick, Beavin, & Jackson, 1967). Multiple meanings may all be in a single domain, or they may reside in different domains. Indeed, there are few cases in which only a single meaning domain is relevant. Whenever more than two people are present, observer as well as subject meanings are possible, especially for the special case where a researcher is one of the observers. And the maintenance of a coherent conversation, even in the privileged subject domain, requires that actors attend to generalized observer meanings, such as who holds the floor.

As a joint enterprise of two or more actors, interaction creates and relies upon *intersubjectivity* of meaning, the last feature to be discussed. Intersubjectivity is a *state* wherein people share common understandings generated by cultural or interaction *processes*. Studies of intersubjectivity can be divided into those focused on the *state* and those focused on the *processes* generating the state. For example, studies of coorientation (e.g., Laing, Phillipson, & Lee, 1966; Pavitt & Cappella, 1979) assess intersubjectivity as a property (state) of relations; studies of identity negotiation (McCall & Simmons, 1978) center on the means (process) by which intersubjectivity is generated.

To regard intersubjectivity as a state or outcome is to acknowledge the possibility that it may vary in *degree*. It is a common experience to have thought we understood someone, only to find later that we were mistaken (Planalp & Honeycutt, 1985). Some approaches to the study of interpersonal communication treat intersubjectivity as simply present or absent, whereas others attempt to assess degrees of intersubjectivity and allow for the possibility of misunderstanding.

In conclusion, the features displayed in Table 10.1 are not merely analytic distinctions: *From the best evidence available, they represent features of interaction people actually use to guide their own activities and to understand the activities of others.* For example, people often take apparent insults as jokes, because the person who insulted them has joked that way in the past (i.e., they infer subject-privileged meaning based on syntagmatic, global beliefs about the relationship). They know at what point in the joke it is appropriate to laugh (i.e., they predict local sequences from a knowledge of global sequences). They know procedures for checking whether they misunderstood and the "joke" really was an insult (i.e., processes for restoring intersubjectivity). The various features and the skills associated with them are an inherent part of interaction management. They have become analytic terms not for academic reasons, but because of their critical place in social life. Other features, as yet undiscovered, may be added.

INTERACTION RESEARCH AND THE
NATURE OF INTERACTION

The features in Table 10.1 are important constituents of communication theory. Most comprehensive theories attempt to encompass many features. Pearce and Cronen's (1980) theory of coordinated management of meaning, for instance, spans local and global structures in both temporal and syntagmatic terms; it focuses on generalized and restricted subject meanings and allows for varying degrees of intersubjectivity as well. Other lines of research concentrate on detailed analysis of particular features. McLaughlin and Cody's (1982) research on awkward silences focuses on local temporal structures in terms of restricted observer meanings.

Interaction analysis methods attempt to measure and to identify relationships among the features. All methods are subject to two crucial limitations. First, to achieve precision, methods are focused on a subset of features. Scales that assess postconversation impressions, for example, index global, syntagmatic perceptions. Even for methods capable of being adapted to many features, particular applications are tailored to only a few specific properties. Second, specific techniques are imperfect representations of actual features or relationships. They are imperfect, in part, due to unreliability of measurement. If unreliability is too great it can render measures invalid and bias analysis. Methods are also imperfect because they are mappings of natural events onto numerical scales or specialized qualitative terminology. Like a photograph or thermometer reading, methods represent events and properties in media different from those in which they naturally occur. Most people do not use coding categories, correlation coefficients, or ethnographic field notes in everyday life; these tools represent features of interpretations and relationships useful for scientific purposes. The ultimate usefulness of methods turns largely on the validity of their mappings. In the classic, technical sense validity refers to whether an instrument actually measures what it is intended to measure or to whether an analytic technique yields an accurate, unbiased estimate of a relationship (Kerlinger, 1973). Validity can also be taken in a larger sense to refer to whether a given method maps the full extent and "richness" of the event or property in question (Poole & McPhee, 1985). Just as a thermometer gives only the barest picture of what happens when something is heated, so some methods may give only one-dimensional pictures of an interaction feature.

In designing and selecting methods it is important to consider which features they refer to and their limitations with respect to other features. Each property of interaction poses unique problems of measurement and analysis, and methods must be tailored to overcome them. This results, necessarily, in specialization: The purposes a method can serve are limited by the features to which it refers. We cannot, for example, make accurate claims about local interaction structure based on global judgments of syntagmatic structure. Although this seems obvious, too often researchers have tried to do just that. Too often they have measured subjects' impressions of cooperativeness or dominance, carefully defining the limitations of their measures in their Procedures section, but then have ventured claims such as "these results suggest subjects *behaved* more competitively in their Discussion section. Such claims are unwarranted because they have no measures of behavior, only measures of global impressions. Instances of the converse problem can also be found: Researchers analyzing local sequential structure have leaped to conclusions about what these structures mean on the global level. Again, these claims are unwarranted because they are based not on global measures but only on local act-to-act sequences. Such errors occur because researchers have not thought through the restrictions on their methods.

It is also important to evaluate the validity of our methods, especially the larger issue of how best to capture a full picture of a given feature. This requires us to go back to the feature anew, to consider it outside the context of the method in question. This is hard, because methods shape how we view features, but it is essential.

OVERVIEW OF THE CHAPTER

This chapter takes a broad view. It concentrates on the assumptions, capacities, limitations, and potentialities of methods, rather than on detailed technical issues. The latter are important, but are already discussed in other excellent sources. We divide methods into two major classes: *quantitative* and *qualitative techniques.* For quantitative techniques we consider both *techniques for observation and measurement* and *methods of analysis.* For qualitative approaches no clear line can be drawn between observation and analysis. Therefore, in that section we discuss two approaches to qualitative analysis— informant-based analyses and formal analyses—and under each we examine specific techniques and analytic issues that arise in employing each approach.

For each technique we will consider its basic assumptions and typical applications, potential problems and whether they can be remedied, what the technique can tell us about interaction, and its limitations. The scheme of interaction features serves as a constant reference point in this undertaking. It helps us to define not just limits on methods, but also new or innovative uses—possibilities along with actualities.

QUANTITATIVE TECHNIQUES

OBSERVATIONAL AND MEASUREMENT TECHNIQUES

Methods are available for observation or measurement of all four levels of meaning. With the exception of mechanical techniques for recording sound-silence patterns (Cappella & Streibel, 1979; Jaffe & Feldstein, 1970) and recognizing key words (Krippendorff, 1980), these methods incorporate human beings as an integral part of the measurement process. Among other things, they rely on people to unitize streams of behavior, to categorize behaviors, to give global judgments of interaction episodes, and to record field observations. Although human components are sometimes inconsistent and unreliable compared to mechanisms, they offer numerous advantages in the study of complex behavior. Human interpreters have the flexibility to take context into account. They can recognize and choose among multiple or ambiguous meanings. They also have a store of cultural knowledge difficult to catalog or program.

With these advantages come potential problems of reliability and validity. Unreliability may result from observers' inconsistent application of rules and instructions, the ambiguity of those rules and instructions, cognitive limitations that prevent effective use of complex observational systems, or the effects of inattention or fatigue. An extensive literature has grown on the causes of and corrections for unreliability (Folger et al., 1984). Problems of validity are not as well formulated at present. They are discussed below, but in general terms, invalidity may result either from inadequate mappings of interaction features or from biases introduced by human observers.

This section presents a critical analysis of two quantitative observational techniques: global ratings and interaction coding. For each we will (1) outline how the technique is commonly used and the features to which it refers; (2) consider the technique's reliability and validity and how to assess these; and (3) discuss limitations, problems, and caveats.

Global evaluations. The first measurement strategy is to assess global descriptions or evaluations of an interaction episode. Typically, observers (and sometimes participants) are asked to judge the episode or its participants on a number of behavioral dimensions; the judgments are expressed in ratings or rankings based on raters' memory of the episode. Ratings are usually collected immediately following the episode, but some studies require raters to make global judgments based on several connected episodes (e.g., a series of group meetings). Individual judgments are then aggregated to yield an overall profile of the episode or its participants. For example, Wish, D'Andrade, and Goodnow (1980) had participants rate people involved in short conversations on 12 bipolar scales that described their behavior, such as cooperative/competitive, cheerful/gloomy, and tense/relaxed. They averaged responses on these scales to aggregate judgments.

This strategy measures global, syntagmatic properties of interaction structure, such as the overall level of cooperative behavior or who in an interaction is dominant. It is capable of covering all levels of meaning: When observers are trained in the researcher's theory, global descriptions represent the restricted observer mode; aggregated ratings from naive observers and participants are data in the generalized subject mode—that is, they represent shared or collective judgments—and individual ratings made by participants represent the restricted subject perspective. This strategy can also generate estimates of the degree of intersubjectivity through tests for agreement among ratings. The coorientation model, with certain qualifications, provides one means of assessing agreement (Cronbach, 1955; Newcomb, 1953). The global evaluation strategy treats intersubjectivity as an outcome or stable trait of interaction. This approach has several advantages for interaction research. First, the constructs it measures are clearly important in their own right. Global perceptions and estimates of the situation are important reference points for both comprehension and action. In addition, the rating procedures take maximum advantage of human skills in sorting through and combining cues and in utilizing contexts for interpretation. Finally, the procedure is quite convenient compared to interaction coding or direct observation.

Certain problems and caveats must be considered as well. If we are to take advantage of raters' skills, the rating task must be consistent with conditions under which they normally make judgments. The "episodes" chosen by researchers should correspond as closely as possible to episodes or units raters would use. This is not problematic for studies that focus on entire social units, such as conversations or meetings. However, the boundaries of other episodes, such as arguments, are hazy. Some units, such as snippets of conversation or 10-minute talk segments, are arbitrary creations of the researcher. If the units are not meaningful to raters, the validity of their responses is questionable. Although some studies have shown that people unitize actions and interaction consistently (Newtson, 1976), the range of units that would be meaningful to raters is not defined. To be safe, researchers should sample only naturally recognized units, such as turns, topics, or episodes (see Forgas, 1979). In addition to "episode" or other unit boundaries, the scales used to assign meaning to these units should be meaningful to raters. There is an extensive body of evidence regarding the dimensions or constructs people use to understand and evaluate interaction (Triandis, 1978; Wish, 1976; Wish & Kaplan, 1977). Problems of scale artificiality can also be eliminated with more "open" methods of data gathering, such as interviewing or paired comparisons (e.g., Poole & Folger, 1981b).

D'Andrade (1974) presented evidence relevant to a second validity problem, the effects of memory biases on ratings. He summarized several studies showing (1) low correlations between observer ratings on a behavioral dimension and immediate codings of the behavior in question (average r's = .34 and .07 for two studies); (2) strong correlations between semantic-similarity rankings of scale anchors and scale intercorrelations (average r's ranged from .60 to .91 across several studies); and (3) low correlations between semantic-similarity rankings of scale anchors and immediate codings of the corresponding behavior (average r's ranged from .03 to .20). D'Andrade summarizes the import of these results:

> The argument presented in this chapter is not just that there is memory drift when people make ratings or rankings of other people's behavior, but that this "drift" is systematic, nonrandom, biased in the direction of the rater's conception of "what is like what.".... Given a series of attributes (such as behavior traits) which can apply to a class of objects (such as other people), there will be systematic shift in the individual's recall of which attributes are possessed by which objects, such that the more strongly the individuals conceive of the attributes as belonging together, the more likely it will be that the individual recalls both attributes as belonging to the same objects. With this type of memory error, any attempt to discover how human behavior is organized into multibehavioral units—such as dimensions or clusters—will result in conclusions which primarily reflect the cognitive structure of the raters. (pp. 176-177)

In short, ratings may not correspond to actual behavior and may be biased in a systematic fashion. It may well be that this bias, based in cognitive structure, is desirable for some purposes because it depicts naturally occurring interpretive biases. However, D'Andrade's results suggest ratings are no substitute for immediate coding.

Aggregation of ratings assumes homogeneous responses across raters, marred only by sampling error, which the aggregation corrects. This implies that researchers should test for homogeneity before aggregating, but few do so. Studies have shown high levels of interrater agreement (reliability); D'Andrade (1974) reports a coefficient of .94 and Carter Haythorn, Meirowitz, and Lanzetta (1951) report an r of .68. However, a study by Poole and Folger (1985) showed that a putatively homogeneous sample of college students actually divided into at least two interpretive sets. Individual differences in responses were also found by Wiggins and Fishbein (1969). Homogeneity cannot be presumed; it must be demonstrated. Depending on the aggregation method, different means of testing for homogeneity are available. Coefficients of interrater reliability can be used if responses are to be aggregated by taking their mean (Winer, 1971). If multidimensional scaling is used to determine aggregate dimensions, several versions allow identification of individual response differences. Lingoes's program PINDIS has a test for individual differences (Borg & Lingoes, 1978); three-mode factor analysis can also be used for this purpose (Tucker, 1966).

Finally, there is the question of whether participants or uninvolved observers are better raters. In part, this depends on the researcher's purposes. Studies have compared observer and participant ratings with uneven results. D'Andrade (1974) reports correlations of .52 and .76 for two sets of observer and participant ratings across six of Bales's (1970) IPA categories. Schneider (1970) reports much lower correlations for ratings on four rather vaguely defined dimensions. Observer and participant ratings seem to be similar for clearly defined scales. Of interest is Gouran and Whitehead's (1971) finding of observer-participant correlations ranging from .62 to 1.00 for ratings of *single* statements on "orientation" and "provocativeness" dimensions.

Interaction coding. This term refers to any systematic method of classifying verbal and nonverbal behavior, ranging from formal category systems such as Bales's (1970) IPA and Fisher's (1970) Decision Proposal Coding System; to systems for classifying speech acts (Searle, 1969; Vendler, 1972); to structured discourse analytic methods, such as the identification of adjacency pairs (Jackson & Jacobs, 1980). These methods have in common the interpretation of utterances according to a (relatively) standard set of rules. They require two analytic stages: division of discourse into discrete units (unitizing) and classification of the resulting units. Three key issues facing interaction analysis are coding system design, reliability, and validity.

In designing category systems it is necessary to establish (1) the appropriate unit of analysis, (2) the degree of latitude left to coders' interpretations, (3) whether the categories will be mutually exclusive or multifunctional, and (4) the level of meaning the system is intended to code. Coding systems capture local rather than global structure, but there is considerable variation in the size of local units. The most common units are the communicative "act," the smallest discriminable segment of behavior that can be classified (Bales, 1970), and the "turn," which includes all actions and/or statements made by a speaker while he or she holds the floor. Some systems code larger units that may include several turns; for example, Mabry (1975) coded one-minute segments. Unitizing is easier with turns or timed segments because units can be identified without reference to content. Conversely, classification may be harder with turns or segments than with acts; if more than one codable act occurs in a turn, which interpretation is to be assigned to the entire unit?

Closely related is the issue of interpretive latitude. To what degree do we wish to rely on coders' judgments? At one end of the scale are mechanical devices and computer software, which eliminate human judgment altogether. Such devices have been used to identify sound-silence patterns in conversation (Cappella, 1979). A less stringent alternative specifies a choice tree that presents a complete set of classifications and a series of simple, binary questions that "lead" the coder to the proper classification (e.g., Anderson, 1983;

Stiles, 1980). Here coders must answer the questions, but their attention is focused on specific cues and classification criteria are clearly delineated. The final and most common method emphasizes utility and pragmatic impact rather than logical completeness. Researchers compile as complete a list of categories as possible (or necessary), write enough rules to enable coders to recognize and distinguish the categories, and rely on coders' native skills for the rest. The categories are often specified by the researcher's theory, as in the case of the Rogers and Farace (1975) relational coding system, and they may also have considerable internal structure, as does Bale's (1970) IPA system. Such systems may also be developed with a "grounded theory" approach to reflect the functions the observer or participants see in the situation, as with Jefferson's transcription rules (Sacks, Schegloff, & Jefferson, 1974) and Hawes's (1972) interview coding system. As opposed to the logically complete approach, this third strategy relies heavily on the coder's interpretive abilities to determine classifications. This is advantageous for complex functions or meanings because it is difficult, if not impossible, to develop complete classification rules. But reliance on coder judgments makes the procedure harder to control and may result in inconsistent classifications if categories are not precise enough. An important determinant of coder latitude is the number of channels coders are asked to monitor. Some systems restrict channels by having coders rely solely on transcripts or audiotapes. In general, the more channels, verbal and nonverbal, coders must deal with, the greater their latitude of judgment.

A third design issue relates to univocal versus multifunctional coding. Many traditional sources recommend that coding categories be mutually exclusive and exhaustive (Lazarsfeld & Barton, 1969). But assigning a single code to each act (mutual exclusivity) may be problematic when language serves more than one function simultaneously (Hawes, 1972). In view of the fact that interaction has multiple layers of meaning, such cases may be more the rule than the exception.

Finally, it is important to specify which domain of meaning the system is intended to code. Coding systems can be designed to pick up any of the four domains of meanings—generalized observer, restricted observer, generalized subject, or restricted subject—and a system attuned to one level may miss meaning on another. For example, Longabaugh's (1963) interpersonal exchange coding system, which encodes restricted observer meanings, may result in quite different interpretations than those the participants would place on the same discourse. Longabaugh's interpretations are valid and useful at their intended level of interpretation, but they do not represent what subjects "see" in the interaction. For most coding systems, the issue of meaning correspondence has received less attention than it merits. Designers have generally relied solely on implicit understandings of what they are trying to code and have neglected to demonstrate explicit connections between categories and particular domains of meaning.

Specifying these connections is important for several reasons. First, categories will be labeled and defined differently depending on the meaning domain for which they are designed. Systems encoding restricted observer meanings may embody technically precise distinctions that are awkward to the layperson; Mabry's (1975) typology for coding group discussions uses terms such as "universality" and "particularity." On the other hand, a system designed to code generalized subjective meanings may rely on lay terms, even at the expense of less clear categorizations; Folger and Puck's (1976) question coding system is based on distinctions sensible to most English speakers, such as dominance. Second, depending on the domain for which a system is designed, different evidence for validation is required. We will come to this point shortly. Finally, the claims a researcher can make from the coded data are limited to the domain or domains for which the system is designed and validated. It would not be legitimate to make claims about subject interpretations based on a system designed to encode the objective meaning domain.

In addition, reliability is a necessary condition for classificatory validity. Although it is generally accepted that users of "formal" interaction coding systems need to establish reliability, researchers employing "informal" systems, such as conversational transcription systems, have been resistant to reliability analysis. However, such approaches also specify display and classification rules that might be flawed or ambiguous, and reliability analysis is the appropriate way to check this possibility. For example, Edelsky (1982) has shown classification problems inherent in Jefferson's conversational transcription rules.

Coding reliability can be separated into two components: *unitizing* reliability, which refers to coders' ability to agree on how the discourse should be parsed into units; and *classificatory* reliability, which refers to the level of agreement on how units should be classified. Folger et al. (1984) provide an extensive discussion of different means of assessing reliability and of special cases in which reliability is particularly critical. One matter especially worth mentioning is the need to establish reliability for individual categories rather than simply assessing reliability for the entire coding scheme. Hewes (1985) shows how category unreliability can bias tests of hypotheses concerning either distributions or temporal dependencies. Moreover, this can occur even when overall reliability is acceptable.

In abstract terms the validity of interaction analysis systems is the degree to which they actually yield the types of information they are designed to obtain. Exactly what constitutes validity and how validity is assessed depends on which domain or domains of meaning the researcher is attempting to code (Folger et al., 1984; Poole & Folger, 1981b). Whichever domain is targeted, the researcher's claims about his or her classifications must be backed by evidence of their validity. Each domain requires different types of evidence. For systems encoding observer-privileged meanings, the classic techniques of assessing construct validity are sufficient (Allen & Yen, 1979; Cronbach &

Meehl, 1955). However, for systems that code both generalized and restricted subject meanings, the researcher also must provide evidence that the data actually represent subjects' interpretations. Several methods for assessing the representational validity of coding systems have been developed (see Folger et al., 1984, for a review; specific studies include Borgatta, 1962; Folger & Sillars, 1980; Poole & Folger, 1981a; Wish et al., 1980).

Establishing the validity of coding systems is very important because researchers may be mistaken about whether they are measuring the constructs they are attempting to measure or tapping subjects' perspectives. Face validity, the traditional resort of interaction analysis, is not sufficient. This is clearly illustrated by O'Donnell-Trujillo's (1982) comparison of two relational coding systems that purported to code the same constructs. He found a very low degree of overlap in codings, suggesting that one or both were "off base." But which one? Without validity assessment it is impossible to know.

Finally, there are several additional considerations. The first concerns the need to report the tailoring of coding systems when applying them to specific cases. Most coding schemes are designed for general use. A relational coding system is meant to apply to many types of relationships, a bargaining scheme to numerous negotiations. In practice, however, each study has its own peculiar requirements and problems, and researchers must adapt coding schemes to these exigencies. Researchers may make special assumptions about what the rules mean; they sometimes drop or add categories, may specify "priority rules" favoring one classification over another, or make any of a number of other changes. Generally, these adjustments are not reported, but they should be because they change the meaning of the data. Cicourel (1980) has recommended that these adaptations should be reported in a methodological appendix, along with more detail on coder background and training than is normally supplied.

A second concern for coding research—and for many forms of qualitative analysis, as well—is the paradox of microanalysis, also discussed by Grimshaw (1982), Labov and Fanshel (1977) and Pittenger, Hockett, and Daheny (1960). Minute and repeated analysis of recordings and transcripts may expose and highlight features that are not important in practice. For example, microanalysis may find incoherence or conflict in interaction, but miss the inattention and work that neutralize such disharmony in practice. "Lengthy concentration of attention on the one event can easily blow up in significance far out of proportion to its original duration and its actual setting. One must not mistake the five-inch scale model for the fly itself" (Pittenger et al., 1960, cited in Labov & Fanshel, 1977, p. 22).

QUANTITATIVE METHODS FOR ASSESSING STRUCTURE

While there are many ways to categorize quantitative methods for assessing structure, we have chosen to use the following divisions: input-output models, experimental techniques, developmental analysis, and act-to-act analyses. Each of these categories provides a distinctive slant on the structure of social interaction as well as manifesting an interesting array of identifiable strengths and weaknesses.

Input-output models. This technique requires observation only of the initial (input) and final (output) conditions potentially reflected in an interaction sequence. The investigator specifies a model of the process that is assumed to transform the initial state into the final state. To test the model, one takes observed initial states, employs the model to predict the final state, and compares predicted with observed outputs. An example will help clarify this.

Davis (1973) was interested in modeling how groups combined their members' individual preferences into a group decision. He posited the Social Decision Scheme (SDS) model as a "picture" of the group's interaction. A decision scheme is a mathematical rule for combining members' preferences into a final group choice; in some cases, though not all, it corresponds to a norm for decision making, such as majority rule. The decision scheme seeks to depict the essence of what occurs in group interaction without direct observation. Davis has tested this model successfully by collecting members' initial opinions, using the SDS model to predict final group decisions for various decision schemes, and then comparing predicted to observed decisions (see Hewes, 1985).

This kind of approach treats interaction as a "black box," substituting the theorist's model of interaction for direct analysis. This restricts input-output models to the analysis of global structures, though they have considerable flexibility with respect to the other dimensions shown in Table 10.1. There are several advantages to this approach. Input-Output modeling is useful when researchers cannot observe interaction or when they lack confidence in their observational methods. For example, a researcher may believe influence attempts will occur but not know how to identify or code them. Rather than going through the tedious and uncertain process of developing and validating a coding system, the researcher could posit a model of the outputs that would result if the hypothesized influence pattern held. This highlights a second advantage of input-output models: They enable the researcher to model a single process in a powerful way, cleanly separating it from other processes or influences. The SDS model permitted Davis to separate the effects of decision rules from those of social influence. If the explanation in question is general and powerful, it is useful to be able to separate its effects from the "noise" created by other influences. Third, an input-output model based on the assumption of no communicative effects can serve as a "baseline" for measuring communicative effects. For example, Hewes (1985) posits a model of no influence as a standard for assessing interpersonal influence.

On the down side, there is no way to determine what is wrong if the model does not fit. All we know is that the model in question does not work; results of this test do not provide any direct insights for improving the model (although indirect evidence can be gained from examining residuals). Interaction processes must be studied directly in order to pin down needed changes in the model. There is an additional problem: Input-output models are not particularly satisfying given the "process" orientation of most communication researchers. These models often seem too abstract, too far removed from interaction processes. The parsimony and power of such models may require staying too far away from the interaction itself.

Experimental techniques. The value of experimentation in interaction research is often underestimated (as in Shimanoff, 1980). Experimental designs are most useful with global, syntagmatic structures (e.g., a system of rules). An adequate set of rules should generate observable behavioral predictions that can be tested by experiment. Furthermore, since rules have a constitutive as well as a regulative function, knowledge of rules can be tested using a host of techniques from cognitive psychology including distortions in recognition and recall (see Planalp, 1985). Experiments can also be used to study individual perceptions of interaction, overall summary interaction patterns (Gouran & Baird, 1972), and "lawlike" propositions about discourse processing (Planalp & Tracy, 1980), normative influence, and so on. Some notable examples illustrate the possibilities.

Planalp and Tracy (1980) hypothesized that the cognitive process of information integration was important in determining what topic shifts in a conversation would be seen as "competent." Their experimental results clearly demonstrated the cognitive structures that stand behind topic changes (see also Tracy, 1983, for a discussion of on-topic talk). Several researchers have used experiments to test rule systems; for example, Donohue (1981) tested a rules theory of negotiation. We recommend Vroom and Jago's (1974) study of leadership rules as an exemplar for rules experimentation.

Experimental studies can also be used to study behaviors per se. Sillars (1980) studied the effects of attributions on conflict strategy choice. College roommates discussed their disagreements and coded the strategies they employed. This "prompted" conflict was orchestrated through a joint interview in a laboratory setting. Montgomery (1984) employed the Social Relations model (Kenny & LaVoie, 1984) to study relational interdependencies. This model, based on analysis of variance, allows the researcher to determine the extent to which a person's behavior is influenced by another and to identify patterns of coordination. The Social Relations model characterizes syntagmatic interaction structure; it is based on participants' perceptions of each other. Thus its definition of interdependence or influence differs from that employed by researchers who observe interaction directly.

The greatest advantage of experimentation is control; the greatest disadvantage, the potential for low external validity. Laboratory situations are not necessarily realistic. Participants may be exposed to unusual situations and be asked to do unusual tasks. Hence, their responses may not mirror what would "naturally" occur. Asking subjects to draw lines at topic shifts on transcripts will not necessarily get at the topics perceived in day-to-day conversation (though see Planalp & Tracy, 1980, for an example of careful background work to establish the validity of their topic-shift data). Because of their potential lack of realism, experiments may lead to problems in the study of subject-centered meanings. Even when designed to assess perceptions, an experiment may put participants in a situation that elicits unrealistic responses (Hewes, 1978).

A good time to use experimental approaches is in the substantiation of findings from less controlled research. For example, qualitative studies or sequential analysis might be used to develop a system of rules that could then be tested experimentally. Despite criticisms of experimental approaches (Shimanoff, 1980), they remain a live option for interaction researchers.

Developmental analysis. This strategy traces the evolution of global or syntagmatic structures over time. Generally, it involves dividing a relationship or interaction sequence into self-marked phases or into discrete time units (e.g., minutes, days), compiling the types of interaction that occur and analyzing changes in these variables across time. Perhaps the most common form of analysis divides a relationship into phases. Relevant behaviors in each phase are measured and a value of occurrence in the phase is calculated. For example, intimacy might be expected to rise through the first four of Knapp's (1983, 1984) phases of relational development and then fall during the fifth phase. Trend analysis can be used to test whether this model fits and whether all relationships follow the same developmental sequence (see Poole, 1981, for an application to group contexts). Other modelling techniques are also available for testing phase models (Poole & McPhee, 1985; Wohlwill, 1973). These techniques are also appropriate for continuous variables, such as affect level. It is also possible to derive typologies of developmental paths. Tucker (1966) developed a procedure that takes a set of curves and groups them based on similarity. Huston, Surra, Fitzgerald, and Cate (1981) have employed this technique to distinguish types of relational development patterns during courtship.

In using developmental techniques, researchers must be careful to choose their time units judiciously or they run the risk of missing crucial details. Poole (1981) provided evidence that this problem existed in group decision-making research: Investigators used too few time periods and missed differences in decision-making paths (for more detail, see Folger et al., 1984). Despite Huston et al's. (1981) success at deriving a typology from the data, developmental analysis should be informed by a theory of what drives development. It is not feasible simply to describe development and hope a theory emerges.

Act-to-act analysis. Act-to-act analysis is probably the most widely used technique for the study of interpersonal interaction. These procedures identify and test for relationships among individual interaction units. For example, a first-order Markov model identifies the probabilities that a given act (A) will be followed by various others acts (A, B, or C), yielding probabilities that various two-act sequences will be observed in a discourse sample. As with all statistical techniques, the results of act-to-act analyses are equivocal; they cannot establish that one act *influences* or *causes* another without a theory or frame of interpretation. These analyses work best with theories or explanations that depend upon or directly imply sequential principles (Hewes, 1979). Three such cases can be distinguished:

(1) Explanations in which the sequence serves as a causal structure can be directly tested with act-to-act analyses. Examples include reinforcement models and social influence models (Hewes, 1985).

(2) In some theories, such as those of the Palo Alto group (Watzlawick et al., 1969), act-to-act sequences constitute or define relationships, and are therefore the central object of interest. The acceptance and rejection of "bids" directly ties sequences to characteristics such as relational control (Rogers & Farace, 1975).

(3) Finally, in some cases we may be aware of larger units or episodes that are made up of sequences. For example, act-act pairs (interacts) can be used to identify phases of problem solving (Fisher, 1970; Poole, 1981).

In all three instances, interpretations of act-to-act analyses are informed by a broader theory or explanatory framework. These frames tell researchers which sequences to seek and undergird causal inferences. Unfortunately, many applications are not so informed. Instead they seem to employ a type of naive causality in their interpretations of act-to-act probabilities or cross-correlations: If Act A follows Act B, it must be a response to B; if it is a response to B, A must be caused or influenced by B. This reasoning is used to support a "shopping trip" through the data. Act-to-act probabilities or spectral correlations are computed and those that turn out to be significant are chosen for interpretation. These are then portrayed as "what has happened" in the interaction. For example, a researcher might code marital conflicts with a category system designed to code conflict responses, calculate the first-order Markov transition matrix, and then attempt to use the transition probabilities to deduce what happened in this and other such conflicts. The problem here is that any conclusions are so closely tied to the sample that their generality is doubtful. Unguided by a theory or explanation of contiguities, the researcher is likely to overstate the significance of some patterns and understate the significance of others. Such studies are useful for exploratory purposes, but they must be followed by confirmatory research that is guided by definite hypotheses and theories.

Three genres of act-to-act confirmatory techniques will be discussed: (1) methods for the analysis of categorical data (Markov modeling and lag sequential analysis); (2) methods for analysis of continuous data (time series and time series regression); and (3) methods for analysis of combinations of categorical and continuous data (semi-Markov analysis, Markovian regression, and interrupted time series).

(1) Methods for categorical data: Markov analysis is not a statistical technique per se, but rather involves fitting a probabilistic model to the data. The Markov chain model requires the researcher to specify a finite number of "states," such as communicative acts. It is then necessary to specify the degree of temporal contiguity that exists among the acts ("order")—that is, the number of states extending into the past we must know in order to predict optimally the current state of the system. Once the order of the process is established, the stability (stationarity) of the observed pattern is determined as well as the stability (homogeneity) of the pattern across different dyads or groups.

Lag sequential analysis (Sackett, 1978) is often treated as though it were unrelated to Markovian models. However, to assert that Behavior A has a "lag 2" relationship with behavior C is to say that one very special form of second-order Markov process exists that generates C from A. Others are possible, though they can be lost through the use of lag sequential technique (Hewes & Kebis, 1986). The lag sequential model is a limited Markov model, and as such, is subject to all assumptions of the Markov model: order, stationarity, and homogeneity (see Dindia, 1986). For a given set of acts, it is first necessary to establish that a Markov process of defined order, stationarity, and homogeneity exists; then lags to the orders that fit can be analyzed. Many users of lag sequential analysis have ignored this requirement. Without evidence that these assumptions are met in the overall process, tracking back individual paths is meaningless. To mention one example, it is questionable whether Gottman's (1979) overall analysis of content and affect patterns in married dyad interaction is meaningful since his Table 6.5 gives clear evidence of a lack of stationarity in his data across nine categories. Since lag sequential data are strongly predicated on this assumption of stationarity, this violation makes it harder to accept his descriptive data as valid. In addition, the common practice of calculating a large number of lags and selecting the significant ones runs the danger of producing spurious results, since many individual tests greatly increase the likelihood of Type 1 error.

(2) Methods for continuous data: Examples of continuous variables of interest to interaction researchers include affect, conflict, or relational involvement. Time series techniques can be used to study developmental patterns for single variables and cross influences between two or more variables. Gottman (1981) provides an introduction to and statistical package for this kind of analysis (best illustrated in Gottman, 1979; Gottman, Markman, & Notarius, 1977). Such techniques offer great promise in the study of the local organization of social interaction. On the other hand, both single variable time series analysis and cross-correlational techniques may unduly rest by a system of

explanation to the temporal antecedents of only one or two variables. While this limitation can be overcome, we suggest that researchers employing these techniques take great care to justify the explanatory closure inherent in these time series studies.

(3) Methods that combine categorical and continuous data: Despite social scientists' best efforts to make the world either purely categorical or purely continuous, the fact remains that it is composed of a mixture of nominal and continuous phenomena. Categorical and continuous data can be combined in three distinct ways: Some techniques model continuous and categorical data simultaneously (as in semi-Markov models); some techniques show the impact of categorical forces or interventions on continuous processes (e.g., interrupted time series); and some techniques show the impact of continuous processes on categorical variables (e.g., Markovian regression).

The first class of techniques models categorical and continuous variables *together,* implicitly showing their relationships. Semi-Markov models incorporate two "motors" for depicting sequential relations: (a) the familiar Markov transition matrix, which governs categorical message-to-message structure in "event time," and (b) two transition matrices that depict influences operating in continuous time—a "waiting-time probability" matrix (which depicts the probability that a transition in the system will occur in a period *longer* than the basic time unit that governs model transitions), and a "holding-time" transition matrix (whose elements indicate the likelihood a transition will occur in exactly n units of time, for n time periods). The model thus takes into account between-transition latencies and within-turn durations. Hewes, Planalp, and Streibel (1980) applied this technique to group interaction and the resulting model fit better than simple Markov models, providing a richer description of local structure than that offered by Markov chains.

The effects of categorical variables on continuous ones can be assessed through a time series experiment or interrupted time series analysis (Campbell & Stanley, 1963; Glass, Wilson, & Gottman, 1975). This design calls for repeated measurements of the dependent variable (in this case, some feature of interaction), yielding a string of observations. At one or more points in this series the independent variable (a categorical occurrence) is introduced. Comparison of the behavior of the dependent time series before and after the independent event allows assessment of the impact of the independent variable. Such designs are ideal for studying "critical events" in interaction (see Evans-Hewes & Hewes, 1975). For example, a researcher might use this design to study changes in relational control patterns resulting from an argument. By looking at an extended time series, the researcher could address several issues he or she could not get at with a simple pretest–posttest design, such as whether apparent changes were random aberrations in the series, whether real changes were temporary or permanent, and how significant such changes were for relational development. The dependent variable in this case can be a direct measure of interaction—e.g., the number or occurrence of certain acts–or an index or structural coefficient—e.g., a measure of control symmetry or an influence measure.

As Campbell and Stanley (1963) point out, simple time series designs without control groups may not be able to rule out competing explanations. In such cases, it is not clear that observed effects are due to the independent variable rather than to some other cause occurring at the same time. Glass et al. (1975) outline a series of designs that provide control by contrasting occasions when the independent variable is present and absent for a single group (also see Simonton, 1977). Another alternative would be a time series design with an equivalent control group. An additional problem with time series designs generally is the difficulty of measuring change and dealing with auto-regression effects (see Poole & McPhee, 1985, for a review).

Regardless of these difficulties, quantitative studies of critical incidents are badly needed. Most quantiative studies focus on continuous influences. Intermittent or single-shot influences are assigned by default to the realm of qualitative inquiry. By neglecting quantitative approaches to critical incidents or discrete influences, researchers may be missing a chance to join empirical and interpretive research strategies.

Finally, we might consider the impact of continuous variables on categorical variables. Perhaps the most common and accessible method in this case is Markovian regression (Sorenson, 1978, pp. 356-380). Here the transition probabilities among categories are "data" to be explained by continuous variables in a regression equation (dummy-coded categorical variables may also be used). For example, Cappella (1979, 1980; Cappella & Planalp, 1981) used regression to determine the effects of occasion and partner on the parameters of Markov transition matrices of dyadic talk-silence patterns (see Spilerman, 1972). Cappella attempted to explain patterns in transitions among categories with continuous variables.

This move is extremely powerful and interesting. It does not simply take the Markov transition matrix as self-evident, but instead treats it as something to be explained. It thus encourages higher-order theory development. This is, we believe, an important advance over most uses of Markov analysis in studies of interpersonal communication. Too often researchers have simply calculated transition matrices and then have attempted to interpret "what they mean." Or they have conducted rather simple and not particularly powerful comparisons of matrices derived from two or three different conditions, unguided by systematic method. Markov regression analysis permits systematic testing of hypotheses about *why* transition matrices take on the values they do.

QUALITATIVE TECHNIQUES

BASIC CONSIDERATIONS

In building a rationale for a qualitative method of interaction analysis, Labov and Fanshel (1977) argue against the use of interaction coding schemes. Their argument rests on a claim that lies at the heart of most qualitative approaches to the study of discourse. They note that "if our understanding of conversation were at the level that permitted us to divide all phenomena into a closed set of 6 to 12 categories, it might be said that all serious problems had been solved already" (p. 19). Parsing interaction into a relatively small set of a priori categories is deemed by most qualitative researchers as problematic because the "serious problems" of discourse analysis are said to defy such reduction.

knowledge that is shared across a community of language users and that gives rise to structure and meaning in interaction. As Garfinkel (1967) put it, the goal is to determine "what any competent speaker knows." Philipsen (1977, p. 44) echoes Garfinkel's statement in his discussion of qualitative design considerations when he states that the objective of ethnography is to "explicate the culturally distinctive common knowledge which one must share in order to use language appropriately in any role in any scene staged in a particular community." The set of presuppositions speakers share and employ is assumed to be broad and complex and this knowledge is said to defy simple, a priori categorization. In this view, coding schemes and other quantitative methods can steer researchers away from the most important sources of information. Different interaction analysis methods have to be used to locate the shared knowledge and pragmatic presuppositions in various social settings.

The methods employed in qualitative studies of interaction are aimed at unraveling participants' knowledge and skills as they are displayed in language-based encounters. Two major methodological approaches have been adopted in this research. Each gives rise to different techniques for data collection and analysis. Figure 10.1 summarizes the two approaches and the investigative techniques that follow from them. One approach attempts to *elicit* the shared, pragmatic knowledge from participants' reports of their own presuppositions. The second approach rests on the researcher's ability to *infer* speakers' shared knowledge through the identification of formal properties of interaction. We will consider both of these methodological approaches in turn. It should be noted at the outset, however, that this distinction is drawn primarily to allow us to situate and examine these investigative methods. Most qualitative researchers do not commit themselves to one specific approach, but draw upon various techniques.

INFORMANT-BASED ANALYSES

One line of qualitative research in social interaction follows the informant-based methods developed in the fields of cultural anthropology and interpretive sociology. This approach focuses on subject-privileged meanings in that attempts are made to elicit interactors' interpretations of messages or the pragmatic knowledge that undergirds their participation in specified social encounters. Although informant-based approaches have not been the most widely used qualitative method in interaction analysis, researchers have recently argued strongly on their behalf. McGregor (1983, p. 272), for example, contends that researchers "need to be much less concerned with developing an integrated formalism for capturing structural properties of verbal interaction." He calls for the adoption of an informant approach because "an examination of what the lay-person has to tell us about 'what is going on' in their own words and other people's verbal interactions promises to be at least as interesting as theoretical introspection about what such activity might constitute" (p. 276).

Figure 10.1 identifies three informant-based techniques. One technique is labeled "meta-pragmatic studies," following McGregor's (1983) discussion of this genre of research. In these studies, respondents are presented with segments of interaction and are asked to comment on, clarify, or explain specified or unspecified aspects of the exchange. In studies that seek restricted subject meanings, respondents react to interaction in which they have participated (Frankel & Beckman, 1982; Hawes, 1972; Kreckel, 1981). In other "eavesdropping" investigations that seek generalized subject meanings, respondents comment on interactions in which they were not involved (McGregor, 1983). The data from both types of studies are "metapragmatic" accounts of the displayed interaction. Such data include interpretations of specific messages (local structures), reactions to the entire speech event (global structures), descriptions of participants' behavior (syntagmatic structure), or rationales for specific interactive moves in the exchange. The key characteristic of these studies is that respondents are asked by the investigator to stand outside social settings and to respond to transcripts and/or recordings of interaction.

A second informant-based technique is employed in ethnographies of communication and rests on open-ended, face-to-face interviews with informants. In these studies, investigators turn to members of the language-using community and pose probing questions about the informants' world. These interviews are usually conducted in the field and are often accompanied by observations of participants' interaction (Lenk-Kruger, 1982; Philipsen, 1975, 1976). The questions posed by researchers in these studies vary considerably. Informants may be asked to comment on previous encounters (based on their own recollections rather than recordings of those exchanges). They may also

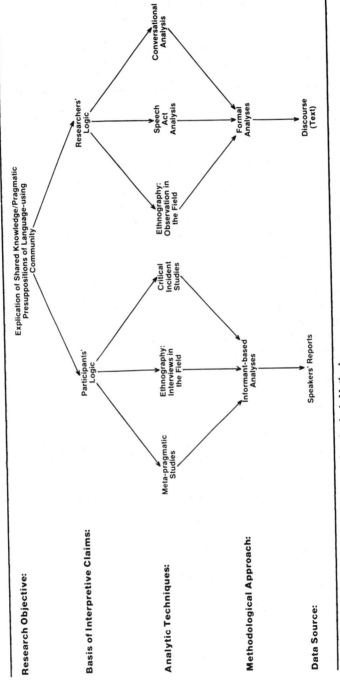

Research Objective: Explication of Shared Knowledge/Pragmatic Presuppositions of Language-using Community

Basis of Interpretive Claims: Participants' Logic | Researchers' Logic

Analytic Techniques: Meta-pragmatic Studies | Ethnography: Interviews in the Field | Critical Incident Studies | Ethnography: Observation in the Field | Speech Act Analysis | Conversational Analysis

Methodological Approach: Informant-based Analyses | Formal Analyses

Data Source: Speakers' Reports | Discourse (Text)

Figure 10.1 Summary of Qualitative Interaction Analysis Methods

be asked to respond to hypothetical scenarios that attempt to map the range of "appropriate" or "expected" responses for certain social situations in a given language-using community. This work most often seeks generalized subject meanings; informants are viewed as spokespersons who can provide interpretations shared across a larger culture or community, thus capturing global and syntagmatic structures that govern interaction in a language-using community.

Critical incident studies are a third informant-based technique employed in qualitative research. In these studies, respondents are asked to focus on some event deemed important or critical and to offer retrospective, interpretive accounts of that event. Critical incident studies acknowledge that certain exchanges carry more "weight" than others in the context of a relationship, an organizational decision, or a group process. This technique allows participants to identify interactions they perceive as crucial and to offer detailed characterizations of these interactions. Because they rely upon participants' idiosyncratic interpretations of significant events, these studies focus on restricted subject meanings. In most instances, participants' responses provide global, syntagmatic analyses of the events rather than message-by-message accounts.

In conducting critical incident studies, researchers usually describe the type of incident the informant is to discuss and the informant chooses the event to fit the investigator's general instructions. Petersen (1979), for example, has used this technique to study interaction in intimate relationships. His procedure for obtaining interaction records in one study relied on the following protocol:

> At the end of each day husbands and wives were to sit down together, discuss the things that had gone on between them that day, and decide on the most important interaction they had. We told them what we meant by an interaction, but let them determine which interactions were "important" for them. Then, on a form we provided, they were to write independent accounts of the interactions from start to finish. The forms asked them to indicate: (1) the conditions under which the interaction took place (Where and when did it happen? How were you both feeling as the interaction began? Were there any previous events which influenced what happened between you?); how the interaction started (Who made the first move? What did the person say or do?); and (3) what happened then (Who did and said what to whom? What were you thinking/feeling as the action went on? What ideas and emotions did your partner seem to have? How did it all come out?). (p. 38)

Critical incident techniques have also been used in studies of organizational conflict (Burke, 1977; Phillips & Cheston, 1979).

In capturing subject-privileged meanings, the three informant-based techniques rely heavily on participants' logic. The participants' reasoning and views form the basis for researchers' conclusions about shared social knowledge and pragmatic presuppositions. Although all the techniques share this common orientation, researchers face two decisions in following informant-based protocols.

One issue centers on the amount of structure researchers should impose on informants' responses during data collection. Investigators differ in how directive they are in eliciting information from interactors. McGregor (1983) recently highlighted this issue in metapragmatic research. He criticized previous studies in which investigators anticipated the important issues in the interaction and pointed informants toward those issues. He argued that "the need to explore the listening behaviors of the native, hearer without attempting to pre-judge or pre-empt what it is he might listen for is paramount" (p. 276). In one study, McGregor made a deliberate attempt to elicit interactors' comments without shaping or prompting responses in any way. His instructions to the informants included only the following comments: "I am going to play you a short extract of talk which I have recorded. At the end of the recording, I will switch the machine off. If you have any comments to make about the extract, I would like to note them" (p. 277). Participants' requests for clarification were diverted by pointing out "the need not to prejudice the outcome of the research by providing information whose significance one could not know in advance" (McGregor, 1983, p. 277).

McGregor's study seeks the broadest possible analytic objectives by trying to determine what everyday language users hear when they listen to conversation. Studies aimed at narrower research questions than those McGregor addresses direct informants' comments to specific issues or specific messages in an exchange. Regardless of the breadth of the investigator's research question, how far investigators can go in structuring informants' responses without threatening the quality of their data is a debated issue in this work. The underlying concern in this debate is whether shaping responses to any significant degree imposes an implied theoretical orientation that turns subject-privileged data into observer-privileged data. Critics such as McGregor are attempting to preserve the subject-based quality of interpretive data. They argue that if respondents are directed toward certain structures in the exchange or are prompted toward meanings that the researcher suspects are present, then the results of the investigation may not be based in subject-privileged interpretations, despite the apparent informant-based method being employed.

The second issue is also concerned with the possible limits that should be placed on the researcher's role, not in data *collection* but rather in data *analysis*. Researchers vary in their willingness to "reduce" informants' accounts when the data from a study are presented. The decision is whether to collapse informants' responses through synopsis or categorization or to present only verbatim extracts of the informants' responses. Studies that reduce informants' accounts to broader classifications (Petersen, 1979; Phillips & Cheston, 1979) are usually led by well-articulated theoretical concerns or are offered in anticipation of quantitative, follow-up research. Studies that present informants' accounts with minimal reduction (McGregor, 1983) are often strongly committed to the need for careful and complete description of the interaction or speech event under investigation.

FORMAL ANALYSES

A second line of qualitative interaction research is shown in Figure 10.1 as "formal analysis." To identify interactors' shared knowledge and pragmatic presuppositions, this approach relies on the researcher's ability to mark structural properties of interaction through close observation and analysis of exchanges. It is based on the assumption that speakers' pragmatic presuppositions are realized in exhibited behavior during interaction. The identification of formal characteristics of exchanges allows the researcher to infer the presuppositions that must be in place for the structural properties to emerge. The researcher's investigative efforts are directed mainly toward obtaining representative segments of interaction, identifying structures in that interaction, and building logical arguments for the presuppositions that must be in place in order for the structures to surface in the verbal exchanges. Formal analyses are based on observer-privileged perspectives. No attempt is made to obtain introspective reports from interactors about their own or another's behavior. Heuristic theoretical frameworks such as Frentz and Farrell's (1976) "language-action paradigm" or Labov and Fanshel's (1977) "comprehensive discourse analysis method" are sometimes employed in this work to guide the researcher's analysis. In these instances, researchers are examining restricted observer meanings because an a priori theoretical framework is applied to offer interpretive claims about the interaction under investigation.

Formal analysis has produced three well-known analytic techniques. In ethnographies of communication, researchers observe interaction in the field (often as participating members of a speech community) to provide detailed descriptions of and explanations for the expected behaviors of participants in specified social settings (Foster, 1974; Hymes, 1972, 1974; Labov, 1972; Philipsen, 1975, 1976). The claims made are in most instances at a global, syntagmatic level. Speech events are examined in an effort to capture how shared knowledge of communicative situations establishes expectations for message exchange and interpretation.

In conversational analysis, researchers work from samples of interaction that are transcribed and become records of the interaction under investigation. These records are closely analyzed for local and temporal structures (e.g., adjacency pairs, story structures, etc.) that can help explain how the interaction is organized and how participants have negotiated the interpretation of individual messages. Conversational analysts have followed the work of Sacks and his colleagues (Sacks, 1972; Sacks et al., 1974; Jefferson, 1973, 1974) and have studied interaction in diverse social settings, including doctor-patient interaction (Frankel, 1983; West, 1983, 1984), classroom interaction (Coulthard, 1977; Gumperz & Herasimchuk, 1972; Mehan, 1979; Phillips, 1972), parent-child interaction (West & Zimmerman, 1977), service encounters (Merritt, 1976), argumentation (Jackson & Jacobs, 1980; Jacobs & Jackson, 1983), and courtroom interaction (Beach, 1985; Nofsinger, 1983; Pollner, 1979). This work is largely premised on the assumption that the researcher should *not* impose an a priori theoretical framework and is thus centered in generalized observer-privileged meanings.

Finally, speech act studies are formal analyses of interaction that emerged independently of ethnographies or conversational analysis. These studies have their roots in linguistic philosophy and the study of pragmatics (Austin, 1962; Searle, 1969; Strawson, 1964). Speech act analyses are aimed at identifying the primary units of language use and inferring the implicit constitutive rules that are in place for the production and recognition of these pragmatic functions. The focus of this work is on local structures; it is premised on a restricted, observer-based perspective in that it imposes the speech act framework on interaction as it is studied. Studies in the speech act tradition have focused on the development of pragmatic competence (Dore, 1974, 1975, 1977; Folger & Chapman, 1978; Garvey, 1975), the specification of constitutive rules governing specific pragmatic functions (Nofsinger, 1975, 1976), and the classification of illocutionary intents (Bach & Harnish, 1979; Hancher, 1979).

The claims offered in formal analyses of interaction rest heavily on the researcher's logic. It is the investigator's reasoning that links the identified structures in interaction (e.g., speech acts) to the claims about "what any competent speaker knows." Although the researcher's logic is paramount in this approach, it is not entirely independent of informant-based criteria for evaluating the adequacy of claims made about speakers' presuppositions. There are two points of contact between formal approaches and informant-based analyses. First, when investigators are members of the language-using community under study, they may choose to rely upon their own knowledge as participants to provide supporting evidence for their analyses. In this case, researchers view themselves as astute informants on the shared knowledge that undergirds pragmatic competency. In other instances, researchers view themselves as "blank slates," either because they are not members of the setting under investigation or because they do not want their implicit assumptions to guide them before completing a formal analysis of interaction.

A second point of contact occurs when the criteria offered for assessing claims drawn from researchers' observations of interaction are tied to informants' judgments of adequacy. Philipsen (1977), for example, notes that when researchers employ their own analytical terms to represent the native speaker's view, these observations should be put to one of two possible tests. The investigator can (1) determine whether the native speaker agrees that the proposed observation is a "reasonable feature of his social world" or (2) assess whether the researcher's insight helps the native speaker "understand his social world better" (Philipsen, 1977, p. 49). Although these "tests of adequacy" are suggested criteria that lie behind formal analyses of interaction, they are rarely applied fully in formal investigations. Rather, there is an assumption in the actual conduct of this work that assessments of adequacy will be made through researchers' ongoing dialectic over specific claims as they are made. Recent criticism of Searle's analysis of the constitutive rules for the performance of speech acts (Frank, 1981; Levinson, 1981; Streek, 1980) illustrates this form of theory testing. Searle's conception of constitutive rules has been challenged on the grounds that it ignores the interactive nature of speech act production and that speakers must rely on a much broader set of inferences to identify acts than Searle's analysis suggests. This debate over the adequacy of constitutive rule analyses has advanced largely through the presentation of examples and counterexamples that illustrate potential problems with Searle's analysis. Informants are not sought to provide evidence on this issue. Indeed, in speech act analyses and many conversational analysis studies, there is an implicit belief that the knowledge the investigator is unearthing through the identification of formal properties may be beyond the informants' expressive capacity.

ISSUES OF VALIDITY AND PROOF

Advocates of qualitative approaches have often posed them as alternatives to quantitative techniques. This is unfortunate, because the two modes of analysis can complement and strengthen each other. It is doubly unfortunate because the rejection of quantitative approaches often has led to a neglect (and sometimes rejection) of the issues of reliability, validity, and proof. Some have argued that qualitative findings are so contextually and historically bound that standards of social scientific method are both inappropriate and impractical. But while one may grant that quantitative approaches distort or oversimplify essential qualities to some degree in order to gain precision, these methods also embody a healthy skepticism of research results. There should be analogs for quantitative reliability and validity in qualitative research. Indeed, a chief advantage of qualitative techniques—their capacity to give a richer, fuller, multifaceted account of interaction—can evaporate in the face of serious questions concerning validity of observation or inference.

Ethnographers have paid the most attention to these issues. In an excellent article, LeCompte and Goetz (1982) discuss problems of reliability and validity in ethnographic research (see also Becker & Geer, 1960; Cicourel, 1964). LeCompte and Goetz explicate analogs for reliability and validity in field research. They outline potential threats to external reliability (the researcher's social position in the community studied, imprudent choices of informants, not controlling for social context effects, and idiosyncratic constructs), internal reliability (high-inference descriptors, low interobserver agreement, lack of cross-checking), internal validity (history and maturation effects, observer effects, selection and regression, mortality, spurious relationships), and external validity (low comparability, setting effects, construct effects, history effects). For each they outline possible preventive and corrective measures. There have been less extensive discussions of these issues for other methods in Figure 10.1 (e.g., see Wootton, 1979, on speech act analysis), however, further work should be placed on the agenda.

Tudor (1976) makes an extremely useful argument relevant to the problems of validation of qualitative results. He criticizes qualitative research on "everyday life" for emphasizing only the "logic of discovery," the creative and inductive derivation of patterns. This is important, he argues, but it must be complemented by a "logic of verification." Patterns and relationships discovered by qualitative research must be tested and validated, preferably in other contexts. Some qualitative approaches, such as grounded theory advocate this step, but few qualitative research programs have carried out both stages. On the other hand, few traditional quantitative researchers expend much energy on the logic of discovery. Taking both phases of inquiry seriously would provide the impetus for combining qualitative and quantitative strategies. quantitative strategies.

REFERENCES

Allen, M., & Yen, W. (1979). *Introduction to measurement theory*. Belmont, CA: Brooks/Cole.

Anderson, P. A. (1983). Decision-making by objection and the Cuban missile Crisis. *Administrative Science Quarterly, 28,* 201-222.

Austin, J. (1962). *How to do things with words*. Oxford: Clarendon Press.

Bach, K., & Harnish, R. M. (1979). *Linguistic communication speech acts*. Cambridge: MIT Press.

Bales, R. F. (1970). *Personality and interpersonal behavior*. New York: Holt, Rinehart & Winston.

Beach, W. (1985). Temporal density in courtroom interaction: Constraints on the recovery of past events in legal discourse. *Communication Monographs, 52,* 1-18.

Becker, H. S., & Geer, B. (1960). Participant observation: The analysis of qualitative field data. In R. N. Adams & J. J. Preiss (Eds.), *Human organization research* (pp. 267-289). Homewood, IL: Dorsey.

Borg, I., & Lingoes, J. (1978). What weight should weights have in individual differences scaling? *Quality and Quantity, 12,* 223-237.

Borgatta, E. F. (1962). A systematic study of interaction process scores, peer and self-assessments, personality and other variables. *Genetic Psychology Monographs, 65,* 219-291.

Bower, G. H., Black, J. B., & Turner, T. J. (1979). Scripts in memory for text. *Cognitive Psychology, 11,* 177-220.

Burke, R. J. (1977). Methods of resolving superior-subordinate conflict: The constructive use of subordinate differences and disagreements. In R. C. Huseman, C. M. Logue, & D. L. Freshley (Eds.), *Readings in organizational communication* (pp. 253-271). Boston: Holbrook Press.

Campbell, D. T., & Stanley, J. C. (1963). *Experimental and quasi-experimental designs for research.* Skokie, IL: Rand-McNally.

Cappella, J. N. (1979). Talk-silence sequences in informal conversations I. *Human Communication Research, 6,* 3-17.

Cappella, J. N. (1980). Talk-silence sequences in informal conversations II. *Human Communication Research, 6,* 130-145.

Cappella, J. N. (1981). Mutual influence in expressive behavior: Adult-adult and infant-adult dyadic interaction. *Psychological Bulletin, 89,* 101-132.

Cappella, J. N., & Planalp, S. (1981). Talk-silence sequences in informal conversations III. Interspeaker influence. *Human Communication Research, 7,* 117-132.

Cappella, J. N., & Streibel, M. J. (1979). Computer analysis of talk-silence sequences: The FIASSCO system. *Behavior Research Methods and Instrumentation, 11,* 384-392.

Carter, L., Haythorn, W., Meirowitz, B., & Lanzetta, J. (1951). The relation of categorizations and ratings in the observation of group behavior. *Human Relations, 4,* 239-254.

Cicourel, A. V. (1980). Three models of discourse analysis. *Discourse Processes, 3,* 101-132.

Coulthard, M. (1977). *An introduction to discourse analysis.* London: Longman.

Cronbach, L. J. (1955). Processes affecting scores on "understanding of others" and "assumed similarity." *Psychological Bulletin, 52,* 177-193.

Cronbach, L. J., & Meehl, P. E. (1955). Construct validity in psychological tests. *Psychological Bulletin, 52,* 281-302.

D'Andrade, R. G. (1974). Memory and the assessment of behavior. In H. M. Blalock (Ed.), *Measurement in the social sciences* (pp. 159-186). Chicago: Aldine.

Davis, J. H. (1973). Group decision and social interaction: A theory of social decision schemes. *Psychological Review, 80,* 97-125.

Dindia, K. (1986). Antecedents and Consequences of awkward silence: A replication using revised lag sequential analysis. *Human Communication Research, 13,* 108-125.

Donohue, W. A. (1981). Development of a model of rule use in negotiation interaction. *Communication Monographs, 48,* 106-120.

Dore, J. (1974). A pragmatic description of early language development. *Journal of Psycholinguistic Research, 4,* 343-350.

Dore, J. (1975). Holophrases, speech acts and language universals. *Journal of Child Language, 2,* 21-39.

Dore, J. (1977). Children's illocutionary acts. In R. Freedle (Ed.), *Discourse production and comprehension* (pp. 227-240). Norwood, NJ: Ablex.

Edelsky, C. (1982). Who's got the floor? *Language in Society, 10,* 383-421.

Evans-Hewes, D. E., & Hewes, D. E. (1975). *Toward a process model of social interaction.* Paper presented at the annual meeting of the International Communication Association, Chicago.

Fisher, B. A. (1970). Decision emergence: Phases in group decision-making. *Speech Monographs, 37,* 53-66.

Folger, J., & Chapman, R. (1978). A pragmatic analysis of spontaneous imitations. *Journal of Child Language, 5,* 25-38.

Folger, J. P., Hewes, D. E., & Poole, M. S. (1984). Coding social interaction. In B. Dervin & M. J. Voigt (Eds.), *Progress in communication sciences* (Vol. 5, pp. 115-161). Norwood, NJ: Ablex.

Folger, J. P., & Puck, S. (1976). Coding relational communication: A question approach. Paper presented at the annual meeting of the International Communication Association, Portland, OR.

Folger, J. P., & Sillars, A. (1980). Relational coding and perceptions of dominance. In B. Morse & L. Phelps (Eds.), *Interpersonal communication: A relational perspective* (pp. 322-333). Minneapolis: Burgess.

Forgas, J. P. (1979). *Social episodes: The study of interaction routines.* New York: Academic Press.

Foster, M. K. (1974). When words become deeds: An analysis of three Iroquois longhouse speech events. In R. Bauman & J. Sherzer (Eds.), *Explorations in the ethnography of speaking* (pp. 354-367). London: Cambridge University Press.

Frank, D. (1981). Seven sins of pragmatics: Theses about speech act theory, conversational analysis, linguistics and rhetoric. In H. Parret, M. Sbisa, & J. Vershueren (Eds.), *Studies in language companion series, Vol. 7: Possibilities and limitations of pragmatics.* (pp. 225-236). Amsterdam: John Benjamins B.V.

Frankel, R. (1983). From sentence to sequence: Understanding the medical encounter through micro-interactional analysis. *Discourse Processes, 7,* 135-170.

Frankel, R., & Beckman, H. (1982). Impact: An interaction-based method for preserving and analyzing clinical transactions. In L. Pettegrew (Ed.), *Straight talk: Explorations in provider and patient interaction* (pp. 71-86). Louisville, KY: Humana Inc.

Frentz, T. S., & Farrell, T. B. (1976). Language-action: A paradigm for communication. *Quarterly Journal of Speech, 62,* 333-349.

Gadamer, H. G. (1975). *Truth and method.* New York: Crossroad.

Garfinkel, H. (1967). *Studies in ethnomethodology.* Englewood Cliffs, NJ: Prentice-Hall.

Garvey, C. (1975). Requests and responses in children's speech. *Journal of Child Language, 2,* 41-63.

Glass, G. V, Wilson, V. L., & Gottman, J. M. (1975). *Design and analysis of time-series experiments.* Boulder: Colorado Associated University Press.

Gottman, J. M. (1979). *Marital interaction: Experimental investigations.* New York: Academic Press.

Gottman, J. M. (1981). *Time-series analysis: A comprehensive introduction for social scientists.* New York: Cambridge University Press.

Gottman, J. M., Markman, H., & Notarius, C. (1977). The topography of marital conflict: A study of verbal and nonverbal behavior. *Journal of Marriage and the Family, 39,* 461-475.

Gouran, D. S., & Baird, J. E., Jr. (1972). An analysis of distributional and sequential structure in problem-solving and informal group discussions. *Speech Monographs, 39,* 16-22.

Gouran, D. S., & Whitehead, J. (1971). An investigation of ratings of discussion statements by participants and observers. *Speech Monographs, 38,* 263-268.

Grimshaw, A. (1982). Comprehensive discourse analysis: An instance of professional peer interaction. *Language in Society, 11,* 15-47.

Gumperz, J. J., & Herasimchuk, E. (1972). The conversational analysis of social meaning: A study of classroom interaction. In R. W. Shuy (Ed.), *Socio-linguistics: Current trends and prospects.* Washington, DC: Georgetown University Press.

Hancher, M. (1979). The classification of co-operative illocutionary acts. *Language in Society, 8,* 1-14.

Hawes, L. (1972). Development and application of an interview coding system. *Central States Speech Journal, 23,* 92-99.

Hewes, D. E. (1978). Interpersonal communication theory and research: A metamethodological overview. In B. Ruben (Ed.), *Communication yearbook 2* (pp. 155-169). New Brunswick, NJ: Transaction Books.

Hewes, D. E. (1979). The sequential analysis of social interaction. *Quarterly Journal of Speech, 65,* 56-73.

Hewes, D. E. (1985). Systematic biases in coded social interaction data. *Human Communication Research, 11,* 554-574.

Hewes, D. E., & Kebis, J. A. (1986). *Messing around with lag-sequential analysis.* Paper presented at the annual meeting of the International Communication Association, Chicago.

Hewes, D. E., Planalp, S. K., & Streibel, M. (1980). Analyzing social interaction: Some excruciating models and exhilarating results. In D. Nimmo (Ed.), *Communication yearbook 4* (pp. 123-144). New Brunswick, NJ: Transaction Books.

Huston, T. L., Surra, C., Fitzgerald, N., & Cate, R. (1981). From courtship to marriage: Mate selection as an interpersonal process. In S. Duck & R. Gilmour (Eds.), *Personal relationships 2: Developing personal relationships* (pp. 53-90). New York: Academic Press.

Hymes, D. (1974). Ways of speaking. In R. Bauman & J. Sherzer (Eds.), *Explorations in ethnography of speaking* (pp. 433-452). London: Cambridge University Press.

Hymes, D. (1972). Models of interaction of language and social life. In J. J. Gumperz & D. Hymes (Eds.), *Directions in sociolinguistics* (pp. 35-71). New York: Holt, Rinehart & Winston.

Jackson, S., & Jacobs, S. (1980). Structure of conversational influence attempts. *Quarterly Journal of Speech, 66,* 251-265.

Jacobs, S., & Jackson, S. (1983). Strategy and structure in conversational influence attempts. *Communication Monographs, 50,* 285-304.

Jaffe, J., & Feldstein, S. (1970). *Rhythms of dialogue.* New York: Academic Press.

Jefferson, G. (1973). A case of precision timing in ordinary conversation: Overlapped tag-positioned address terms in closing sequences. *Semiotica, 9.1,* 47-96.

Jefferson, G. (1974). Error correction as an interactional resource. *Language in Society, 3,* 181-191.

Kenny, D. A., & LaVoie, L. (1984). The social relations model. In L. Berkowitz (Ed.), *Advances in experimental social psychology* (Vol. 18, pp. 141-182). New York: Academic Press.

Kerlinger, F. N. (1973). *Foundations of behavioral research* (2nd ed.). New York: Holt, Rinehart & Winston.

Knapp, M. L. (1983). Dyadic relationship development. In J. M. Wiemann & R. P. Harrison (Eds.), *Nonverbal interaction* (pp. 179-207). Newbury Park, CA: Sage.

Knapp, M. L. (1984). *Interpersonal communication and human relationships.* Boston: Allyn & Bacon.

Kreckel, M. (1981). *Communicative acts and shared knowledge in natural discourse.* London: Academic Press.

Krippendorff, K. (1980). *Content analysis.* Newbury Park, CA: Sage.

Labov, W. (1972). Rules for ritual insults. In D. Sudnow (Ed.), *Studies in social interaction* (pp. 120-169). New York: Free Press.

Labov, W., & Fanshel, D. (1977). *Therapeutic discourse: Psychotherapy as conversation.* New York: Academic Press.

Laing, R. D., Phillipson, H., & Lee, A. R. (1966). *Interpersonal perception.* New York: Harper & Row.

Lazarsfeld, P. F., & Barton, A. H. (1969). Quantitative measurement: A codification of techniques unique to social science. In L. I. Krimerman (Ed.), *The nature and scope of social science* (pp. 514-549). New York: Appleton-Century-Crofts.

LeCompte, M. D., & Goetz, J. P. (1982). Problems of reliability and validity in ethnographic research. *Review of Educational Research, 52,* 31-60.

Lenk-Kruger, D. (1982). Marital decision making: A language action analysis. *Quarterly Journal of Speech, 68,* 273-287.

Levinson, S. (1981). The essential inadequacies of speech act models of dialogue. In H. Parret, M. Sbisa, & J. Vershueren (Eds.), *Studies in language companion series, Vol. 7: Possibilities and limitations of pragmatics* (pp. 473-492). Amsterdam: John Benjamins B.V.

Longabaugh, R. (1963). A category system for coding interpersonal behavior as social exchange. *Sociometry, 26,* 319-344.

Mabry, E. A. (1975). The sequential structure of interaction in encounter groups. *Human Communication Research, 1,* 302-307.

McCall, G. J., & Simmons, J. L. (1978). *Identities and interactions* (rev. ed.). New York: Free Press.

McGregor, G. (1983). Listeners' comments on conversation. *Language and Communication, 3,* 271-304.

McLaughlin, M., & Cody, M. (1982). Awkward silences: Behavioral antecedents and consequences of the conversational lapse. *Human Communication Research, 8,* 299-316.

Mehan, H. (1979). What time is it, Denise? Some observations on the organization and consequence of asking known information questions in classroom discourse. *Theory into Practice, 18,* 122-135.

Mehan, H., & Wood, R. (1975). *The reality of ethnomethodology.* New York: John Wiley.

Merritt, M. (1976). On questions following questions in service encounters. *Language in Society, 5,* 315-357.

Montgomery, B. M. (1984). Individual differences and relational interdependencies in social interaction. *Human Communication Research, 11,* 33-60.

Mosenthal, J. H., & Tierney, R. J. (1984). Cohesion: Problems with talking about text. *Reading Research Quarterly, 19,* 240-244.

Newcomb, T. M. (1953). An approach to the study of communicative acts. *Psychological Review, 60,* 393-404.

Newtson, D. (1976). Foundations of attribution: The perception of ongoing behavior. In J. H. Harvey, W. J. Ickes, & R. F. Kidd (Eds.), *New directions in attribution research* (Vol. 1, pp. 223-247). Hillsdale, NJ: LEA.

Nofsinger, R. E. (1975). The demand ticket: A conversational device for getting the floor. *Speech Monographs, 42,* 1-9.

Nofsinger, R. E. (1976). On answering questions indirectly: Some rules in the grammar of doing conversation. *Human Communication Research, 2,* 172-181.

Nofsinger, R. E. (1983). Tactical coherence in courtroom conversation. In B. Craig & K. Tracy (Eds.), *Conversational coherence: Studies in form and strategy* (pp. 243-258). Newbury Park, CA: Sage.

O'Donnell-Trujillo, N. (1982). Relational communication: A comparison of coding systems. *Communication Monographs, 48,* 91-105.

Olson, D. H. (1978). Insiders' and outsiders' view of relationships: Research strategies. In G. Levinger & H. L. Rausch (Eds.), *Close relationships* (pp. 115-135). Amherst: University of Massachusetts Press.

Pavitt, C., & Cappella, J. N. (1979). Coorientation accuracy in interpersonal and small group discussions: A literature review, model, and simulation. In D. Nimmo (Ed.), *Communication yearbook 3* (pp. 123-156). New Brunswick, NJ: Transaction Books.

Pearce, W. B., & Cronen, V. E. (1980). *Communication, action, and meaning.* New York: Praeger.

Peterson, D. R. (1979). Assessing interpersonal relationships in natural settings. In L. R. Cahle (Ed.), *Methods for studying person-situation interactions* (pp. 33-44). San Francisco: Jossey-Bass.

Phillips, E., & Cheston, R. (1979). Conflict resolution: What works? *California Management Review, 21,* 76-83.

Phillips, S. (1972). Participant structures and communication competence. In C. B. Cazden, D. Hymes, & V. P. John (Eds.), *Functions of language in the classroom.* New York: Teacher's College Press.

Philipsen, G. (1975). Speaking "like a man" in Teamsterville: Cultural patterns of role enactment in an urban neighborhood. *Quarterly Journal of Speech, 61,* 13-22.

Philipsen, G. (1976). Places for speaking in Teamsterville. *Quarterly Journal of Speech, 62,* 15-25.

Philipsen, G. (1977). Linearity of research design in ethnographic studies of speaking. *Communication Quarterly, 25,* 42-50.

Pittenger, R. E., Hockett, C. F., & Daheny, J. J. (1960). *The first five minutes.* Ithaca, NY: Paul Martineau.

Planalp, S. (1985). Relational schemata: A test of alternative forms of relational knowledge as guides to communication. *Human Communication Research, 12,* 3-29.

Planalp. S., & Honeycutt, J. M. (1985). Events that increase uncertainty in interpersonal relationships. *Human Communication Research, 11,* 593-604.

Planalp, S., & Tracy, K. (1980). Not to change the topic, but . . . A cognitive approach to the management of conversation. In D. Nimmo (Ed.), *Communication yearbook 4* (pp. 237-258). New Brunswick, NJ: Transaction Books.

Pollner, M. (1979). Explicative transactions: Making and managing meaning in traffic court. In G. Psathas (Ed.), *Everyday language: Studies in ethnomethodology* (pp. 227-256). New York: Irvington.

Poole, M. S. (1981). Decision development in small groups I: A comparison of two models. *Communication Monographs, 48,* 1-24.

Poole, M. S., & Folger, J. P. (1981a). A method for establishing the representational validity of interaction coding schemes: Do we see what they see? *Human Communication Research, 8,* 26-42.

Poole, M. S., & Folger, J. P. (1981b). Overture to interaction research: Modes of observation and the validity of interaction coding systems. *Small Group Research, 17,* 477-494.

Poole, M. S., & Folger, J. P. (1985). *How shared are "shared" interpretations?* Unpublished manuscript, Department of Speech Communication, University of Minnesota.

Poole, M. S., & McPhee, R. (1985). Methodology in interpersonal communication. In M. L. Knapp & G. R. Miller (Eds.), *Handbook of interpersonal communication* (pp. 100-170). Newbury Park, CA: Sage.

Rogers, E., & Farace, R. (1975). Analysis of relational communication in dyads: New measurement procedures. *Human Communication Research, 1,* 222-239.

Sackett, G. P. (1978). The lag sequential analysis of contingency and cyclicity in behavioral interaction research. In J. Osofsky (Ed.), *Handbook of infant development* (pp. 300-340). New York: John Wiley.

Sacks, H. (1972). On the analyzability of stories by children. In J. J. Gumperz & D. Hymes (Eds.), *Directions in sociolinguistics* (pp. 325-345). New York: Holt, Rinehart & Winston.

Sacks, H., Schegloff, E. A., & Jefferson, G. (1974). A simplest systematics for the organization of turn-taking in conversation. *Language, 50,* 696-735.

Schneider, B. (1970). Relationships between various criteria of leadership in small groups. *Journal of Social Psychology, 82,* 253-261.

Searle, J. R. (1969). *Speech acts: An essay in the philosophy of language.* Cambridge: Cambridge University Press.

Shimanoff, S. B. (1980). *Communication rules: Theory and research.* Newbury Park, CA: Sage.

Sillars, A. L. (1980). Attributions and communication in roommate conflicts. *Communication Monographs, 47,* 180-200.

Simonton, D. K. (1977). Cross-sectional time-series experiments: Some suggested statistical analyses. *Psychological Bulletin, 84,* 489-502.

Sorenson, A. B. (1978). Mathematical models in sociology. *Annual Review of Sociology, 4,* 345-371.

Spilerman, S. (1972). The analysis of mobility processes by the introduction of independent variables into a Markov chain. *American Sociological Review, 37,* 277-294.

Stiles, W. B. (1980). Comparison of dimensions derived from rating versus coding of dialogue. *Journal of Personality and Social Psychology, 38,* 359-374.

Strawson, P. F. (1964). Intention and convention in speech acts. *Philosophical Review, 73,* 439-460.

Streek, J. (1980). Speech acts in interaction: A critique of Searle. *Discourse Processes, 3,* 133-154.

Tracy, K. (1983). The issue-event distinction: A rule of conversation and its scope condition. *Human Communication Research, 9,* 320-334.

Triandis, H. C. (1978). Some universals of social behavior. *Personality and Social Psychology Bulletin, 4,* 1-16.

Tucker, L. R. (1966). Learning theory and the multivariate experiment: Illustration by determination of generalized learning curves. In R. B. Cattell (Ed.), *Handbook of multivariate experimental psychology* (pp. 416-501). Chicago: Rand-McNally.

Tudor, A. (1976). Misunderstanding in everyday life. *Sociological Review, 24,* 479-503.

Vendler, Z. (1972). *Res cogitans: An essay in rational psychology.* Ithaca, NY: Cornell University Press.

Vroom, V. & Jago, A. (1974). Decision-making as a social process: Normative and descriptive models of leader behavior. *Decision Sciences, 5,* 160-186.

Watzlawick, P., Beavin, J., & Jackson, D. D. (1967). *Pragmatics of human communication.* New York: Norton.

West, C. (1983). Small insults: A study of interruptions in cross-sex conversations between unacquainted persons. In B. Thorne, C. Kramarae, & N. Henley (Eds.). *Language, gender, and society* (pp. 86-111). Rowley, MA: Newbury House.

West, C. (1984). When the doctor is a "lady": Power, status and gender in physician-patient encounters. In N. Denzin (Ed.), *Symbolic interaction,* (Vol. 7, pp. 87-106). Greenwich, CT: JAI Press.

West, C., & Zimmerman, D. H. (1977). Women's place in everyday talk: Reflections on parent-child interaction. *Social Problems, 24,* 521-529.

Wiggins, N., & Fishbein, M. (1969). Dimensions of semantic space: The problem of individual differences. In J. G. Snider & C. E. Osgood (Eds.), *Semantic differential technique* (pp. 183-193). Chicago: Aldine.

Winer, B. J. (1971). *Statistical principles of experimental design* (2nd ed.). New York: McGraw-Hill.

Wish, M. (1976). Comparisons among multidimensional structures of interpersonal relations. *Multivariate Behavioral Research, 11,* 297-324.

Wish, M., D'Andrade, R., & Goodnow, J. E. (1980). Dimensions of interpersonal communication: Correspondences between structures for speech acts and bipolar scales. *Journal of Personality and Social Psychology, 39,* 348-360.

Wish, M., & Kaplan, S. (1977). Toward an implicit theory of interpersonal communication. *Sociometry, 40,* 234-246.

Wohlwill, J. (1973). *The study of behavior development.* New York: Academic Press.

Wootton, A. (1976). *Dilemmas of discourse.* New York: Holmes and Meier.

Chapter 11

COMMUNICATION IN INTERPERSONAL RELATIONSHIPS
Social Penetration Processes

Dalmas A. Taylor and Irwin Altman

COMMUNICATION IS CRITICAL in developing and maintaining interpersonal relationships. Several studies point to strong association between good communication and the general satisfaction of relationships (Markman, 1981; Murphy & Mendelson, 1973; Navran, 1967). In a longitudinal study of couples prior to and during marriage, Markman (1981) found that couples who had positive communication prior to the marriage were more likely to have happier marriages after five years than couples who had not established positive communication prior to marriage. Good communication or "openness" has also been associated with positive mental health (Jourard, 1964) and liking (Jourard & Landsman, 1960; Jourard & Lasakow, 1958). These studies suggest that making the self accessible to others through self-disclosure is intrinsically gratifying. Gratification, in turn, leads to the development of positive feelings for the other person. Research on married couples by Levinger and Senn (1967) also reveals a positive correlation between marital satisfaction and self-disclosure. In a more recent study of marital satisfaction, McAdams and Vaillant (1982) reanalyzed longitudinal data collected in the 1950s and 1960s on male Harvard graduates. Intimacy motivation (derived from TAT stories) correlated highly with marital happiness. Men high in intimacy motivation in early life were more likely to report happiness and stability in their marriages at midlife than men who were low in intimacy motivation. Thus communication and disclosure intimacy appear to be the sine qua non of developing satisfying interpersonal relationships. In their theory of social penetration, Altman and Taylor (1973) explicate the role of self-disclosure, intimacy, and communication in the development of interpersonal relationships. Further, their theory describes the role of these variables in the dissolution of relationships—depenetration. In this chapter, we will review the status of social penetration theory using as a backdrop the empirical literature that has emerged since its publication.

More than a decade of research has dealt with issues or topics initially raised in social penetration theory. Many of these studies are somewhat peripheral to the theory, but nonetheless examine concepts that are critical to a further understanding of communication and developing relationships. Some of this literature includes studies testing hypotheses derived from social penetration. The objective of this chapter is to review this research literature as a basis for providing commentary on some of the ideas and concepts that we began to formulate approximately 20 years ago.

The approach employed here is similar to a propositional inventory in that we have organized our discussion around major aspects of the theory, and secondarily around subordinate issues as they relate to the research literature. This approach not only allows us to determine aspects of social penetration theory that have been confirmed empirically, but also to ascertain features of the theory that have not been confirmed, as well as those which have been ignored by researchers.

To generate articles for this review, a bibliography consisting of all journal publications that cited "social penetration theory" between the years 1973-1985 was compiled. The *Social Science Citation Index* yielded 193 items. A less useful secondary source was a computer search based on key words from the theory. The chief difficulty with this approach was the inability to key on the term "social penetration." Nonetheless, we generated another 150 articles, many of which had already been identified through the *Social Science Citation Index*. The resulting bibliography contained only studies that reported empirical data—we eliminated theoretical articles and those attempting to develop or validate instruments. Only studies reported in the English language were used, and we omitted books, chapters, technical reports, and dissertation abstracts. Approximately 100, or one-third of the articles identified by this procedure, are included in this review.

The article abstracts included a detailed casting of the hypotheses, both conceptual and operational. A description of the research participant population (sex, age, size, etc.), methods and procedures, and the statistical analyses employed was also included. Finally, results and conclusions were extracted and evaluated. Key words from each article were used to form topical categories reflecting the major variables and categories in social penetration theory. As might be expected, many studies fit into more than one category.

SOCIAL PENETRATION THEORY

DEVELOPMENT AND DISSOLUTION

Social penetration theory focuses on relationship development. It deals primarily with overt interpersonal behaviors occurring in social interaction and the internal cognitive processes that precede, accompany, and follow relationship formation. The theory is developmental in that it is concerned with the growth (and dissolution) of interpersonal relationships. Social penetration processes proceed in a gradual and orderly fashion from superficial to intimate levels of exchange as a function of both immediate and forecast outcomes. Forecasts involve estimates of potential outcomes in areas of more intimate exchange. This factor causes relationships to move forward in the hope of finding new and potentially more satisfying interactions. For example, people generally move only gradually from discussions of work situations to those concerning their fears, or from comparable superficial issues to details of their sexual problems.

The earliest stage *(orientation)* of interaction is postulated to occur at the periphery of personality in "public" areas. During these initial encounters, individuals make only a small part of themselves accessible to others. At this stage there is very little evaluation; instead, individuals make concerted efforts at conflict avoidance. The overall tone is cautious and tentative, as each party to the relationship scans one another in accordance with socially conventional formulas.

The next stage *(exploratory affective exchange)* represents an expansion of richness of communication in public-outer areas; aspects of personality that were guarded earlier are now revealed in more detail, and less emphasis is placed on caution. Relationships at this stage are generally more friendly and relaxed, and movement toward intermediate areas of intimacy is begun.

Close friendships and romantic relationships characterize the next stage *(affective exchange)* of social interaction. Here, interactive engagements are more freewheeling and casual. Interaction at outer layers of personality is open, and there is heightened activity at intermediate layers of personality. Although some cautions are employed here, generally there is little resistance to open explorations of intimacy. The importance of this stage is that barriers are being broken down and dyad members are learning a great deal about each other. This stage is transitional to the highest level of intimacy exchange possible.

A final stage *(stable exchange)* of development in growing relationships is characterized by continuous openness, as well as richness across all layers of personality. Both public and private communication become efficient—dyad members know one another well and can reliably interpret and predict the feelings and probable behavior of the other. In addition to verbal levels, there is a good deal of nonverbal exchange and environmentally oriented behavior.

The dynamics of the theory include verbal, nonverbal, and environmentally oriented behaviors, each of which has substantive and affective or emotional components. Verbal exchanges include self-disclosure and other communication processes; nonverbal behaviors involve body postures and gestures, smiling, touching, and eye gaze. Environmentally oriented behaviors include use of personal space and physical objects, as well as interpersonal distance, as ways of managing social relationships. The more a relationship approaches friendship and love, the greater the probability that intimate distances will be experienced. Close relationships should permit easier transitions between physical distance, in much the same way that movement to and from intimate and superficial areas on a verbal continuum is easier once barriers have been crossed. Facial expressions and other bodily postures will also have different manifestations in close relationships than in superficial ones. In close relationships, dyad members are more willing to allow each other to use, have access to, or know about very private intimacies and belongings.

Conflict is viewed as an essential part of development. Relationship growth occurs during periods of compatibility, and relationship deterioration occurs in response to crises and other stresses. These conflict processes are hypothesized to operate in accordance with the same factors (reward/cost, personal, and situational) involved in development. However, once set in motion, the exchange processes that occur in the dissolution of an interpersonal relationship are the reverse of those occurring in developmental phases. They are systematic and proceed gradually, this time from inner (intimate) to outer (nonintimate) levels of exchange. In one sense depenetration is a failure of conflict management.

Few studies have directly examined the development process in social penetration. Altman, Vinsel, and Brown (1981) note that the studies done to test the theory "have consistently demonstrated that the growth of relationships follows the hypothesized course of development from peripheral, superficial aspects of personality to more intimate ones. The disclosure of superficial information usually takes place rapidly during the early stages of a relationship whereas exposure of intimate aspects of the self occurs only gradually and at later stages of a relationship" (p.110).

A good deal of the evidence for this contention is based on inferences from studies that address only the results of relationships, not their development (e.g., Berg, 1983, 1984; Chaiken & Derlega, 1974; McAllister & Bregman, 1983; Morton, 1978; Sabatelli, Buck & Dreyer, 1982, 1983). For example, two separate studies, one of dating couples (Berg, 1983) and another of college roommates (Berg, 1984), confirmed predictions about the final outcomes of relationships using data that were collected at the initiation of the relationships (early) and again after the passage of several months (later). Using discriminant analysis, Berg found that the late measures were no better predictors of final outcome than were the early measures. He concluded that people make decisions about the nature of their relationships early, and there is insignificant change over time. At both time points persons who were satisfied with their relationships reported a greater number of social exchanges—more communication about the relationship, more problem-solving behaviors, more self-disclosure, and greater satisfaction with the relationship than expected. Aries and Johnson (1983) and Chaiken and Derlega (1974) infer relationship growth or development from distinctions made between casual acquaintances and close (intimate) friends. Similarly, Baxter and Wilmot (1983) extracted information on growth and development from 116 diaries kept by one member of each relationship over a two-week period.

In contrast to the above studies and interpretations, however, there is modest support for a gradual development in relationship building from studies conducted in the context of mate selection (e.g., Kerckhoff & Davis, 1962; Murstein, 1970). This research preceded the publication of social penetration theory, but is quite compatible with its tenets. Potential partners pass through a series of successive stages (called filters) in which initially external characteristics are important, then value consensus, and finally role matching. Although the evidence for this approach has been deemed weak (Rubin & Levinger, 1974), other studies offer stronger support of a gradual development of friendships and romantic relationships (Braiker & Kelley, 1979; Davis, 1976; Hays, 1984, 1985; Levinger & Snoek, 1972).

In a 13-week longitudinal study of college roommates, Taylor (1968) investigated shifts in self-disclosure of intimate and nonintimate behaviors. His findings confirmed several hypotheses derived from social penetration theory: progressive development in exchanges over time, with less rapid development in intimate behaviors than nonintimate ones, and a general slowing down of the process at later time periods. No one has actually studied development directly since Taylor's (1968) study. A laboratory analogue of self-disclosure development (Davis, 1976) and two longitudinal studies on friendship formation by Hays (1984, 1985) constitute partial exceptions to this assertation.

Davis (1976) tested the social penetration hypothesis that there is a monotonic increase over time of the breadth and depth of self-disclosure. However, a more specific interest was to determine whether this monotonic function would apply to the minute-by-minute transaction in a brief encounter. Three general findings confirmed social penetration theory:

(1) The intimacy of topics disclosed increased linearly as encounters progressed, without appearing to reach an asymptote. This outcome was interpreted as supporting the temporal features of social penetration theory applicable within a brief encounter just as much as between the encounters of a developing relationship.
(2) Partners matched the average intimacy levels of their disclosures an their rates of increase of intimacy, an outcome supportive of the "dyadic effect."
(3) The dyadic effect was not due to mutual reciprocity but rather to a role differentiation in which the more disclosing member of the dyad took the lead and the less disclosing one tended to take his or her cue accordingly.

In two separate studies, Hays (1984, 1985) asked new students to select two same-sex others whom they had not known before but with whom they thought they might become good friends during the school year. On three subsequent occasions, at three-week intervals, respondents were asked to report the amount of casual and intimate exchange they had with the target students. The exchanges dealt with communication, companionship, affection, and consideration. Overall behavioral exchange (intimate and nonintimate) increased over time among pairs rated as "close" at the end of the semester but not among those who were rated as "not-close."

For the most part, the studies reviewed above simply address the issue of relationship development by comparing brief samples of people's behavior in long-term versus short-term relationships (e.g., Berg, 1983, 1984), by making inferences based on casual acquaintances compared with intimates (e.g., Chaiken & Derlega, 1974), or by examining verbal and nonverbal communication between short-term and long-term cohabiting couples (Sabatelli et al., 1982). Longitudinal studies of development (e.g., Hays, 1984, 1985), as prescribed by Altman and Taylor (1973), are rare. This has been a neglected approach for the study of relationships by social psychologists and other students of relationships.

The issue of dissolution (depenetration) has received far less attention than has development. Our review uncovered only one study in the literature that attempted to assess the dynamics of relationship dissolution. Tolstedt and Stokes (1984) hypothesized that in depenetration, as intimacy decreased, self-disclosure breadth and depth would decline and the valence of self-disclosure would become more negative, particularly at low levels of intimacy. The correlational results confirmed the reversal hypothesis of social penetration theory for breadth and valence of self-disclosure: As intimacy decreased, so did breadth; similarly, as intimacy decreased, valence became more negative. Contrary to the depenetration hypothesis, however, depth of self-disclosure tended to increase as intimacy decreased for both descriptive and evaluative depth. The latter finding may be due in part to experimental demands and the respondent population.

Tolstedt and Stokes's respondents were facing crisis points in their relationships and were asked to discuss these relationships. In these cases, increased depth was also associated with negative valence. Therefore, the increased depth may be temporary; and as depenetration continues, decreased depth may accompany decreased intimacy. On the other hand, the social penetration prediction for depth may be incorrect. The pain and anger that accompany the loss of an intimate relationship may engender self-disclosures of considerable depth. Such couples, already at such low intimacy levels, could feel that they have less to lose and that communication of negative thoughts and feelings may lead to an improvement in their relationship. Due to the procedural limitations of this study, however, these interpretations must be viewed with some skepticism.

Unfortunately, there are no other studies on depenetration that could provide a basis for evaluating the above conjectures. As noted earlier, a number of studies have confirmed the value of communication in the development and maintenance of interpersonal relationships. More research is needed to inform us of the dynamics of relationship dissolution.

REWARDS AND COSTS

The second broad category of the theory involves a description of the role of rewards and costs in the social penetration process—the dyadic effect. Interpersonal rewards and costs are motivational in that rewards form the basis for maintaining or continuing a relationship to deeper levels of exchange, whereas costs lead to a winding down or dissolution of relationships.

The meaning of rewards and costs in social penetration theory is principally derived from the theories of Thibaut and Kelley (1959) and Homans (1950, 1961). These theories assume that parties in social exchanges seek to maximize gains and to minimize losses. However, since all relationships inevitably involve costs, parties typically evaluate costs relative to the rewards they may obtain. Therefore, the overall outcome of a relationship is a function of both its rewards and its costs:

RELATIONSHIP OUTCOMES = REWARDS - COSTS

Altman and Taylor derived their definition of rewards and costs, in part, from the social psychology of Thibaut and Kelley (1959):

> By rewards, we refer to the pleasures, satisfactions, and gratifications the person enjoys. The provision of a means whereby a drive is reduced or a need fulfilled constitutes a reward. . . . By costs, we refer to any factors that operate to inhibit or deter a performance of a sequence of behavior. . . . Thus cost is high when great physical or mental effort is required, when embarrassment or anxiety accompany the action, or when there are conflicting forces or competing response tendencies of any sort. (pp. 12-13)

Additional inputs to the definition come from a similar approach to rewards and costs. Homans (1950) relies upon economic-based ideas of profit and loss. Rewarding interaction involves a positive exchange of objects, symbolic signs, and attitudes and feelings. Costs come from negative experiences deriving from an aversive stimulus, or from the withdrawal of a pleasant one. Homans's (1961) concept of *distributive justice* deals with interactants' perceptions of equity and fairness in the distribution of rewards and costs:

> A man in an exchange relationship with another will expect that the rewards of each man be proportional to his costs—the greater the rewards, the greater the costs—and that the net rewards, or profits, of each man be proportional to his investments—the greater the investments, the greater the profits. (p. 32)

For Homans, relationship outcomes are described in terms of profits. The overall evaluation of a relationship is in terms of distributive justice:

PROFIT (RELATIONSHIP OUTCOME) = REWARDS - COSTS

The combined formulations of rewards and costs by Thibaut and Kelley (1959) and Homans (1950, 1961) have been incorporated into social penetration theory in five propositions:

(1) *Reward/cost ratio* refers to the balance of positive and negative experiences in a social relationship (i.e., the relative number of rewards to costs). The greater the number of rewards to costs, the more satisfying the relationship.

(2) *Absolute reward and cost properties* involve the absolute magnitude of positive and negative experiences in a relationship. For example, two social relationships might have the same relative reward/cost ratios but differ in absolute amounts of rewards and costs and, consequently, in psychological characteristics.

(3) *Immediately obtained rewards and costs* refer to the set of rewards and costs that accrue from a finite, temporally bound, relatively immediate social interaction. The temporal locus is "what just happened."

(4) *Forecast rewards and costs* are projections to future rewards and costs. Such forecasts play an important role in propelling relationships foward or in slowing them down and even reversing their growth. The forecasting process is similar to the Thibaut and Kelley (1959) concepts of comparison level (CL) and comparison level for alternatives (CL_{alt}) in that one component of forecasting includes a comparison of a present relationship to some standard, or to alternative relationships.

(5) *Cumulative rewards and costs* refer to the cumulation of rewards and costs throughout the history of a dyad. Conceptually, they can be represented as a reservoir or pool of positive and negative experiences up to a given point in time and extending back to the point of a relationship's formation.

Thus rewards and costs are consistently associated with mutual satisfaction of social and personal needs. Relationship outcomes are not necessarily the same as satisfaction with a relationship. In order to predict how satisfied persons will be in a relationship, we need to take into account their experiences and expectations. Outcomes received in past experiences are often critical to knowing and understanding the kinds of outcomes expected in the future. Finally, gains and losses from an interpersonal relationship cover a broad spectrum, from anxiety and security to status and power, group identification, and other sociopsychological phenomena.

The greater the ratio of rewards to costs, the more rapid the penetration process. Stated differently, the growth of a relationship will be a direct function of the extent to which good or satisfying aspects of the experience outweigh bad or unfavorable ones. In addition to a proportional analysis of rewards and costs, their absolute magnitude must also be considered. Assuming a similar ratio of favorable to unfavorable experiences, a greater absolute magnitude of rewards should yield a faster-growing, more intimate relationship. In this regard rewards are probably more important than costs in that the driving force that propels relationships forward is most likely the search for and reaction to achieved rewards rather than the avoidance of costs. This assertion does not rule out the importance of cost factors, but only suggests a different subjective emphasis. In maximizing their own reward characteristics, people often make it difficult for others to learn about their negative characteristics. Thus cost assessment is less certain and cost information is in a less accessible form—the positive aspects of each individual are most salient.

The early exchange theorists (i.e., Homans, 1950; Thibaut & Kelley, 1959) were principally concerned with the preconditions of relationship formation, not development. In social penetration theory the concept of reward/cost assessment is viewed as the motivational basis for relationship growth through the various stages of development. Continuous exchanges (communication, self-disclosure, etc.) occur as long as individuals mutually experience a favorable reward/cost balance. Further, as relationships progress, the exchanges become more intimate, a process illustrated in Figure 11.1. If exchange processes are sustained or increased over time, individuals must be "profiting" from the relationship (Taylor, 1968). The process begins with a first encounter in which individuals communicate at fairly superficial levels. These communications are evaluated in terms of rewards and costs, and forecasts are made regarding future exchanges. Two events occur here: (1) a reward/cost assessment, analogous to Thibaut and Kelley's (1959) concept of comparison level (CL); and, (2) an extrapolation that takes into account the projected relationship and alternative relationships—a comparison level for alternatives (CL_{alt}). The process continues throughout the history of the interaction.

Studies uncovered in this review, while ignoring the developmental focus of social penetration, confirm the importance of rewards and costs in social exchanges, similar to early application of these principles. The reinforcement or motivational interpretations of rewards and costs are augmented with cognitive explanations of the assessment of forecasted and retroactive analyses of rewards and costs (see Figure 11.1). Rewards are operationalized as positive experiences (e.g., liking, agreement, compatibility) and costs are translated as negative experiences (e.g., dislike, disagreement, tension).

An important application of rewards and costs in an interpersonal context can be found in studies on communication. For example, McLaughlin, Cody, and Rosenstein (1983) describe what they call *account sequences,* a mechanism by which parties to an initial encounter deal with the discovery of dissimilarity and other conversational disagreeables (costs). They conclude that there is a structural preference for agreement in conversations, especially for new acquaintances. Through the use of account strategies parties to a relationship

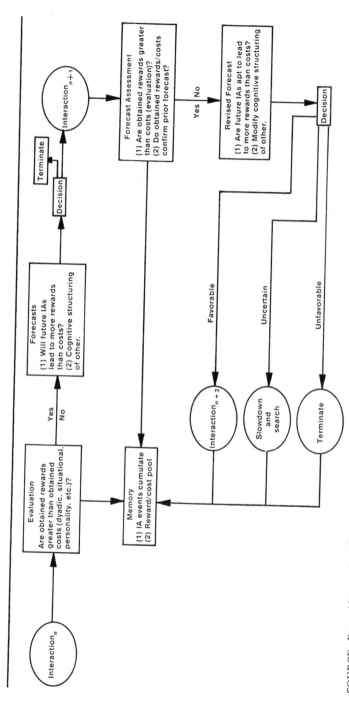

Figure 11.1 Interpersonal Reward/Cost Aspects of the Social Penetration Process

attempt to maintain harmony in conversations. When this is not effective for a particular topic, there is a tendency to drop the subject, or otherwise change the conversation. In more intimate contexts positive correlations have been found between marital satisfaction and verbal, affective, and physical intimacy (Tolstedt & Stokes, 1983); attitude similarity (Hendrick, 1981); quality nonverbal communication (Honeycutt, Wilson, & Parker, 1982; Markman, 1981; Murphy & Mendelson, 1973; Navran, 1967; Sabatelli et al., 1982); and openness as indicated by personal self-disclosure (Levinger & Senn, 1967).

In investigating the matching hypothesis through lonely hearts advertisements, Harrison and Saeed (1977) operationalized attractiveness and financial security as rewards. Rosenfeld (1979) explored cost factors in communication by examining self-disclosure avoidance. Even though self-disclosure has many potential benefits (rewards) and is essential to relationship development, it appears to be a small part of the communication process. Rosenfeld found that males tend to avoid self-disclosure to maintain control over their relationships, whereas females avoid disclosing themselves to prevent personal hurt and other problems. In both instances disclosure appears to be perceived as a cost rather than a reward. This conclusion, however, should be viewed with caution since the finding is not tied to a developmental stage. Taylor and Altman (1966) found that disclosure intimacy is inversely correlated with social desirability and therefore can be potentially rewarding or costly. McAllister (1980), for example, describes the social reward potential and resulting attraction that could result from sending and receiving communications. Premature and/or inappropriate disclosure intimacy is often costly, whereas disclosure intimacy that is synchronized with target and stage of development can have beneficial effects for a relationship (see Chelune, Sultan, & Williams, 1980). We will return to these considerations later in discussing reciprocity and intimacy.

Taylor, Altman, and Sorrentino (1969) went beyond the demonstration of basic reward/cost effects by exploring expectations (confirmed and disconfirmed) as a function of prior reward/cost experiences; that is, how do individuals react to communications that are consistently favorable (rewarding) and unfavorable (costly) versus those that are initially unfavorable and end up being favorable, and vice versa? Mixed reward/cost experiences seem to produce a contrast effect. Positive messages that immediately follow initially negative ones are enhanced by this context. Evidence for the reverse of this sequence is equivocal. Aronson and Linder (1965) have described this phenomenon as a "gain-or-loss" effect; gains and losses have more impact on attraction than consistent evaluations. McAllister and Bregman (1983) tested an integration theory model against gain-loss theory and found more evidence for integration theory. Integration theory models predict that sequences increasing or decreasing in intimacy should have less impact on attraction than constant intimate or nonintimate disclosures. Although the McAllister and

Bregman finding was not interpreted as consistent with social penetration theory, it is consistent with exchange theory. It simply suggests an alternative hypothesis concerning what is more rewarding—constant high intimacy disclosures versus a sequence of increasingly intimate disclosures. More important, these studies show that a reward (or cost) is not an absolute entity but is assessed in relation to its context (Taylor, DeSoto, & Lieb, 1979), potentially or real existing alternatives (Berg, 1984), and sequence (Aronson & Linder, 1965; McAllister & Bregman, 1983; Taylor et al., 1969). Moreover, they provide support for the Thibaut and Kelley concept of comparison level for alternatives (CL_{alt}).

RECIPROCITY AND INTIMACY

A final topic of importance to the social penetration framework concerns the reciprocity of exchange between persons in a relationship. Will one person's disclosure, or behavior, increase the probability that the other person will disclose? According to social penetration theory, one organizing principle for communication in initial encounters is the *norm of reciprocity* (Gouldner, 1960). This norm asserts that we feel obligated or indebted to return disclosures received. A second question for the social penetration process is concerned with whether we like another person because he or she has disclosed to us, or whether we disclose to others because we like them. In social penetration theory, we argued that while a norm of reciprocity seems to exist, it is not the sole determinant of the social penetration process. Further, we speculated that reciprocity derives from the dynamics of the encounter between people, the level of intimacy of topics discussed, the properties of the situation, and the characteristics of the participants. Altman and Taylor (1973) concluded that reciprocity is a set of behavioral events, not necessarily an explanation of those events (p. 56).

Altman (1973) later expanded upon the concept of reciprocity by proposing a model that incorporates the norm of reciprocity and social reward as motivational determinants of mutual disclosure. In this model an obligation to reciprocate disclosure is hypothesized to be more important in early stages of a relationship than in later stages. At early stages, reciprocal disclosure is presumed to occur independent of social consequences. Instead, reciprocal disclosure was postulated as a basis for establishing trust. Once trust has been established, reciprocation is no longer considered important since unilateral disclosures carry little risk of vulnerability. Thus nonintimate disclosure probably operates more in accordance with a norm of social reciprocity than do highly intimate disclosures.

This outcome leads to the prediction of an inverse relationship between stage of relationship and degree of reciprocity. Further, the intimacy of the disclosed topic interacts with the stage of a relationship so that nonintimate reciprocity is at a maximum among strangers and declines as a relationship develops. Conversely, reciprocity of intimate disclosures is predicted to reach a peak in the middle stages of a relationship. At early and late stages reciprocity of intimate disclosures will be minimal or nonexistent. In two separate studies, Won-Doornick (1979, 1985) directly tested and found support for Altman's hypotheses on reciprocity. Evidence from Cohn and Strassberg (1983) corroborates and adds to the generalizability of the disclosure reciprocity effect. In the early stages of relationships reciprocity is thought to be important because it demonstrates and establishes trust (Altman, 1973; Rubin, 1975). This explanation, however, has been challenged by others (Berg & Archer, 1980, 1982; Jones & Archer, 1976; McAllister, 1980).

Jones and Archer (1976) tested modeling versus trust explanations for reciprocity, and added an additional explanation—equitable exchange. Equitable exchange is presumed to operate when a recipient feels obligated to reciprocate personal information to pay for disclosures received. According to these authors a special variant of equitable exchange, personalism, engenders exclusive trust. Personalistic disclosures are held to be more valuable than disclosures shared with others (Taylor et al., 1981). Jones and Archer, therefore, hypothesized that personalistic disclosure leads to liking because the recipient feels that she or he has been singled out as trustworthy and is a candidate for an intimate relationship. Trust was ruled out as a possible mediating variable in disclosure reciprocity. In a series of studies of the special effects of personalism and intimacy, Taylor and his colleagues (Taylor, Gould, & Brounstein, 1981; Taylor & Hinds, 1985) found that highly intimate disclosers were liked most when they attributed their disclosure behavior to characteristics of the disclosers, whereas low-intimacy disclosers who attributed their disclosure to characteristics of the disclosees, were liked least.

Up to now the research studies reviewed give clear evidence that reciprocity in relationship development depends on early reward/cost experiences and intimacy. Participants' perceptions of the impact of their own communication and other exchanges have implications for their understanding of how mutual liking and trust develop, and how these in turn promote increased intimacy (Berg & Archer, 1983; Brewer & Mittelman, 1980; Hill & Stull, 1982; Petty & Mirels, 1981; Shaffer, Smith, & Tomarelli, 1982). Whether the relationship proceeds to an intimate stage depends on the accuracy of perception and the ability of the parties in the relationship to assess and to sustain favorable reward/cost outcomes. There is disagreement, however, among theorists on the application and interpretation of intimacy in interpersonal relationships:

> The principles of the interpersonal marketplace are most likely to prevail in encounters between strangers and casual acquaintances, and in early stages of the development of relationships. As an interpersonal bond becomes more firmly established, however, it begins to go beyond exchange. (Rubin, 1973, p. 86).

Others criticize the implications of "emotional bookkeeping" and the crass weighing of rewards and costs in strict conformity with exchange principles

(Clark, 1984; Clark & Mills, 1979; Clark, Ouellette, & Milberg, 1984; Mills & Clark, 1982; Murstein, 1971, 1973; Murstein, MacDonald, & Cerreto, 1977; Rubin, 1973). On the other hand, Walster and her colleagues (Walster, Berscheid, & Walster, 1973; Walster, Walster, & Berscheid, 1978) have steadfastly defended exchange interpretations of intimate relationships: "We contend that, even in the most intimate relations, considerations of equity will influence strongly the viability and pleasantness of a relationship" (Walster et al., 1973, p. 170).

Recall that Altman's (1973) hypotheses on reciprocity state that reciprocity will be greater for superficial, nonintimate messages than for intimate ones. Qualifications on equity applications to intimate relationships by Walster et al. (1978) support that distinction. Specifically, intimates are predicted to tolerate more imbalance in exchange than do casual acquaintances. These variable effects in intimacy reciprocity, however, have not been consistently supported in the literature (e.g., Caltabiano & Smithson, 1983; Dalto & Ajzen, 1979; Davis & Perkowitz, 1979). The analysis of intimacy reciprocity by Caltabiano and Smithson (1983) identifies two qualifying variables that may account for the mixture of findings in the research literature: valence and gender. Positive disclosures were seen as more appropriate than negative disclosures, and females were more receptive to disclosure than males.

Patterson (1976) proposed an arousal model of interpersonal intimacy that presumes variations or changes in intimacy produce changes in arousal level. Furthermore, the change in arousal is thought to be a mediating mechanism for adjustments in reciprocated intimacy. If the arousal is labeled negative (e.g., anxiety, discomfort), the resultant behaviors are designed to lessen the negative affective state. If the arousal is perceived as positive (e.g., liking, love, relief), it is predicted that the intimacy will be reciprocated. In two separate studies, Taylor and his colleagues (Moriarty & Taylor, 1986; Taylor & Belgrave, 1986) found that negatively labeled messages diminished the effect of reciprocation. These findings taken together with those of Caltabiano and Smithson (1983) demonstrate that disclosure reciprocity is sensitive not only to the intimacy of received disclosure but also to the valence of that disclosure. Further considerations of reciprocity effects in interpersonal communication should incorporate or examine the impact of valence.

Caltabiano & Smithson's (1983) observation on gender effects and self-disclosure is consistent with a pervasive finding in the literature. Although gender effects were not originally dealt with in social penetration theory, the effect is now one that cannot be ignored. A persistent finding among the studies examining the self-disclosure process in relationship to social penetration theory is that females disclose more, and are more open, than males (Aries & Johnson, 1983; Arlett, Best, & Little, 1976; Chelune, 1976; Cozby, 1973; Little, 1968; McGuire & Padawer-Singer, 1976; Pelligrini, Hicks, Meyers-Winton, & Antal, 1978; Rosenfeld, Civikly, & Herron 1979; Taylor & Hinds, 1985; Thase & Page,

1977; Walker & Wright, 1976). Jourard and his colleagues (Jourard & Lasakow, 1958; Jourard & Richman, 1963) reasoned that females are socialized to be more open, self-disclosing, and empathic than males. The male role, according to Jourard and his associates, requires greater control of emotion and concealment of self-disclosure intimacy, and is therefore a "lethal" role.

Despite the persistence of this finding, it has been challenged and subject to modification by a number of contradictory and/or equivocal findings (Dies & Greenberg, 1976). In a major literature review on sex differences, Maccoby and Jacklin (1974) state that the evidence does not justify concluding that men and women differ in self-disclosure. The differences in self-disclosure between men and women are influenced by the target person's sex (Komarovsky, 1976; Wheeler & Nezlek, 1977), social desirability (Zanna & Pack, 1975), marital status (Booth & Hess, 1974), and topical content (Komarovsky, 1976). Rosenfeld et al. (1979) similarly state, "It becomes clear that the conclusion 'females disclose more than males' is inaccurate" (pp. 108-109). These authors conclude that the consideration of four factors could lead to less equivocal findings regarding male-female disclosure. These factors are anatomical/psychological sex, a clear operational definition of intimacy, control over disclosure topics, and an unambiguous specification of the relationship between subject and target. It may, therefore, be necessary to keep these four considerations in mind as we review sex differences and disclosure in social penetration processes.

Knapp (1978) has extended the social penetration framework to emphasize communication phenomena. Specifically, he proposes going beyond considerations of depth and breadth of exchange to examine synchronized communication and efficiency. Within this context, Baxter and Wilmot (1983) investigated the communication characteristics of relationships of differing growth rates, and looked at how these characteristics vary as a function of the sex of respondent. They found sex differences in several aspects of communication including encounter personalness, topic breadth, encounter importance, and enactment of talk for talk's sake; all were consistent with traditional sex-role socialization described above.

Derlega, Durham, Gockel, and Sholis (1981) conducted a series of experiments on disclosure intimacy and gender that may be responsive to the gender-disclosure issues raised earlier by Rosenfeld et al. (1979). These studies manipulated sex of subject, disclosure topic, intimacy target gender, and degree of friendship. Derlega et al. predicted that males would disclose more than females on traditionally masculine topics; females would disclose more than males on traditionally feminine topics; and males and females would disclose at the same level for "neutral" topics (those considered equally appropriate for either sex). Women did disclose more than men on feminine topics, emphasizing personal concerns and vulnerabilities. However, males did not differ from females on masculine topics or neutral topics. These findings also generalized to strangers as target persons. Therefore, the robustness of the traditional male-female differences was demonstrated in a variety of settings with the kinds of controls advocated by Rosenfeld et al. (1979).

SUMMING UP

In this chapter, we have reviewed literature relevant to social penetration theory and communication and developmental phenomena. The theory is developmental in its concern with the growth and dissolution of interpersonal relationships. Four stages of interpersonal exchange and communication were identified: (1) orientation, (2) exploratory affective exchange, (3) affective exchange, and (4) stable exchange. A second aspect of the theory involves rewards and costs as motivational components of establishing and sustaining stable interpersonal relationships. Finally, the dynamics of reciprocity and intimacy were assessed as to how they influence interpersonal relationships. A large number of studies that referenced social penetration were analyzed as a way of determining the impact of the theory.

The most glaring conclusion to be derived from this review is that many researchers have been influenced by the ideas from social penetration theory, but few have directly tested propositions from the theory. To assess development—the major focus of the theory—researchers need to employ longitudinal research strategies. These approaches are not in vogue in social psychology; moreover, it is difficult to gain access to appropriate populations for research. A direct challenge to the efficacy of the theme of "gradual development in relationship formation" was found in the work of Berg and his colleagues (Berg, 1983, 1984: Berg & Clark, in press). The conclusions from their studies indicate that many aspects of close relationships develop quickly rather than gradually. Berg cites evidence that measures of attraction and social exchange obtained early in a relationship predict the state of the relationship almost as well as the same measures taken later in the relationship. However, Berg also acknowledges the need for further longitudinal research in order to clarify these observations.

Although a number of studies examined development by inference, we were able to find only one study in the literature that attempted to assess the dynamics of relationship dissolution (depenetration). It is quite likely that the same procedural challenges that discourage investigators from making direct tests of developmental hypotheses are at issue here. These omissions point to opportunities in tracking growth and dissolution in interpersonal relationships. The *dyadic effect* has been confirmed by numerous studies, but reciprocity and intimacy analyses have broken new ground with the introduction of Patterson's (1976) intimacy arousal model and studies on personalistic disclosure (e.g., Jones & Archer, 1976; Taylor et al., 1981). It is hoped that these efforts will not only sharpen and improve our knowledge about reciprocity in interpersonal contexts but will also be used to understand better relationship buildup and breakdown.

REFERENCES

Altman, I. (1973). Reciprocity of interpersonal exchange. *Journal for the Theory of Social Behavior, 3,* 249-261.

Altman, I., & Taylor, D. A. (1973). *Social penetration: The development of interpersonal relationships.* New York: Holt, Rinehart & Winston.

Altman, I., Vinsel, A., & Brown, B. B. (1981). Dialectic conceptions in social psychology: An application to social penetration and privacy regulation. In L. Berkowitz (Ed.), *Advances in experimental social psychology* (Vol. 14, pp. 107-160). New York: Academic Press.

Aries, E., & Johnson, F. (1983). Close friendship in adulthood: Conversational content between same sex friends. *Sex Roles, 9,* 1183-1196.

Arlett, C., Best, J. A., & Little, B. R. (1976). Influence of interviewer self-disclosure and verbal reinforcement on personality tests. *Journal of Clinical Psychology, 32,* 770-775.

Aronson, E., & Linder, D. (1965). Gain and loss of esteem as determinants of interpersonal attractiveness. *Journal of Experimental Social Psychology, 1,* 156-171.

Baxter, L., & Wilmot, W. (1983). Communication characteristics of relationships with differential growth rates. *Communication Monographs, 50,* 264-272.

Berg, J. H. (1983). *Attraction in relationships: As it begins so it goes.* Paper presented at the annual meeting of the American Psychological Association, Anaheim, CA.

Berg, J. H. (1984). Development of friendship between roommates. *Journal of Personality and Social Psychology, 2,* 346-356.

Berg, J. H., & Archer, R. L. (1980). Disclosure or concern: A second look at liking for the norm-breaker. *Journal of Personality, 48,* 245-257.

Berg, J. H. & Archer, R. L. (1982). Responses to self-disclosure and interaction goals. *Journal of Experimental Social Psychology, 18,* 501-512.

Berg, J. H., & Archer, R. L. (1983). The disclosure-liking relationship: Effects of self-perception, order of disclosure and topical similarity. *Human Communication Research, 10,* 269-281.

Berg, J. H., & Clark, M. S. (1986). Differences in social exchange between intimate and other relationships: Gradually evolving or quickly apparent? In V. J. Derlega & B. Winstead (Eds.), *Friendship and social interaction.* New York: Springer-Verlag.

Booth, A., & Hess, E. (1974). Cross-sex friendships. *Journal of Marriage and the Family, 36,* 38-47.

Braiker, H. B., & Kelley, H. H. (1979). Conflict in the development of close relationships. In R. L. Burgess & T. L. Huston (Eds.), *Social exchange in developing relationships* (pp. 135-169). New York: Academic Press.

Brewer, M., & Mittelman, J. (1980). Effects of normative control of self-disclosure on reciprocity. *Journal of Personality, 48,* 89-102.

Caltabiano, M., & Smithson, M. (1983). Variables affecting the perception of self-disclosure appropriateness. *Journal of Social Psychology, 120,* 119-128.

Chaiken, A. L., & Derlega, V. J. (1974). Variables affecting the appropriateness of self-disclosure. *Journal of Consulting and Clinical Psychology, 42,* 588-593.

Chelune, G. J. (1976). A multidimensional look at sex and target differences in disclosure. *Psychological Reports, 39,* 259-263.

Chelune, G. J., Sultan, R. F., & Williams, C. L. (1980). Loneliness, self-disclosure, and interpersonal effectiveness. *Journal of Counseling Psychology, 27,* 462-468.

Clark, M. S. (1984). Record keeping in two types of relationships. *Journal of Personality and Social Psychology, 47,* 549-557.

Clark, M. S., & Mills, J. (1979). Interpersonal attraction in exchange and communal relationships. *Journal of Personality and Social Psychology, 37,* 12-24.

Clark, M. S., Ouellette, R., & Milberg, S. (1984). *Recipient mood, relationship type, and helping.* Paper presented at the Second International Conference on Personal Relationships, Madison, WI.

Cohn, N. B., & Strassberg, D. S. (1983). Self-disclosure reciprocity among preadolescents. *Personality and Social Psychology Bulletin, 9,* 97-102.

Cozby, P. C. (1973). Self-disclosure: A literature review. *Psychological Bulletin, 79,* 73-91.

Dalto, C. A., & Ajzen, I. (1979). Self-disclosure and attraction: Effects of intimacy and desirability on beliefs and attitudes. *Journal of Research in Personality, 13,* 127-138.

Davis, J. D. (1976). Self-disclosure in an acquaintance experience: Responsibility for level of intimacy. *Journal of Personality and Social Psychology, 33,* 787-792.

Davis, D., & Perkowitz, N. T. (1979). Consequences of responsiveness in dyadic interaction: Effects of probability of response and proportion of content-related responses on interpersonal attraction. *Journal of Personality and Social Psychology, 37,* 534-550.

Derlega, V. J., Durham, B., Gockel, B., & Sholis, D. (1981). Sex differences in self disclosure: Effects of topic content, friendship, and partner's sex. *Sex Roles, 7,* 433-447.

Dies, R., & Greenberg, B. (1976). Effects of physical contact in an encounter group context. *Journal of Consulting and Clinical Psychology, 44,* 400-405.

Gouldner, A. W. (1960). The norm of reciprocity: A preliminary statement. *American Sociological Review, 25,* 161-178.

Harrison, A. A., & Saeed, L. (1977). Let's make a deal: An analysis of revelations and stipulations in lonely heart advertisements. *Journal of Personality and Social Psychology, 35,* 257-264.

Hays, R. B. (1984). The development and maintenance of friendship. *Journal of Social and Personal Relationships, 1,* 75-97.

Hays, R. B. (1985). A longitudinal study of friendship development. *Journal of Personality and Social Psychology, 48,* 909-924.

Hendrick, S. (1981). Self-disclosure and marital satisfaction. *Journal of Personality and Social Psychology, 40,* 1158-1159.

Hill, C. T., & Stull, D. E. (1982). Disclosure reciprocity: Conceptual and measurement issues. *Social Psychology Quarterly, 45,* 238-245.

Homans, G. C. (1950). *The human group.* New York: Harcourt Brace Jovanovich.

Homans, G. C. (1961). *Social behavior: Its elementary forms.* New York: Harcourt Brace Jovanovich.

Honeycutt, J., Wilson, C., & Parker, C. (1982). Effects of sex and degrees of happiness on perceived styles of communicating in and out of the marital relationship. *Journal of Marriage and the Family, 44,* 395-406.

Jones, E. E., & Archer, R. L. (1976). Are there special effects of personalistic self-disclosure? *Journal of Experimental Social Psychology, 12,* 180-193.

Jourard, S. M. (1964). *The transparent self.* New York: Van Nostrand.

Jourard, S. M., & Landsman, M. J. (1960). Cognition, cathexis, and the "dyadic effect" in men's self-disclosing behavior. *Merrill Palmer Quarterly, 9,* 141-148.

Jourard, S. M., & Lasakow, P. (1958). Some factors in self-disclosure. *Journal of Abnormal and Social Psychology, 56,* 91-98.

Jourard, S. M., & Richman, P. (1963). Disclosure output and input in college students. *Merrill Palmer Quarterly, 9,* 141-148.

Kerckhoff, A. C., & Davis, K. E. (1962). Value consensus and need complementarity in mate selection. *American Sociological Review, 27,* 295-303.

Knapp, M. L. (1978). *Nonverbal communication in human interaction* (2nd ed.). New York: Holt, Rinehart & Winston.

Komarovsky, M. (1976). *Dilemmas of masculinity: A study of college youth.* New York: Norton.

Levinger, G., & Senn, D. J. (1967). Disclosure of feelings in marriage. *Merrill Palmer Quarterly, 13,* 237-249.

Levinger, G., & Snoek, J. D. (1972). *Attraction in relationship: A new look at interpersonal attraction.* New York: General Learning Press.

Little, K. B., (1968). Cultural variations in social schemata. *Journal of Personality and Social Psychology, 10,* 1-7.

Maccoby, E. E., & Jacklin, C. N. (1974). *The psychology of sex differences.* Stanford, CA: Stanford University Press.

Markman, H. J. (1981). Prediction of marital distress: A 5-year follow-up. *Journal of Consulting and Clinical Psychology, 49,* 554-567.

McAdams, D., & Vaillant, G. E. (1982). Intimacy motivation and psychosocial adjustment: A longitudinal study. *Journal of Personality Assessment, 46,* 586-593.

McAllister, H. A. (1980). Self-disclosure and liking: Effects for senders and receivers. *Journal of Personality, 48,* 409-418.

McAllister, H. A., & Bregman, N. J. (1983). Self-disclosure and liking: An integration theory approach. *Journal of Personality, 51,* 202-212.

McGuire, W. J., & Padawer-Singer, A. (1976). Trait salience in the spontaneous self-concept. *Journal of Personality and Social Psychology, 33,* 743-754.

McLaughlin, M. L., Cody, M. J., & Rosenstein, N. E. (1983). Account sequences in conversations between strangers. *Communication Monographs, 50,* 102-128.

Mills, J., & Clark, M. S. (1982). Exchange and communal relationships. In L. Wheeler (Ed.), *Review of personality and social psychology* (Vol. 3, pp. 121-144). Newbury Park, CA: Sage.

Morton, T. L. (1978). Intimacy and reciprocity of exchange: A comparison of spouses and strangers. *Journal of Personality and Social Psychology, 36,* 72-81.

Moriarty, B. F., & Taylor, D. A. (1986). *Intimacy and valence effects in self-disclosure reciprocity.* Paper presented at the annual meeting of the Eastern Psychological Association, New York.

Murphy, D. C., & Mendelson, L. A. (1973). Communication and adjustment in marriage: Investigating the relationships. *Family Process, 12,* 317-326.

Murstein, B. I. (1970). Stimulus-value-role: A theory of marital choice. *Journal of Marriage and the Family, 32,* 465-481.

Murstein, B. I. (1971). A theory of marital choice and its applicability to marriage adjustment and friendship. In B. I. Murstein (Ed.), *Theories of attraction and love* (pp. 100-151). New York: Springer.

Murstein, B. I. (1973). A theory of marital choice applied to interracial marriage. In I. R. Stuart & L. E. Abt (Eds.), *Interracial marriage: Expectations and realities* (pp. 19-35). New York: Grossman.

Murstein, B. I., MacDonald, M. G., & Cerreto, M. (1977). A theory of the effect of exchange-orientation on marriage and friendship. *Journal of Marriage and the Family, 39,* 543-548.

Navran, I. (1967). Communication and adjustment in marriage. *Family Process, 6,* 173-184.

Patterson, M. L. (1976). An arousal model of interpersonal intimacy. *Psychological Review, 83,* 235-245.

Pelligrini, R. J., Hicks, R. A., Meyers-Winton, S., & Antal, B. G. (1978). Physical attractiveness and self-disclosure in mixed sex dyads. *Psychological Record, 28,* 509-516.

Petty, R. E., & Mirels, H. L. (1981). Intimacy and scarcity of self-disclosure: Effects on interpersonal attraction for males and females. *Personality and Social Psychology Bulletin, 7,* 493-503.

Rosenfeld, L. B. (1979). Self-disclosure avoidance: Why I am afraid to tell you who I am. *Communication Monographs, 46,* 63-74.

Rosenfeld, L. B., Civikly, J., & Herron, J. (1979). Anatomical and psychological sex differences. In G. J. Chelune & Associates, *Self-disclosure* (pp. 80-109). San Francisco: Jossey-Bass.

Rubin, Z. (1973). *Liking and loving: An invitation to social psychology.* New York: Holt, Rinehart & Winston.

Rubin, Z. (1975). Disclosing oneself to a stranger: Reciprocity and its limits. *Journal of Experimental Social Psychology, 11,* 233-260.

Rubin, Z., & Levinger, G. (1974). Theory and data badly mated: A critique of Murstein's SVR theory and Lewis's PDF model of mate selection. *Journal of Marriage and the Family, 36,* 226-231.

Sabatelli, R. M., Buck, R., & Dreyer, A. (1982). Nonverbal communication accuracy in married couples: Relationships with marital complaints. *Journal of Personality and Social Psychology, 43,* 1088-1097.

Sabatelli, R., Buck, R., & Dreyer, A. (1983). Locus of control, interpersonal trust, and nonverbal communication accuracy. *Journal of Personality and Social Psychology, 44,* 399-409.

Shaffer, D. R., Smith, J. E., & Tomarelli, M. (1982). Self-monitoring as a determinant of self-disclosure reciprocity during the acquaintance process. *Journal of Personality and Social Psychology, 43,* 163-175.

Taylor, D. A (1968). The development of interpersonal relationships: Social penetration processes. *Journal of Social Psychology, 75,* 79-90.

Taylor, D. A., & Altman, I. (1966). Intimacy-scaled stimuli for use in studies of interpersonal relations. *Psychological Reports, 19,* 729-730.

Taylor, D. A., Altman, I., & Sorrentino, R. (1969). Interpersonal exchange as a function of rewards and costs and situational factors: Expectancy confirmation-disconfirmation. *Journal of Experimental Social Psychology, 5,* 324-339.

Taylor, R. B., DeSoto, C. B., & Lieb, R. (1979). Sharing secrets: Disclosure and discretion in dyads and triads. *Journal of Personality and Social Psychology, 37,* 1196-1203.

Taylor, D. A., Gould, R., & Brounstein, P. (1981). Effects of personalistic self-disclosure. *Personality and Social Psychology Bulletin, 7,* 487-492.

Taylor, D. A., & Hinds, M. (1985). Disclosure reciprocity and liking as a function of gender and personalism. *Sex Roles, 12,* 1137-1153.

Taylor, D. A., & Belgrave, F. Z. (1986). The effects of perceived intimacy and valence on self-disclosure. *Personality and Social Psychology Bulletin, 12,* 247-255.

Thase, M., & Page, R. A. (1977). Modeling of self-disclosure in laboratory and nonlaboratory interview settings. *Journal of Counseling Psychology, 24,* 35-40.

Thibaut, J. W., & Kelley, H. H. (1959). *The social psychology of groups.* New York: John Wiley.

Tolstedt, B. E., & Stokes, J. P. (1983). Relation of verbal, affective, and physical intimacy to marital satisfaction. *Journal of Counseling Psychology, 30,* 573-580.

Tolstedt, B. E., & Stokes, J. P. (1984). Self-disclosure, intimacy, and the depenetration process. *Journal of Personality and Social Psychology, 46,* 84-90.

Walker, L. S., & Wright, P. H. (1976). Self-disclosure in friendship. *Perceptual and Motor Skills, 42,* 735-742.

Walster, E., Berscheid, E., & Walster, G. W. (1973). New directions in equity research. *Journal of Personality and Social Psychology, 25,* 151-176.

Walster, E., Walster, G. W., & Berscheid, E. (1978). *Equity theory and research.* Boston: Allyn & Bacon.

Wheeler, L., & Nezlek, J. (1977). Sex differences in social participation. *Journal of Personality and Social Psychology, 35,* 742-754.

Won-Doornick, M. J. (1979). On getting to know you: The association between the stage of a relationship and reciprocity of self-disclosure. *Journal of Experimental Social Psychology, 15,* 229-241.

Won-Doornick, M. J. (1985). Self-disclosure and reciprocity in conversation: A cross-national study. *Social Psychology Quarterly, 48,* 97-107.

Zanna, M. P., & Pack, S. J. (1975). On the self-fulfilling nature of apparent sex differences in behavior. *Journal of Experimental Social Psychology, 11,* 583-591.

Chapter 12

HOW TO LOSE FRIENDS
WITHOUT INFLUENCING PEOPLE

Steve Duck

FOR SOMETHING LIKE 10,000 years, people have been warring with other tribes, fighting other nations, sparring with their neighbors, hating their colleagues, quarrelling with their loved ones, arguing with one another, and suffering the pangs of despised love without the benefit of scientific research into relationships and their problems. Since Hinde's (1979) seminal treatise on relationships, a body of scientific research has developed that casts light on the conduct of these often turbulent daily relationships. It is only recently, within that newly growing body of work, that study of the decline and deterioration of relationships in general has been added to the already existing diffuse and variegated research on divorce and marital turmoil. This chapter is about that research and its development, both past and future. Since I am an apostate social psychologist it will begin, predictably enough, with an account of the social psychological threads of the work. However, it will also stress my growing belief that the future development of the field of personal relationships lies in its acquisition of a multidisciplinary flavor. In my view (Duck, 1985; Duck & Perlman, 1985), the major element in this growth has been, and will be, supplied by the communication scientists. Therefore, this chapter will emphasize the contribution of communication to understanding these complex issues.

Nobody knows for sure why people fall out nor do they know how to prevent it. It would be surprising, then, if we were to find that the new research had come up with many definitive answers to humankind's 10,000-year-old problem. Nevertheless, although every reader knows that the final sentence of this chapter will be some variant of "much more research needs to be done," some clarification has emerged from the fog of obscure possibilities and the precise areas for the "much more research" have become easier to delineate.

RUNNING WITH BOTH FEET IN CEMENT

People are rarely surprised to note that a large chunk of research on breakdown of relationships has a demographic style to it. Of course it makes sense to find whether couples who marry at a more advanced age or who have more education and fewer children also stand a higher risk of relational disturbance. Nonetheless, such research may do no more than refine the problems; it hardly explains the reasons for their occurrence. At worst it can mislead us into simple generalizations. For instance, studies showing that marriages between younger partners were less stable or longlasting (e.g., Bentler & Newcomb, 1978) were believed by those who felt that the young were an unreliable lot who had not yet stabilized their lives and could not be expected to make a success of something as serious as marriage. This was often so believed even despite the evidence suggesting a confound of age with level of education and socioeconomic status (Mott & Moore, 1979; Renne, 1970)—obviously the younger the couple, the greater the chances that they are lower on both! A hidden confound is likewise provided by the different cohorts to which the older and younger couples belong.

There were, in truth, some elements in the frame that recurred in many studies; for instance, it appeared that a consistent decline in satisfaction with marriage occurred during the first 10 years or so (Rollins & Feldman, 1970). Those couples that marry despite heterogeneity of demographic background are more prone to instability in the ensuing marriage (Burgess & Locke, 1953; Cattell & Nesselroade, 1967; Jaffe & Kanter, 1979). Black marriages are more prone to disruption than are white ones unless one compares white and black *males* only and controls for socioeconomic factors (Renne, 1970). In general, however, black married men are less satisfied with their lives than are black single men (Ball & Robbins, 1984). Growing up in a home disrupted by divorce also predicts higher rates of divorce for the adult (Mott & Moore, 1979), although at least one study has failed to confirm this widely held belief (Bentler & Newcomb, 1978). However, it is not always clear whether findings of this kind increase our grip on the causal influences behind relational distress.

Research on demographic variables on the smaller and more personal scale produces equally problematic results. For example, the greater the number of premarital sexual partners, the higher the likelihood of disruption to the person's marriage (Athanasiou & Sarkin, 1974), presumably because of the likely continuance of sexual excesses into extramarital liaisons after the marriage. Curiously enough, extramarital affairs are traditionally regarded in this literature (e.g., Newcomb & Bentler, 1981) as precipitators of marital disruption rather than as indicators that the participating individual is somehow commenting on the unsatisfactory nature of the marriage by embarking on extramarital relationships in the first place! An extramarital affair is itself some sort of deescalation of the marriage, while perhaps ultimately becoming a cause of its final dissolution. To believe this, however, one has to assume that any given relationship is best understood in some context of other relationships and that any communications about it and within it are likewise best understood in the same sort of way. That latter point has been somewhat neglected and will become a central one in later discussion.

Other work in like manner records likelihood of marital instability following on premarital cohabitation, and various historical and personal background features of the relationships in question. It is extremely rarely, or only recently, that one comes across a more satisfactory level of analysis that relates such historical factors to current *behavior* in the actual interactions of the relationship itself. It is even more unusual to find studies that relate present communication to the relational history or communicative background of the relationship as it developed, but some are now beginning to appear (Kelly, Huston, & Cate, 1985; Lloyd & Cate, 1985a, 1985b).

In reviewing contemporary studies, Newcomb and Bentler (1981) concluded that the lack of theory and the lack of concern for dyadic levels of analysis were prejudicial to progress, and one can only but agree. The most defensible general conclusion from such work is that we are very little further forward in preventing or curing the problem and we have probably failed to analyze it sufficiently well. It is fine to assume that some structural feature of people's lives—their demographic background, for instance—exerts an inevitable determinism upon their marriages and friendships, but it is not really all that plausible, especially when some people from the selfsame background demonstrate the problem and others do not. In part this comes from a failure to analyze the effects of such global variables on the internal communicational dynamics of relationships, and we really did not learn a lot about such internal differences between the relationships of different ethnic or demographic groups or groups with different personal and relational histories. (Indeed, we still do not know much about this.) What is needed here is some research into the relatively obvious question of whether premarital cohabitors differ in their communications with one another vis-à-vis those who married without cohabiting. Do blacks and whites enact their marriages differently or use a different pattern of communication? Do the younger, the less well off, and the less well educated *do* something differently from the older, the better off, and the more educated couples—and, if so, does that behavior or communication account for the instability of their marriages?

This is only a part of the problem, however, although it is, like the other parts, one about which communication research can add to our store of knowledge. In part, the problem comes from regarding "a relationship" or "the relationship under scrutiny" as an entity with concrete form and out of its dynamic context—rather like looking at stuffed elephants and hoping to learn about *life* in African game parks. There is an implicit tendency in much research to look at relationships in vitro rather than in vivo and, more perniciously, to view them as equivalent from all possible perspectives, rather than to look at them as a part of the phenomenal and communicational experience of each partner. In addition, there has been a failure to look at them from a dyadic level; instead, research has taken a simplistic approach to their dependency on, and emergence from, the characteristics of the individuals who are in them (Duck & Sants, 1983). Such a fault is present even in the slightly more penetrating research conducted by social psychologists on the effects of personality.

In such work at least the researchers emphasized the individual characteristics of the actors and often suggested that such characteristics might influence behavior (Thelen, Fishbein, & Tatten, 1985). It was rarely claimed that there was any particular need to explore the ways in which such attitudes and personality characteristics might influence communicational features of the relationship nor yet how they might communicate themselves to the partners (but see Cappella, 1984; Duck, 1977, 1985). It was assumed that if happy partners were similar or complementary then that was itself a sufficient explanation for their satisfaction; little work was done on the effects of such variables (or states) on communication, nor have we learned how similarity and complementarity were communicated by partners to one another. At best it was suggested that the characteristics' influences on behavior could somehow spill over in an untidy way into communications that might pass between the two partners, but usually the implication was that this caused more problems than it solved and was not really a center of much attention.

Lacking or underemphasized in much social psychological work, then, was a dyadic level of analysis that indicated the bearing of one person's personality on the behavior of another. It is surprising that social psychologists could do so much work under the assumption that the two partners came together but did not really consider or influence one another's behavior in interactions, nor did their communications affect communications made in response. On the other hand, communication writers such as Applegate (1983), Clark and Delia (1979), Norton (1983), and others stressed the functional impacts of communication on the form of a relationship, and hence on its quality, and hence back again to the style of communication within it. The essential argument in these cases is that style of communication is functional for partners and serves their achievement of relational goals. Communicators' beliefs thus influence communications and their interpretation. They can influence the style and structure of communication—and this changes as the relationships develop or change.

By contrast, social psychologists' concerns with intrapersonal and relatively nondynamic personal characteristics merely offered us another version of the "demographic styles" by suggesting that relationships are simple and predictable products of the cognitive characteristics or properties of persons at the individual level and of the way the particular pieces of their separate jigsaw puzzle fitted with one another (perhaps elaborated into simple models of time's influence on the jigsaw, e.g., Levinger, 1974). This is rather like assuming that success at driving a car is determinable from the height and proportions of the driver relative to the vehicle in which that person is placed, and as if successful arrival is guaranteed by turning on the ignition switch! If you have x attributes and so do I (or y needs and I do not) then the relationship will (1) occur, (2) develop, and (3) be a success, these three rather different consequences of the initial conditions being very frequently treated in the literature as identical. Dating agencies and their clients still believe this, although Woll (1986) has shown that even in video dating agencies the characteristics that partners actually pay most to attention are the age and physical attractiveness of their potential partners. For dating agencies and in the stated, but not enacted, view of the person in the street, then, relationships are products of some matching of the two actors' personality characteristics that preexisted the relationship, rather than a result of their communication or behavior relative to one another in a present relationship. More recently and more interestingly, Huston, Surra, Fitzgerald, and Cate (1981) and Kelly et al. (1985), for the development of relationships, and Hagestad and Smyer (1982) and Lloyd and Cate (1985a, 1985b), for the dissolution of relationships, have suggested that behavior is the relevant variable through which these psychological forces and properties have whatever determining effects they have. In this recent work, emphasis is placed on the ways that partners negotiate about conflict or on the ways that personality characteristics influence the conjoining of partners' lives through negotiation of shared activity patterns. When social psychologists begin to stress behavior in relationships, communication scientists have every right to feel smug. However, the theme of this work still remains determinist and accepts the belief that behavior (i.e., handling of conflict levels) at the courtship stage can affect the survival of the ensuing marriage assessed five years later (Kelly et al., 1985).

Proponents of such work have, even so, focused mostly on the start of relationships ("caused by" characteristics of actors) and their success (dependent on behavior) as if, once started, their future is entirely or largely determined by the past rather than by present behavior, needs, or thoughts. Two elements are omitted from such a notion: First, it overlooks the probability that people *think* about relationships and that in turn influences their present behavior (Duck, 1980); have temporary strategies that we enact in communications with one another (Applegate, 1983); create and strive to achieve momentary goals (Clark & Delia, 1979); form relational hopes, fears, and doubts; experience remorse about past behavior and try to change it in the future, and so on. This work perhaps treats such things in only the most mechanical and dispassionate ways and fails to attribute them their real, living significance. Yet presumably our assessment of the success of our present relationships must be made against the criteria of such beliefs, and interactional behavior will be so guided or influenced. Second, such work focuses unduly on the start of relationships and on those that develop in intimacy. By contrast, and additionally, we should perhaps begin to explore not only developing but extant and more stable relationships, whether or not they are voluntary or intimate (Delia, 1980). What characterizes the communications, strategies, and behaviors of persons conducting these everyday parts of life?

One answer is that uncertainty reduction is the normative goal (see Berger & Bradac, 1982; and Berger, this volume). Presumably, then, in the conduct of everyday relationships that are not developing in intimacy, the stability comes from a constancy of (un)certainty levels. Presumably also, relationships decline when uncertainty increases unexpectedly, and, as Planalp and Honeycutt (1984) note, not all new information does decrease uncertainty, as Berger and Bradac (1982) may have supposed. For instance, if a friend confesses to having AIDS or if a marital partner admits infidelity, the hearer gains new information but simultaneously uncertainty is increased. Work in this tradition, though, stresses the influences of a person's "cognitive work" about relationships and the active role of communication in stabilizing and, to some extent, determining those thoughts. Work from a rhetorical framework that also naturally stresses the role of such thoughts in relationships has been extended to relational dissolution (Miller & Parks, 1982). From this perspective, one partner's task is to persuade the other person to allow them both to part. By contrast, the present argument is that such conscious and strategic work is only a part of the process of dissolving relationships.

It is clearly true that people do often sit down and think about their relationships, but this is by no means what they always do—very often they just gossip (Emler & Fisher, 1982) and the result is not always uncertainty reduction so much as increased stress (Duck, 1982, 1984) or increased uncertainty about the future of the relationship (Duck & Miell, 1984; Duck, Miell, & Miell, 1984). This is likely to be true especially of relationships that are falling apart or are about to do so—a thought to which we shall return. Thus although we need some further work on the cognitive aspects of relationships, I believe we need to supplement work on pure cognition that is divorced from social-communicative realities with work that focuses on communication patterns over time in the real interactions of real relationships.

Against this background the terrain for this chapter becomes a little more obvious. The main problems with this previous social psychological work on dissolution of relationships are that it usually fails signally to make precisely those assumptions that a communication scientist takes for granted: that a dyadic level of analysis is necessary; that the phenomena are complex and dynamic just because they are interpersonal; that people's backgrounds and personality probably influence relationships through the medium of communication style, which therefore needs to be explored; and that people have both long-term and temporary plans or relational goals that influence relational communication and need to be taken into account.

Where other researchers have looked at the influences of global variables such as demographic background and personality factors or attitude structure as the ultimate honey or vinegar of relationships, communication scientists would naturally ask how such things actually indicate themselves in the day-to-day behavior of relational partners. They are thus in a much better position to answer one key question, "What is it about a particular *relationship* that ends up being problematic?" rather than, "What is it about the partners, isolated from that relationship, that could account for their difficulties?" This incidentally helps to identify the correct level for answering why it is that a given person can succeed in some relationships and not others, even though, to all intents and purposes, that person's background and personality stay the same in every relationship (give or take a few scholarly provisos). One already stated thesis of this chapter is that a communicational level of analysis of such issues has been both necessary and productive, and I will now put some flesh on that bone.

In addition, I also want to suggest some new avenues for such work predicated on the argument that researchers have frequently acted naively in relation to the dissolution of relationships and have treated dissolution as if it were an event—as if the marriage breaks up on the day the court pronounces divorce, or the friendship goes wrong on the day that one of the partners ups and leaves the shared apartment. By contrast, this chapter will review the notion—and the growing body of evidence—that dissolution of relationships is a process extensive not only in time but also in the psychological experience of the dissolving couple. I will argue that such processes probably show themselves in characteristic modifications to communicative actions both intentionally and willy nilly. In the development of this point it will become clear that much early work overlooked partners' intentions and goals in communicative encounters.

Finally, I will claim that even if most communication is purposive, not all purposes lead to the dissolution of relationships and not all dissolution of relationships is purposive or strategic. After a period that tended to regard all communication as purposive and functional (Applegate, 1983), it is now clear that humans often do not really know what is going on (Duck & Miell, 1984) and even more often they do know but make simple mistakes anyway! Indeed it is surprising, after at least 5,000 years of recorded experience of the phenomenon, that the human capacity for error has so far eluded systematic attention equally in theories of communication and in theories of everyday social life.

This is a particularly important point in the present context in that much of the most significant communication work in relational dissolution derives from a rhetorical framework in which dissolution is seen as an act of interpersonal influence (Miller & Parks, 1982) during which one partner attempts to persuade the other to dissolve the relationship. Though there are undoubtedly circumstances for which this model works effectively—and indeed it may account for more instances than any other model—it perhaps assumes too great a rational control of the chaos of relationships. There is now work (Baxter, 1984; Baxter & Wilmot, 1985; Lee, 1984) that tells us how persons frequently deescalate relationships by accident or error—or sometimes without knowing that it is happening! This is due in part to the fact that information can serve several simultaneous functions in relationships (Duck, 1976) and can often bear more than one simultaneous interpretation in a relational context depending on the perspective of the observer (Duck & Sants, 1983). Therefore deescalation of relationships is only sometimes due to the skills and quite often due to the entire lack of skills of relevant actors, only sometimes due to a deescalative strategy and quite often due to unforeseen consequences of other plans and strategies of life. In any case, it is not necessary to view persuasion or interpersonal influence as the only element in dissolving personal relationships. Quite often I suspect that it "just happens"—but that would not mean that it has no features that are of interest to communication researchers.

TALKING...AND POSSIBLY WALKING

I have argued broadly that a communicational level of analysis is a productive way out of the dilemmas and entrenchments created by the predominant style of the social psychological work in this field. In the present section I will fill this out by showing that uncertainty reduction is not the only aspect of communication relevant to our understanding of personal relationships (PRs). I will also attempt to rescue the reputation of social psychology by showing how some new lines of research there could point us in exciting directions for future empirical and theoretical communicational work in the PR field. In a later section I will show how this general reconceptualization has special relevance to the dissolution of relationships and is thus a broader approach to PRs.

There is plenty of work on communicative elements of relationships, some of it relevant, if not yet actually applied directly, to relationships in trouble. For instance, Roloff (1976) argues that we communicate in order to affect our environment; one specific example of this is provided by Bell and Daly (1984), who indicate that partners' goals or intentions to establish relationships influence the communicative strategies they adopt. Bell and Daly claim that we use a number of affiliative strategies to make people like us and that most of these strategies influence our communication with partners. For instance, we may use a strategy giving us visibility in an interaction (i.e., we increase our communicative inputs to the exchange) or one that gives us greater control (i.e., we issue more "one-up" messages).

This style of work could be applied to both deterioration of relationships (i.e., a decline in the perceived quality) or to their dissolution. An individual using any given strategy with the goal of improving the relationship or enhancing his or her own role in it is likely to be a sensitive monitor of the effects of that strategy. Shortfall between desired goal and actual achievement is likely to lead to perceived decrements in the attractiveness of the relationship or at least to awareness of one's lack of success. My guess is that such a realization would lead most persons to a redoubled affiliative effort followed (if this is unsuccessful) by decreased attraction to the relationship and hence toward dissolution.

The point is a simple one: Any communicational enterprises aimed at the goal of creating satisfactory relationships will, if they fail, bring about dissatisfaction with the relationship. Hence work on the satisfactory conduct of relationships is also causally extendable to the deterioration and dissolution of relationships. If patterns of communication are manipulated to create relationships, then we can expect also the converse to be true: When such strategies are ineffective, a change in patterning is likely to be detected. We can store this point for future use in the argument that follows.

As a slight variation on this point, we can note that while this would be most notable when we have a plan to carry out, communication affects our environment whether we intend the effects or not and many effects are actually accidental. On numerous occasions (see Hatfield & Traupmann, 1981), persons do not formulate a persuasive intent but merely act inequitably in a relationship such that the partner picks up a message and leaves, whether that message was purposely communicated or not.

A further lesson for use later in this argument is provided by the various pieces of work carried out by Baxter and her colleagues, especially with Wilmot. While simultaneously exploring the communicative aspects of breakdown and dissolution of relationships (e.g., Baxter, 1984, 1985), Baxter has worked on the dark side of the conduct of successful relationships. Baxter and Wilmot (1984), for example, looked at the "secret tests" we use to establish the status of our relationships. A common strategy is the use of jealousy-evoking statements so we can assess the reaction made by our partner and hence assess his or her commitment to the relationship with us. Again, we can see this as an example of the ways in which the content and the pattern of communication are a useful source of information about relationship quality and commitment, and that this may have implications for dissolution even though not yet directly applied there. As a final example, we can note that Baxter and Wilmot (1985) examined "taboo topics"—those topics that partners choose to avoid in order to prevent any destabilization of the relationship. Topics such as past relationships can threaten the present one because they imply that the person can feel as intensely about someone else and has actually done so in the past. The patterning of content in an interaction is thus of interest here, too, and can serve to indicate the status of a relationship or to prompt the partners toward its reassessment. Again, then, the point is that we may assess our relationships or carry out other life tasks that lead to the deescalation of the relationship as a secondary consequence rather than as a conscious and strategic result.

So although a large part of my point here is that much good work in communication has illuminated aspects of relationships not touched by social psychology, I also want to emphasize the communicative effects of the relational strategies and "accidents" uncovered by such work. We should therefore attend to the effects upon communication that are exerted by *changes* in strategy and circumstances (e.g., by a change from developing a relationship to deescalating it). Also implicit in this coverage is the notion that the pattern of content, rather than the individual items of content, should occupy our research attention in a communicative approach to PRs.

These are thus some valuable and interesting pieces of work with some lessons for us both in terms of their strategic approach to the area and in terms of specific topics of interest. I wish, indeed, to consider the point that they presage a general approach to relationships that could be developed in communication studies and that provides a base for later research about relationship dissolution.

Although "old" work continues, perhaps with reduced vigor as it becomes plainer that it does not produce a magic key to the problem, more recent work has taken other routes. Morton (Morton, Alexander, & Altman, 1976; Morton & Douglas, 1981), for instance, foreshadowing some of the arguments of Huston et al. (1981), argued that relationship development grew from mutuality of relationship definition. Every viable social relationship requires mutuality of control between participants and this will be defined through interpersonal communication. As relationships develop, so modes of exchange will tend to expand and diversify with evidence being provided by changes in the style of communication between persons. Any development in a relationship implies a change in the relational definition accepted by the partners, and this in turn involves a change in the nature of interdependence that will be reflected in a restructuring of communicative exchanges.

This is a rather interesting set of ideas, particularly in this context, since Morton et al. (1976) define mutuality and nonmutuality of relationship largely in terms of their communicative manifestations, and since they stress that the transitional nature of *all* forms of relationship development and deterioration is based on communicative actions, whether verbal, nonverbal, or symbolic—e.g., changes to patterns of interdependent action. The work emphasizes the relational effects of *style* of communication and the central role of communication style in affecting and mediating relational change.

Such a level of analysis is more noticeably dyadic or relational than some of the preceding work and it introduces us to a whole new set of considerations. It emphasizes the fact that demographic or personality characteristics influence relational form only through some sort of mediation by communication, for instance. Cappella (1984) argues at a finer level that communication mediates certain large elements of relationships. For example, if partners are similar to one another in personality, we would expect them to show it by matching in NV means. Thelen et al. (1985) have recently argued that the reason for the puzzling lack of progress in the similarity-complementarity debate is the fact that behavioral/interactive consequences of alleged personality traits were never assessed. Using a communicative task, these authors show that those couples whose *behavior* complements one another predictably from their personality questionnaires are those most satisfied with their relationship.

If individuals have not only life goals, plans, and considerations of their own, along with expectations for their outcomes from a given relationship, then they may also have similar goals, plans, considerations, and expectations for the form of the relationship itself and the interactions that constitute it (Davis & Todd, 1985). These may be relative to some sociocultural norms for relating—e.g., we know what a "perfect marriage" *ought* to look like or to some personal expectations for relating—e.g., we know what we personally usually expect to get out of relationships and can see if it is happening in the present instance.

These reference points, one familiar to sociologists and one to psychologists, are each capable of mediation through communicative means. It is the concept of relational definition through communicative style in the relationship that frames that particular jigsaw puzzle. For instance, if satisfaction in a relationship derives in part from the partners' joint creation of a relational form that reflects their desires, expectations, and interactions, then we ought to be able to assess satisfaction in parallel with relational form; that is to say, satisfaction should relate to communicative features of a relationship and dissatisfaction likewise. Indeed, we find that this is the case. Gottman (1982), Noller (1985), and Noller and Venardos (1986) have all shown the close connection between the timing of communication and relationship satisfaction, between negative reactivity cycles and dissatisfaction, and between nonverbal and verbal patterns (on the one hand) and marital satisfaction or dissatisfaction (on the other hand). It is now clear that communication in relationships is not an epiphenomenon but is both a reflection and a cause of the levels of (dis)satisfaction in that relationship. What remains for further exploration, however, is systematic work on the *changes* to such variables as relationships deteriorate; previous work tends to have used comparisons of groups already known to be satisfied or dissatisfied, and so patterns of change characterizing the move from satisfaction to dissatisfaction—or vice versa—have not been explored.

Thus while Morton et al.'s (1976) argument has been largely supported both directly in some empirical work and indirectly in terms of the directions taken by the field as it has developed, it remains for it to be extended systematically to the process of relationship dissolution.

To my mind, these arguments about content patterns and style can usefully be put together with the recent developments in social psychological theory and research that emphasize joint actions and everyday patterns of behavior. Such work has recently begun to observe the patterns of everyday life interactions among varieties of persons, but has typically recorded gross variables such as number of persons present in an interaction, sex of the parties, length of interaction, and so on. These have then been related to other gross variables such as physical attractiveness or loneliness. Using such an approach, Wheeler and Nezlek (1977) and Duck and Miell (1982, 1984) have shown that physically attractive persons meet more others during the day, that lonely persons typically meet more males, and that the most frequent type of conversation among friends is nonintimate chat about other persons. However, the details of communicative patterns and styles have not yet been fully explored in similar ways.

Communication in relationships has at least four elements, some of which have been extensively studied at the expense of others. *Content patterns* are an obvious set of items to study. For any given relationship or type of relationship, we could explore the kinds of topics typically covered in any given interaction or that typically characterize everyday interactions in that relationship. Thus, for example, we could characterize a given exchange as primarily task-related or sociable, but we could also determine the content patterns that are typical of a given sort of relationship. In what ways are the content of friends' conversations typically different from those of strangers? Equally, another part of communication that has clear importance is *style*—that is, emotional tone, dominance, control (Millar & Rogers-Millar, 1976). From the saturation of conflict or amiability in a given interaction we learn a lot about the nature of the partners' relationship (Fitzpatrick, 1977, 1984; Norton, 1983). However, two other aspects of communication have received less attention. One is *context*—that is, in PRs, the relational history, the situational setting, the likelihood of a given style of response given a particular communication, what went before and came after, the setting, the context of its history, and so on. Another is *ordering* of communication, by which I mean partly the frequency of communication with a given other or a given type of other: How often does X talk to (1) neighbors (2) friends, (3) strangers? and what about? However, I also intend some reference to the fact that the number of a person's communications on a given day is, from anecdotal experience, influenced by circumstances, mood, tasks, life events, and so on. Irrespective of content, for example, there is something significant, illustrative, and informative about the fact that on a given day I spoke only to police officers, lawyers, and prison officers rather than to friends and neighbors as usual!

My sense is that we do not yet know enough about those four aspects of communication as they relate to the everyday relationships that make up daily lives. Equally, we do not yet know how each of them is affected by the changing circumstances that arise in the deescalation of relationships.

LIVING, LOVING, AND LEAVING

The recent change in social psychological work to a focus on everyday life exchanges is a good signpost for future work in this field by communication scientists. From the foregoing, then, we can see that a communicational level of analysis alters our perspective on relationships in significant and useful ways. But we also see that to change and improve the level of analysis is not the same as to take a broader and improved view of the base phenomena. Recently it has been argued that the processes of relational dissolution embrace many elements and, by implication, communicative analyses can be applied in more than one place. The foregoing section has tended to imply that the partner's communicative exchanges with one another are all that count, but on top of that we need to map a more sophisticated view of the deescalation of relationships in everyday life. Duck (1982, 1984) has claimed that there are different phases to relational dissolution (see Figure 12.1). The present chapter extends this point to claim that an analysis of communication at each phase is potentially fruitful.

Duck's (1982) argument is that the dissolution of relationships proceeds from a *Breakdown Phase* (in which one or both partners conclude there is a problem with the conduct of the relationship) to an *Intrapsychic Phase* (in which one partner broods privately about the relationship, or gripes about it to some unrelated person or to a confidant who is not known to both partners or who is expected not to convey the complaint to the other partner). If the problems with the relationship are still perceived to persist, then after the Intrapsychic Phase comes a *Dyadic Phase* in which one person presents the complaint to the partner and discussions of its importance and correctness proceed. If the partners do not thereby resolve their differences and decide not to repair the relationship, or are unable to do so, then the next stage is the *Social Phase* in which other members of the network are included in the discussion of the relationship and allies for the argument are sought. Finally, if the relationship is dissolved, there is a *Grave-Dressing Phase* in which partners and their network associates create and "market" a version of the story about the end of the relationship that favors their side of the case. This model of breakdown leads to a related view of the correct means of attempting to repair a relationship at a given phase (Duck, 1984), but for present purposes, the significance of the approach lies in what it suggests about changes in communication during relationship deescalation.

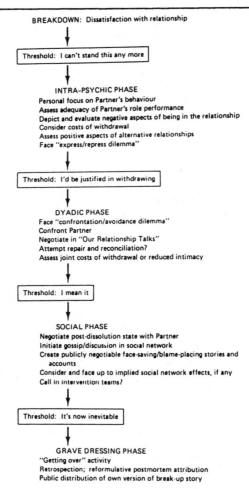

BREAKDOWN: Dissatisfaction with relationship

↓

Threshold: I can't stand this any more

↓

INTRA-PSYCHIC PHASE
Personal focus on Partner's behaviour
Assess adequacy of Partner's role performance
Depict and evaluate negative aspects of being in the relationship
Consider costs of withdrawal
Assess positive aspects of alternative relationships
Face "express/repress dilemma"

↓

Threshold: I'd be justified in withdrawing

↓

DYADIC PHASE
Face "confrontation/avoidance dilemma"
Confront Partner
Negotiate in "Our Relationship Talks"
Attempt repair and reconciliation?
Assess joint costs of withdrawal or reduced intimacy

↓

Threshold: I mean it

↓

SOCIAL PHASE
Negotiate post-dissolution state with Partner
Initiate gossip/discussion in social network
Create publicly negotiable face-saving/blame-placing stories and
    accounts
Consider and face up to implied social network effects, if any
Call in intervention teams?

↓

Threshold: It's now inevitable

↓

GRAVE DRESSING PHASE
"Getting over" activity
Retrospection; reformulative postmortem attribution
Public distribution of own version of break-up story

SOURCE: From Duck, S. W. (Ed.) (1982). *Personal relationships 4: Dissolving personal relationships* (p. 16). © 1982 Academic Press. Reprinted by permission.

Figure 12.1 A Sketch of the Main Phases of Dissolving Personal Relationships

The above view is that relational deescalation is a complex process that is influenced by, and in turn influences, not just isolated cognitive parts but rather the rest of the communicative lives of the two partners. We need to view it all in the context of the other elements of the persons' lives rather than treating it as test-tube, desanitized deescalation—as if people conducted that part of their relational existence without reference to any other part of their daily activities, projects, or concerns.

If we now revisit some points made earlier in this chapter, we can see that such everyday life experiences as thoughts about relationships, reinterpretations of past events, speculations on future events, intentions, goals, uncertainty, and so on will be vastly significant to the communication that occurs in deescalating relationships in everyday life. One problem obscuring the turbulence of relationship dissolution, however, has been our general tendency to overlook the human inclination to come up with logical "stories" for events experienced at the time as chaotic (Duck & Sants, 1983). Thus persons may give accounts of relationship dissolution that stress a strategic design or pattern where one is less obvious to outside observers. Nonetheless, we could expect some changes to communicative content patterns, viewed with a bird's eye, manifested *by an individual.* Rather than looking dyadically at the communication with a specific partner (itself a worthy, lengthy, and rare research enterprise) we should also expect that a person's communicative patterns will be affected by progress through the phases of dissolution.

For one thing, at the Intrapsychic Phase we might expect a decline in the amount of communication with the partner, relative both to the usual level and to that carried out with the person's network of friends and acquaintances. At this stage the person is complaining *about* the partner to other people and also to himself or herself. In other words, at this phase we might expect a redeployment of the "statistics" of communication content. Samter & Burleson (1984) have explored an important tip of this particular iceberg by examining the ways in which persons comfort others who are distressed. Comforting is particularly conceived to comprise messages that have "the intended function of alleviating or lessening the emotional distress arising from a variety of everyday hurts and disappointments" (Samter & Burleson, 1984, p. 1). The authors found that an important influence on both quality and quantity of comforting was presented by the extent of differentiation of participant's constructs of the situation, but the participants were all female and the situation involved comforting a stranger in the laboratory—although it did have the merit of being a face-to-face encounter. We have to start somewhere in such research and this study is interesting. Since it opens the door on some intriguing possibilities, there is a clear need for strong development of this work and work on other related topics such as forgiving, reconciliation, and acceptance.

My thought here is that the pattern of such communicative content is also a relevant concern in comforting and indeed probably ties this area of research to the blossoming area of social support. Indeed, in this latter domain, the actual delivery of support—rather than the sense of felt support—needs further close attention. This is important because of the communicative techniques persons use in everyday life to extract comfort and support and the techniques that comforters and advisors typically use to give it in a face-saving way. Even when comforting intentions are clear, the achievement of them may not be direct. Glidewell, Tucker, Todt, and Cox (1982) found that teachers in need of advice about their schoolwork did not ask for it explicitly in an advice center but approached the issue obliquely. Specifically, they told anecdotes that indicated their predicament without specifically asking for advice. In helping them out, the advisors usually adopted the same technique; namely, they told anecdotes indicating how they had coped with a relevant problem rather than giving prescriptive or direct advice. Accordingly, I suspect we shall find many interesting communicative devices when we begin to explore the Intrapsychic Phase from a communicational perspective.

At the Dyadic Phase we would expect an increase in communication with the partner, since the two persons are coming together to negotiate their difficulties. Indeed, Baxter (1979, 1980, 1984, 1985) has charted such confrontational communication. She finds, as have others, a notable amount of oscillation between reconciliative efforts and conflictive communication in such encounters. The style and content of such interactions are notable for their inconsistency and the absence of any clear goals, but such inconsistencies are data about the psychological states of the partners as well as being informative about the state of the relationship. Clearly there may be a strategic element to changes in style and content, since goals are different here and so is the audience at different stages. However, the very fact that the stages may differ and that we could typologize them according to these dimensions is the point at issue.

We would also expect a change in the style and content of communication at this stage. My prediction is that there should be an increased occurrence of "I" statements, "you" statements, and "our relationship" statements, relative to the frequency of those statements in stable relationships and relative to other phases of dissolution. Furthermore, my hunch is that there would be more frequent mention of expectations and goals or hopes. Style is likely to be more negative, in general terms, and the overall pattern of communication is likely to be different, both at the level of pattern within an interaction and at the level of the individual's total ordering of communication acts (with partner versus with others). At the Dyadic Phase, then, we can expect some quite dramatic shifts of communicative phenomena.

At the Social Phase similar and related changes in communication can be expected. The most pronounced change will be that the person alters the ordering of communication so that the more communication is directed at others in the network. However, other predictable consequences are that the content of interactions will turn toward discussion of the person's partner and the relationship between them. Style of communications is likely to be complaining, accusatory of the partner, and self-justificatory. Hindsight and "postprediction" of the difficulties are also likely to increase and to provide a transition to or preparation for the next phase, in which accounts of the dissolution are to be marketed.

At the Grave-Dressing Phase the main purpose (Duck, 1982, contends) is to get over the breakup and to ensure that one survives the experience with one's social face intact (LaGaipa ,1982). Accordingly, we could predict that the content of interactions will consist more of the swapping of stories about the ex-partner, comparison of the ex-partner with others, accounts of the advantages of being separated, and so on. Weber (1983) has indicated that a substantial part of such accounts consists of the person's claim to have known all along that the relationship would not work out: It had some fatal flaw from the beginning and despite the person's valiant efforts to overcome or ignore it, the flaw proved too fatal and the partner too unwilling to change. At this phase, too, then, we can see some relatively obvious features of the communicative terrain will be characteristically influenced by the phase the dissolution has reached.

CONCLUSIONS ABOUT CONCLUDING

From the foregoing section it is clear that dissolution is a complex process with different foci at different stages, and that communication will be affected in broad ways by the different parts of the process. Present work perhaps errs on the cognitive, intentional, purposive side in that it seems to assume that persons have control over the outcomes and a clear sight of their goals. We should not accept this view naively. If we accept the general point argued above—that deescalation must be seen in the context of the matrix of people's lives—then we need not uniformly assume that deescalation always occurs on purpose, nor that the communicative contribution to deescalation is always strategic. Indeed, disengagement may be accidental or may be purposeful but unannounced or unskillfully done—as well as being strategically conceived and skillfully executed. What is clear, however, is that communication plays a central role in these processes, and it is equally clear that we do not yet have a strong enough understanding of the details of such a role.

I wrote at the beginning that I would conclude that more research needs to be done. Although such a conclusion was always predictable, the foregoing discussion has pointed to several specific avenues that such self-propelling endeavors could follow. Let us hope it does not take another 10,000 years for us to come up with the answers.

REFERENCES

Applegate, J. (1983). *Constructs, interaction goals, and communication in relationships.* Paper presented at the PCP Congress, Boston.

Athanasiou, R., & Sarkin, R. (1974). Premarital sexual behaviour and postmarital adjustment. *Archives of Sexual Behaviour, 3,* 207-225.

Ball, R. E., & Robbins, L. (1984). Marital status and life satisfaction of black men. *Journal of Social and Personal Relationships, 1,* 459-470.

Baxter, L. A. (1979). Self-disclosure as a relationship disengagement strategy: An exploratory investigation. *Human Communication Research, 5,* 215-222.

Baxter, L. A. (1980). *Communication apprehension and disengagement of interpersonal relationships.* Unpublished manuscript, Department of Communication, Lewis & Clark College, Portland, OR.

Baxter, L. A. (1984). Trajectories of relationship disengagement. *Journal of Social and Personal Relationships, 1,* 29-48.

Baxter, L. A. (1985). Accomplishing relationship dissolution. In S. W. Duck & D. Perlman (Eds.), *Understanding personal relationships* (pp. 243-265). Newbury Park, CA: Sage.

Baxter, L. A., & Wilmot, W. (1984). Secret tests: Social strategies for acquiring information about the state of the relationship. *Human Communication Research, 11,* 171-202.

Baxter, L. A., & Wilmot, W. (1985). Taboo topics in close relationships. *Journal of Social and Personal Relationships, 2,* 253-269.

Bell, R. A., & Daly, J. A. (1984). The affinity seeking function of communication. *Communication Monographs, 51,* 91-115.

Bentler, P., & Newcomb, M. (1978). Longitudinal study of marital success and failure. *Journal of Consulting and Clinical Psychology, 46,* 1053-1070.

Berger, C. R., & Bradac, J. (1982). *Language and social knowledge: Uncertainty in interpersonal relationships.* London: Arnold.

Burgess, E. W., & Locke, H. J. (1953). *The family.* New York: American Book.

Cappella, J. (1984). The relevance of the microstructure of interaction to relationship change. *Journal of Social and Personal Relationships, 1,* 239-264.

Cattell, R. B., & Nesselroade, J. R. (1967). Likeness and completeness theories examined by sixteen personality factor measures on stable and unstable married couples. *Journal of Personality and Social Psychology, 7,* 351-361.

Clark, R. A., & Delia, J. (1979). Topoi and rhetorical competence. *Quarterly Journal of Speech, 65,* 187-206.

Davis, K. E., & Todd, M. (1985). Assessing friendship: Prototype, paradigm cases and relationship descriptions. In S. W. Duck & D. Perlman (Eds.), *Understanding personal relationships* (pp. 17-38). Newbury Park, CA: Sage.

Delia, J. (1980). Some tentative thoughts concerning the study of interpersonal relationships and their development. *Western Journal of Speech Communication, 44,* 97-103.

Duck, S. W. (1976). Interpersonal communication in developing acquaintance. In G.R. Miller (Ed.), *Explorations in interpersonal communication* (pp. 127-147). Newbury Park, CA: Sage.

Duck, S. W. (1977). *The study of acquaintance.* Farnborough: Gower.

Duck, S. W. (1980). Personal relationship research in the 1980s: Towards the study of complex human sociality. *Western Journal of Speech Communication, 44,* 114-119.

Duck, S. W. (1982). A topography of relationship disengagement and dissolution. In S. W. Duck (Ed.), *Personal relationships 4: Dissolving personal relationships* (pp. 1-30). London: Academic Press.

Duck, S. W. (1985). Social and personal relationships. In M. L. Knapp & G. R. Miller (Eds.), *Handbook of interpersonal communication* (pp. 655-686). Newbury Park, CA: Sage.

Duck, S. W., & Miell, D. E. (1982). *Charting the development of relationships.* Paper presented at the First International Conference on Personal Relationships, Madison, WI.

Duck, S. W., & Miell, D. E. (1984). Towards an understanding of relaionship development and breakdown. In H. Tajfel, C. Fraser, & J. Jaspars (Eds.), *The social dimension: European perspectives on social psychology* (pp. 228-249). Cambridge: Cambridge University Press.

Duck, S. W., Miell, D. E., & Miell, D. K. (1984). Relationship growth and decline. In H. E. Sypher & J. L. Applegate (Eds.), *Communication by children and adults* (pp. 292-312). Newbury Park, CA: Sage.

Duck, S. W., & Perlman, D. (1985). The thousand islands of personal relationships: A prescriptive analysis for future exploration. In S. W. Duck & D. Perlman (Eds.), *Understanding personal relationships* (pp. 1-15). Newbury Park, CA: Sage.

Duck, S. W., & Sants, H.K.A. (1983). On the origin of the specious: Are personal relationships really interpersonal states? *Journal of Social and Clinical Psychology, 1,* 27-41.

Emler, N., & Fisher, S. (1982). *Gossip.* Paper presented at the BPS Social Psychology Section Conference, Oxford.

Fitzpatrick, M. A. (1977). A typological approach to communication in relationships. In B. Ruben (Ed.), *Communication yearbook 1* (pp. 263-275). New Brunswick, NJ: Transaction Books.

Fitzpatrick, M. A. (1984). A typological approach to marital interaction: Recent theory and research. In L. Berkowitz (Ed.), *Advances in experimental social psychology* (Vol. 18, pp. 1-47). New York: Academic Press.

Glidewell, J. C., Tucker, S., Todt, M., & Cox, S. (1982). Professional support systems: The teaching professions. In A. Nadler, J. D. Fisher, & B. M. DePaulo (Eds.), *Applied research in help-seeking and reactions to aid* (pp. 139-162). New York: Academic Press.

Gottman, J. M. (1982). *Temporal form in personal relationships.* Paper presented at the First International Conference in Personal Relationships, Madison, WI.

Hagestad, G. O., & Smyer, M. (1982). Dissolving long-term relationships: Patterns of divorcing in middle age. In S. W. Duck (Ed.), *Personal relationships 4: Dissolving personal relationships* (pp. 155-188). London: Academic Press.

Hatfield, E., & Traupmann, J. (1981). Intimate relationships: A perspective from equity theory. In S. W. Duck & R. Gilmour (Eds.), *Personal relationships 1: Studying personal relationships* (pp. 165-178). London: Academic Press.

Hinde, R. A. (1979). *Towards understanding relationships.* London: Academic Press.

Huston, T. L., Surra, C., Fitzgerald, N., & Cate, R. (1981). From courtship to marriage: Mate selection as an interpersonal process. In S. W. Duck & R. Gilmour (Eds.), *Personal relationships 2: Developing personal relationships* (pp. 53-88). London: Academic Press.

Jaffe, D. T., & Kanter, R. M. (1979). Couple strains in communal households: A four factor model of the separation process. In G. Levinger & O. Moles (Eds.), *Divorce and separation* (pp. 71-96). New York: Basic Books.

Kelly, C., Huston, T. L., & Cate, R. M. (1985). Premarital correlates of the erosion of satisfaction in marriage. *Journal of Social and Personal Relationships, 2,* 167-178.

LaGaipa, J. J. (1982). Rules and rituals in disengaging from relationships. In S. W. Duck (Ed.), *Personal relationships 4: Dissolving personal relationships* (pp. 189-210). London: Academic Press.

Lee, L. (1984). Sequences in separation: A framework for investigating endings of the personal (romantic) relationship. *Journal of Social and Personal Relationships, 1,* 49-73.

Levinger, G. (1974). A three level approach to attraction: Toward an understanding of pair-relatedness. In T.L. Huston (Ed.), *Foundations of interpersonal attraction* (pp. 99-120) New York: Academic Press.

Lloyd, S.A., & Cate, R.M. (1985a). Attributions associated with significant turning points in premarital relational development and dissolution. *Journal of Social and Personal Relationships, 2,* 419-436.

Lloyd, S. A., & Cate, R. M. (1985b). The developmental course of conflict in dissolution of personal relationships. *Journal of Social and Personal Relationships, 2,* 179-194.

Millar, F. E., & Rogers-Millar, L. E. (1976). A relational approach to interpersonal communication. In G. R. Miller (Ed.), *Explorations in interpersonal communication* (pp. 87-103). Newbury Park, CA: Sage.

Miller, G. R., & Parks, M. (1982). Communication in dissolving personal relationships. In S. W. Duck (Ed.), *Personal relationships 4: Dissolving personal relationships* (pp. 127-154). London: Academic Press.

Morton, T., Alexander, J. F., & Altman, I. (1976). Communication and relational definition. In G. R. Miller (Ed.), *Explorations in interpersonal communication* (pp. 105-125). Newbury Park, CA: Sage.

Morton, T., & Douglas, M. A. (1981). Growth of relationships. In S. W. Duck & R. Gilmour (Eds.), *Personal relationships 2: Developing personal relationships* (pp. 3-26). London: Academic Press.

Mott, F. L., & Moore, S. F. (1979). The causes of marital disruption among young American women. *Journal of Marriage and the Family, 41,* 335-365.

Newcomb, M. D., & Bentler, P. (1981). Marital breakdown. In S. W. Duck & R. Gilmour (Eds.), *Personal relationships 3: Personal relationships in disorder* (pp. 57-94). London: Academic Press.

Noller, P. (1985). Negative communication in marriage. *Journal of Social and Personal Relationships, 2,* 289-301.

Noller, P., & Vernardos, C. (1986). Communication awareness in married couples. *Journal of Social and Personal Relationships, 3.*

Norton, R. (1983). *Communicator style.* Newbury Park, CA: Sage.

Planalp, S., & Honeycutt, J. (1984). *When uncertainty increases in relationships.* Paper presented at the annual meeting of the International Communication Association, San Francisco.

Renne, K. S. (1970). Correlates of dissatisfaction in marriage. *Journal of Marriage and the Family, 32,* 54-67.

Rollins, B. C., & Feldman, H. (1970). Marital satisfaction over the life cycle. *Journal of Marriage and the Family, 32,* 20-28.

Roloff, M. E. (1976). Communication strategies, relationships, and relational change. In G. R. Miller (Ed.), *Explorations in interpersonal communication* (pp. 173-195). Newbury Park, CA: Sage.

Samter, W., & Burleson, B. (1984). *When you're down and troubled...have you got a friend?* Paper presented at the annual meeting of the International Communication Association, San Francisco.

Thelen, M., Fishbein, M. D., & Tatten, H. (1985). Interpersonal similarity: A new approach to an old question. *Journal of Social and Personal Relationships, 2,* 437-446.

Weber, A. (1983). *Breaking up.* Paper presented at the Nags Head Conference, Nags Head, NC.

Wheeler, L., & Nezlek, J. (1977). Sex differences in social participation. *Journal of Personality and Social Psychology, 35,* 742-754.

Woll, C. (1986). So many to choose from: Decision strategies in video dating. *Journal of Social and Personal Relationships, 3.*

ABOUT THE CONTRIBUTORS

IRWIN ALTMAN received his Ph.D. in social psychology from the University of Maryland, College Park, in 1957. He is currently Professor of Psychology and Vice President for Academic Affairs at the University of Utah. His research interests focus on the development of interpersonal relationships, and physical environmental aspects of relationships such as privacy regulation and cross cultural features of homes. Some of his most recent books are *Culture and Environments* (1980), *Home Environments* (1985), and the forthcoming *Handbook of Environmental Psychology*.

CHARLES R. BERGER is Professor of Communication Studies at Northwestern University. He received his Ph.D. in communication from Michigan State University. His research interests include the role of uncertainty reduction in interaction, and cognitive plans as predictors of communication phenomena. He coauthored (with J. Bradac) *Language and Social Knowledge: Uncertainty in Interpersonal Relationships*, coedited (with M. E. Roloff) *Social Cognition and Communication,* and coedited, most recently, (with S. Chaffee) the *Handbook of Communication Science*. He has also served as the editor of *Human Communication Research*.

ELLEN BERSCHEID is Professor of Psychology at the University of Minnesota. She is currently editor of *Contemporary Psychology* and author and coauthor of a number of articles and books in the relationship area, including *Close Relationships,* published by Freeman in 1983.

FRANKLIN J. BOSTER is Associate Professor of Communication at Michigan State University and was Associate Professor of Communication at Arizona State University prior to moving to Michigan State. He received his Ph.D. from Michigan State University in 1978. His research focuses on the relationship between persuasive strategies and interpersonal relationships, the impact of various persuasive strategies on attitude change, and small group decision making.

VALERIAN J. DERLEGA is Professor of Psychology at Old Dominion University, Norfolk, Virginia. He received his doctoral degree in social psychology from the University of Maryland in 1971. He edited *Communication, Intimacy, and Close Relationships* (1984), *Friendship and Social Interaction* (1986), and *Self-Disclosure: Theory, Research and Therapy* (in press). His interests include personal relationships, communications, sex roles, and applications of social psychology to mental health issues.

STEVE DUCK, formerly Senior Lecturer in Psychology at the University of Lancaster in England, is now Daniel and Amy Starch Research Professor in Communication Studies at the University of Iowa in Iowa City. He is the author or editor of 15 books and editor of the *Journal of Social and Personal Relationships.*

JOSEPH P. FOLGER is an Associate Professor in the Department of Speech, Temple University. He received his Ph.D. in communication arts from the University of Wisconsin—Madison. His current work is in the area of interpersonal communication, with a focus on conflict resolution processes. He has published in *Communication Yearbooks 5 and 6,* and in national communication journals, and is coauthor (with M. S. Poole) of *Working Through Conflict: A Communication Perspective.*

MICHAEL GREENSPAN is a recent graduate in psychology from Old Dominion University, Norfolk, Virginia. He is currently enrolled in the doctoral program in clinical psychology at Auburn University, Auburn, Alabama. His research interests are mainly in the area of sports psychology.

DEAN E. HEWES is Associate Professor of Speech Communication at the University of Illinois, Urbana-Champaign. He received his Ph.D. from Florida State University. His interests include cognitive/interpretive approaches to interpersonal communication, small group communication, persuasion in message campaigns, rumor, interaction analysis, research methodology, and fishing. He has published in *Human Communication Research, Communication Monographs, Quarterly Journal of Speech, Communication Research, Journal of Communication,* and four volumes of the *Communication Yearbook* as well as in numerous edited volumes.

KATHY KELLERMANN is Assistant Professor of Communication at Michigan State University. She received her Ph.D. from Northwestern University in 1984. Her research interests include cognitive predictors of information exchange, individual and small group decision making, research methodology, and mathematical modeling. She has published in *Human Communication Research, Communication Monographs, Communication Research,* and the *Communication Yearbook.*

GEORGE J. McCALL is Professor of Sociology and Public Policy Administration at the University of Missouri—St. Louis. Among his several works on the interplay between selves and interpersonal communication, best known is his book (with J. L. Simmons) *Identities and Interactions.*

FRANK E. MILLAR is Associate Professor of Communication at Cleveland State University. He received his Ph.D. from Michigan State University. His research interests include the description of recursive loops in interpersonal systems. He coauthored (with D. Millar) *Messages and Myths* and has published articles in *Communication Monographs, Communication Yearbook, Family Processes, Human Communication Research,* and *The Handbook of Discourse Analysis.*

GERALD R. MILLER is Professor and Chair, Department of Communication, Michigan State University. A past editor of *Human Communication Research* and *Communication Monographs,* he has authored and edited a number of works in interpersonal communication, including *Between People,* with (Mark Steinberg); *Explorations in Interpersonal Communication,* a Sage Annual published in 1976; and, most recently, *Handbook of Interpersonal Communication,* with Mark Knapp.

MARSHALL SCOTT POOLE is Assistant Professor of Speech Communication at the University of Minnesota. He received his Ph.D. from the University of Wisconsin—Madison in 1980. His research interests include group and organizational decision making, organizational communication, conflict management, organizational climate, communication theory, and interaction analysis methodology. He has recently coedited a Sage book entitled *Communication and Group Decision-Making* (with Randy Hirokawa). He serves on the editorial boards of *Human Communication Research* and the *Journal of Applied Communication Research.*

L. EDNA ROGERS is Professor of Communication at Cleveland State University. She received her Ph.D. from Michigan State University in 1975. Her research interests include family communication processes and their effect on relational satisfaction. She is currently the President of the International Communication Association and has served as the chairperson of the interpersonal communication divisions in both the International Communication Association and the Speech Communication Association. Her work has been published in *Communication Monographs, Communication Yearbook, Human Communication Research, Family Processes,* and *The Handbook of Discourse Analysis.*

MICHAEL E. ROLOFF is Professor of Communication Studies at Northwestern University. He received his Ph.D. from Michigan State University in 1975. His research interests include social exchange within intimate relationships, persuasion, interpersonal conflict resolution, and bargaining and negotiation. He wrote *Interpersonal Communication: The Social Exchange Approach,* and coedited *Persuasion: New Directions in Theory and Research* (with Gerald R. Miller) and *Social Cognition and Communication* (with Charles R. Berger).

DAVID R. SEIBOLD is Professor of Speech Communication at the University of Illinois, Urbana-Champaign. He received his Ph.D. from Michigan State University in 1975. His research interests include attribution theory, interpersonal influence processes, group decision making, health communication, and program evaluation methods. A coauthor of *Attitudes and Behavior* (Praeger) and published widely, he serves on the editorial boards of several communication journals. He currently is Chairperson of the Interpersonal Communication Division, International Communication Association.

ALAN L. SILLARS is Assistant Professor of Interpersonal Communication at the University of Montana. He received his Ph.D. from the University of Wisconsin—Madison. His research interests include family and marital conflict. He has published in *Communication Monographs, Communication Research, Communication Yearbook, Human Communication Research,* and the *Journal of Social and Personal Relationships.*

DALMAS A. TAYLOR is Dean of the College of Liberal Arts at Wayne State University. He received his Ph.D. in social psychology from the University of Delaware in 1965. He coauthored (with Irwin Altman) *Social Penetration: The Development of Interpersonal Relationships.* He and Altman have collaborated on a number of studies that addressed the dynamics of developing relationships. In addition to his interests in self-disclosure, intimacy and relationship formation, he is pursuing research in group conflict and the reduction of prejudice.

JUDITH WEISBERG is a doctoral candidate in the Department of Communication at Ohio State University. Her research interests include marital and family communication patterns and themes and metaphors in family interaction.

BARBARA A. WINSTEAD is Associate Professor of Psychology at Old Dominion University, Norfolk, Virginia. She received her doctoral degree in personality psychology from Harvard University in 1980. She recently coedited (with V. Derlega) *Friendship and Social Interaction* (1986), which includes her chapter, "Gender and Same-Sex Friendships." She also coauthored (with T. Cash and L. Janda) a body image survey (July 1985) and report of results (April 1986) for *Psychology Today.* Her interests include friendship, body image, and the psychology of women.

PAUL T. P. WONG received his Ph.D. at the University of Toronto. Currently, he is Professor of Psychology at Trent University and Adjunct Professor at the University of Toronto and Queen's University in Canada. His research interests include close relationships, coping behavior, and aging.

NOTES

NOTES